Right Reverend New Dealer: JOHN A. RYAN

Right Reverend New Dealer

JOHN A. RYAN

Francis L. Broderick

THE MACMILLAN COMPANY, NEW YORK

COLLIER-MACMILLAN LTD., LONDON

© Francis L. Broderick 1963

First Printing

The Macmillan Company, New York
Collier-Macmillan Canada, Ltd., Galt, Ontario
Divisions of The Crowell-Collier Publishing Company

Printed in the United States of America

Library of Congress catalog card number: 62–19419

Designed by Mina Baylis

FOR BARBARA

Preface

The seventeen years since Monsignor John A. Ryan's death have confirmed, even enlarged, his reputation as a pioneer social reformer. National policy at home and abroad has moved along lines congenial to his teaching, and the statements of Catholic spokesmen, both in the United States and in Rome, have continued to follow his trail. More than any other single figure in the Catholic Church in America, he is responsible for the progressive stands adopted by official Catholic spokesmen in our time. Some of these men are former students of his; many were trained in an atmosphere he helped to create. It is time to assess his contribution, and this book is an essay directed toward that goal.

Since historians, like the public figures they describe, are deeply involved in their times, this essay does not claim to be objective. Like all historians, I cannot escape from my biases, from those unstated, hidden presuppositions that undermine objectivity. Perhaps the reader can compensate for them in his own mind if I state frankly here that, like Monsignor Ryan, I am a Catholic well disposed to the reforming urge that inspired the progressive tradition in America and led to the New Deal.

Although this is not an authorized biography, I have enjoyed the fullest cooperation from those who knew Ryan best, both his family and his colleagues at the Catholic University of America and at the National Catholic Welfare Conference (NCWC). At no time, however, has anyone tried to guide my pen, and I am sure that those who knew Father Ryan best will have reason to quarrel with some of my judgments.

My debts are many and varied. The greatest is to John A. Ryan's brother, Monsignor Lawrence F. Ryan, who gave permission for my use of all available material and spared no effort in assisting me in my research in St. Paul. Father Lawrence and his sisters, the late Sister Constance and Sister Mary John, both Sisters of St. Joseph, spent many hours answering my questions and directing me to additional sources. Father Lawrence was very close to his brother, and the narrative that follows indicates the value of his cooperation.

At the Catholic University in Washington, where the Ryan papers are housed, a generous scholarly community went out of its way to help. Monsignor William J. McDonald, the rector, gave me unrestricted access to the university's archives; Eugene P. Willging, Director of University Libraries, went well beyond the normal courtesies to visitors; Fathers Henry J. Browne, Patrick W. Gearty, and Robert Trisco, who were in charge of the archives and manuscript collections at different times during my research, did everything they could to make my task easy. As I made the rounds of archival deposits, others helped: Father J. Joseph Gallagher in Baltimore, Father Thomas T. McAvoy, C.S.C., and Philip Gleason at the University of Notre Dame, Father Henry W. Casper, S.J., in Omaha. Leonard Rapport guided me in the Archives of the United States and generously shared some of his own notes with me. In addition, the staffs at the libraries of the University of Wisconsin and the State University of Iowa, Widener Library at Harvard University, the Minnesota State Historical Library, the New York Public Library and the Boston Public Library, the Davis Library at Phillips Exeter Academy, and the Archbishop Ireland Memorial Library at the St. Paul Seminary gave me generous and efficient help. Father Raymond A. McGowan, Monsignor Ryan's assistant and then successor at the NCWC, and Monsignor George G. Higgins, Father McGowan's successor, have both been wonderfully helpful in orienting me to the work of the Social Action Department and in sharing their memories of Father Ryan with me. In St. Paul, Monsignor James P. Shannon, president of St. Thomas College, permitted me to make my headquarters at the college for a period of time well beyond that regarded by Benjamin Franklin as safe for visitors and fish, and Father John Fitzpatrick allowed me to use his unpublished article on Ryan.

I have had scores of interviews with people who knew John A. Ryan: his students, colleagues, friends, relatives. It is not possible to acknowledge my debt to each by name; I am grateful to them all. Several interviews proved especially fruitful: those with Monsignor Maurice S. Sheehy, Father E. Harold Smith, Jane Hoey, Carlton J. H. Hayes, and Roger Baldwin.

I owe a great debt to four scholars who read the entire manuscript as it neared completion: Monsignor John Tracy Ellis, Father Joseph A. Broderick, O.P., Walter P. Metzger, and Henry F. Bedford. I know that it is conventional to disentangle them from any responsibility for what appears in the book. I bow to the convention. I wish also to go beyond this customary disclaimer, for none of them saw the book in its final form, and I did not take all their suggestions. Hence, though I appreciate more than they know the assistance they gave me—every page shows marks of their skill—they must be held blameless for what appears. Let no one say of any of them, "At least *he* should have known better."

Finally, I wish to thank William G. Saltonstall, Principal of Phillips Exeter Academy, and the trustees of the Academy for a sabbatical leave that made this book possible, and my wife, Barbara Baldridge Broderick, whose critical approval is hard to win and is all the more valued for that reason.

FRANCIS L. BRODERICK

Exeter, New Hampshire
April, 1962

Contents

Right Reverend New Dealer: JOHN A. RYAN

Irish-American
Farm Boy

FOR WEEKS JOHN A.
Ryan had been in a hospital in St. Paul, Minnesota, his life
ebbing away. One morning in mid-September, 1945, his
doctors permitted him to go out, not because he was better,
but because his condition was beyond hope. So John's
younger brother, the administrator of the St. Paul Cathedral,
drove him eight miles south to the little town of Vermillion.

Vermillion was the farming town near which the large
Ryan family, six boys and four girls, had grown up. Although the Ryan place had long since passed out of the
family, John Ryan liked to visit it when he returned to
St. Paul, for his roots were there, and he knew how deep a
mark his early years had left on him. As the eldest son on
a busy farm, he had learned about hard work, and he had
learned blunt speech—as well as barnyard humor—that never
left him. The land was rich, but in the late nineteenth century had hardly yielded enough to keep a large family
solvent. Low prices and high costs had put prosperity just
beyond the farmers' grasp. Blaming the power of big business and the greed of the railroads, farmers had turned hopefully to the state to redress the balance for the common

2

man. Some Americans had called this radicalism; the farmers had called it a quest for justice. Young John had heard them and, to some extent, had understood them. As he grew up, his Catholicism had strengthened his longing for social reform. And in the deep piety of his family, he had found encouragement for his vocation to the priesthood, in which he was to serve for almost fifty years.

During those years as a priest the farm boy had achieved fame as the Right Reverend John A. Ryan, domestic prelate, moral theologian, Catholic pioneer in America's struggle for social reform, author of a famous controversial statement on the relations between church and state. He had quarreled with a President and a Cardinal; he had been honored by another President and by a Pope. Stubborn yet flexible, gruff but affectionate, learned and simple, he had survived four decades of controversy with humor and with friends. Now his career was about to end. It had been, as a Supreme Court justice noted, a "life greatly lived."

A Minnesota farm worked by an Irish Catholic family during a period of agrarian discontent: the setting shaped John Ryan's early years.[1] His parents were both Irish immigrants. William Ryan, the father, had emigrated from County Tipperary in 1834. Arriving in America, William's family found its way to Great Barrington, Massachusetts, where various members found work in the textile mills. In the rush to California after 1848, the young Irishman went along: by steamer to Panama, across the narrows of the Isthmus of Panama, then up the Pacific Coast to the goldfields. In California, Ryan saw more Irishmen than nuggets, and contractors paid workers with unkept promises. Wearied by three years of drudgery, William left behind the $100 owed to him in wages and headed east to Minneapolis. The city was accessible by railroad. His sister was already there, married and well settled in the Diocese of St. Paul, which, under Bishop Joseph Cretin, was becoming a Catholic island in the Midwest. Once in Minneapolis, William looked around cautiously and finally found a suitable farm in the little township of Vermillion. His sister's husband, William Murnane, was making a farm in the area pay, so Ryan bought 160 partially improved acres from the railroad, paying partly in cash, partly with a mortgage. His mind wandered back

[1] This account of Father Ryan's youth is based on interviews with his sisters, Sister Constance and Sister Mary John of the Sisters of St. Joseph, on extended talks with his brother, Monsignor Lawrence F. Ryan, on his autobiography, *Social Doctrine in Action* (New York, 1941), pp. 1–61, and on scattered items in the John A. Ryan Papers at the Catholic University of America, Washington, D.C.

regretfully, then and many times afterward, to the $100 left behind in California.

A bride accompanied him to their new home. Maria Elizabeth Luby, the only daughter in a family of four children, had emigrated from Ireland with her uncle's family during the famine. With a little capital, the clan had made a successful life as farmers in the Golden Valley west of Minneapolis. Maria's own parents followed when their Fenian activities cost them most of their property in Ireland. Maria met the stiff, formal William Ryan, the only son in a family of four children, at the infrequent socials at the old St. Anthony's Church in Minneapolis, and on June 28, 1868, they were married.

Their new home was three or four miles out into the "prairie," the area beyond what local inhabitants still call hills. Vermillion had been organized as a township only ten years earlier. Though it lacked churches, several schools were operating every term.[2] The soil was rich and black, well suited to spring wheat, the principal crop, and hospitable to clover, oats, and barley as rotation crops, and later to corn when wheat from the great acreages of the Dakotas flooded the market. Along both sides of the dirt road and around the house William planted careful rows of poplars to restrain the fury of cyclones. His currant bushes and strawberry vines grew near the house, the apple trees somewhat farther out. Until the children were old enough to help, he regularly employed one man, more at harvest time.

As quickly as possible, William put up his house and barn, then his chicken coops. The barn, an innovation in its day, had a high, steep, pointed roof designed to resist cyclones. Seventy-five feet away, the house stood facing the dirt road. The front door opened on the parlor. To the rear, a lean-to attached to the house served as a kitchen, and later on, a separate summer kitchen was added. The parents lived in a small room off the living room, and overhead, up stairs so steep they were practically a ladder, the boys used one room, the girls the other. John was the first child, born on May 25, 1869. Christened "Michael John," he dropped the "Michael" during his school days. Ten more children followed over the next twenty years, six boys and four girls. Of the eleven children, ten survived as adults.

The Ryans were conspicuously Irish. Both husband and wife still had relatives in the old country. Some news filtered through by mail, and the *Irish World and Industrial Liberator*, a weekly published in New

[2] W. H. Mitchell, *Dakota County* (Minneapolis, 1869), pp. 96–97.

York and regularly received in the Ryan household, carried detailed reports, county by county, of conditions "back home." The closest neighbors were all Irish immigrants, almost invariably first-generation—the Moores and Kings and Rices and Callahans and the O'Learys with all the daughters. When the Ryans bought a second farm, the Coughlins, Russells, Barretts, Murphys, Careys, and Noonans were all close by. The names of nearby communities, Rosemount and Inver Grove, harked back to the old country.

Sunday mass gave the Irish "exiles," as they called themselves, a chance to meet and talk. During John's youth, mass was celebrated every fourth Sunday in St. Agatha's Church, three-quarters of a mile east of the Ryan place, just across from the public school. On the other three Sundays, the Ryans almost invariably went west seven miles to Rosemount rather than mingle with Luxemburgers at the German-language church at Vermillion, two miles closer. In the frame church at Rosemount they were among their own, and after mass the talk was in English: politics, crops, family news to catch up on. On Sundays the nine or ten Methodist families in the neighborhood went up the hill toward Rich Valley, and over to the west was the German Lutheran church. Everyone knew his neighbors by name, for they met in town on market day, coming in or out of John Gearaghty's store or Hynes' saloon; but no one visited the home of a neighbor from a different national or religious group.

In the Ryan home, morning prayers came before breakfast. On those infrequent Sundays, perhaps three or four all winter, when fresh snow or windswept drifts kept the family from church, they prayed together at home. During Lent the family said the Rosary together each evening, and William read from a devotional book; and on Sunday everybody went off on his own to read about the life of Christ, either in the Scriptures or in a popularized form. Piety, strong in both parents, took complementary forms in each, the father stern in the mood of the Old Testament, the mother joyous in the spontaneous and reiterated love of the New. To William, the father more respected than loved, religion was the duty of sinful men given to weaknesses of the flesh. Like so many Irishmen tainted with Jansenism, he felt an unsmiling seriousness about his unworthiness in God's sight. For years he received Holy Communion only once a year; the required minimum seemed the desirable maximum until his wife finally won him over to more frequent Holy Communion. The children learned their religion from their mother. Her warm, intuitive understanding embraced areas of Catholic thought that did not yield to her husband's more formal approach.

Strict with the children, especially with the boys, William looked for instant obedience. At the table he was silent, a wispy beard, stylish and common in the period, adding to the severity of his thin face. His children were more likely to recall his hatred for a lie than his love for his family. He worked hard, never smoked or played cards, abhorred liquor. He was never seen inside Hynes' saloon, even for a sociable chat. And yet when his father-in-law, always called Grandpa Luby, visited Vermillion, William always stocked a small keg of beer, and if the older boys stole a taste he managed not to notice. He lacked humor and he lacked warmth; these were the qualities in which his wife abounded.

Maria Ryan was slight but strong. Her thin neck gave her a delicate appearance all out of keeping with the rigors of farm life, and a poignant sadness hung about her eyes—the "Luby sadness," the Ryan family called it. At the dinner table she was gay in conversation. Careful never to cross her husband openly, she did restrain his authority in many ways the children were aware of and probably in many more as well. Her gentleness gave way to sarcasm only in the presence of pomposity; her eldest son's dislike for sham was, by general assent in the family, a legacy from her. A busy wife and mother, she still kept in regular touch with the Luby clan, catching the milk train to Minneapolis in the morning, selling a few items, shopping, visiting, returning the same day. In later years, after her children grew up, she held them together through a voluminous correspondence, little of which has survived.

As the years passed, the Ryans found it hard to accumulate money. William never wrote a check, never had a bank account, indeed never went into a bank except to make a payment on his mortgage. As late as 1896 he was still paying interest as high as 12 percent, for the state legislature persistently refused to pass adequate laws against usury. With prices on some staples declining 50 percent between 1870 and 1890,[3] he had to raise an increasingly larger crop to produce the same number of dollars. As a result, he found it hard to get ahead of his debts. The "milk checks" provided the only regular cash—perhaps thirty dollars a month. Once in a while pigs or cows were taken to St. Paul for slaughter, and a few eggs and some butter might be sold at the general store in Hastings or Rosemount. But generally barter was more economical. Every general store had two prices for items it bought—a dozen eggs

[3] Fred A. Shannon, *The Farmer's Last Frontier* (New York, 1945), p. 294.

brought five cents in cash or six in trade, a pound of butter twelve cents in cash, sixteen in trade. Money was needed for taxes, for the mortgage, and for items as miscellaneous as the weekly newspaper and the support of the Church. Otherwise barter was quite effective. Two competing millers in Hastings ground the farmers' wheat; part of the flour paid the millers for their labor; the rest established credit at the general store.

As the family grew large and older, it gained self-sufficiency: hands enough for plowing, harvesting, and binding. While William drove his two horses behind the plow, the girls took care of the chickens and the ducks. The boys milked the cows or stored underground the butter that their sisters and mother had churned. When all else was done, William, meticulous about his fruit trees and bushes, pruned and weeded.

School was in session only seven months a year; in the remaining months the children were kept hopping. Even after John went off to the seminary in St. Paul, he spent almost every summer at work on the farm. After the Murnanes' only son drowned, they sold their farm to the Ryans and went back to Minneapolis. As a result, the Ryans' work load doubled, perhaps more than doubled, for William added eighty acres to the Murnanes' 153 acres. The "other place"—which was what the Ryans always called the Murnane farm—was a couple of miles away along a mud road even now barely passable after a heavy rain, so the Ryans usually left a little colony of their young there, John probably in charge, and David or Mary Jane along to take care of the cooking. This they called "batching," and though fun, it was also hard work.

Yet recreation balanced work. When William hauled a load of pigs into St. Paul, a few youngsters always went along. On the slow trip in, the old Lutheran Church on Dodd Road, the halfway mark, took a long time to appear. But the trip back was a wild and joyous ride, for Papa always had fast horses, and his children never had to urge him on. When tickets to ship milk were needed, someone had to go to the Great Western station at Rich Valley. A saddle was available, but the lucky messenger almost invariably rode bareback. Farming did not encourage an extensive social life, yet basket suppers at church, lyceums at the school, Sunday visits with Irish neighbors broke the routine. And, naturally, a family with ten children drew on its own resources for entertainment.

Maria unabashedly made a favorite of her eldest, and many of the landmarks in John's life survive only in the affectionate, perhaps indulgent, memories that she passed along to her eldest daughter, Mary

Jane.[4] At the age of two, John set his parents off on a frantic search when he was lost toward evening in a thick woods near a stream on the Murnane farm. At four, John knew his letters. At five, he entered an ungraded public school, three-quarters of a mile down the road, where one instructor coped with a class of forty or fifty children from five to eighteen years old. Occasionally the teachers were local men as ungraded as the class they taught. More often they were competent professionals with normal-school certificates, so good in fact that the small township frequently lost them to more lucrative positions. They boarded locally as paying tenants with families anxious for ready cash. At six, John could read. One evening in the school lyceum he scored a great hit by reciting "The Charge of the Light Brigade" as if he were the sole survivor of the six hundred. As elocution ranked high as an art in the small community, the boy rode home in triumph on his father's shoulders. "His father could not do any better than John did," his sister Mary Jane, who was there, has reported. At eight he was already using the fourth-grade reader, and he hounded his mother about getting back to classes: "When will it be Monday again so I can go to school?" (Believe what you like. Family tradition is firm on this point.) John's adroitness in his schoolwork soon created a neighborhood problem. Other parents feared that the teachers gave this bright pupil more than his share of their time. When these complaints reached William's ears, he kept Johnnie at home.

John was an athlete as well as a scholar. Never a tall lad, he was inclined to be pudgy, though years on the farm had given him strong hands and broad shoulders. During recess at school he excelled in any sort of ball game. Two prominent front teeth won him the nickname "Big Tooth"; no one recalls why he was also called "Sambo." At home he was ready to try anything, his eldest sister has recalled. Once when he heard about three men who had been hanged in Ireland, he threw a noose over a tree, stood on a box under it, stuck his head in the noose, and kicked away the box. His terrified sister got the box back under his feet in time to save John from joining the three Irishmen. Discreet, she never reported this incident to their parents. Maria and William did discover the fact that John on another occasion had pushed a plank out the top door of the barn, perhaps forty feet above the ground, and then had hung from the plank by his feet. Both Ryan parents believed

4 Interviews with Sister Constance, April, 1958; and Sister Constance to author, May 8, 1958, in my possession.

in spankings "as the occasion demanded." This occasion no doubt "demanded."

An important part of John's education came from reading at home. Few books were available. In his autobiography Ryan lists the Bible, a life of the Virgin Mary, an item entitled *Ireland as She Is, as She Has Been, and as She Ought To Be,* and *The Lectures and Sermons of the Reverend Thomas N. Burke,* one of the greatest Dominican preachers of the century. A different stream of thought came from Patrick Ford, editor of the *Irish World and Industrial Liberator,* a bulky weekly newspaper. Ford "hid an essentially conservative mind behind colorful rhetoric,"[5] yet as the Knights of Labor and, later, the American Federation of Labor, matched organized labor against large industrial corporations, the *Irish World* put itself on the workers' side, detail and invective hammering home the main points.

Young John responded to Patrick Ford's attack on big business, for the National Farmers' Alliance, of which his father was a loyal though undemonstrative member, was waging a similar war on the railroads. The Alliance, with branches all through the Mississippi Valley and the southern states, was organized in 1880 as a protest against the nation's railroad system, which was denounced as "a virtual monopoly . . . defiant of all existing law . . . oppressive alike to the producer and consumer, corrupting to our politics, a hindrance to free and impartial legislation, and a menace to the very safety of our republican institutions."[6] Actually, freight rates went down during the 1880's and 1890's. But the price of grain fell even faster. American farms were producing more grain for declining international markets; at the same time, a stable, contracted currency was doing service for a population still doubling every thirty years. The fall in wheat prices in 1884–1885 stimulated the Alliance's growth and encouraged radical ideas such as inflation of the currency and governmental ownership of one or more transcontinental railroads. Hard times in the next few years brought in thousands of new members, preparing the way for the Populist party that would compete seriously for the Presidency in 1892 and would capture the Democratic party in 1896.

For the Ryans deflation and declining prices meant a pinch, and if they forgot their woes momentarily, conversations after church or a

[5] Thomas N. Brown, "Irish-American Nationalism, 1848–1891," Ph.D. dissertation, Harvard University (1956), p. 90.
[6] Quoted in John D. Hicks, *The Populist Revolt* (Minneapolis, 1931), p. 99.

Fourth of July oration by Ignatius Donnelly, the official Alliance orator, snapped them back to their troubles. Donnelly was quite a figure to John Ryan. Donnelly's home was in Nininger, the neighboring township, and his spectacular career—lieutenant governor at twenty-eight, a member of the House of Representatives for six years, organizer of the Anti-Monopoly party, state senator, state orator for the Farmers' Alliance—gave him a special local prestige. A young elocutionist like Ryan knew a master when he heard one. Writing in 1941, Ryan recalled Donnelly as the most effective and entertaining political stump speaker he had ever heard. Others had their points perhaps, he said, but Donnelly "excelled them all in quick thinking, wit, repartee, and a kind of sarcasm that was always effective and rarely biting or bitter."[7]

Johnnie rarely missed a chance to hear adult conversation about farmers' grievances. After Mass on Sunday when Hugh McGuire, the town radical who subscribed to a daily St. Paul paper—an extravagance unusual in the community—harangued about the railroad monopoly, John was always nearby. If neighbors dropped in to talk over Alliance issues with William, John was at hand, his mouth sagging as his energy went into keeping his ears open. When they dared, the younger children, and perhaps his mother as well, teased him, and in time a quip about John standing with his mouth open became a stock family joke.

Withdrawn from the District 36 school, John grew restive under his father's continuous discipline. After one stormy tiff, the sixteen-year-old boy ran away. He walked the eight miles to St. Paul along the railroad tracks and, worn out by the journey, went to the police station for the night. The next morning he found work piling laths. For twenty-five cents a day, he was ruining his clothes, so he went on to Minneapolis, deciding upon his uncle's house as a base. When his mother realized that he had really left, she hitched up the team and went after him. Playing a hunch, she headed directly for her brother's house. On the way she found John looking up at the tall buildings in downtown Minneapolis. "Johnnie, what are you doing here?" she asked quietly. "You come right home with me." The previous day had not been a great success. Running away at sixteen was overrated. John jumped upon the wagon and went home.

That fall he enrolled in the Cretin School in St. Paul, an elementary and high school run by the Christian Brothers. His uncle, Maurice Luby, made room for him on his forty-acre farm at Highland, five miles from

[7] Ryan, *Social Doctrine in Action*, p. 13.

the center of town, and five days a week Johnnie went off to the old cathedral, a stubby yellow-brick building with green shutters. The Christian Brothers were part of a baker's dozen who ran three schools in the city. Their students called them "Nickies" behind their backs, perhaps because of the Brothers' "incessant reference" to St. Nicholas, the patron of children, but the boys jumped when the figures in plain black habits, square-toed shoes, tricornered hats, and flapping mantles ("bibs" to the irreverent) came into a classroom. In the five classrooms the brothers dispensed a simple fare of reading, writing, a "dabbling of arithmetic," and religion.[8] As the year progressed, John sensed that he had a religious vocation. The Christian Brothers urged him to join their ranks, but John soon made up his mind in favor of the diocesan priesthood. With his parent's consent and his grandfather's gift of $200 for tuition, young John switched in September, 1887, to St. Thomas Seminary.

The seminary's twenty acres were as attractive as the Cretin School was dreary. Well out in the country toward Minneapolis, the three-year-old seminary occupied uninhabited, unspoiled grounds. Woods banked the campus on every side, and trees shaded the areas already in use. Brown thrushes and robins, gophers and rabbits, cranes, even an occasional deer appeared near the main seminary building. The Mississippi was only a few minutes' walk away, with the Falls of Minnehaha a few steps beyond that. The main seminary building was a solid four-story brick structure, its wings forming three sides of a square, its imposing tower, a symbol of elegance in its day, rising ninety feet. When the breeze was strong enough to turn the seminary's windmills, students could expect hot and cold water in all parts of the building. As modern as a cable car, the college was lighted by gas and heated by steam. "In fact," an admiring account in the Milwaukee *Catholic Citizen* pointed out, "the inclemencies of the weather are utterly banned here, and the comforts of the natural man regulated down to a nicety by taps and screws." The food, like the food in the officially sponsored statement of every college, was abundant and delicious. It was served by "female help," who never entered the dining rooms or met the students. The college had facilities for rowing and skating on nearby Lake Mennith; its gymnasium was fully equipped; and what was more, the "finest base-ball grounds in the state" were right there on the property.[9]

[8] Brothers of the Christian Schools, *Mississippi Vistas* (Winona, 1948), pp. 182–187.
[9] Quoted in *Northwestern Chronicle*, Jan. 1, 1892. The origins of the seminary are traced in William Busch, "The Diocesan Seminary Project in St. Paul," *Acta et Dicta* (St. Paul), October, 1935, pp. 56–82.

Founded primarily to train candidates for the priesthood, the seminary prepared young men for other careers as well. Its college department, covering six years, gave generous attention to English language and literature, science, and German. A number of students spoke German as a first language, for many Catholic families in the diocese had recently emigrated from Germany. Futhermore, John Ireland, Bishop of St. Paul (Archbishop after 1888), was recruiting young clerical candidates in Germany to meet the needs of his German-speaking parishes. For this group there were special classes. After the college level, the "classical course," as it was called, came six years of the "clerical course."

When John entered St. Thomas, the seminary had seventy-five students, less than half of them clerical students, and a faculty of eight priests and three laymen.[10] He studied five years as a classical student before going on to the clerical department. From the start he did exceptionally well in everything but conduct. At the end of his second year, he received "first distinction" in Latin and Greek, and "special merit" (an even higher rating) in Christian doctrine, English, history, and geometry. Among the awards for "excellence in general deportment," however, John's name did not appear. His academic excellence continued all the way through, and even his grade for deportment advanced: "second distinction" in 1889–1890, "special merit" in 1890–1891. In his final year, he put together quite a record: his languages—German, Latin, Greek, and English —all in the middle 90's, Christian doctrine, 100; and "application to study," 96, one point better than conduct.[11] When he gave the class's valedictory address, "On High Ideals in Education," the Northwestern Chronicle warmly applauded the "good appearance in his style and delivery."[12] By this time, Johnnie was twenty-three, already a voter, but not too grown up to enjoy the warm pride that his parents, and especially his mother, felt at this achievement.

Studies did not take all his time. He became the regular first baseman for the seminary's Base Ball Association, and in his last two years, he was manager and then captain of the team. As official representative of the students, he welcomed a delegation of visiting bishops in December, 1889. In a brief appearance in a four-act drama called Sir Thomas More, he did not distinguish himself as an actor, but when he returned as

[10] Northwestern Chronicle, Nov. 17, 1887.
[11] Catalogue of St. Thomas Aquinas Seminary, 1889–1890 (St. Paul, 1890), and subsequent volumes; St. Thomas Seminary "Roll of Honor," 1891–1892, p. 16.
[12] Northwestern Chronicle, July 1, 1892.

Biblius in *The Hidden Gem,* the *Northwestern Chronicle* could not deny that he was splendid in the part.[13] John had one other activity: he was the seminary's most inveterate trolley rider. Whenever the legislature was in session, John looked for every chance to take the twenty-minute trolley ride to the center of St. Paul to watch the solons at work. "Sambo" and "Big Tooth" were heard no more. Now his friends called him "Senator."

While John was in college, controversy within the Catholic Church in the United States was creating two groups loosely known as "liberals" and "conservatives," distinctions rooted in the immigrant history of American Catholics. The first mass wave of newcomers, largely Irish and partly German, arrived in the generation preceding the Civil War. They immediately faced the intense antipathy of native American non-Catholics hostile to the immigrants and, by extension, to the Church as well.[14] In the 1850's antipathy became violence on numerous occasions —in Louisville, Kentucky, in 1855, scores of Catholics were killed—and in most state organizations of the Know-Nothing party, anti-Catholicism was a basic principle.

From the Civil War to the end of the century, however, the Church in America began a reconciliation with the surrounding culture. In this approach the Irish performed a central role. After initial struggles with the native American and then French prelates who held the episcopal sees, the Irish gradually began to dominate the American Church, taking over both the rectories and the bishops' houses. English-speaking themselves, they had no major language barrier, and they developed a loyalty to their new homeland as intense as their former devotion to Ireland; like their cousins in the old country, they became patriotic with a religious fervor. This new loyalty spurred their desire for assimilation into the American culture and encouraged their efforts to mediate between Catholicism and the Protestant and the secular cultures that surrounded it. Most of them did not become farmers, as they had been in Ireland; the city dwellers adjusted to the mores of American urban life, adapting with special aptitude to American politics. Catholicism as practiced among the Irish seemed less foreign to American eyes. Will Herberg has noted: "It was English-speaking, 'puritanical,' democratic, popular, and activistic, with little of the traditional Catholic inwardness,

---

[13] *Ibid.,* Jan. 3, 1890; June 29, 1888; June 26, 1891.
[14] Brown, "Irish-American Nationalism, 1848–1891," pp. 60–62.

but also with little of the aristocratic conservatism or the baroque excesses that characterized so much of nineteenth-century Continental Catholicism."[15] Though originally a church of the poor, Catholicism began to achieve middle-class respectability as its members began the social climb characteristic of successive waves of immigration to America.

German-American Catholics developed differently. From the beginning they held aloof from the surrounding culture. Divided from their neighbors by language, they clustered in parishes of their own, protecting their children's heritage and faith with German-language schools, newspapers, and benevolent societies, eyeing with suspicion the pressure toward assimilation within an American culture that might force them to surrender their German heritage. Even within the Church itself they encountered pressures little to their liking, for the Irish-Americans in control were creating an institution that was taking on the color of its environment at the expense of the traditional Catholicism the German immigrants had known in their native land. They feared not only the loss of their ethnic identity but also the integrity of Catholic truth itself. In this view even some of the Irish prelates joined, men conditioned either by personality, training, or the special circumstances of their dioceses.

European influences reinforced the division in America. Henry Cardinal Manning in England, where Catholics faced a comparable problem of acceptance as a minority group, supported the liberal position taken by Americans. Some Continental Europeans shared this view, welcoming the example of the United States as a demonstration that even without a privileged position the Church could thrive. Perhaps the bulk of Continental opinion, however, leaned to the other side. In France and Italy, where laic states evidenced hostility to the Church, conservative European Catholics were unsympathetic to the American attempts to make soft-spoken advances to Protestants and others outside the Church. These differences were evident even in the Vatican.[16]

By the later 1880's the situation in the United States had clarified into two fairly clear, and fairly clearly conflicting, positions. On essential points of doctrine and Church discipline, the two wings agreed. Their differences lay rather in programs for the Church in America. The conservatives, reluctant to adapt to the American environment too rapidly,

15 Will Herberg, *Protestant—Catholic—Jew* (Garden City, 1960), p. 145.
16 Robert D. Cross, *The Emergence of Liberal Catholicism in America* (Cambridge, 1958), pp. 19–21, 182–189.

regarded the Church as the jealous custodian of truths challenged by the surrounding secular and Protestant influences. The liberals regarded America as a great missionary area where congenial institutions lent themselves to the extension of the Church's influence; they argued for flexibility in contacts with non-Catholic elements. The conservatives feared corruption by a secular society. The liberals feared stultification by confining American Catholics within a European framework. Liberals thought that conservatives were imprudent reactionaries. Conservatives suspected liberals of heresy. The two groups fought not only in private meetings and in correspondence but also in the public press.[17]

The struggle between the two wings came to focus in the bitter disagreements between John Ireland, Archbishop of St. Paul, and Michael A. Corrigan, Archbishop of New York. Others in the hierarchy were more outspoken perhaps—Bernard J. McQuaid, of Rochester, New York, for the conservatives; John Lancaster Spalding, of Peoria, Illinois, for the liberals—but the two archbishops, because of their rank as metropolitans of provinces, were more readily heard, both in this country and in Rome. Corrigan, a methodical administrator of his diocese and an active builder, battled secret societies and, like a jealous shepherd, guarded against liberal tendencies in his province. Ireland, a former Civil War chaplain, joined the American Civic Federation, supported the Republican Party with outspoken loyalty, fought political corruption and the liquor interests. As priest and then as prelate, he organized total-abstinence societies, purchased railroad lands to stimulate colonization projects for immigrants, worked intently to make the Church friendly to America and America friendly to the Church. "The consecrated blizzard of the Northwest," he was aptly called. Between the two wings stood James Cardinal Gibbons, Archbishop of Baltimore, the gentle mediator who, though leaning toward the liberals, sought to compromise differences and to avoid an open break.[18]

John Ryan, along with everyone else, knew the arguments, and he found his sympathies with the liberals. While he was in college and in the seminary, the liberals elicited his enthusiasm on three occasions. In 1887, when the Vatican was considering the inclusion of the Knights of Labor among secret societies that Catholics might not join, Gibbons, Ireland, and

[17] *Ibid.*, *passim.*
[18] *Ibid.*, 38; John Tracy Ellis, *The Life of James Cardinal Gibbons* (Milwaukee, 1952), 2 vols.; James H. Moynihan, *The Life of Archbishop Ireland* (New York, 1953); Frederick J. Zwierlein, *Letters of Archbishop Corrigan to Bishop McQuaid* (Rochester, 1946).

Keane, supported by seventy of the seventy-five American bishops, warned Rome that condemnation would be imprudent and unjust because of the reality of the grievances of the working class; it would endanger the reputation of the Church and might lead to persecution; it would cruelly undermine the authority of the American bishops, who were known to oppose such drastic action by Rome.[19] In his autobiography, Ryan recalls his delight when Rome's decision not to condemn the Knights "vindicated the vigilance and social vision of Cardinal Gibbons and the American hierarchy."[20]

Two years later Ireland called more specifically for action. Speaking at the hundredth anniversary of the American Catholic hierarchy, Ireland bade the Church make America Catholic and "solve for the Church universal the all-absorbing problems with which religion is confronted in the present age." "What if at times we do blunder?" he went on. "Success is not the test of merit. If we never venture, we never win. The conservatism which wishes to be ever safe is dry rot. . . . It is deplorable that Catholics grow timid, take refuge in sanctuary and cloister, and leave the bustling, throbbing world with its miseries and sins to the wiles of false friends and cunning practitioners. . . . These are days of action, days of warfare. . . . Into the arena, priest and layman! Seek out social evils, and lead in movements that tend to rectify them. Speak of vested rights, for this is necessary; but speak, too, of vested wrongs, and strive, by word and example, by the enactment and enforcement of good laws, to correct them."[21] The words sparkled for a college sophomore; they came with the double authority of their source and their essential justice.

About the time of his graduation in 1892, and perhaps accidentally, as he ransacked the library for material for his valedictory, John came across Bishop Spalding's *Education and the Higher Life.* Spalding, whom Ryan called in 1941 "undoubtedly the greatest literary artist" produced by the American hierarchy,[22] was also probably the most determined to effect a reconciliation between the Church and nineteenth-century American democracy. He hailed democracy as the best government, and he looked to religion to connect democratic culture with eternal truth. Religion

[19] Henry J. Browne, *The Catholic Church and the Knights of Labor* (Washington, 1949), pp. 239–242.

[20] Ryan, *Social Doctrine in Action*, p. 20.

[21] John Ireland, *The Church and Modern Society* (Chicago, 1896), I, 55, 71, 78, 79. These passages are marked in Ryan's copy of the book, now in Mullen Library, Catholic University of America.

[22] Ryan, *Social Doctrine in Action*, p. 28.

"gives new vigor to the cultivated mind," he said; "it takes away the exclusive and fastidious temper which a purely intellectual habit tends to produce; it enlarges sympathy; it teaches reverence; it nourishes faith, inspires hope, exalts the imagination, and keeps alive the fire of love."[23] In addition to being a rich source for a valedictory, Spalding's book introduced John to the most articulate liberal in the American hierarchy.

Ryan had the happy experience of being propelled into his career as an American social reformer by his Catholicism. His boyhood, shaped by Donnelly, Ford, and the Alliance movement, made him sensitive to social evils. Then the great liberal prelates guided him without tortured reflection toward social reform. Trained in this tradition, Ryan could never understand people, inside or outside the Church, who set Americanism and Catholicism in opposition to each other.

In the fall of 1892, his "classical course" completed, John had to decide whether to go on to the "clerical course." For a lad with Irish ancestry, generations of reverence for the figure of the priest as a religious leader, as an educated font of authority on all sorts of questions, and as a symbol of Irish resistance to English overlords, invested a religious vocation with special grandeur. Irish parents who yielded a son to the priesthood felt an immense joy, bred in the memories of hundreds of years of religious loyalty and social alienation. A young man like John fell heir to this tradition as he considered a life of religious service, his cultural heritage supporting the call that Catholics regard as a summons from God. For John the final decision did not come easily; he weighed alternative careers, he thought about getting married. Awed by the dignity of the high calling of the priesthood, he could not suppress a momentary longing to have the burden of decision on other shoulders. Yet this choice he had to make himself. Proud of his freedom to choose, he chose.[24]

Now he was a seminarian in the formal sense. For the first year he simply moved from the "classical" to the "clerical" wing of the main building at St. Thomas's. By the fall of 1893, however, the seminary crossed Summit Avenue to its new home, the $500,000 gift of the railroad builder James J. Hill, a friend of Archbishop Ireland. The college section of St. Thomas Aquinas Seminary now became the College of St. Thomas; the seminary was dedicated as the St. Paul Seminary. Four red-brick

[23] Quoted in *ibid.*, pp. 29–30.
[24] Ryan, "Journal," 1892–1898, Oct. 2, 1892, Oct. 18, 1892. (All items not specifically located elsewhere are in the Ryan Papers at Catholic University.)

dormitories—"Jim Hill's boxcars," the students used to call them—an administration building, and a classroom building clustered together among the trees. A stone church, ample enough to accommodate the entire faculty and student body in choir stalls, was set off from the other buildings both in location and in construction. Time has dealt kindly with the buildings: Hill's passion against frills saved the campus from the extravagances of the era, and the years have brushed warmth into the red brick. The seminary opened on September 6, 1894, flooded with sunshine and archiepiscopal eloquence. The *Chronicle* hoped for "another Oxford in its palmy days."[25]

The curriculum called for two years of philosophy and four years of theology. As a token response to the injunction of Leo XIII to teach seminarians about social problems, St. Paul's tacked economics and sociology onto its philosophy courses. English—reading, writing, and speaking—was part of the regular course, and in addition, Archbishop Ireland required all his seminarians to learn German. In deference to Hill's wishes, science courses and well-equipped laboratories were provided. The archbishop kept a close check on his seminary, visiting regularly, presiding at final oral examinations, giving frequent inspirational talks to his seminarians.[26]

For Ryan the training was long. Twenty-three when he started, he would be twenty-nine before ordination. Graduate work would stretch out his apprenticeship even further. He wanted to accelerate this unhurried pace to his ministry, but the faculty was not willing, and he stayed the full time.[27] Unafraid of exacting hard work, he pored over his writing style, always ready to exchange "brilliant ornament and graceful rhetoric" for unadorned clarity and conciseness. In his journal small essays, written and rewritten, improved steadily as he struck out superfluous words, especially fancy words. No waste, no sham, no curlicues— Ryan was training for his later years. The same journal revealed mutterings of impatience. A combination of resignation and exasperation lay behind the comment on his philosophy course: "Surely it must have some compensating reward or so much time would not be devoted to it."[28]

[25] *Northwestern Chronicle*, July 14, 1893.

[26] James Michael Reardon, *The Catholic Church in the Diocese of St. Paul* (St. Paul, 1952), pp. 313–314. Many of these talks have been reprinted in John F. Duggan, comp., "The Education of a Priest," *Ecclesiastical Review*, October–December 1939, pp. 289–300, 385–398, 495–504.

[27] Ryan, *Social Doctrine in Action*, p. 60.

[28] Ryan, "Journal," Nov. 22, 1892.

Ryan's inner religious life never became public property. Though he wrote a great deal during his career, he rarely touched on mystical or even purely religious topics. His closest friends went through decades knowing nothing about his private spiritual reading; his brother Lawrence, a priest, can only hint at John's spiritual life. Even in his private journal, John had little to say, as though his distaste for sham made him uneasy lest he grope toward piety in a self-important way. His journal spoke only of a practical view of perfection, directed outward rather than inward. If we cannot attain the perfection of loving our neighbors as ourselves, he wrote, "let us see that our love and appreciation for self does not become openly injurious and offensive to others. In this way we shall avoid sin against others if not against ourselves."[29] Christianity embraces both a call to individual perfection and a social ethic. Already in Ryan's writings, the social ethic was taking the more conspicuous place.

Twice a month the seminary conducted a "public academy" at which the best papers prepared in class seminars were read and discussed. Ryan won this honor with his paper on "The Influence of Jewish Theories of Inspiration on Christian Exegesis." He became president of the Lacordaire Literary and Debating Club. On one festive occasion he delivered a tribute to the founder of the seminary at a public forum.[30] (Ryan's autobiography does not mention his eulogy of James J. Hill.)

Politics continued to interest him. As a sympathetic observer, he followed the Populist revolt, its failure in 1892, its surprising triumph in the Democratic convention of 1896, and its defeat the following November in the national election. He visited the gallery of the legislature downtown less frequently, but newspapers were a partial substitute. They did not carry a hopeful story. After the election of 1892, he mourned the Populist defeat: "Time servers and hypocrites are rewarded while honest patriots are made the object of mercenary ridicule. When will the eyes of the masses be opened?" Two years later Ryan's journal could have served as a Populist handbook: "The money power is the real enemy of the people's prosperity; yet the people, misled by a hireling press and plutocratic orators, have voted to continue the power of Wall Street. . . . Great is the influence of Mammon and misrepresentation." Only a strong faith in the ultimate good sense of the people saved a man from despair. The Democratic party was dead—killed (presumably) by President Grover Cleveland's refusal to coin silver. When the Republicans failed,

[29] *Ibid.*, Nov. 17, 1892.
[30] *Saint Paul Seminary Register* (St. Paul, 1897), pp. 37–43.

Ryan predicted, the people would turn finally to the People's party or to a successor with a different name but similar principles. This change must come within twenty-five years, he said, and when it does, it will bring a "complete transformation in our economic relations": state absorption of natural monopolies, shorter workdays, and revolution in land tenure. "Forward then, is the watchword, with renewed hope and determination; for the change is inevitable."[31]

The striking new departure of Ryan's seminary years was his interest in the labor problem. Though Patrick Ford had been his early tutor on this subject, the critical moment came early in 1894 when he read, apparently for the first time, Pope Leo XIII's great social encyclical *Rerum novarum* ("On the Condition of Labor"). The encyclical appeared in May, 1891, but Ryan, a busy junior in college, did not notice it, even though Archbishop Ireland's five sermons on it appeared in full in the *Northwestern Chronicle*. When Ryan came to *Rerum novarum* three years later, what led him to recognize the encyclical as a seminal document on which a whole social program could be based? A recognition of Populism's limitations after the failure of 1892? More intimate contact with an urban population? Violent labor disputes like the Homestead massacre of 1892, in which strikers at the Carnegie Steel Company had a pitched battle with armed guards from the Pinkerton Detective Agency? Ryan's memory does not help. He sees all his previous training leading to the moment when the requirements of his course led him to a careful reading of *Rerum novarum*.[32] At that moment his career stretched out before him.

The encyclical stated as a "first and most fundamental principle" the inviolability of private property, then went on to the corollary "that the main tenet of Socialism, the community of goods, must be utterly rejected." Leo also denied the idea of class struggle, that employers and employees are naturally hostile. In fact, he said, the exact contrary was true: "Each requires the other; capital cannot do without labor, nor labor without capital." Each had its rights and obligations. A laborer had the natural right to enough of the world's goods to maintain himself in "reasonable and frugal comfort," and in turn he owed his employer an honest day's work. An employer had the reciprocal obligation to pay a reasonable wage and the right to expect a fair output in return. But Leo acknowledged that despite these principles derived from the natural law, "by degrees it has come to pass that Working Men have been given over,

[31] Ryan, "Journal," Nov. 11, 14, 1892; Nov. 11, 1894.
[32] Ryan, *Social Doctrine in Action,* pp. 43–45.

isolated and defenseless, to the callousness of employers and the greed of unrestrained competition," so that "a small number of very rich men have been able to lay upon the masses of the poor a yoke little better than slavery itself." To meet this condition, the Pope called employers to a recognition of their obligations, and endorsed workingmen's associations as instruments of achieving just wages, decent working conditions, and the benefits of the ownership of property. And he affirmed that the state has the obligation to guarantee the rights of all its citizens: "Whenever the general interest of any class suffers, or is threatened with evils which can in no other way be met, the public authority must step in to meet them."[33]

For Ryan, the encyclical contained much that was old, much that was new. The condemnation of socialism and the reaffirmation of the natural right to private property were familiar to anyone who had followed Catholic social comment. But the Populist in Ryan must have been struck by the Pope's harsh words about the rich. Even more impressive was the extraordinary field for state action that the Pope seemed willing to tolerate. Leo's statement that whenever rights could not be protected in any other way, the state had the obligation to use its might in safeguarding each of its citizens was for its time an advanced view, quite contrary to dominant orthodox opinion. Ryan was delighted to see his own sympathetic view of the regulation of industry by the state ratified by the highest authority in Christendom: "The doctrine of state intervention which I had come to accept and which was sometimes denounced as 'socialistic' in those benighted days, I now read in a Papal encyclical." In the state of American Catholic social thought around 1890, Ryan noted later on, "Leo's teaching on the state seemed almost revolutionary."[34] The young seminarian also noted with satisfaction that the encyclical provided specific principles for the workingman: a living wage, enough to allow a man to live in "reasonable and frugal comfort," as a natural right, and labor unions as legitimate instruments for securing these rights.

Today the student, tomorrow the teacher. Barely finished with his paper on *Rerum novarum*, Ryan wrote a letter to the *Northwestern Chronicle* on the right to work. Adopting the pen name "Olney Overton," he laid out the basic principles: Man had a right to life, and the state must protect that right. In the present organization of society, that right meant the right to work. If men lost the opportunity to find a job, if the state allowed "the greed and usurpations of some other men—the 'Pluto-

---

[33] "Five Great Encyclicals," pamphlet (New York, 1939), pp. 1–30 *passim*.
[34] Ryan, *Social Doctrine in Action*, pp. 44–45.

crats' for instance—" to make working impossible, then the state had a positive obligation to find jobs. Relief was no solution, for as Henry George said, "Charity is a poison when taken as a substitute for justice." Ryan insisted that the state's obligation to secure its citizens' welfare was not new; novelty occurred only in applying an old principle to new conditions.[35]

This letter anticipated Ryan's future career in a remarkable way. A living wage, guaranteed by the state if necessary, was the idea most intimately associated with his name for the next half-century. Always at the core of his social philosophy was the natural law as expounded by Leo XIII.

The young seminarian spent the summer of 1894 studying economics. He came upon *Principles of Political Economy*, an English translation of the elementary text by the Italian Jesuit Matteo Liberatore. It gave Ryan a sense of the field of economics; at the same time, it judged economic attitudes and institutions by Catholic standards. William S. Lilly, an English Catholic writer, taught Ryan about the limitations of property ownership. Much property in Europe, Lilly wrote in his popular ethical tract *On Right and Wrong*, had its source in robbery; but even property legitimately acquired owes an obligation to the community. Lilly also thought that the moral law demanded the reorganization of industry. Reassuring Ryan that radical economic ideas were in line with Catholicism, Lilly continued as a favored author all through Ryan's later seminary years. The records in the library show Ryan turning to Lilly again and again, occasionally even to the same book. Richard T. Ely's *Socialism and Social Reform* also found a place in Ryan's summer reading. It gave him his first glimpse of a systematic program of social reform: government ownership and operation of natural monopolies (railroads, telegraphs, forests, and coal mines); graduated taxes on land held for speculative purposes; labor legislation—an eight-hour day, accident insurance, abolition of child labor; a flexible currency. Ely made some key definitions that showed how reformers and socialists could agree on social change even though they did not share the same premises. The socialist's incorrect premise did not invalidate his conclusion, Ryan came to see, if this same conclusion could be reached by deduction from a valid premise.[36]

In Europe Catholic leaders were beginning to make the protest against

---

[35] *Northwestern Chronicle*, March 2, 1894.
[36] Ryan, *Social Doctrine in Action*, pp. 46–54.

social injustice heard: Bishop Wilhelm von Ketteler in Germany, Gaspard Cardinal Mermillod, first in Switzerland, later in Rome; Karl Vogelsang in Austria-Hungary, Albert de Mun and Jean Paul Villeneuve-Burgemont in France, Cardinal Manning in England. The climactic encyclical of Leo XIII authoritatively ratified their criticisms. In the United States a comparable assault on the industrial capitalist system was spelled out in detail by Walter Rauschenbusch, a prominent Protestant clergyman. The American Catholic hierarchy readily affirmed the dignity of labor and the worker's right to a decent wage, but rarely did they translate these benign ideas into explicit reforms.[37] Most Catholic writers recoiled from the specter of socialism, condemning it as a diabolic program that demolished God and property. People devoted to the *status quo* readily tagged every reform as "socialistic," and for the timid and the uninformed the tag stuck. Thus the alternatives appeared to be individualism, which created monstrous social evils, and socialism, which was unacceptable to the Christian mind.

As a menace feared by Catholics, Henry George's single tax ran socialism a close second. In *Progress and Poverty* (1879) George pointed to the anomaly of increased wealth and increased poverty in modern society. He put his finger on the cause: rent absorbed the wealth that society produced. His solution was as simple (some would say as simplistic) as his diagnosis: a tax on land large enough to absorb the rent that society's development allowed property-holders to charge. Land that yielded large, unearned gains would thus return to society through taxes the value that society had created. This "single tax" could replace other taxes and thus free the majority from the burden of taxation. A rash of Single Tax clubs soon showed that George's ideas had immense appeal both in the United States and in Great Britain.[38]

George first aroused the suspicion of articulate Catholic leaders because socialists had supported him in 1886 when he ran for mayor of New York City against an aging Democrat, Abram S. Hewitt, and the new Republican light, Theodore Roosevelt. Because socialists supported George, Catholics generally were against him. An even more direct Catholic repudi-

---

[37] Clarence J. McCabe, "The Background of *Rerum novarum*," M.A. dissertation, Catholic University (1941); Michael P. Fogarty, *Christian Democracy in Western Europe, 1820–1953* (Notre Dame, 1957), pp. 149–178; James Edmund Roohan, "American Catholics and the Social Question: 1865–1900," Ph.D. dissertation, Yale University (1952), pp. 398–409, 425–426; Sister Joan de Lourdes Leonard, "Catholic Attitudes Toward American Labor, 1884–1919," M.A. dissertation, Columbia University (1940), pp. 50–52.

[38] Charles Albro Barker, *Henry George* (New York, 1955), *passim*.

ation of George arose because of the case of Father Edward McGlynn, of New York, an articulate exponent of George's ideas. In the course of this well-publicized fracas, which finally centered on ecclesiastical discipline rather than on social ideas, Archbishop Corrigan suspended McGlynn and tried to have *Progress and Poverty* put on the *Index of Forbidden Books.* He failed, and four professors at Catholic University found nothing opposed to Catholic doctrine in McGlynn's defense of Henry George's ideas. A papal ablegate, Archbishop Francesco Satolli, ordered Corrigan to reinstate McGlynn. Yet the controversy made the Single Tax so suspect among Catholics that a recent student of George's influence has observed that in this period "many Catholic ideas and solutions for the labor problem began as rebuttals for Georgism."[39]

Young Mr. Ryan faced the problem that despite Ely's useful distinctions, Lilly's reforming urge, and Leo XIII's imperative command, American Catholics turned their backs on two programs, socialism and the single tax, that sought to solve the social question, and they failed to give positive support to any alternative that went beyond pious aphorism.

In the winter of his second year of theology, Ryan defined the problem in three articles for the *Northwestern Chronicle.* The social question, he said, was almost identical the world over—the quest for "a more equitable distribution of material blessings." The question was fraught with possibilities for good or for ill, for "the masses will not be satisfied today with homilies on the emptiness of human life, and the blessedness in store for them beyond the clouds." People were weary of these "drafts upon eternity." Past remedies no longer satisfied: "We must bear in mind that the discoveries of physical science and the tendency toward the elimination of the supernatural from religion have given the world—the here and now—an importance not realized before."

Individualism provided no solution, Ryan went on. Events had dispelled the illusion that social freedom resulted from individual freedom. The American tradition of laissez faire in the struggle for survival stood condemned as "unChristian and unjust." Socialism appeared by a law of reaction, and the growing number of socialists in England and Germany attested to the potency of its appeal as a solvent of problems that capitalism refused, or was unable, to meet. Denunciation of socialism solved nothing: "Genuine social reform suffers more injury at the hands of

[39] *Ibid.*, pp. 464–466, 486–489; Stephen Bell, *Rebel, Priest and Prophet* (New York, 1937), pp. 30–205; James Jeremiah Green, "The Impact of Henry George's Theories on American Catholicism," Ph.D. dissertation, University of Notre Dame (1956), p. 188.

24

flippant fools who rush in to demolish socialism *a priori* than from the extreme vagaries of the most wide-eyed Socialist."

Is socialism wrong? In asking this question, Ryan entered the slippery area that produced, on the one hand, papal condemnation of socialism, and on the other hand, an American bishop, James A. McFaul, of Trenton, who spoke approvingly of "Christian socialism."[40] Catholic theologians, such as the distinguished Jesuit moralist Viktor Cathrein, thought that socialism vitally depended on the materialism of Karl Marx. At this point Ryan, guided by Ely, groped for new ground. Socialism itself did not suffer because the materialist concept of history and the Marxian theory of value were false, Ryan asserted. Many socialists were irreligious; socialism was not. In Germany, was not religion regarded as a private matter among socialists? The chief purpose of socialism, Ryan argued, was distributive justice, the allotment of material goods among the members of a society in a way that did not violate the principles of justice. When Christian theology affirmed the right to private property, it did not necessarily mean private ownership of land or of the means of production; it meant private property to be used for the necessities and comforts of life. If a collective state guaranteed these, justice was satisfied. Knowing that he was on unconventional ground, the young seminarian added promptly that his conclusion was drawn, not out of friendship for socialism, but out of friendship for truth, "which is of more importance than any system or any refutation."[41]

Later in the year Ryan replied to an attack on George in the *Irish Ecclesiastical Review* by Father Sylvester Malone, a Brooklyn pastor generally identified with the liberal wing. The young seminarian moved cautiously, too unsure of his ground to defend George unequivocally. To the extent that George denied the right to private property in land, he was wrong, Ryan conceded, for the alternative to private property was barbarism, and the right to private property in land was as valid as the right to any other kind of private property. At the same time, Ryan went on, George's unnecessarily harsh language and his errors in argument did not reverse the fact that "the practical principles of the single tax theory contemplate nothing intrinsically unjust or opposed to Catholic teaching." George wanted merely to reclaim for the community what the com-

[40] Leonard, "Catholic Attitudes Toward American Labor 1884–1919," *loc. cit.*
[41] "R.A." (pseud.), "What is the Social Question?" "Individualism and Socialism," "Is Socialism Wrong?" *Northwestern Chronicle,* Dec. 6, 27, 1895; Jan. 17, 1896.

munity had created, Ryan explained; this argument had satisfied the papal ablegate who ordered Father McGlynn's reinstatement. Therefore (the conclusion was unstated but abundantly implied) it should have been enough for everyone else.[42]

While still a seminarian, Ryan wrote nothing more on the social question. His journal was all but silent. On one occasion he observed that the Church could break through people's indifference to religion by emphasizing the social side of Catholicism. "Draw their attention, win their sympathy, and their native yearning for religious truth will do the rest."[43] This was the only entry in a three-year period. In the whole of his final year of seminary training, he borrowed from the seminary library no work bearing directly on the social question. His reading turned to the theological treatises of Camillo Cardinal Mazzella and Father Thomas J. Bouquillon and to Cardinal Manning's *Vatican Council and Its Definitions*. He read Blaise Pascal and St. Francis de Sales, St. Thomas Aquinas and St. Augustine. Just before ordination he turned increasingly to devotional works on the priesthood and on the sacrament of the Holy Eucharist.[44]

Finally, on June 4, 1898, Ryan was ordained to the priesthood by Archbishop Ireland. All the Ryan family, parents and nine other children, attended the ordination upstairs in the class building at the seminary. After the ceremony, William Ryan warned all his children that it was to be "Father John" from now on, and no one was to call Father John "stupid" to his face. The children duly obeyed—all except David, the youngest and least tractable son—and thus was born that respectful formality with which members of the Ryan family always referred to their siblings in the religious state.

For his first solemn mass, Father John planned to use the church at Rosemount, which was larger than the little frame building of his own parish. But the neighbors would not hear of it. They insisted on his saying his first public mass at St. Agatha's. To accommodate all who wished to attend, they removed one side of the church and put up a canvas-covered platform large enough for the overflow from the church itself. The canvas cover was a happy idea: it rained that morning. After the Mass, the rain having stopped in time, the whole crowd returned to an open-air feast at the Ryans'. A brass band in full uniform came over from Vermillion. The new priest was well liked in the neighborhood, and the

[42] Ryan, "Georgism and Justice," *ibid.*, April 24, 1896.
[43] Ryan, "Journal," Oct. 10, 1897.
[44] St. Paul Seminary, "Library Journal," 1895ff.

occasion was memorable, especially for Maria Ryan, who felt herself returning her first son to God.

During the summer months, Ryan was sent to the parish of Belle
Creek, the only parochial assignment in his priestly career. That fall
Archbishop Ireland sent him for graduate training in moral theology to
the Catholic University of America in Washington as preparation for
teaching moral theology at the St. Paul Seminary.

Student, Teacher, Scholar

WHEN HE LEFT St. Paul for Washington, Father John Ryan moved toward a center of ecclesiastical bickering. From its beginning the Catholic University of America had been caught in the controversies that divided liberal and conservative Catholics. Its principal supporters were prominent liberals. If credit for the creation of the university belonged to any one man, it was Bishop Spalding of Peoria; few leading prelates gave it greater support than Archbishop Ireland; its first rector, Bishop John J. Keane, had drawn the conservatives' special wrath by his appearance in episcopal garb in Harvard's Appleton Chapel. More by coincidence than by conviction, Archbishop Corrigan showed up in the opposing camp, with Bishop McQuaid lending him powerful support. McQuaid was sensitive to the competition that the university might offer to his own project, St. Bernard's Seminary in the Diocese of Rochester. Corrigan was building a diocesan seminary, and the Jesuit university at Fordham was also in its formative years. Both men objected to the tone of the university, which they viewed as the creature of the liberals. Cardinal Gibbons, a warm partisan of the university once it was set up, played his usual compromiser's role, attempting to keep peace between the factions without causing too much of a stir in Rome.[1]

Prominent professors at the university had taken publicly controversial roles. Two, Joseph Pohle and Joseph Schroeder, had supported the conservative sentiment that ran through German areas of the Church in America. They had spoken frequently at German-American conventions, and in regular summer trips abroad had rallied support among European Catholics. Since Monsignor Schroeder's influence carried to the Roman Curia, he had been a figure to reckon with in the United States. Both men had been forced out of the university before Ryan came.[2] On the other side, Father Bouquillon, professor of moral theology at the university, had energetically defended Archbishop Ireland's controversial arrangement that provided for parochial and public education in the same buildings in Faribault, Minnesota.[3] This support made liberals grateful and conservatives irate. Bouquillon had also served on the four-man committee that, in giving Father McGlynn a clean bill, had furnished Archbishop Satolli with the warrant to order McGlynn's reinstatement. Of these four, Thomas O'Gorman had since become Bishop of Sioux Falls, South Dakota, but Bouquillon and the other two, Edward A. Pace and Thomas J. Shahan, were still at the university. Father William J. Kerby, professor of sociology, fit easily into their ranks.

Two years before Ryan arrived in Washington, the liberals had received an unmistakable rebuke when Rome abruptly and unexpectedly ended Keane's rectorship. His successor, Monsignor Thomas J. Conaty, passed muster by avoiding clear identification with either wing of the hierarchy. An active organizer of and president of the Catholic Total Abstinence Union of America, he had served in a cause that drew the ardent allegiance of Ireland and Keane. At the same time, he had headed the Catholic Summer School at Cliff Haven, near Plattsburgh, New York, an experiment in popular education enjoying Corrigan's special favor. And Satolli—now Cardinal Satolli, Prefect of the Congregation of Studies —was reported to have been charmed by Conaty. Enjoying this wide-

[1] John Tracy Ellis, *The Formative Years of the Catholic University of America* (Washington, D.C., 1946).

[2] Colman S. Barry, *The Catholic Church and German Americans* (Milwaukee, 1953), pp. 230–235.

[3] Thomas J. Bouquillon, "Education: To Whom Does It Belong?" pamphlet (Baltimore, 1892); Daniel F. Reilly, *The School Controversy, 1891–1893* (Washington, D.C., 1943).

spread favor, Conaty brought to the university a modicum of educational experience rather than any pronounced theological or social views.[4]

The year after Ryan's arrival, the liberals—at the university and elsewhere—suffered their most stunning blow: a papal letter of January, 1899, *Testem benevolentiae*, addressed to Cardinal Gibbons. The letter condemned what was known among European churchmen as "Americanism." Without stating that anyone in the United States actually held the views he condemned, Pope Leo XIII warned against the argument that "in order the more easily to bring over to Catholic doctrine those who dissent from it, the Church ought to adapt herself somewhat to our advanced civilization, and, relaxing her ancient rigor, show some indulgence to modern popular theories and methods," this indulgence extending even to "the doctrines in which the *deposit of faith* is contained." He warned against views that the direct action of the Holy Spirit served as a substitute for the guidance of the Church; that natural virtue was adequate without the sanctifying addition of divine grace; that the needs of modern times have established the superiority of "active virtues" over "passive virtues" and that therefore religious vows, while suitable for an earlier age, now "avail little for Christian perfection and the good of human society, and rather obstruct and interfere with it."[5] The controversy over Americanism had reached white heat in France, where Catholics who wished to effect a rapprochement with the French Republic pointed to the growth of the Church in the United States as evidence that the faith could thrive under a secular state. Conservative leaders of the Church in France, hostile to the republican government, resisted this view, pointing out that the Church in the United States was thriving only at the cost of purity of doctrine. The publication abroad of a careless French translation of Walter Elliott's *Life of Father Hecker*, together with a provocative introduction by Abbé Félix Klein, jarred nerves made sensitive by the struggle within the French Church and gave a convenient focus to issues that went far beyond it. With his letter to Gibbons, Pope Leo was attempting to still the controversy on both sides of the Atlantic. In the United States, the conservatives were jubilant about what they regarded as the repudiation of their liberal opponents. The liberals, stung by the letter, insisted that it condemned ideas prevalent in France, that it had no relevance to

4 Peter E. Hogan, *The Catholic University of America, 1896–1903* (Washington, D.C., 1949), pp. 13–27.
5 The encyclical is reprinted in Ellis, ed., *Documents of American Catholic History* (Milwaukee, 1956), pp. 554–562.

anything being taught in the United States—a conclusion difficult to reconcile with its having been directed to Cardinal Gibbons. The liberals readily accepted the ideas of the letter, protesting—with some justice, it now seems—that they had never taught what the letter condemned. Still, the Vatican had raised a note of caution against the tendency of their thought; the line of danger was closer to them than to the self-confidently orthodox conservatives.[6]

Ryan, in his first year of graduate work when *Testem benevolentiae* appeared, felt the characteristically liberal reaction: "Of course, these doctrines are wrong, but who holds them in the United States? Surely not the Paulists."[7] The conservatives viewed this liberal response as sheer dissembling, but in fact Rome probably looked for this type of reaction. The Pope wanted to raise a monitory finger against dangerous tendencies, not to provoke schisms by branding prelates as heretics.

Despite these setbacks, the tone of the university remained liberal. Father Joseph McSorley, a Paulist whose student days at the university overlapped Ryan's, has recalled that the atmosphere was heavy with liberalism.[8]

The university in 1898 consisted of three buildings in Brookland, a suburb of northeast Washington several miles from the Maryland border. About three miles from the Capitol, the campus included an ample sixty acres perched on a hill that looked over to the Soldiers' Home. The Baltimore and Ohio ran a spur within a few hundred yards of the buildings, and a trolley line up North Capitol Street and along Michigan Avenue right onto the grounds of the university made access to the city quite easy. The little village of Brookland clustered around a few stores about a ten-minute walk to the east.

The university's two main buildings were of heavy gray local sandstone, rectangular in shape, and adorned with the period's arches, pillars, and busywork. McMahon Hall housed classrooms, offices, and a library. Caldwell Hall, the first building, served all purposes. It contained classrooms and bedrooms, a kitchen and dining room, and a chapel ringed about with twelve small altars at which the priests on the faculty and among the students celebrated their daily Masses. A third building, tall

[6] Thomas T. McAvoy, *The Great Crisis in American Catholic History, 1895–1900* (Chicago, 1957); John Joseph Kenny, "The Influence of Father Hecker on French Catholic Thought," M.A. dissertation, University of Maryland (1960), pp. 83–87.

[7] Ryan, "The Congregation of St. Paul," MS. of article (1933).

[8] Interview with Joseph McSorley, May 7, 1958.

and gawky Keane Hall (now Albert Hall), housed both faculty and students.

The priest-students and two Sulpician priests made up the community known as Divinity College. Though the discipline at Caldwell Hall was not so strict as at St. Paul, the Sulpicians were expected to maintain a fairly close check on their charges' hours and habits. Ryan, now almost thirty years old, may have chafed under this quasi-monastic routine, but many years spent under clerical discipline had trained him to accept it.

The university, a charter member of the Association of American Universities, was primarily a graduate school in sacred studies—theology, canon law, philosophy—but in recent years it had added law and science courses as possible sources of revenue. The various departments were still rather small. In Ryan's second year only thirty-three theological students lived in Caldwell Hall, though this number was swelled by at least as many more course auditors from the religious houses that had begun to cluster around the university—the Paulists, the Congregation of Holy Cross, and the Marists, for example. A staff of four professors of moral theology, one associate professor, and one instructor taught these men— a rather too generous faculty-student ratio.

Ryan had some able teachers whose names would become known beyond the university. Father Kerby, who taught sociology, later helped found the National Conference of Catholic Charities. Charles P. Neill, the economist, went on to the post of United States Commissioner of Labor. In moral theology, Ryan studied principally with Bouquillon, whom he knew to have international standing as a leading contemporary theologian.

During his first year Ryan studied moral theology, canon law, sociology, and political economy. He had to continue canon law for a second year to satisfy the requirements for his licentiate in sacred theology (a canonical license to teach the sacred sciences), but then he dropped it and concentrated on moral theology and economics. He had a splendid record all the way through, winning his licentiate *maxima cum laude*. Occasionally he faltered a bit in attendance, especially in canon law, but his achievement grades were invariably "4," the top of a scale from 1 to 4. In his final year, he was given no grades, just comments. Two of these gave a telling preview of Ryan's subsequent career: he was awarded an "excellent" in moral theology but only a "good" in economics.[9]

Father Bouquillon, Ryan's "major professor," was a swarthy Belgian

[9] Catholic University of America, "Record of Students, 1896–1902," p. 167, Catholic University Archives.

with a round face, a badly rumpled soutane, and some skill at the pool table. His students noticed that he invariably stopped in the chapel before he went on to class. Tenacious in argument, he never failed in courtesy. He lacked color in the classroom, for a hesitating manner delayed his statements until he had the words to match the precision of his thought. He entered each class with a "passion for exactness, for accuracy, and for thoroughness," and he expected his students to pick up these qualities. One of his students even noted that his mind, in becoming too cold and logical, became "the victim of its own insight and grasp."[10]

Bouquillon tried to understand the sociology and the economics of a problem before passing on to its morality. He complained that existing theological manuals were out of touch with contemporary life, and he warned that moral theology would not regain its position of true distinction until theologians intelligently applied Judeo-Christian principles to the social, religious, and civil problems of the modern individual. To do this, he said, moral theology had to profit by constant contact with all the social sciences. Bouquillon followed his own injunction, as his part in the McGlynn case and in the controversy over parochial schools in Minnesota showed. At the same time, however, he opposed confining the study of moral theology to current problems. Remembering that the *Summa Theologica* of St. Thomas was a harmonious whole, a "living organism," he warned that "the attempt to study one portion of the field of theology . . . to the neglect or exclusion of any other, must be fatal."[11] Ryan later remembered Bouquillon as the most erudite man he had ever known.[12]

A second influence, considerably less overpowering, was Ryan's sociology professor, Father Kerby. Kerby, an Iowan one year Ryan's junior, took his doctorate at the Catholic University of Louvain in Belgium and then returned to Catholic University of America for a long career as an educator and social reformer. Keenly aware that unless society solved industrial problems "the socialist will have been a prophet with a mission," Kerby spoke favorably of unions, of identifying labels on products produced by union labor, and of the Consumers' League, which was just starting its fight for decent working conditions. Though much of his comment was directed against socialism, Kerby was also capable of outlining the Church's affirmative role in solving the social question:

[10] "Thomas Joseph Bouquillon," and "Memorial Exercises for Dr. Bouquillon," *Catholic University Bulletin*, January, 1903, pp. 152–163.

[11] Bouquillon, "Moral Theology at the End of the Nineteenth Century," *ibid.*, April, 1899, pp. 244–268.

[12] Ryan, *Social Doctrine in Action*, p. 63.

We who are in and of the Catholic faith feel and know that we have the truth, and with it a superb and active organization which is the greatest social power on earth; we must rise to the occasion and meet it. We must study social science and fit ourselves; we must study the organic relation of the Church to society and form a social conscience; we must bravely follow its dictates and assist in the work of reform. The Church has already done this in Europe, but it must be done here. The age is drifting to the conviction that the last decisive test of any religion is its power to solve the social question. The test should be welcomed by us, for the Catholic Church can meet the situation and bring social peace.[13]

Between them, Bouquillon and Kerby spoke words prophetic for the direction of Ryan's thought. Though Ryan never reached Bouquillon's depth of learning in the theological classics, the older priest succeeded in forcing Ryan's attention onto the political, social, economic context of theological problems. For Ryan parts of that context were blank. He knew agrarian problems with the passion of a participant, and he learned about industrial problems from his reading. But his training in history never went beyond the few books he had read as a seminarian in St. Paul; the number of these not directly related to the history of the Church would not have crowded a quite small desk. Ryan never filled in this gap in his knowledge; he never developed a real historical sense.

Yet during the years in Washington he at least began his education in economic history. William J. Ashley's *Introduction to English Economic History and Theory* introduced him to the medieval guilds and to the medieval canonists' tracts on the morality of economic practices. Here he learned the concept of the just price, that elusive standard that promised justice to all parties to a transaction. Here in a period in which no man, except possibly the king, owned land outright, Ryan learned about the social responsibility of property. Living in a period of separation of religion and economics, Ryan looked back enthusiastically, though not wistfully, to an era when their close interaction served Christendom. John A. Hobson carried this story up to date in his *Evolution of Modern Capitalism* (1897), and then in *The Economics of Distribution* (1900) he supplied the basis for the most striking theme of Ryan's economic writings. Hobson argued that when the balance between profits and wages tilted too decisively in favor of profits, workers lacked the money to buy industrial goods. Capitalists, looking for an outlet for their profits, created new

[13] William J. Kerby, "The Laborer and His Point of View," *American Catholic Quarterly Review*, January, 1901, p. 109, and "The Socialism of the Socialist," *ibid.*, July, 1901, pp. 476, 485.

productive facilities that added even further to the oversupply of goods. Hobson said briefly, "We save too much and consume too little." Hobson's analysis did not command wide attention until the depression of 1929, but it convinced Ryan as soon as he saw it. An absorbing seminal idea, this theory of underconsumption became central to Ryan's thinking. When he published his fullest moral treatise, *Distributive Justice*, in 1916, he thought seriously of dedicating it to John A. Hobson.[14]

Father Ryan's initial two years at the university ultimately stretched into four. He received his S.T.B. (bachelor in sacred theology) at the end of the first year, and his S.T.L. (licentiate in sacred theology) at the end of the second. During the summers he returned home. Without a parochial assignment, he read and studied a good deal, especially since his brothers were sufficiently grown to take care of the farms. In September, 1899, he preached at a Labor Day observance at the Cathedral of St. Paul, quite an honor for a priest ordained just over a year. His new learning at the university proved useful: the Fathers of the Church and the medieval canonists had unhesitatingly condemned irresponsible wealth, and Leo XIII had made their pleas as contemporary as the telephone. If Ryan was urging the consolations of religion on labor, he was as pointedly talking to churchmen, reminding them of their responsibilities.[15]

In the fall of 1900, Archbishop Ireland went abroad, thoughtlessly having left without giving Ryan an assignment. With more brashness than logic, the young priest assumed that he was to return to the university. He did—and got away with it. Ireland allowed him to remain four years in all—the happiest four years of his life, Ryan recalled toward the end of his career. At some point, there was talk of bringing him home to teach Latin, but someone in the St. Paul chancery interceded in time to prevent it.[16]

After he returned to the university, Ryan's name appeared in the *Catholic World*, the *Catholic University Bulletin*, and the *International Journal of Ethics*, first with book reviews, then with formal articles. His first appearance, a review of Henry Demarest Lloyd's *A Country Without Strikes*, was the lead article in the *Catholic World* for November, 1900. Lloyd was favorably describing New Zealand's compulsory arbitration of labor disputes. Ryan approved. Of course, this interference limited

[14] Ryan, *Social Doctrine in Action*, p. 64.
[15] St. Paul *Catholic Bulletin*, Sept. 8, 1899.
[16] "High Honors for Monsignor John A. Ryan," *Catholic University Bulletin*, March, 1934, p. 4.

free contract, he said, but the laborer's right to a fair wage, which involved basic human rights, was more fundamental than a free contract. Anyway, "free contract" was a misnomer: the employer had the distinct economic advantage over a "comparatively powerless" laborer not really free to reject a job that he needed in order to live. Noting that New Zealand's labor courts generally favored the workers, Ryan said that the state acted justly in helping the weaker side.[17]

For the *International Journal of Ethics* he added a further indictment of capitalism, based on his licentiate dissertation, "The Ethics of Speculation." The route of his argument was tortuous and detailed, but the conclusion was clear: "Speculation as an institution is *economically* of doubtful validity; *socially* it is productive of great and widespread evils; *morally* it is vitiated by a very considerable amount of dishonest 'deals' and practices."[18]

That same month he pulled together some of his notes for his doctoral dissertation to answer the question, "What is a living wage?" The article sagged under the weight of citations, but he came up with a good statement of the principle of the living wage and a detailed household accounting that set two dollars a day as the irreducible minimum.[19]

When Ryan finished his four years at the university he hoped for a fifth. He had completed his course work with distinction, but he was not ready for comprehensive examinations, nor was his dissertation written. Once again his special interests may have distracted him from the routine. The Capitol and the Library of Congress may have filled too many hours. His degree was to be in moral theology; the area of his special interest, the virtue of justice, particularly in economics, formed only a small part of that whole. Much remained to be done, and he wanted another year. After Bouquillon died in Brussels in the summer of 1902, the School of Theology offered Ryan a teaching fellowship in moral theology, a stopgap appointment while he completed his degree.[20] But the Archbishop of St. Paul, who had made a substantial investment in Ryan for the benefit of

[17] Ryan, "A Country Without Strikes," *Catholic World*, November, 1900, pp. 145–157; Aaron I. Abell, "The Catholic Factor in the Social Justice Movement," in McAvoy, *Roman Catholicism and the American Way of Life* (Notre Dame, 1960), p. 73.

[18] Ryan, "The Ethics of Speculation," *International Journal of Ethics*, April, 1902, p. 347.

[19] Ryan, "The Laborer's Right to a Living Wage," *Catholic University Bulletin*, April, 1902, pp. 156–174.

[20] "Report of the Dean of the Faculty of Theology to the Secretary of the Academic Senate," *n.d.*, in "Academic Senate: Reports," Catholic University Archives.

the local seminary, was unwilling to extend Ryan's absence. The St. Paul Seminary needed a professor of moral theology; Ryan was canonically licensed to teach it. No more time away. Furthermore, Ireland was already losing one member of his faculty to the university in the fall of 1902—Thomas F. Shields, professor of psychology. So Ireland was adamant concerning Ryan's return.

An obedient subject of his ordinary, grateful for the opportunities for graduate work, Ryan returned ungrudgingly. St. Paul, city and seminary, was home, and Ryan felt a strong sentimental attachment to it. Before he left Washington, one of his professors asked him whether he worried about getting into trouble in St. Paul, his social and economic views being notably at variance with Archbishop Ireland's.[21] He would find the answer in St. Paul.

That fall Ryan started his classes, back in familiar rooms. Still a student, as he would ever be, he was now a teacher as well.

At thirty-three, Father Ryan was old to be inaugurating his productive career, young to be a professor of moral theology at an important seminary, the only diocesan seminary formally affiliated with the Catholic University of America. St. Paul's was growing steadily. When Ryan was in college, the clerical students just filled one wing of St. Thomas College. When the seminary opened in 1894, the seventy-five suites for students seemed adequate. During the thirteen years, 1902–1915, that the young theologian spent on the faculty, the student body passed two hundred,[22] and a new residence hall was added to accommodate the overflow from the original two. Ryan was there in the period of the seminary's greatest growth. The only major addition since has been the handsome Archbishop Ireland Memorial Library.

Archbishop Ireland regarded an assignment to the seminary as tremendously important. An exacting supervisor, he insisted on his professors' presence at all seminary functions, chapel as well as classes. At the same time, he protected the faculty from the weekend parochial assignments—helping out in a parish with confessions on Saturday and public Masses on Sunday—that would have deprived the professors of leisure for their own work and recreation.[23] Furthermore, the seminary followed a

[21] "High Honors for Monsignor John A. Ryan," *loc. cit.*, p. 4.
[22] *Catholic Bulletin*, Feb. 22, 1913.
[23] Reardon, *The Catholic Church in the Diocese of St. Paul.* p. 313.

normal academic year, so that Ryan had his summers free for work and travel.

For three or four years John Ryan did not wander far from the seminary. He had to prepare lectures from scratch—a formidable job, especially since he wrote them out rather fully. His courses at Catholic University had given him a backlog on which to build, of course, but those had been graduate courses, and here he was dealing with seminarians approaching moral theology for the first time. Preparing his courses—he also taught English—consumed most of the first two years. Thereafter he stuck to the same basic framework for the rest of the time he taught at St. Paul's.

Father Ryan's students remember him as amiable enough out of class, but intense, businesslike, dry, even dull in class. He lectured hurriedly, impatient to pass on quantities of his own learning. He never had any success in conducting class as a discussion. What his students regarded as easy questions led him off into long monologues, for he was wary of simple solutions to nice moral questions. He acquired a new nickname, "Fogy Ryan," partly because he exuded an air of wisdom beyond his years. Many of his colleagues took on the status of "characters," in seminary chatter; not Father Ryan. He had no special reputation as either a hard or an easy teacher. He played tennis on the seminary court, neither good enough tennis nor bad enough to attract an audience. Among his colleagues, he quickly established a reputation as a hard worker. Father Nicholas Stubinitsky, who taught German, liked to stop by for an evening chat. But he was greeted coolly. Each time Ryan pointedly held his finger to mark the place in his book, glanced up from his desk, peered out over his pince-nez, and asked curtly, "What do you want?" This was enough to chill further conversation, so "Stubie" and everyone else stopped coming. That suited Father Ryan. He did not welcome interruptions from the seminarians, either. When he was dean of South Hall, that is, the resident professor in charge, he cowed noisy seminarians into silence by standing at the foot of the stairwell and barking "Quiet!" so authoritatively that his voice filled the whole building. Then, order restored, he resumed his work at his secondhand typewriter with the circular keyboard.

With his lectures completed, Ryan devoted the next eighteen months to his doctoral dissertation on the ethics of the living wage, which he finished in the fall of 1905. During these months he published five articles in Catholic magazines. Three were based on the dissertation; indeed, two of these were actually chapters from the larger work. And the other two dealt with topics that would be of continuing interest to him: small families and the morality of labor unions.

In the fall of 1903, President Theodore Roosevelt set off a national debate by warning America of race suicide: its best citizens were not providing an adequate number of children for the next generation. Avoiding the overtones of Anglo-Saxon racial superiority in Roosevelt's statement, Ryan wrote in the *Ecclesiastical Review*, an unofficial trade journal for American Catholic priests, that the sacrifice of moral fiber for luxury and sensual pleasure was causing an abnormal decline in the American birth rate. He scorned an anonymous writer for the *North American Review* who insisted that the happiness of parents was the primary purpose of marriage, the rearing of children being desirable only to the extent that it contributed to that end. This was worthy of a place in Thomas Carlyle's "Pig Philosophy," Ryan wrote. The small family was generally immoral, he asserted, because the positive means of achieving it—"and in the overwhelming majority of instances the means are positive"—were "often criminal—the murder of the unborn offspring—and always perverse, unnatural, and degrading." He mocked the pretense of a fuller life as an excuse for small and childless families; actually what was meant was more luxury, which spoiled the children and weakened the *ésprit* of the nation. Ryan noted that the declining Anglo-Saxon population in the United States failed to provide a selection large enough to produce leaders. In a sentence somewhere between a taunt and a threat, he observed that the time was "not distantly remote" when, if Catholics remained true to their consciences and traditions, "mere preponderating numbers will enable them to dominate American life."[24]

About the same time Ryan used the anthracite coal strike of 1902 as an occasion for comments in the *American Catholic Quarterly Review* on "The Morality of the Aims and Methods of Labor Unions." Skeptical of the automatic harmonies of unlimited competition, he insisted that laborers could not leave their fate to employers and consumers. He regarded the argument for the "right to work" as pious pretense designed to weaken labor unions without actually guaranteeing workers anything substantial. Without being oversanguine about the wisdom of the proletariat, he

[24] Ryan, "The Small Family and National Decadence," *Ecclesiastical Review*, February, 1904, pp. 140–155; Paterfamilias (pseud.), " 'Race Suicide' and Common Sense," *North American Review*, June, 1903, pp. 892–900.

recognized the usefulness of unions in improving conditions for some workers. Because of his well-established enthusiasm for the medieval guild system, he approved generally of the closed shop. He even tolerated limitation of output to the extent that it protected the worker against pressure for an excessive day's work. While approving of unions as such, especially as a safeguard against socialism, he viewed the strike and the boycott as dangerous, though in an inherently unjust situation the injustice might warrant these extreme recourses.[25]

In all these judgments Ryan was applying the traditional canons of justice to twentieth-century conditions. Precise knowledge of moral principles came first, followed by wide acquaintance with economic institutions. Only then could a theologian translate moral principles into specific programs of action. This combination of moral principles and economic fact was the young professor's goal in his doctoral dissertation, "A Living Wage: Its Ethical and Economic Aspects."[26]

In his dissertation, Ryan argues that every man, because he is "endowed by nature, or rather, by God, with the rights that are requisite to a reasonable development of his personality," has a natural right to share in the earth's products. The primary natural right to subsist on the bounty of the earth exists at all times; in an industrial society the right takes the form of a living wage. When a wage earner has expended his energy in some useful task, he has met the reasonable prerequisite to a decent livelihood. Subsistence, a bare livelihood, is the product of man's right to life; a "*decent* livelihood" is demanded by man's dignity.

The primary obligation for the living wage, Ryan says, falls on the employer as a "reasonable consequence of his position in the economic organism." The employer cannot escape his duty by getting his workers to agree to work for less, for the so-called "free contract" is consistent with extortion. "The underpaid laborer does not *willingly* sell his labor for less than the equivalent of a decent livelihood, any more than the wayfarer willingly gives up his purse to the highwayman." In assessing rights, Ryan says, superior economic force has no more ethical validity than superior physical force. The employer cannot base his pay rates on a worker's productivity, for that is usually unknowable, and anyway it is "always inferior to needs as a canon of distribution." Only a genuine

[25] Ryan, "The Morality of the Aims and Methods of Labor Unions," *American Catholic Quarterly Review*, April, 1904, pp. 326–355.

[26] My quotations are all from the published version: Ryan, *A Living Wage: Its Ethical and Economic Aspects* (New York, 1906).

inability to pay a living wage releases an employer from his obligation. An employer's right to his profit, like the investor's right to his interest, is a real right, but it is subordinate to the worker's essential needs.

Consumers have an obligation, too: to pay a fair price for goods, a price that enables the producers to be "decently remunerated." If, without undue convenience, they can patronize a business that carries a union label over another known to sweat its workers, they are morally bound to do so. The rule is slippery, yet it imposes a real obligation: ". . . the consumer is morally answerable for insufficient wages in proportion to his power to make reasonable efforts toward bettering them."

The rich have a special duty. Quoting the Christian tradition from Paul to Basil to Thomas Aquinas, and finally to Leo XIII, Ryan asserts that superfluous goods are a "trust to be administered for the benefit of the needy." By "superfluous goods" Ryan means what remains after the satisfaction of reasonable wants; "reasonable wants" are those short of desires involving injury to health, mind, or character: excessive drink, or houses and clothing directed more to ostentation than to comfort or aesthetics. Because so many workers in America approach "extreme and grave need" as defined by the theologians, Ryan agrees with Andrew Carnegie, the steel manufacturer, that all superfluous goods should be used as a trust for the poor. Like Carnegie, Ryan wants, not direct gifts of money, but subsidies to activities that would improve the workers' condition. Unlike Carnegie, who poured money into the construction of free libraries, Ryan calls for financial aid for organizing and maintaining labor unions; industrial education; hospitals for "insufficiently remunerated laborers" and their families; subsidized housing projects. If these are strange ideas of the stewardship of property, Father Ryan says, it is past time for somebody to remind Christians of them, for they are the traditional teachings of Christianity. The trouble lies not in the teachings, which admittedly are demanding, but in the age, so callous to human suffering that it accepts human misery as the unquestioned price of natural economic laws. The obligation to help rests especially on the lenders and landowners who profit from underpaid workers, for while the obligation of most wealthy men is solely one of charity, the obligation of landowners and lenders derives from the virtue of justice.

Turning to the role of the state, Ryan observes, with more optimism than the facts warranted, that the "baneful heritage" of laissez faire no longer holds any considerable following. Thus the way is clear for him to assert: "As an abstract proposition, the State has both the right and the duty to compel all employees to pay a Living Wage." On the authority of Sidney and Beatrice Webb, the English Fabians, he is convinced that a national minimum wage is no more open to economic objection than the factory legislation already on the books. He foresees political barriers, but he is not willing to surrender to them. A "perverse individualism which prefers irrational liberty and industrial anarchy to a legal regime of order and justice" makes it difficult to carry through the changes in state and federal constitutions necessary for legislation. But happily, the progressive movement, personified by President Roosevelt, is "very rapidly" changing its attitude toward the "legislative repression of abuses." Once an amendment adequate to regulate corporations is passed, a modification allowing wage commissions to fix minimum rates of pay will follow easily.

Sensing that the legally guaranteed minimum wage is a long way off, Ryan suggests intermediate measures: minimum-wage levels in public services or in private work done by contract for the government; a similar measure on all "quasi-public industries of a monopolistic character" such as railroads, telephones and express companies. In addition, there are indirect methods—limit working hours to eight hours a day, subsidize public housing, pay old-age pensions, this last "in fact, a part of the Living Wage that is due him [the worker] for his life work." To pay for these measures, Ryan grasps gladly at Carnegie's endorsement of heavy inheritance taxes, and adds his own defense of a graduated income tax.

Ryan invokes moral suasion to back up social effort. If clergymen set forth the duty of paying a living wage as vigorously as they expound other duties that are no more important, if they withhold the privileges of church membership from recalcitrant employers as they do from any persistently disobedient members, if writers condemn in specific terms employers who could pay a living wage and do not, then moral suasion would reveal a power not yet tapped. Moral suasion and concerted social action—both are necessary; together they would yield astonishing results in moving the community toward social justice.[27]

One chapter, "The Obligation of the Laborer," gives the expectation

[27] The term "social justice" was not widely used before its frequent appearance in Pius XI's encyclical *Quadragesimo anno* (1931). Its precise meaning in theological writing varies. For Ryan, it meant the "common good" understood as the welfare of all and of each. Patrick W. Gearty, *The Economic Thought of Monsignor John A. Ryan* (Washington, D.C., 1953), pp. 112–117. On the term itself, see Leo W. Shields, *The History and Meaning of the Term Social Justice* (Notre Dame, 1941), and William Ferree, *The Act of Social Justice* (Washington, D.C., 1942), especially pp. 80–141.

of balancing a worker's duties against his rights, but this expectation is disappointed. Ryan notes that saving, temperance, and increased productive efficiency may help labor some in isolated cases, but little compared to what might be accomplished by unions, especially industrial unions reaching down to the least skilled and most exploited workers. The bulk of the chapter denounces economists and moralists who urge workers to practice "what is somewhat euphemistically termed 'sexual self-restraint.' " Advocacy of a lowered birth rate has become a pose that saves the comfortable from a true view of their responsibility to pay a living wage, he complains; the blame is sloughed off on workers who are viewed as creating their own problems by giving unrestrained scope to their passions.

To establish his thesis, Ryan uses both moralists and economists to back him up. Looking back into European history, he jumps hastily to the conclusion that earlier ages accepted "an objective standard of justice." Drawing on Ashley's *English Economic History*, he finds in the Middle Ages a deeply ethical sense of the just price, and he traces in the Fathers of the Church and in medieval theologians the fixed idea that "every human being has an imperishable right to a livelihood from the common bounty of nature." He thinks that medieval writers, even St. Thomas, were disappointingly imprecise in defining a just price for labor. Yet later moralists, especially Luís de Molina, S.J., and Juan Cardinal de Lugo, in the seventeenth century, set a standard not far removed from the essentials of a reasonable wage. He deplores modern manualists whose applications of medieval teaching to modern conditions confirms the judgment of classical economists. Taking medieval phrases like "customary wage" and "common estimate," they equate them with "current wages" and with the result of the higgling of the marketplace. The French Jesuit Charles Antoine argues that the laborer is entitled to remuneration that would replace the energy expended in his employer's service. This principle, Ryan argues, readily adapts itself to sweatshops where, in fact, workers manage to reappear day after day; it could readily exist side by side with David Ricardo's iron law of wages.

Ryan takes on more formidable opinion when he challenges the traditional Christian view of the just price based upon the "social estimate," the judgment of society as to what is reasonable. However satisfactory theoretically, the social estimate lacks definiteness in a society that has lost the common moral moorings of medieval society, he says. Older formulas about paying the worker the "worth," "equivalent," or "value" of his labor need more precise formulation adjusted to modern industrial society. Leo XIII's definition of the living wage in *Rerum no-varum* meets this need, in Ryan's view, for it takes cognizance both of a man's right to life and of the social obligation of those who hold property, and it is geared to modern society. Its clear pronouncement that a worker deprived of an income sufficient for "reasonable and frugal comfort" is the "victim of fraud and injustice" opened a new era. This encyclical, Ryan says, "converted the Living Wage from an implicit into an explicit principle of Catholic ethics."

At one point, Father Ryan goes beyond the standard set by Leo XIII. Did the Pope's definition of a living wage include wages sufficient to maintain a family in reasonable and frugal comfort? An inquiry directed to Rome just after *Rerum novarum* appeared was answered by Tommasso Cardinal Zigliara, O.P., an official of the Roman Curia credited with drafting the first version of the encyclical.[28] He stated that an employer was not bound in strict justice to pay a familial living wage, although he might act contrary to charity in failing to do so. Rather brashly, Ryan declared that the cardinal's explanation "leaves something to be desired, both in clearness and in conclusiveness." The worker's right rests on his dignity as an individual. This dignity undoubtedly includes the right to marry and to procreate as the essential condition of normal life. If justice is satisfied by a wage sufficient only for the celibate, the majority of men will lack the means necessary to meet the demands of their normal condition. They are forced to choose between a living wage and a normal family life. Hence, Ryan asserts, a familial living wage is indeed demanded by justice.[29] In concrete terms, based on a careful breakdown of living expenses, Ryan suggests $600 as the *minimum* acceptable in any American city for decent living. In 1906 the average wage for urban workers (that is, excluding farm labor) was $571; about 60 percent of America's industrial labor force fell below that acceptable minimum.[30]

The ethical standard defined, Ryan turns to the economics of the living wage. He sees little to cheer him. Wages have risen since 1865, but in the most recent quarter-century the upward trend has leveled off. To break down the defense of this situation by orthodox economists who argue for the free contract between worker and employer, Ryan

[28] Henry J. Browne, *The Catholic Church and the Knights of Labor*, p. 347.
[29] A subsequent work, pursuing Ryan's idea here, is John D. Callahan, *The Catholic Attitude Toward a Familial Living Wage* (Washington, D.C., 1936), especially pp. 61ff.
[30] Paul Douglas, *Real Wages in the United States, 1890–1926* (Boston, 1930), p. 391; *Northwestern Chronicle*, Nov. 13, 1906.

invokes the Webbs and John A. Hobson. Indeed, most of his arguments come from English sources, for he elects to regard England as "typical of the greater part of Europe and of the whole of North America," an assumption that does violence to the variant roles of both Germany and the United States. He protests against the notion of economic law as an independent force demanding obedience. Actually, economic law is, in the words of Alfred Marshall, the English economist, no more than "a statement that a certain course of action may be expected under certain conditions from members of an industrial group." Ryan senses the play upon the word "law": economists accept Marshall's definition; then in practice they infer that economic law directs a course of action. What is only descriptive becomes normative, if not mandatory. This switch in meaning then leads to the confident dictum that wages cannot be modified by human effort. In practice, wages determined by the tenets of classical liberalism represent simply the relative bargaining power of the contracting parties. Ryan draws on Hobson and Friedrich Engels, on Thomas Carlyle and John Ruskin, to show that classical liberalism has led the English working class to poverty while their employers grew wealthy, to starvation while wives and children took men's jobs. Ryan concedes that classical economics enjoys a presumption in its favor because of the writings of economists and of the legislation based on those writings. But that presumption vanishes, he says, when careful analysis exposes the deceptive ambiguities of economic law and the fanciful hopes of legislative policy. What remains, nakedly, is the selfishness of the middle class.

Distribution, not production, is the essential problem, Ryan thinks as the result of his reading in Hobson. America already has the physical capacity to produce enough for all. Adequate wages would permit workers to buy what industry produced; the increased demand for goods would create a need for new factories; these in turn would create still more jobs. The economy would expand. A living wage paid to all workers would move the economy onto this upward spiral and undercut the perpetual danger of overproduction that plagues individualistic competitive capitalism. Yet Ryan dejectedly predicts that the economic fallacies that held back the upward movement of wages would "be with us for many years yet," for the great majority of economists are captivated by the value of productivity as such.

Father Ryan's striking synthesis of economics and morality never went beyond a narrow area of each. In economics, he drew principally on economic historians like Ashley and the Webbs, on Hobson for his theory of underconsumption, and, of course, on Ely and Lilly for the discussions that touched both fields. His old attraction to Henry George was apparent in the chapter on rent, though George's name appeared neither in the text nor in the footnotes and bibliography. As Ryan looked upon the claims of rent, profits, interest, and wages, he drew his official readers at the university through a précis of the fundamentals of economics that he had had to master himself. Ryan had much to learn about economics. Though he went on studying all his life, there were always areas, like the theory of money, that he never penetrated.

In the field of morality, he drew principally on manuals of moral theology and the encyclicals of the popes. He cited relatively few basic theological texts, and suprisingly enough, he had only the vaguest idea of the preliminary work leading to *Rerum novarum*—the decades of ferment created by Ketteler, Vogelsang, De Mun, Pottier, and Manning. His only reference to them came from a secondary source, and of the five, only Pottier, author of a formal treatise in moral theology, appeared in Ryan's own ample bibliography. The same was true of Christian socialists like Charles Kingsley and F. D. Maurice in England and Walter Rauschenbusch and Washington Gladden in the United States.[31]

The work completed, Ryan sent it off to Ely for advice. Ely, in turn, immediately looked for a publisher. Turned down a couple of times, he finally talked The Macmillan Company into handling the book if Ryan would pay for the printing plates.[32] Then Ely wrote an introduction warmly endorsing the work, while Ryan got in touch with the theological faculty in Washington to arrange for his degree. Suddenly difficulties arose. First, the faculty, having approved the thesis, refused to accept it if it was published before Ryan's final defense of it. (It was scheduled to appear in April.) Ryan pleaded that the arrangements for publication were already too far advanced to admit any change. The faculty relented. Then it objected to Ely's introduction because it "conveyed the impression that he was defining Catholic doctrine." Ryan agreed to have Ely phrase his praise more discreetly.[33] As problems surrounding the dissertation dissolved, problems concerning the list of propositions

---

[31] On the latter two, see Charles Howard Hopkins, *The Rise of the Social Gospel in American Protestantism* (New Haven, 1940), *passim*.

[32] Ryan, *Social Doctrine in Action*, pp. 80–81.

[33] "Acta Facultatis Theologicae Universitatis Catholicae Americae," Jan. 22, March 5, March 14, April 2, 1906. Catholic University Archives.

Ryan was to defend in the course of his examination remained. These, too, had to be negotiated in detail. Even the date of the examination created bickering.[34]

When all the details were settled, copies of the dissertation were mailed to the major eastern seminaries and to the headquarters of the largest religious orders, along with invitations to join in the examination.[35] When the day finally arrived, Ryan's examiners pushed him hard to topple him off his position, but few of them could match him in the field he had made his own, and he "stood fore-square to every wind that blew."[36] Father Ryan became also Dr. Ryan, and the St. Paul professor began his career as a national figure in the Catholic Church and in the American reform movement.

Once published, the book was widely noted here and abroad, even as far as India. Many reviewers got their comments out of Ely's introduction. Ely hailed the work as "the first attempt in the English language to elaborate what may be called a Roman Catholic system of political economy." Ely especially welcomed the attempt by a religious teacher "to get beyond vague and glittering generalities to precise doctrine, and to pass from appeals to sentiment to reasoned arguments."[37] Catholic journals varied in their reception of the book. Canon William Barry, writing in the *Catholic Times* of Liverpool, approved overwhelmingly (as well he might, since he was expressing similar views in England). The Chicago *New World* and the Buffalo *Catholic Union and Times* echoed this view. The *Tablet* of London doubted the obligation to pay a living wage when it was not earned, and it especially irked Ryan by calling his writing foggy. The reviewer for the *Catholic University Bulletin* apparently had participated in Ryan's oral examination; he engaged in a full and technical discussion to show that the obligation to pay a living wage was not binding in strict justice. The *Ecclesiastical Review* was more generous: perhaps Ryan carried the notion of the right of strict justice too far, but the work brought tremendous credit to the university.[38]

[34] *Ibid.*, Oct. 20, Nov. 23, 27, 1905; Jan. 15, 22, April 2, Jan. 22, Feb. 5, 1906.
[35] *Ibid.*, May 15, 1906.
[36] *Catholic World*, August, 1906, p. 688.
[37] Richard T. Ely, Introduction to Ryan, *A Living Wage*, pp. vi, vii.
[38] Liverpool *Catholic Times*, Sept. 14, 1906; Chicago *New World*, May 12, 1906; Buffalo *Catholic Union and Times*, Sept. 6, 1906; London *Tablet*, Jan. 5, 1907, Feb. 16, 1907; *Catholic University Bulletin*, July, 1907, pp. 470–475; *Ecclesiastical Review*, April, 1907, pp. 465–466.

A similar range of opinion appeared in secular journals. *Dial* and the *Annals of the American Academy of Political and Social Science* gave warm approval, but the *American Journal of Sociology* foresaw a secular refusal to accept the terms of reference of the book: to those for whom such an argument was necessary, Ryan's work was not convincing; to those whom his argument would convince, the argument was not necessary. The *Liberty Review* in London was blunter. Discounting Ryan's "vague and gratuitous assumptions," it announced confidently: "Economics having no real relation with ethics, ethical economics cannot be scientific." The London *Pioneer* observed that Ryan, far from opposing socialism, was actually "preaching the creed in its entirety." The Minneapolis *Tribune*, obviously delighted with its local celebrity, greeted his work as "undoubtedly the clearest exposition and summing up of the truly fundamental question of the labor problem from a religious standpoint ever published in this country." The Minnesota *Union Advocate*, the labor paper soon to become the official organ of the Minnesota Federation of Labor, was equally enthusiastic. Assuming that the book's acceptance by Catholic University secured at least "qualified approval" of the Church, the paper asserted that Ryan's effort would place his Church in the front rank of the forces working for "a true solution of the problems of humanity which organized labor has brought to the front in our time." The paper promised to return to the book for a fuller analysis later and to follow Ryan's future career with interest.[39] The first intention fell by the wayside, but over the next decade the *Union Advocate* had reason to make good on the second.

[39] *Dial*, May 1, 1907, p. 288; *Annals of the American Academy of Political and Social Science*, January, 1907, pp. 234–235; *American Journal of Sociology*, January, 1907, pp. 561–563; London *Liberty Review*, August, 1906, n.p.; London *Pioneer*, June 9, 1906; Minneapolis *Tribune*, May 6, 1906; Minnesota *Union Advocate*, May 25, 1906.

A Theological Voice
for Reform

THE STIR CREATED by his first book led Father Ryan to further speculation. If the living wage was to stand, either morally or economically, the parts of the total economy that it jostled had to face similar scrutiny. Traditional moral principles governing economic practices abounded in theological volumes. But principles had meaning only in a concrete situation, and for all practical purposes ethical thinking had lagged behind in the agrarian, handicraft age. On most modern economic practices, the Church had not yet spoken officially, and the few moralists within the Catholic Church with proper training and appropriate interest were neither exhaustive nor unanimous. So Ryan boldly set about the difficult chore of making the Church catch up. Stating his own positions frankly, he was prepared to let theological controversy carry the issue from there. As in *A Living Wage*, his material came in about equal parts from the traditional theological manuals and from economic texts like the *Report of the United States Industrial Commission*, a massive survey of the American economy that finally filled nineteen volumes.

For Ryan, as for other progressives, monopolies were a prime concern, for they violated justice by raising prices after having eliminated competitors. The state's obligation to protect the general welfare from evils beyond the control of individuals justified the Sherman Antitrust Act as a legitimate exercise of public power, Ryan said, and since the railroads were among the most prominent beneficiaries of monopoly organization, his approval embraced the Interstate Commerce Act as well. Indeed, Ryan went even further concerning railroads. As quasi-public institutions, they were bound by the same rigorous rules of distributive justice that required the state itself to achieve justice for all its citizens. Ryan condemned equally a genuine monopoly and a pooled arrangement in which independent dealers, by dividing a market and keeping prices high, achieved the advantages of a monopoly.[1] Thus far no progressive would have disagreed.

The implication of *A Living Wage* carried its author further. The older theological manuals taught that prices became immoral when they went higher than the "normal" competitive price, that is, the price reached by natural action of the market. Ryan pointed out that this standard was acceptable for the Middle Ages when the "just price" protected the interests of both the consumer and the producer. But the modern world no longer heeded the obligations of the just price: the laborer normally did not receive a fair return for his work. In this situation, the competitive price frequently failed to provide a decent wage. Borrowing from Adolphe A. Tanquerey, S.S., professor of theology at St. Mary's Seminary in Baltimore, Ryan restated the basic rule: "The objective rule of justice is that a thing should be sold at a price sufficiently high to remunerate fairly all who have contributed to the production of the thing. . . ." A fair price thus provided a living wage for all workers, with a higher wage for greater skills; a fair profit for businessmen; and a fair rate of interest for capital. The social utility of capital, measured by the interest produced in a genuinely competitive business, created the right to interest. In practice, Ryan said, monopolies were immoral because they disregarded these standards, raised prices to the level the traffic would bear, and even then failed to pay workers an adequate wage.[2]

[1] Ryan, "The Moral Aspect of Monopoly," *Irish Theological Quarterly*, July, 1908, pp. 273–292.
[2] Ryan, "Monopoly, Moral Aspects of," *Catholic Encyclopedia* (New York, 1911), X, 497–498.

The limitation of corporate profits became a topical political issue when the Hepburn Act (1906) empowered the Interstate Commerce Commission to fix maximum rates, allowing a just profit to the railroads' owners. Two questions arose: What is a fair rate of profit? What is the base to which that rate is to be applied? Senator Robert M. La Follette, of Wisconsin, pointed out in the debate over the Hepburn bill that the ICC must have the authority to appraise the railroads' property before it could set rates that could be defended in the courts. But his voice was not heeded, and the commission did not receive this power until 1913.[3]

A widespread debate argued the relative merits of basing rates on the original cost of building the railroads or on their reproduction cost, that is, the cost of 1906 of rebuilding them. Reproduction costs yielded the lower figure. Railroad interests naturally favored an estimate of the original cost. Reformers generally favored the cost of reproduction. If 8 percent was regarded as a reasonable return on an investment, a railroad valued at $1,000,000 (reproduction cost) could charge rates that would yield an annual profit of $80,000. For the same railroad valued at $2,000,000 (original cost), "reasonable" rates would have to be set at a level high enough to yield a "reasonable" return of $160,000.

Ryan stood with the reformers in favor of reproduction costs, though he acknowledged that rates based on original cost could not be conclusively branded as unfair. The market value of any business depended on what a rival would have to invest to set up a comparable competitor—in other words, on reproduction costs, Ryan said; this simple economic fact determined which moral principles applied. Rates based on original cost legalized stock-watering, he said, and the resultant tax on the consumer went beyond the norm of justice. A double offense occurred if the state lent its authority to this injustice, for rates set by the state enjoyed the presumption of fairness.[4]

In discussing monopoly and stock-watering, Ryan was breaking new ground in theological discourse, reapplying old principles to modern conditions in a consciously original way. Since his topics were new, he did not have to buck the weight of accumulated theological opinion.

When he turned to the morality of interest, the going was tougher. A dense literature surrounded the topic, and priests everywhere half remembered from their days in the seminary that the Church condemned

[3] George E. Mowry, *The Era of Theodore Roosevelt, 1900–1912* (New York, 1958), p. 206.
[4] Ryan, "Is Stock-Watering Immoral?" *International Journal of Ethics,* January, 1908, pp. 151–167.

usury. Yet modern business rested overwhelmingly on credit mechanisms, and Rome was moving toward tolerating practices that seemed to fall under the ban of medieval theologians. Was Rome reversing itself? Or was the ban in medieval times consistent with modern toleration of interest?

Ryan answered "No" to the first question, "Yes" to the second. Drawing again on Ashley, he recalled that the loans that drew medieval condemnation were those made mainly for consumption. A peasant suffering from a blighted crop borrowed to survive until the next harvest. A lender, having more than enough for himself, took advantage of this misfortune to exact a profit. This act was usurious, in the full pejorative sense of the word, a violation of justice, to say nothing of charity. As economic conditions changed, however, the morality of moneylending changed with it, not because moral principles changed, but because new conditions altered the application of moral principles. Money lent to, or invested in, a new enterprise that opened new markets or created new products occupied a different status than money lent to a starving peasant, for it created opportunities from which all might gain. As theologians accepted money as "virtually productive" and loans as potential contributions to the general welfare, the weight of opinion tipped in favor of interest as tolerable. Without arguing the point at length, Ryan suggested that even loans made for consumption had come to enjoy an equally favorable moral position.

Ryan did not label his opinions as conclusive. He consulted the theological manuals, reviewed the answers given by the Sacred Congregations in Rome to specific questions placed before them, and studied the concrete facts of industrial life. Then carefully staying within the evidence as he understood it, he said that no current argument proved that interest on capital was required by strict justice; nor could the contrary be established. The true test was the general welfare. To gauge that, he added with some impatience, theologians must forget their "metaphysical, artificial, irrelevant, inadequate way of regarding money," and realize that in modern times "the value of money which is borrowed for a year is . . . equal to the capital goods for which it will exchange, plus a year's use of these capital goods." This was the economic aspect of the situation, he added, "the only one that has any relevancy for the moralist."[5]

These abstruse discourses, carried on in learned journals like the

[5] Ryan, "The Church and Interest-Taking," pamphlet (St. Louis, 1910), p. 28 *et passim.*

Irish Theological Quarterly and the *International Journal of Ethics*, gave added weight to Ryan's more popular arguments, either in lectures or in magazines like the *Catholic World* that circulated more widely. Young Dr. Ryan's reputation depended largely on his skill in directing his attention first to one, then to the other. The learned articles drew more attention from his clerical brethren because they had come across his name in other contexts; and the reception of his popular articles and lectures carried more weight because of what he was—perhaps the most learned American Catholic moral theologian in the field of social problems.

The preparation of his articles took a great deal of his time. They were frequent, and more often than not, carefully prepared and well argued. Ryan wrote a solid, unadorned prose. Graceful metaphor or vivid turn of phrase had disappeared during the late seminary years. Literary or historical allusions, other than those in the history of economic thought, were infrequent. Clarity was his strongest point: precision in his distinctions, accuracy in his choice of words.

His lectures carried the same impact: his forthright speaking style, blunt, factual, original, held audiences even if they preferred more eloquence and wit. The Minnesota *Union Advocate*, which chronicled his lectures and writings, caught just the tone Ryan wanted: he was a "gentleman of great force of character and goes to the bottom of every subject that interests him." He was an "exhaustive and thoughtful student, a close and reflecting observer and a strong, positive and direct controversialist."[6] (Ryan would, however, have regretted the *Advocate*'s careless use of commas.)

His ambition not confined to St. Paul Seminary, Father Ryan moved eagerly into a larger arena. His position at the seminary, and especially the archbishop's dim view of absences in term time, restricted his movements. Yet even in term time he could be away from his rooms on the first floor of South Hall for weekends and for local meetings. In addition, there were always vacations. Through lecture tours and popular articles, Father Ryan extended his own reputation to a national audience. Catholics urgently needed education in the social question. The industrial world had been changing rapidly for over fifty years. Did Catholic leaders, clerical or lay, know enough about the new industrial world to say anything useful? Ryan's answer was an emphatic "No."

The clergy was busy with many chores. Successive waves of im-

[6] Minnesota *Union Advocate*, July 30, 1909.

migrants had left pastors frantically coping with numbers and with the national differences within their flocks. Aware of poverty, they were attempting to relieve it as a Christian obligation. When priests turned their thoughts to the larger social questions, most of them confidently denounced socialism and asserted that only Christian principles could solve the problems of society.

Father Ryan warned his brethren that these nostrums were not enough. Catholics spent too much time answering Marx, too little solving the contemporary social problems that gave Marx his worldwide audience. Ryan respected the careful analysis that went into Cathrein's *Socialism and Christianity*, yet he regretted that such an effort blurred the "valuable truth" in Marx's crude and exaggerated economic determinism—that is, the immense importance of economic factors in history. Catholics had gotten caught in a curious trap. They were "so preoccupied refuting Socialism and defending the present order, that they go to the opposite extreme, understating the amount of truth in the claims of the Socialists and overstating the rights of property and the advantages of the present system."[7]

The solution was as clear to Ryan as the problem. Priests must know their industrial world, and their education must start in the seminary. At St. Paul Seminary, Father Ryan gave over one-fourth of his two-year course in junior moral theology to economic history and to political economy. This not only trained the seminarians in these two areas; it had the additional value of presenting social studies as an intellectual discipline, Ryan said, "an antidote, if the term be permissible, to the ultra-deductive habits of mental activity which are frequently apt to plague the seminarian."

After ordination, the new priests—indeed all priests—had to read and study, finding time in their busy days, Ryan went on. Especially must they understand the position of the wage earner, or they would see their authority as teachers of morality lessened, perhaps ultimately destroyed. The American clergy flattered itself on avoiding European dangers; it patronized the French Church for refusing to accept democracy. (No one had done this more spectacularly than Archbishop Ireland.) The Church in the United States had never antagonized political democrats and, unlike its European counterpart, it was not identified with any privileged class. The supreme question, therefore, was "Shall democ-

[7] Ryan, "The Marxian Theory of Productivity and of Value, II," *Catholic Fortnightly Review*, November, 1909 (first issue), pp. 613–616.

racy become convinced that its vital aims are in harmony with and safest under the protection of the Catholic Church?" The clergy, Ryan thought, would do much to answer this question in the next generation.

Ryan looked around at his own brethren in the common room at the seminary. Their knowledge of social problems came from conservative journals generally hostile to reform. Journals advocating industrial reforms were likely to be radical, and therefore distasteful, in moral questions, in religion, and in educational policy. Priests, troubled by the doctrinaire liberalism of these journals, avoided them, turning instead to safe conservative papers that did not offend their relegous taste. But these conservative journals, viewing social problems from the standpoint of laissez faire, discredited social reform. Hence the priest, generally sympathetic to social betterment for his flock, rarely, if ever, read a fair-minded presentation of the aims of reform movements.

Catholics, Ryan warned, smugly assumed that the alienation of the worker from Christianity was a Protestant problem, as the most aggressive voices within the Protestant community, from Charles Stefle to Walter Rauschenbusch, unceasingly preached. Catholic clergymen erred in thinking that the problem did not affect them as well. Let them talk to intelligent Catholic trade unionists if they thought that large parts of the labor force were not slipping away from the Church, he said. Then perhaps they would develop a sense of urgency about injustices in the industrial system.

Ryan did not want the Church to become simply an organization for social welfare. He said explicitly that it was not the job of the bishops to adopt formally any particular program of social reform. But the Church had to become interested and informed, both because of the genuine moral questions involved and because of the danger of losing the working class to an unchurched mentality. Either motive was compelling. Together they should be overpowering. Yet, Father Ryan said in his bluntest manner, "The bishops who have made any pronouncement in the matter [of the social teachings of the Church] could probably be counted on the fingers of one hand, while the priests who have done so are not more numerous proportionately."[8]

The clergy had to undertake the basic theological job. The laity had to carry the torch of reform. Ryan was no more satisfied with the one than with the other. The absence of laymen from the reform tradition signified

8 Ryan, "The Study of Social Problems in the Seminary," *Ecclesiastical Review,* August, 1908, pp. 113–121; "The Church and the Workingman," *Catholic World,* September, 1909, pp. 776–782.

a double tragedy: it meant, first, that Catholics were aloof from the new directions of American thought and policy, and second, that reform movements lacked the tempering guidance of Catholic moral principles.

The Catholic laymen tapped to lead the movement for social justice were busy getting and spending. Something of the farm boy persisted in Ryan when he looked at the prevailing standards of middle-class life. Writing of "The Fallacy of Bettering One's Position" in November, 1907, he mocked the materialism that made families hunger for more comfort each time their income increased. Remembering the modest scale of his family's farm, he lacked sympathy with ostentatious living. Ryan had read Thorstein Veblen's *The Theory of the Leisure Class* (1899), which burlesqued the American middle-class yearning for ostentatious proof of wealth and position. Looking at the society around him, Ryan arrived at the same image. "No matter how much a person spends in meeting these wants [for shelter, food, clothing, 'society,' and amusement], he can still maintain, in accordance with the language and standards of the day, that he had merely 'bettered his social position.' . . . Since life is merely, or at any rate chiefly, an aggregate of sensations, more abundant life means the multiplication of sensations, possessions, and pleasurable experiences." Ryan wrote this for the Catholic readers of the *Catholic World,* and he did not soften the charge as it applied to them: "Even the majority of Catholics seem to hold to the Christian conception only theoretically and vaguely, not clearly and practically." In a follow-up article three months later, Ryan laid his charge on the line: "Throughout the article the writer has had chiefly in mind Catholics. For they are, to a deplorable extent, under the delusion that valuable life consists in the indefinite satisfaction of material wants."

What was excessive expenditure? Ryan was quite explicit: the best conditions for Christian life for a majority of American families involved an annual expenditure of $3,000–$5,000, with $10,000 as an outside limit. Beyond that amount, the principal effect of spending was "to increase not legitimate comfort, but pride, vanity, waste of time, and unsocial feelings of superiority." Excessive spending corrupted a wealthy family, scandalized the rest of society, and diverted a part of the national income from the rest of the population, most of whom suffered along on considerably less than $1,500 that he regarded as the irreducible minimum for an average urban family.

Ryan indicted Catholics for their indifference to charity. "The contributions to religion, charity, or education by Catholics who live sumptuously, by all Catholics indeed who exceed the bounds of simple and moderate living—are generally speaking, utterly inadequate as compared with their incomes. Herein consists the *inordinate attachment* to wealth which is contrary to Christian principle." The Catholics' failure to perform the works of charity called for by their Faith not only caused scandal but incapacitated them for the "clean, vigorous, healthy lives" that Theodore Roosevelt saw as the health of the state.[9]

But almsgiving only began to touch the problem. In the modern world the most effective charity required Christians "to attack the social causes of distress," as European Catholics already realized. The Centralverein and the Center Party in Germany had a constructive program of social reform, including compulsory insurance and old-age pensions. The French were borrowing from the National Consumers' League in the United States. The Catholic Social Guild in England had reprinted a summary pamphlet of Ryan's *Living Wage*. Where were the counterparts in the United States? Ryan asked. Every diocese, indeed almost every parish, had institutions for the relief of want, but few had any activity looking toward the prevention of want. There was not even a Catholic periodical devoted to social and economic questions. Were American Catholics going to wait until the social question became as acute in the United States as it was in England? Even that date might be less remote than most Americans thought.[10]

The decades of progressivism were giving birth to a great variety of organizations for social betterment. Settlement houses, such as Jane Addams' Hull House in Chicago, brought trained social workers into the neighborhoods of the poor to provide help for the underprivileged, frequently the immigrant. In St. Paul itself the Associated Charities coordinated the activities of a variety of welfare organizations. The National Conference of Charities and Corrections was increasingly partial to professional social workers to replace untrained volunteers who loved their fellow men but offered aid rather than solutions for their problems. The National Consumers' League was organizing a pressure group of purchasers to improve working conditions. The Protestant churches created the Federal Council of Churches of Christ in America in 1908, and four years later issued a formal and very progressive program outlining the demands for a Christian society.

[9] Ryan, "The Fallacy of 'Bettering One's Position,'" *Catholic World*, November, 1907, pp. 145–156; "The Cost of Christian Living," *ibid.*, February, 1908, pp. 575–588.
[10] Ryan, "Catholic Social Activity in Europe," *Catholic University Bulletin*, February, 1908, pp. 167–185. On the Catholic Social Guild, see Georgiana P. McEntee, *The Social Catholic Movement in Great Britain* (New York, 1927), pp. 152–240.

Where were the Catholics? Ryan was distressed: conspicuously inactive in nonsectarian reform movements, they were equally inactive in setting up their own parallel groups. In an undated speech given sometime during his stay in St. Paul, he spoke of the virtues of the settlement-house movement, mentioning especially Jane Addams. It was a good method of reaching the poor, but it took professional help and could not be the side activity of a parish. Catholics held aloof because they thought that settlement houses were hotbeds of socialism. Of course they were, Ryan said; therefore Catholics had to hurry into the field, not stand aloof with pious distaste.[11]

In the summer of 1909 Father Ryan put together for the *Catholic World* a comprehensive program for reconciling American institutions with social justice.[12] Called "A Programme of Social Reform by Legislation," it picked up the theme of state intervention characteristic of his whole career. The first of two lists called for labor legislation:

1. Legal minimum wage
2. Eight-hour law
3. Protective legislation for women and children
4. Legislative protection for peaceful picketing and boycotting
5. Unemployment insurance and employment bureaus
6. Provision against accident, illness, and old age
7. Municipal housing

These proposals owed much to recent English reform. A part, especially the proposals on housing and on unions, dated back to Benjamin Disraeli, the Tory prime minister who had competed with the Liberals in the previous generation for the votes of newly enfranchised workers. More came from the revivified Liberal party, enjoying strong labor support, which was still in power as Ryan wrote his program. The Trades Disputes Act (1906) granted unions the right to picket and to boycott, and protected their funds from suits for damages. An old-age pension act gave allowances up to five shillings to people over seventy. A system of government labor exchanges dispensed information on opportunities for employment. The Trades Boards Act looked toward a legal minimum wage throughout Great Britain. A plan for insurance against sickness and

[11] Ryan, "Catholic Social Principles and Practical Social Remedies," *Fortnightly Review*, March, 1912, pp. 143–145; "Nature and Scope of a Settlement House," MS of undated speech, *ca.* 1909; Charles Howard Hopkins, *The Rise of the Social Gospel in American Protestantism*, pp. 302–317.

[12] Ryan, "A Programme of Social Reform by Legislation," *Catholic World*, July, August, 1909, pp. 433–444, 608–614.

unemployment did not pass in Parliament until 1911, but it had been introduced when Ryan wrote his program. From Australia and New Zealand came additional examples. Ryan regarded their successful experience with a legal minimum wage as overpoweringly feeble objections based on an outdated individualistic, laissez-faire philosophy. Australia had also shown how to ease industrial disputes; even compulsory arbitration, despite great obstacles, might work in the United States.

Of Ryan's many proposals, the minimum wage predictably headed the list. He envisioned a national act which could be adjusted by the states for local conditions. He recognized that under existing constitutional interpretation a minimum wage law would require an amendment to the Constitution; so would any satisfactory regulation fulfilling the state's proper function in providing for the physical and moral health of the people. Ryan assumed that the theory of nonintervention exercised a stronger influence in the United States than in England because it had been "incorporated into the National Constitution, and in the Constitution of most of the states"[13]—a reference to the Supreme Court's decisions on the "due process" clause of the Fifth and Fourteenth Amendments, decisions that Ryan regarded as authoritative and final.

An amendment was worth struggling for, because legislation could accomplish more than trade unions. Father Ryan always supported labor unions. In 1910 the *Catholic Encyclopedia* published his article, "Labour Unions, Moral Aspects of," which enshrined in that standard reference work the advanced views that Ryan had expressed six years before. Yet he never gained (or sought) the status of "labor priest" like his contemporary, Father Peter E. Dietz, of Ohio. Ryan acknowledged that labor unions had advanced the condition of the workingman. He regarded their strength as a prerequisite for effective conciliation in industrial disputes. He looked past immediate industrial struggles to the time when unions would specialize in education and insurance instead of consuming all their energies in fighting management. At the same time, he saw the state as a superior instrument of social reform, for its responsibility and power extended to the welfare of all, not simply to the interest of one special group.[14] Enjoying a special status conferred by natural law, the state could move more decisively in promoting the general welfare.

A substantial part of the general welfare was the welfare of women,

---

[13] Ryan, "Labour and Labour Legislation," *Catholic Encyclopedia* (New York, 1910), VIII, 723.

[14] Mark Perlman, *Labor Union Theories in America* (Evanston, 1958), p. 57.

and Ryan looked to a minimum wage law as a means of eliminating women from the working force. Ryan had no truck with the economic independence of women. In a speech given just about this time, he insisted that both women and society as a whole would improve if women did not engage in "extra-active" occupations. These chores, in which they competed with men, caused physical damage to the women and injury to the race; they left women unprepared for marriage; they depressed wages. Men would never be paid an adequate living wage while women were available to replace them. And conversely, if men were paid a decent wage, their women would not have to work.[15] For Father Ryan, the living wage had wide ramifications.

Ryan's program went beyond labor legislation to a second list of proposals:

1. Public ownership of public utilities
2. Public ownership of mines and forests
3. Control of monopolies, either by breaking them up or fixing their prices
4. Progressive income and inheritance taxes
5. Taxation of the future increase in land values
6. Prohibition of speculation on the stock and commodity exchanges

These items owed considerably more to the native American reform tradition. They passed as common currency among Populists and progressives, and Ryan's advocacy of them deserves special note, mainly because they placed him among the more radical progressives like Henry Demarest Lloyd rather than with Theodore Roosevelt. In fact, Ryan's ideas were more radical than the program of a good many moderate dues-paying socialists.[16]

For a Catholic to take this stance required a self-conscious defense. Ryan knew what would be said: this program was socialistic. Yet he was not arguing for the collective ownership of the means of production; nor did he seek to introduce his reforms by the "Socialist method," by which he presumably meant revolutionary violence. While the measures were perhaps paternalistic, he said, they were not opposed to "sane individualism" that offered every individual a reasonable measure of opportunity. If the state had to intervene to ensure that individualism, the

[15] Ryan, "Unreasonable Burdens upon Women and Children," MS of undated speech, ca. 1910.
[16] Ira Kipnis, *The American Socialist Movement, 1897–1912* (New York, 1952), pp. 425–428.

"tyranny of an exploded laissez-faire philosophy" should not create a barrier.

Ryan made a bold effort, both here and in the *Catholic Encyclopedia* the following year, to capture "individualism" as a slogan. Set against paternalism, it created an apparent choice between freedom and despotism, liberty and subjugation, the free citizen and the subject, and, of course in religion, the Protestant rebel against the Church of Rome. As a polemical tool it was too good to leave for the opposition. The fight was half lost if "individualism" became identified with laissez-faire philosophy. The Catholic tradition correctly viewed the state not as a necessary evil but as the "normal, natural, and necessary" instrument for promoting individual progress, Ryan said. "Sane individualism" thus carried no presumption against state activity. The test of state intervention was the welfare of society and of its citizens; this was "entirely a question of expediency" determined by experience, not by "any metaphysical theory of the appropriate functions of the state . . ." he said. "Many individualists, and others likewise, who oppose state intervention . . . are victims of a fallacy. In their anxiety to safeguard individual liberty, they forget that reasonable labour legislation, for example, does not deprive the labourer of any liberty that is worth having, while it does ensure him real opportunity, which is the vital content of all true liberty; they forget that, while state control and direction of certain industries undoubtedly diminishes both the liberty and the opportunity of some individuals, it may increase the opportunities and the welfare of the vast majority."[17] Thus rejecting both socialism and laissez-faire liberalism, Ryan sought to appropriate their potent appeals—reform of the industrial order and "sane" individualism—as buttresses for his own program.

Over the years 1909–1914, Ryan said more about land policy and taxation. His recommendation in 1909 for taxation of future increases in land values showed both the influence of the Lloyd George budget in Great Britain and the persistent pull that Henry George had on him. In a way, of course, these two influences were actually one, for the Liberal budget also drew inspiration from Henry George. By 1912 Ryan expanded his catalog of land reforms considerably. From the National Conservation Congress in 1910, he picked up the idea that the state or the national government should retain title to all mineral, timber, and water-power lands not already alienated. Those already lost should be subjected to close supervision to avoid unreasonable private profits from land originally bought from the government for next to nothing. From

17 Ryan, "Individualism," *Catholic Encyclopedia* (New York, 1910), VII, 762.

New Zealand and Australia came the idea of government loans to efficient farmers. From France and Germany, he developed an urgent sense that cities should retain land, or buy it up if they did not already own it, to provide municipal housing at rates that would restrain the avarice of private landlords. Even a conservative theologian like Heinrich Pesch, the German Jesuit, supported such a plan.

When Ryan turned to taxation policy, the influence of Henry George persisted. Ryan wanted no sudden changes, for they would disrupt existing property relationships without comparable social gains. But eventually the government should eliminate all taxes except those on land, income, and inheritance. A protective tariff created a multiple inequity: it protected industries that no longer needed protection, and it imposed an uneven burden on consumers, particularly on the poor who were already paying out a greater proportion of their income in taxes than the wealthy and the comfortable. Ryan wanted to abolish internal taxes entirely, though he made an exception of the tax on liquor, which should be "retained for social reasons connected with public order and sobriety." Municipal and state personal property taxes he would have abolished altogether as "antiquated, inequitable, and largely uncollectable." Heavy taxes on land he endorsed without compromise. Unimproved land should be taxed at the same rate applied to surrounding land. Exceptionally large individual or corporate holdings should sustain a surtax, as they did in Australia. The income tax he endorsed as the fairest of all taxes, for it compelled men to pay according to their ability.[18]

Ryan's tax policy tied in with a familiar goal: release the purchasing power of the poor for consumption; make up the loss by taxing those whose greater share of the earth's wealth gave them both the means and the duty to contribute more to the general welfare. Just as he tried to rescue the word "individualism" from the advocates of laissez faire and to invoke the power of the state to promote "sane individualism," so also he redefined equality in taxation as a burden bearing equally on all members of society according to their station in life.

In scope and daring, Ryan's program probably went beyond what any other prominent Catholic had offered. Radical and detailed, it set a standard by which proposals of others could be measured.

A number of able allies were doing parallel missionary work at about the same time. In 1910 Father Kerby and Thomas J. Shahan, now rector

[18] Ryan, "Methods of Reforming Our Land System," *Catholic World*, October, November, 1912, pp. 1–18, 156–169.

of Catholic University and a bishop, called the first meeting of the National Conference of Catholic Charities. For the next decade the group met biennially, gradually weaning charitable work away from volunteers who dispensed alms, and putting it into the hands of trained professionals. On the initiative of Father Dietz, the American Federation of Catholic Societies set up in 1911 a Social Service Commission, presided over by Peter J. Muldoon, Bishop of Rockford, the most progressive prelate in the American hierarchy right up to his death in 1927. Until then the federation had been a tame convention-going group which had provoked even the *Catholic Bulletin* to criticism of its endless talk and sparse action. Dietz immediately took on the posts of secretary of the commission and editor of a section of the federation's *Bulletin*. A "power-house of action," Dietz sent weekly press reports to Catholic and trade-union papers, lectured wherever he could gain a hearing, and established close ties with local representatives of the American Federation of Labor. At about the same time, he was organizing his Militia of Christ for Social Service, a national group designed to spread the social gospel, especially among Catholic trade unionists. Handicapped by lack of funds and the inertia of Catholic trade unionists, the Militia never reached the proportions of a mass movement, though it did succeed in irritating the socialists. In the Midwest the German Roman Catholic Central Verein, drawing on the rich inheritance of Ketteler, turned away from parochial charity and insurance systems to infuse Christian principles in all phases of American life. The guiding spirit of its Central Bureau in St. Louis, Frederick P. Kenkel, editor of its periodical, *Central Blatt and Social Justice*, bent the Verein away from mere opposition to socialism toward support of trade unionism and ultimately toward a society organically organized by occupations. In Chicago, a Jesuit at Loyola University, Frederic Siedenburg, set up a lecture bureau for the dissemination of Christian principles of industrial society. Across the nation other priests and laymen were active: Father Joseph Husslein, S.J., at Fordham University in New York, Father Peter C. Yorke in San Francisco, and David Goldstein everywhere.[19]

[19] John O'Grady, *Catholic Charities in the United States* (Washington, D.C., 1931), pp. 427–434; Sister Mary Harrita Fox, *Peter E. Dietz, Labor Priest* (Notre Dame, 1953), pp. 29–35, 43–68; *Catholic Bulletin*, Sept. 9, 1911; Sister Mary Liguori Brophy, *The Social Thought of the German Roman Catholic Central Verein* (Washington, D.C., 1941), pp. 72–83. On this whole topic, see Marc Karson, *American Labor Unions and Politics, 1900–1918* (Carbondale, Ill., 1958), pp. 212–284; and Aaron I. Abell, *American Catholicism and Social Action* (Garden City, New York, 1960), pp. 90–188.

Aware of these activities, Ryan cooperated with them as much as his obligations in St. Paul permitted. He attended the first National Conference of Catholic Charities, commented on a paper on the dependent family, and found himself elected to the executive committee of the permanent group. He used the biennial meetings to promote familiar causes. In 1914, in an address on "The Social Side of Charity," he paraphrased Tanquerey: Traditional works of mercy were entirely praiseworthy, but present-day conditions made expedient, and even necessary, certain social works of charity. He showed that the 1909 report of the Committee on Standards of Living and Labor of the nonsectarian National Conference of Charities and Correction laid out a program paralleling that of Leo XIII. (As well it might: Ryan wrote most of it.) From there he went on to rue the small share of influence that Catholics held in secular betterment groups. Only when they participate fully would they "command that measure of social and civic prestige which they ought to possess"— a subtle play on the Catholic sense of inferiority.[20]

Ryan met Muldoon at meetings of the American Federation of Catholic Societies, and he praised Dietz's Militia for Christ as a splendid idea with "great possibilities for good," though he did fear that inert Catholic unionists and "discouragement from above" would make Dietz's road a troubled one. Dietz wanted Ryan to edit the Militia's journal, *Social Service*, but Ireland was not willing to have Ryan surrender that much time from his work at the seminary. Ryan did, however, put together a short summary of his own program of reform for publication in an early issue of *Social Service*.[21] With Kenkel at the Central Verein, Ryan maintained friendly rapport throughout their long careers. Only on one occasion, the fight over the child-labor amendment in 1924, did they openly part company. In 1909 Ryan called attention in the *Catholic Fortnightly Review* to the Central Verein's social program: scholarly study in the social sciences and encouragement of trade unions (all-inclusive unions, not Catholic unions) as instruments of social progress. Scholarly work was important, yet Catholics took little part in professional scholarly meetings, Ryan noted. Catholics would be welcome; but insensitive to the value of Catholic principles, they accepted no responsibility to spread them. As for trade unions, Catholic workers belonged

[20] Ryan, "The Social Side of Charity," Third Biennial Meeting of the National Conference of Catholic Charities, *Proceedings* (Washington, D.C., 1914), pp. 269–273.
[21] Ryan to Dietz, Feb. 18, 1911, quoted in Fox, *Peter E. Dietz, Labor Priest*, p. 49; Ryan to Dietz, March 25, 1911, *ibid.*; Ryan, "Have We Any Catholic Solutions of Social Problems?" *Social Service*, January, 1911, pp. 147–152.

in them, both as a service to the unions and as a service to the Church. He wrote articles occasionally for the *Central Blatt*, and in 1911 the Central Verein published his pamphlet on the minimum wage.[22] He saw Siedenburg and Husslein infrequently, but managed to lecture at Husslein's Social Study Course at Fordham in the summer of 1912 and at Loyola University during the winter of 1914.[23]

The local character of all these activities lessened their impact. Ryan, believing that a genuinely national group should take up the cause of social justice with fervor, went after the Knights of Columbus, a Catholic fraternal order to which he belonged, as a group ready-made for his purposes. It had a national organization and a magazine, both going concerns. Late in 1913 he urged them to get the facts. Read John Graham Brooks, *Social Unrest;* Thomas S. Adams, *Labor Problems;* Frank H. Streightoff, *Distribution of Income in the United States.* Then act. Adopt the program of the Committee on Standards of Living and Labor; it was certainly not too liberal, though it would be many years before it was enacted. The Knights should become engaged in the fight, for "there is a good deal of truth in the charge that American Catholics have not yet developed a social sense," he said. "They participate actively, and on the whole adequately, in religious movements, in political movements, and in the charitable activities which are under Catholic auspices, but they have not yet begun to identify themselves sufficiently with those general movements for social welfare which are non-religious and non-political. . . . As a consequence, the latter are deprived of the assistance and the guidance that they should receive from a strong Catholic membership, while Catholics themselves are without adequate agencies of expression and achievement. Moreover, the absence of Catholics from these societies leads a large proportion of our non-Catholics to the conclusion that we are not vitally interested in works of social betterment."[24] If Father Ryan really expected the Knights to respond, he misjudged his audience. Like most Catholics, they held aloof, leaving the struggle to a noisy platoon of clergy and laymen.

A number of barriers made this work more difficult. One was the notion that poverty was part of the nature of things. "The poor you

[22] Ryan, "Two Important Points in the Social Program of the Central Verein," *Catholic Fortnightly Review,* March, 1909, pp. 130–132; Ryan, "A Minimum Wage by Legislation," pamphlet (St. Louis, 1911).
[23] *Catholic Bulletin,* Aug. 17, 1912; Jan. 24, 1914.
[24] Ryan, "The Knights of Columbus and Social Reform," *Columbia,* January, 1914, n.p.

always have with you," Christ said. Through the ages poverty had been seen as a route to sanctity, just as wealth had been a barrier. Did not the religious orders, with their vow of poverty, endorse its spiritual character? Ryan did not regard Jesus's words as a recommendation of hunger and thirst as a rule for future generations, and, in any case, abundant poverty would remain after men, by taking thought, removed what they could. As for the virtue that poverty promoted in religious orders, Ryan pointed out that this was voluntary poverty, a burden accepted consciously for the love of God; in any case, it rarely fell below minimum human needs. The poor who were helped would have plenty of opportunity to practice virtue more beneficial than the "compulsory humility" forced on them by inadequate income.[25]

A second prejudice reinforced the first. Was organized charity, especially when staffed by professional social workers, not making a mockery of the traditional corporal works of mercy? John Boyle O'Reilly, editor of the Boston *Pilot*, caught the accent of this view when he spoke of:

> The organized charity, scrimped and iced,—
> In the name of a cautious, statistical Christ.[26]

The only answer to such a view was that unorganized almsgiving treated conditions without removing causes and that nonprofessional social workers were inadequate in numbers and training. This was certainly the view of Father William J. White, supervisor of Catholic Charities in Brooklyn. He wanted more and more trained Catholic social workers, despite frowns from the conservative members of the charitable St. Vincent de Paul Society. He did not have enough Sisters to do the job. Nor were they nearly so well trained as good lay workers. Like Ryan, he argued that professionally trained social workers were necessary to attack the problem of poverty fundamentally.[27] Yet this idea created a serious difficulty—"the psychological inability to understand how a person could legitimately earn money helping others."[28]

[25] Ryan, "Poverty and Pauperism," *Catholic Encyclopedia* (New York, 1911), XII, 327–330.
[26] Quoted in Francis J. McManamin, "The American Years of John Boyle O'Reilly, 1870–1890," Ph.D. dissertation, The Catholic University of America (1958), p. 242.
[27] William J. White to Ryan, Feb. 18, 1908.
[28] Abell, "Preparing for Social Action," in Leo R. Ward, *The American Apostolate* (Westminster, Md., 1952), p. 25.

Catholic wariness in dealing with Protestant or secular groups, a legacy from the previous generation, created a larger barrier. The "conservative" wing of the hierarchy held aloof from the contaminations of American society. Distrusting the secular or Protestant society around them, they drew back into Catholic isolation and looked with distaste on the ventures of their more "liberal" brethren. Catholic laymen, quick to sense discrimination, expected anti-Catholic sentiment, looked for it, and, as often as not, found it. In 1913 an indignant "Fair Play" charged in the St. Paul *Catholic Bulletin*, the diocesan paper, that the Associated Charities in that city discriminated against Catholics in appointments to its board of directors. The charge touched a sensitive nerve in Father Ryan, and he replied heatedly and at length.

In this particular case, Ryan said, "I wish I were as confident of my eternal salvation as I am that religious bias had no place among those causes" that kept Catholics off the board. For one thing, not every individual organization could be represented. For another, the Catholic on the board during the previous year, a representive of the St. Vincent de Paul Society, had attended only two meetings and contributed nothing of value. No interested Catholic had suggested another name for next year's board, and the head of the St. Vincent de Paul Society had seen the proposed roster and had made no suggestions. Two prominent Catholics were on the roster—and declined to serve.

Then speaking more generally, Ryan noted that Catholics did not enter civic and social organizations in sufficient numbers in any capacity to make themselves known—"a sober and saddening fact." The few Catholics who did join, like Ryan himself, frequently were given a place of prominence beyond their merits because no other Catholic was available, and there they served, again like Ryan himself, "lonely and isolated in these excellent organizations." Ryan repudiated "the ugly hypothesis of bigotry" that came so swiftly to Catholic minds: "This is the refuge of weaklings and of men of bad will, not of manly men and Christians. It is the attitude of slaves, not of self-respecting and self-reliant freemen. It springs from a mixture of indolence, incompetence, mean-spiritedness, and the demoralizing traditions of persecution and ostracism. The remedy for it is manly self-assertion, knowledge, fairmindedness, and efficiency." The following week John W. Willis, a prominent Catholic lawyer and one of the founders of the Associated Charities, endorsed what Ryan had written.[29]

[29] *Catholic Bulletin,* Oct. 25, Nov. 1, 8, 1913.

Later that same year a group of Catholic laymen objected to Father Ryan's appearance at Ford Hall in Boston because objectionable speakers had appeared on that platform in the past year. The laymen had the tacit backing of William Cardinal O'Connell, Archbishop of Boston. Ryan protested that he had spoken there twice before, that on the earlier of those occasions, he had followed a Jesuit speaker. In conversations with priests on those occasions, there had been no suggestion of any impropriety. Father Ryan added that he would, of course, break the engagement if O'Connell insisted. A friendly priest in Boston told Ryan "He" would take no action if Ryan came. Ryan did, and according to the Boston *Globe*, scored a great triumph, "staggering" the socialists by the frankness and fullness of his answers. "He never once dodged a question." From Ryan's point of view, the meeting had done some good: the Catholic viewpoint had been forcefully put forward, socialist arguments had met courteous rebuttal, the Church had gained, social reform had gained. He was given to understand, however, that the cardinal would not approve of any subsequent engagements at Ford Hall.[30]

Ironically enough, the socialist issue itself constantly created a major hurdle for Ryan. Though he regarded his social program as the most devastating answer to the socialist threat, less well disposed observers saw him surrendering to the evil he nominally opposed. The difficulty was that Ryan would not give the time of day to a routine denunciation of socialism, while to many Catholics such a denunciation disposed of social questions. Ryan could reject socialism with the best of them, but he was more anxious to come up with a coherent program of reform. In practice, much of the program directly paralleled the socialists' call.

A hostile critic of Ryan could take this view: Look again at Ryan's denunciation of socialism: he does not give it a blanket condemnation. He distinguishes its philosophy, its account of society, and its remedies. Many of the last he endorses. A good deal of its account of society he does not dissent from. Only its philosophy does he condemn. Yet even on this last point, is he really reliable? When Father Cathrein demolished socialism in his *Christianity and Socialism*, did not Father Ryan speak of his wasting time? Perhaps Father Ryan is not a socialist; after all, he is a Catholic priest. Yet his own program goes so much in that direction that only logic-choppers can see the difference.

[30] Members of Common Cause Society of Boston to Ryan, Nov. 28, 1914; C. J. Sullivan to P. J. Waters, Nov. 13, 1914; Ryan to Alvin E. Sexton, Dec. 5, 1914; Joseph Fitzgerald to Ryan, n.d.; George W. Coleman to Ryan, July 14, 1915; Boston *Globe*, Feb. 17, 1915.

Nobody went this far, for Ryan's speeches and writings did not command that much attention, nor provide the occasion for a full review. Yet as early as 1906, *A Living Wage* had evoked the charge, and as Ryan gained national prominence among Catholics, the charge kept cropping up. Archbishop Ireland repeatedly heard criticism from conservative members of his flock.[31] He undoubtedly knew of an attack in *Der Wanderer*, a local German-language paper. Edward F. McSweeney, a member of the Massachusetts Industrial Accident Board, made the rounds of Catholic groups in Boston in 1912 and 1913 denouncing the "Minimum Wage and Other Economic Quackeries" as pagan and socialistic. He had Ryan quite explicitly in mind.[32] Ryan, in reply, called McSweeney's comments "a surprising combination of misleading assertions, irrelevant statements, and futile arguments."[33] Rome G. Brown, a Minneapolis lawyer who had submitted a brief opposing the minimum wage in Oregon, followed the more genteel pattern of criticism. He respected Ryan's ethical views and his "valiant work in combatting the propaganda of socialism"; but, Brown warned, Ryan's "enthusiasm for the minimum wage carries him, in effect, into an unconscious alliance with the very socialism which, as such, he abhors."[34]

A look at the record was Ryan's best defense. Whenever he had spoken of socialism, he had opposed it. He insisted on the natural right to private property, and in practice this extended to private property in the means of production. When the Lloyd George budget revived interest in the single tax, Ryan plowed back through the Henry George controversy: "The Ethical Argument of Henry George Against Private Ownership of Land" for the general readership of the *Catholic World*, and "Why Private Landownership Is a Natural Right" for the more specialized audience of the *Catholic University Bulletin*.[35] The articles generally ended up with the same result: George was wrong about the private ownership of land—actually it was a natural right—but for the rest there is nothing unacceptable in his social program. For those who remembered the George controversy through the apoplectic image created by Arch-

[31] Interview with Lawrence F. Ryan, April 23, 1958.
[32] *Der Wanderer* (St. Paul), Feb. 24, 1910; Edward F. McSweeney, "The Minimum Wage and Other Economic Quackeries," *Columbiad*, April, 1913, pp. 3–4.
[33] Ryan, "The Case Against the Minimum Wage," *Central Blatt and Social Justice*, October, 1912, p. 139.
[34] Rome Brown, letter to editor, *Survey*, April 10, 1915, pp. 57–58.
[35] Ryan, "The Ethical Argument of Henry George Against Private Ownership of Land," *Catholic World*, July, 1911, pp. 483–492; "Why Private Landownership Is a Natural Right," *Catholic University Bulletin*, March, 1912, pp. 228–236.

bishop Corrigan, Ryan was skating pretty close to the socialist path trod by Father McGlynn. But the fact was that George was not a socialist, whatever other kind of radical he may have been, and Corrigan's view of his writings had not been shared in Rome nor by the committee of four at Catholic University. Still, the epithet "socialist" was hard to put aside. It was a useful tool for conservatives like Brown or McSweeney who knew the value of a scare word and the impatience of most people for the niceties of precise argument.

Here opinion on Father Ryan rested right up until New Deal days: not technically enough of a socialist to draw the formal censure of his ecclesiastical superiors, but too radical for most of his coreligionists. Ryan's view was simpler: He was about as radical as Leo XIII.

A more serious yet remoter danger for Ryan was "modernism." It is difficult to characterize briefly this complicated movement that struck the Church in Europe, and especially in France and Italy, in the late nineteenth and early twentieth centuries. Hints of it had already appeared in the Americanism controversy in the 1890's.[36] Modernism affirmed that the Church must adapt itself—in its theology, its dogma, its government— to the spirit of the age. It must accept evolution not merely in the physical world but in its habits of thought and in its doctrine. A reliable Catholic authority has spoken of its spirit: "A spirit of complete emancipation, tending to weaken ecclesiastical authority; the emancipation of science, which must traverse every field of investigation without fear of conflict with the Church; the emancipation of the state, which should never be hampered by religious authority; the emancipation of the private conscience, whose inspirations must not be overridden by papal definitions or anathemas; the emancipation of the universal conscience, with which the Church should be ever in agreement . . ."[37] In his *Syllabus of Errors* (1864) Pius IX had listed some of the principal tenets worthy of condemnation, and in 1907 Pius X sought to end the controversy within the Church finally with his decree *Lamentabili* and the encyclical *Pascendi Dominici Gregis*.

While the Catholic Church rejected the idea of swaying with passing intellectual currents, it did not regard its teaching as stagnant, as complete at one stage of its history. Even in doctrine, it recognized "development," a "gradual unfolding" leading to a clearer statement of its dogmas. "Such

36 See above, pp. 29–30.
37 A. Vermeersch, "Modernism," *Catholic Encyclopedia* (New York, 1911), X, 416.

unfolding takes place," Father Vermeersch wrote from the Catholic University of Louvain, "not only in the study of the tradition of the dogma but also in showing its origin in Jesus Christ and the Apostles, in the understanding of the terms expressing it and in the historical or rational proofs adduced in support of it."[38] The Immaculate Conception of the Virgin Mary and Papal Infallibility, defined authoritatively in 1854 and 1870, were examples of the development of dogma. If dogma itself developed, how much more the application of moral principles toward conspicuously changing institutions?

These conflicting principles—the changelessness of Catholic teaching and the development of doctrine—operated in a dense area of theology where even Catholic theologians disagreed. To borrow from Gilbert and Sullivan, a theologian, like

> every boy and every gal
> that's born into the world alive
> is either a little Liberal
> or else a little Conservative.

Where one saw a tampering with the deposit of doctrine another saw adaptation to changing conditions. A doubt of the divinity of the historical Jesus was clearly tampering. The idea of the "just price" in the Middle Ages was as clearly adaptation. But what of the middle ground? The "Americanism" controversy had indicated that honest men could differ when viewing the same evidence.

In this atmosphere Ryan reviewed *Le péril religieux,* by Father A. M. Weiss, a conservative European Dominican, in May, 1907, just before the pope issued *Lamentabili* and *Pascendi Dominici Gregis.* Ryan observed with satisfaction that Father Weiss did a thorough study of modernism without mentioning Ireland, Keane, and Spalding as offending liberals; they were apparently not "the genuine article." Drawing on the English Dominican Vincent McNabb, he defined "legitimate liberals" as "those who, while not taking from authority anything that certainly belongs to it, believe that truth and righteousness will be better promoted by giving a wide scope to individual freedom than by the opposite course."[39] The tone of the definition, and of the article as a whole, clearly aligned Ryan with the liberal view.

[38] *Ibid.,* p. 417.
[39] Ryan, "Is the Modern Spirit Anti-Religious," *Catholic World,* May, 1907, pp. 185, 188.

Because Ryan was on the liberal side, he sometimes struck conservatives as going too far. He published an article in the *New York Review*, a theological magazine published by young priests, many of them Paulists. While no one had attacked the magazine as modernist, its staff, with a prudent sense shared in the archdiocesan office of New York, discontinued it after the papal statements in 1907. Ryan's article in the *Review*, "The Method of Teleology in Ethics," warned against testing the morality of an act in terms of its remote end to the exclusion of any detailed consideration of the acts themselves. Ryan feared that moralists would stress remote ends so much and proximate norms of conduct so little that they would convey the impression that the definition of the remote end would always and readily furnish sufficient guidance concerning the moral quality of a particular action.[40] The article made a reasonable enough point. Yet another seminary professor, Father Charles Plater, S.J., promptly warned that Ryan's reasoning led directly to a Kantian empty form.[41]

Another argument started up in the *Ecclesiastical Review*. Father Thomas Slater, S.J., a renowned English writer on moral theology, defended the attempts in the standard manuals to keep pace with modern business practices. After all, he said, the general principles there stated were readily adaptable to any problem that arose. When a tough moral question came up, a thorough grasp of basic moral principles yielded the answer. Doubtful cases could be solved, therefore, by reference to the basic principles as outlined in "the pages of good, old Gury, or the more recent Sabetti."[42]

Ryan gave his retort in the following issue. General principles of moral theology did not solve problems without concrete information about how the modern economy worked. Older writers had written their manuals with economic practices then current in mind. Now a later generation used these manuals unquestioningly. But the problems had changed. Why should seminarians plow through lengthy discussions of mohatra, a tricky and long-obsolete device designed to avoid the prohibition of usury, when monopoly, stock-watering, unions, and just wages cried out for close moral analysis? Ryan argued that these topics were not adequately treated

[40] Ryan, "The Method of Teleology in Ethics," *New York Review*, January–February, 1907, pp. 409–429.
[41] Charles Plater, "A Starting Point in Ethics," *ibid.*, July–August, 1907, pp. 145–162.
[42] T[homas] Slater, "What Is Honest Business?" *Ecclesiastical Review*, November, 1907, pp. 528–530.

in any of the standard manuals except Tanquerey's, and even there the treatment was briefer than it should have been.[43]

Two years later Slater reopened the fight. After Ryan's articles on stock-watering appeared, Slater showed irritation about Ryan's rebuke to existing manuals—"compendiums made and fashioned with a somnolency almost senile, without a trace of profound study or exact criticism"—then hinted that Ryan's views moved in the direction of an evolutionary morality.[44] In other words, of modernism. In other words, of heresy. Ryan replied mildly, denying that he wanted anything more than the application of principles, themselves stable, to moral issues that would trouble priests in their twentieth-century parochial work.[45] There the matter rested.

In practice, Ryan worried rather little, as an incident described in his autobiography illustrates:

When I was in Rome in the summer of the year 1911, I took advantage of a dinner party given in my honor in the rectory of the English Catholic Church of San Silvestro to ascertain, if possible, whether my social teaching was liable to "get me into trouble" with the authorities of the Church. One of the dinner guests was a distinguished Irish Franciscan who had lived a long time in Rome, Canon Peter Fleming. To him I mentioned the fact that some three years earlier I had rallied Rev. Francis E. Gigot, the celebrated Scripture scholar, concerning the danger that confronted men in his field on account of the recent condemnation of Modernism. His reply was: "It is easy for you to joke about that matter but your time is coming; one of these days you will be censured for your economic doctrine." Canon Fleming's comment was entirely reassuring: "So long as your teaching avoids the stigma or implication of Socialism, you have nothing to fear. There is much more freedom of teaching in the Catholic Church than most persons outside the Church, and many persons within it, assume." The correctness of Canon Fleming's judgment I never doubted. Complete and overwhelming and final testimony on the point was provided, twenty years later, by the encyclical of Pope Pius XI, *Quadragesimo Anno*.[46]

After all, Ryan believed that the massive authority of *Rerum novarum* stood behind his social program. It is hard to be more orthodox than the Pope.

[43] Ryan, "Business Ethics in Our Manuals of Moral Theology," *ibid.*, December, 1907, pp. 653–654.

[44] Slater, "Dr. Ryan and the Moral Aspect of Stockwatering," *ibid.*, April, 1909, pp. 479–488.

[45] Ryan, "Father Slater's Rejoinder on Stockwatering," *ibid.*, June 1909, pp. 746–756.

[46] Ryan, *Social Doctrine in Action*, pp. 116–117.

The many barriers—the flaccid acceptance of poverty, the prejudice against social work, the disinclination to cooperate with non-Catholics, the specter of socialism, the danger of modernism—seemed formidable, especially when aided by the inertia of the *status quo*. Yet, though different in kind, Ryan's barriers were probably not much larger than those that confront any reformer. To balance them, Ryan had certain advantages. Not the least was his own prudence. In addition, others were doing the same work. And finally, influential members of the hierarchy gave him comforting support.

Ryan did not see himself as St. George out to flay reactionary dragons. After all, he was a professor of moral theology at a major American seminary. If economics and economic history accounted for one-fourth of his course, three-fourths were devoted to the traditional corpus of moral theology. On many controversial questions, his stand did not differ from the conservatives'. Like them, he never ceased to attack artificial contraception as metaphysically wrong, as well as contrary to public welfare. His attack on materialist standards for the good life drew on a long Christian tradition. When some critics of *A Living Wage* protested that a living wage sufficient to support a family went beyond the canons of strict justice, Ryan reviewed his own argument and moderated his own judgment.[47] When a decree of the Consistorial Congregation in 1910 required an oath against modernism from all seminary professors, Ryan had no hesitancy in taking it.

He was embarrassed and uncompromising in the face of any attempt to make him appear hostile to the Church. After Ryan's address to the Yale chapter of the Intercollegiate Socialist Society in 1915, a critic reported that Ryan had asserted his determination to make up his own mind regardless of authorities, this last said with a nod in the direction of Rome. The critic went on to observe that Ryan was openly critical of "Roman Catholic" authorities, and as further evidence of Ryan's alienation from the Church, observed that his talk had gone unreported in the Catholic press. Ryan was quick to reply. No Catholic, he said, ever speaks of the "Roman Catholic Church." His remarks critical of the Church referred to the French clergy before the Revolution, and were old stuff, all of it available in Hilaire Belloc and W. S. Lilly. As for shaking his head toward Rome when he spoke of making up his own mind regardless of constituted authorities, he was referring to self-constituted authorities; he did not even know which direction Rome was

47 Ryan, "Compensation," *Catholic Encyclopedia* (New York, 1908), IV, 185–186.

from the platform from which he spoke. And for the clincher, he noted that a full account of his talk had appeared in the *Catholic Transcript* of Hartford together with favorable editorial comment on it.[48]

Ryan never forgot that he was a priest and that his business was the salvation of souls. The remaking of the social order was a means to that end, and not the end in itself. He took the occasion of a meeting of the National Conference of Social Work, a secular gathering, to reject excessive demands that the Church enter the social arena. He was explicitly critical of his friend Rauschenbusch, who, he felt, went too far in this direction. "The primary function of the Church," he said, "is to save souls, to bring the human soul into such relation to God, and into such harmony with God and his purposes, that it will be fit for a permanent union with God in the life to come. That may be old-fashioned and other-worldly; but it is certainly the theory of the Church to which I belong; and it is the prevailing theory in most of the churches that I know anything about." Now it was true that man could not be in right relationship to God unless he had right relations with his neighbors, he said. The dual command was to love God and your neighbor. Therefore, right conduct was the Church's business, and the Church must concern itself, rather more than it had, with the social order. But it could never lose sight of its function: to bring souls to God.[49] This conviction went as deep in Ryan as his insistence on social justice. He said more about social problems mainly because others were saying so little.

Ryan was not alone, and he drew strength from what others were saying: Kenkel and Dietz, Siedenburg and Husslein, Kerby and O'Grady and Shahan. Cardinal Gibbons was vice president of the Maryland branch of the National Consumers' League, and both he and Archbishop Ireland were remembered as friends of organized labor because of their leadership in the fight over the Knights of Labor. Bishop Muldoon stood out from the hierarchy by vigorously supporting specific reforms.

Even greater inspiration came from abroad. When Father Heinrich Pesch published his five-volume work on "solidarism," *Lehrbuch der Nationalökonomie*, which argued that the economic interests of individuals are subordinate to the needs of society and stand in need of supervision as well as protection by society, Ryan greeted it as "the greatest single

[48] New Haven *Journal Courier*, Feb. 4, 18, March 4, 1915, *et al.*; New York *Call*, Feb. 24, 1915.
[49] Ryan, "The Church and Social Work," National Conference of Charities and Corrections, *Proceedings* (Fort Wayne, Ind., 1913), pp. 156–158.

work in existence on political economy."[50] The Catholic Social Guild in England, the Central Verein in Germany—these provided inspiration to American Catholic social thinkers. As these nations were further along the road of social legislation than the United States, they provided institutional models as well as social theory. And behind them all stood Leo XIII, whose *Rerum novarum* gave a general mandate for state intervention that could be adapted to different uses in different nations.

Finally, Ryan could count on the support of his own ordinary, John Ireland. Not a genuine progressive himself, certainly not one to translate general statements into concrete programs, Ireland nevertheless gave Ryan free rein in his teaching and in his varied activities. As a regular examiner for the seminarians at the conclusion of their two-year stint with Ryan as mentor, Ireland could see Ryan's thoughts being passed along. "Nevertheless," Ryan comments in his autobiography, "he did not even once declare or intimate that my teaching was unorthodox, or too 'radical,' putting dangerous ideas into the heads of the young men who within two or three years would be elevated to the priesthood and empowered to teach my doctrines (in reality, the traditional doctrines of the Catholic Church) from their pulpits."[51]

In the balance between difficulties and compensations, then, Ryan had a safe margin. His personal orthodoxy, recognized by his own ordinary and confirmed by the example of others up to and including the Holy Father himself, were more than enough to protect him against hostile forces. If he did not expect some routine buffeting along the way, he had no business being a reformer.

[50] Ryan, "A Great Catholic Work on Political Economy," *Fortnightly Review,* May, 1910, pp. 289, 322.
[51] Ryan, *Social Doctrine in Action,* p. 28.

In League with
the Progressives

ALWAYS A DE-
voted son and brother (and rapidly becoming a doting
uncle as well), Father Ryan never let his activities smother
his concern for his family. As William Ryan aged and some
of his grown sons went off, the farm had become too much
of a burden, and the senior Ryans had moved to St. Paul
where William earned his living hauling. It was not an easy
life, but an old farmer who had broken the soil of Minnesota had known worse. Three of his sons, John, Maurice,
and Lawrence, had gone to St. Thomas College and had
never returned to the farm to live. Their education was
their share of the patrimony. Lawrence had turned up in
Father John's classes at the seminary. He was ordained in
1910. Young William and Thomas held the farm for a
while; then William moved to Portland, Oregon. Mary Jane
had joined the Sisters of St. Joseph, taking the name Sister
Constance. Another daughter had married; only the youngest, Katherine, had remained at home. Then she too applied
for admission to the Sisters of St. Joseph. With her last child
leaving, Maria Ryan wrote a note to her eldest son: "I feel
that I can never thank God enough for all His goodness

to me during my lifetime. I am well paid for all my hardships in the good children God gave me. . . . [Now Kate will be leaving.] Though I am perfectly resigned, I cannot bear to think of the separation. . . . You can guess what a time I shall have, lonely and lonesome, but I will offer it all up to God, and thank Him for His goodness to us all."[1] Soon thereafter William and Maria moved to Portland too. Their departure broke Father John's strongest tie to St. Paul, making it easier to think about returning to Washington. The rigor of the Minnesota winter made it easier still.

With his brother Lawrence, the brotherhood of the clerical life created a special bond. The priests at St. Paul Seminary used to say that no two brothers were "more identically different." Father John was gruff, chubby, earthy; Father Lawrence, polite, lean, ascetic. Except for his brief summer pastorate, John spent his whole priestly life in teaching; Lawrence was assigned to the seminary only after a long career in parochial work, much of it at the Cathedral of St. Paul. The legend persists, in clerical circles at least, that they never quite approved of each other, John insensitive to the problems of parish life and to Lawrence's role in the construction of the cathedral, Lawrence a bit dismayed by John's radicalism. Lawrence was usually pictured as laying a restraining hand on John's arm, and saying, "Now John, now, John . . ." The image is charming, but probably not accurate. The two men were different, and their careers diverse. Yet a strong current of affection ran between them. John felt a deep pride in his brother's success in St. Paul. Lawrence, not active in the social apostolate, never doubted John's cause or his orthodoxy. He had no difficulty in approving the career that John later characterized as "social doctrine in action." When John wrote the manuscript of his autobiography, he characteristically turned to Lawrence for a critical reading, and, on most questions of inclusion and exclusion, he accepted Lawrence's judgment.

In the summer of 1911, John and Lawrence, together with their sister Katherine, who was to enter the convent in the fall, went off to Europe. In Rome the three attended a public audience with Pope Pius X, since canonized as St. Pius X. One of the treasures now in the Ryan family is a handsome ebony and bronze crucifix blessed by the pope-saint. The trip had its lighter side as well. Lawrence was a teetotaler. John was not. John urged upon his brother the familiar slogan, "When in Rome

---

[1] Maria Ryan to Ryan, May 25, 1910.

. . .," and, when Lawrence contracted a slight fever, repeated the advice. Lawrence yielded neither time, preferring on the second occasion to consult a doctor. John had the last word: the doctor's prescription started with a brandy base. Once Lawrence recovered, John bustled him and their sister through an exhausting program of sight-seeing. Katherine was on the trip for her health. Lawrence had had his bout with Roman fever. But John was robust and insistent on company. Their efforts to contain his energy were more strenuous than successful.

During other summers John became a stranger to South Hall within hours after his last class. In the summer of 1912, for example, he went from the convention of the National Conference of Charities and Correction in Cleveland to give a series of lectures on the rise of the modern wage-earning class at the Catholic Summer School at Cliff Haven. And from there he went south to lecture on "The Wage Problem" at the Catholic Chautauqua sponsored by the Central Verein at Fordham University.[2] The next year his travels took him west, combining business with a visit to his relatives on the Pacific Coast. He was a delegate to the Charities and Correction convention in Seattle in July; then he returned to Milwaukee in August to speak to the American Federation of Catholic Societies on the living wage.[3] Even in the brief midyear recess, which traditionally began on the feast of St. Paul (January 25th), he rarely stayed at home. His schedule for 1915 was perhaps busier than that of most years. He went from the cathedral in Des Moines to engagements at St. Ambrose College in Davenport, Iowa; then on to Loyola University in Chicago; to St. Joseph's Seminary, Dunwoodie, the diocesan seminary in New York; then on to Yale, to Melrose, Massachusetts, and to Boston.[4] And then, of course, back to St. Paul Seminary to attend the solemn high Mass opening the second term.

Even in termtime, he managed to get about. The reception that the Minnesota *Union Advocate* had given to *A Living Wage* foreshadowed his welcome in labor circles, though he did not enjoy the close rapport with labor leaders in Minnesota that Father Dietz had in Ohio. In 1911 he talked the St. Paul Trades and Labor Assembly into supporting a minimum wage bill in the Minnesota legislature.[5] The following year the *Union Advocate* noted that Ryan was "steadily widening and elevating

[2] *Catholic Bulletin*, July 6, Aug. 17, 1912.
[3] *Ibid.*, July 19, June 14, 1913.
[4] *Ibid.*, Jan. 23, 1915.
[5] Minnesota *Union Advocate*, Jan. 20, 1911.

his reputation as a profound student of economics and a clear, logical and forcible speaker on the subject."[6] In approaching labor audiences, Ryan was not talking only to the already converted. His major message was the obligation of society to guarantee a living wage to every worker, a proposition that to laborers needed little proof. At the same time, he was proclaiming the Church's concern with the worker's welfare and the worker's need for religious guidance. Every time clergymen spoke for social justice, they blurred the socialists' image of religion as the tool of reaction.

Ryan moved easily among the secular and nondenominational groups into which he constantly coaxed the Catholic laity and clergy. He attended the regular meetings of the Saturday Lunch Club in Minneapolis, a primarily non-Catholic group of professional men who met as a "nonpartisan open forum . . . for free discussion of social, economic, and political issues." Most of the members were alien to conservatism; one socialist and two single-taxers gave the club a genuinely radical flavor. They welcomed Father Ryan, initially with surprise: "Most of the Catholics that they knew were either political and economic reactionaries or quite devoid of interest in the civic and social problems which were discussed in the Saturday Lunch Club." The few Catholics in the group were delighted by his attendance; most outside the group looked askance at Ryan's presence in that "radical bunch." Local politicians, weary of heckling by the members after the meal, spoke of the group as the "Saturday Grouch Club," and at least one Republican in town would have been happy to line up the whole lot and shoot them.[7]

Minnesotans active in social reform came to expect the professor from the seminary at their meetings. When Ryan made his pointed defense of the Associated Charities in 1913, he had already been active in the group for at least five years, three of them as vice-chairman. The organization helped the needy, bringing Catholics, Protestants, and Jews together in a common effort for social betterment. Ryan liked both its aim and its method. Though he regarded his contribution to the group as "neither great nor conspicuous," it led him easily to the coordinating state body, the Minnesota Conference of Charities and Correction, and this in turn to the federal body, the National Conference of Charities and Correction (NCCC).

[6] *Ibid.*, June 28, 1912.
[7] Ryan, *Social Doctrine in Action*, pp. 125–126; William E. Leonard, "The Saturday Lunch Club of Minneapolis," pamphlet (Minneapolis, 1927).

When the national conference held its annual meeting in Minneapolis in 1907, Ryan urged it to ascertain in precise dollars-and-cents terms the minimum normal standard of living for an American family and to learn how many American families fell below that standard.[8] Two years later the Conference's Division on Occupational Standards appointed a committee, of which Ryan was a member, to set up a standard of minimums in modern industrial society. The following year Ryan issued his own interim report, first to the National Consumers' League and later to the NCCC. He set the minimum for the decent maintenance of a family in a small city at $700. This went up to $900 in an expensive area like New York City. Considerably less than one-half the adult male wage earners of the nation were making this amount.[9] The full committee's report, issued in 1912, was less specific on figures, but shared many of Ryan's basic ideas: a living wage large enough to support a family and to ensure against sickness and old age; an eight-hour day and a six-day week; factory inspection against hazards to health and safety; insurance against old age, injury, and unemployment; an end to child labor and a limitation of female labor. As a platform written by social workers, however, the report expressed a level of aspiration, and not much more.[10] Perhaps in tribute to Ryan's share in writing it, he was elected chairman of the committee the following year. He became president of the Minnesota branch in 1912 and served on the executive committee of the national board in 1913.

He also worked actively with the National Child Labor Committee and the National Consumers' League. The Child Labor Committee, organized in 1904 by some distinguished social reformers—Florence Kelley, John G. Brooks, Brooks Adams, Samuel McC. Lindsay, Felix Adler, as well as Cardinal Gibbons—spread to Minnesota in 1908 when Ryan, as head of twenty-eight delegates from groups within the state, formed a committee. This organization did not move into an active campaign at this time, preferring first to build up a strong community base and to confer with elected officials.[11] The Consumers' League, founded by Mrs. Kelley and other women, tried to rally consumers to exert pressure for decent working conditions for laborers. Their program was education

[8] Ryan, "Standard of Living and the Problem of Dependency," National Conference of Charities and Correction, *Proceedings* (Fort Wayne, 1907), pp. 342–347.

[9] Ryan, "A Minimum Wage and Minimum Wage Boards," *ibid.* (1910), pp. 457–475.

[10] The entire platform is reprinted in William J. Kerby, *The Social Mission of Charity* (New York, 1921), pp. 67–72.

[11] National Child Labor Committee, *Proceedings* (n.p., 1908), p. 251; Josephine Goldmark, *Impatient Crusader* (Urbana, 1953), pp. 50–65, 78–92.

through research and publicity. Their most famous gimmick was a white consumers' label on goods that the league certified as having been made under fair working conditions.[12] In 1909 the league began to move more vigorously.

The time seemed ripe, for the Supreme Court's decision in Muller *v.* Oregon (1908) pointed to a fissure in the Constitution that allowed state intervention in the economy. Lochner *v.* New York (1905) had stifled the hopes of social reformers, for in denying the New York State Legislature's right to set maximum hours of work for bakers, the Supreme Court had used the "due process" clause of the Fourteenth Amendment to protect freedom of contract from New York's police power to protect the health of its citizens. Now, three years later, the brilliant brief of Louis D. Brandeis—scant law and abundant sociology—induced a bare majority of the Court to lean in the opposite direction, permitting Oregon to set maximum hours of work for women. Brandeis' "logic of facts" had convinced the Court that long hours did indeed impair the health of women and that the state could legitimately deal with this situation.[13] If maximum hours, why not minimum wages? At its 1909 convention, the league appointed a committee to study the possibilities of a sustained campaign for legislation. The committee, made up of Father Ryan, Professor Arthur Holcombe, of Harvard; and Emily Greene Balch, the famous peace advocate, gave the reply expected, and in 1910 the league committed itself to a ten-year fight for legislation guaranteeing minimum wages.[14]

The fight was on. Ryan, as a member of the committee on minimum wages, helped to draw up a model bill based on the British Trades Boards Act of 1909. With the help of a seminarian at St. Paul's who had been a lawyer, he drew up a similar measure and had it introduced into the Minnesota legislature in 1911. Referred to committee, it stayed buried in the committee's files. So much for Minnesota—at that time at least.[15]

In Wisconsin, meanwhile, with a stronger progressive tradition, the fight was at least a fight. John R. Commons, the expert on labor at the University of Wisconsin, drafted the bill, the first that had been presented to any American legislature. Ryan appeared at the legislative hearing on the bill, and a Catholic lawyer named Carpenter, representing the

---

[12] Maud Nathan, *The Story of an Epoch-Making Movement* (New York, 1926).
[13] Lochner *v.* New York, 198 U.S. 45; Muller *v.* Oregon, 208 U.S. 412.
[14] John O'Grady, *A Legal Minimum Wage* (Washington, D.C., 1915), pp. 80–106; Goldmark, *Impatient Crusader*, pp. 132–179.
[15] George W. Lawson, *History of Labor in Minnesota* (St. Paul, 1955), p. 204.

Milwaukee Merchants and Manufacturers Association, was on hand to oppose him. Ryan argued for the bill on familiar moral grounds. Carpenter replied that the obligation to pay decent wages was a matter of conscience, a matter for the confessional not for the legislature. Ryan replied mildly that workers could not count on such an attitude in all employers. He also pointed out that manufacturers in Australia, where a comparable law was on the books, did not want it repealed. But this bill too failed to pass. The Milwaukee *Daily News* reported that this result was satisfactory to the bill's backers: they needed time to educate the public and were therefore content to postpone action for two years until the next legislature.[16] There is no evidence that Ryan concurred in this view.

Nevertheless, the idea of minimum wage laws caught on. Massachusetts passed its law in 1912, eight more states in 1913. These eight included Pennsylvania and Wisconsin, in both of which Ryan testified; Oregon, where the bill was written and lobbied by Father Edwin V. O'Hara, a former student of Ryan's; and Minnesota itself, where a revised version of Ryan's bill went through with the tepid support of the Minnesota Federation of Labor without arousing the organized opposition of careless industrialists.

The situation in Minnesota was far from typical. In some large industrial states, the active hostility of employers plus the indifference of workers (as in Ohio) or the active opposition of workers (as in California) created a combination sufficiently strong to stifle minimum wage bills. Organized labor preferred to get its wage through organization, not through legislation. It feared that legislative relief would discourage union membership and that a legally stated minimum would in practice set the maximum rate as well as the minimum.[17] Ryan finally felt that he must deal with these fears openly. In 1912, responding directly to a statement in the press by Samuel Gompers of the American Federation of Labor, he warned the AFL in the *Central Blatt and Social Justice* that the unions of skilled workers had no clear awareness of the acuteness of the unskilled workers' needs, especially the needs of women and children. Organization worked splendidly for skilled workers, but for the many,

---

[16] Elizabeth Brandeis, "Labor Legislation," in John R. Commons, *History of Labor in the United States*, 4 vols. (New York, 1935), III, 501–539, especially 512–513; Gertrude Schmidt, "History of Labor Legislation in Wisconsin," Ph.D. dissertation, University of Wisconsin, 1933, pp. 226–231; Milwaukee *Daily News*, April 7, 1911.

[17] Commons and John B. Andrews, *Principles of Labor Legislation* (New York, 1916), p. 215.

"It is too slow, and they are too numerous and too precious."[18] Again in 1915, for the wider reading public reached by *Survey*, he tried to quell the fears of "that occasional labor leader who opposes the legal minimum wage." Even if organized labor were to meet with tremendous success in the next three decades, he argued, its gains would still not reach women, and it was women who benefited from these laws. The choice for women was not a minimum wage by legislation or a minimum wage by organization. It was a minimum wage by legislation or starvation wages. Nor would he concede that legislative action discouraged union membership. Quite the contrary. The minimum wage by law would give "an increased measure of courage, ambition, consciousness, and financial power, all of which make for organization, and it would demonstrate the value of organized cooperation with public officials." Finally, wages were in no danger of being held to the minimum. Such an assertion was a *non sequitur*, and anyway it had not happened. Besides, Ryan added dryly, if anti-labor forces had the power to lower wages, they would not need a precedent.[19] Ryan's argument was strong. But organized labor remained unconvinced.

Most of the bills that passed in 1912 and 1913 put a real bite into their provisions. Massachusetts, the exception, enacted a mealymouthed statute that set up a minimum wage commission charged to determine the cost of decent, healthful living. But it lacked effective machinery for enforcement. The commission could do no more than publish the names of noncomplying employers. In other states, including Minnesota, the minimum set by the commission had the force of law, and employers who failed to pay those rates were liable to fine and imprisonment.

Ryan's law in Minnesota differed from the others mainly by affirming that wages for women and children (none of the laws applied to men) should be adequate to provide the "necessary comforts and conditions of reasonable life." The law set up a board of three: the state commissioner of labor, an employer of women, and a woman representing the public. Advisory boards, representing equally employers, employees, and the "public," were set up, one for mercantile and office occupations, one for factories, laundries, restaurants, and hotels. Father Ryan was chairman of the first of these advisory committees. Ryan wanted the minimum wage set on the assumption that a woman lived in a home of her own, but he could not carry his board on this issue. On many matters the

[18] Ryan, "Far-Fetched Argument of Mr. Gompers Against a Minimum Wage," *Central Blatt and Social Justice*, April, 1913, pp. 11–12.
[19] Ryan, "Fears of the Minimum Wage," *Survey*, May 22, 1915, p. 184.

female representative of employees let him down. The woman workers, despite the high expectations of Florence Kelley, were reluctant to serve on the board, and when they did they were sufficiently overawed by the employer or insufficiently class-conscious or too unused to this type of proceeding to vote as their interest dictated. Ryan found that "club women," the type of middle-class reformer so prevalent in the National Consumers' League, were much more reliable in insisting on a reasonable minimum. His board finally suggested $9.00 a week as the minimum wage. Even this paltry sum went beyond the usual pay of most women who worked in Minnesota. Accepting the bulk of Ryan's committee's recommendations, Minnesota's board issued its first minimum wage orders in October, 1914. It allowed the $9.00 figure for larger cities, but shaded it to $8.50 in smaller cities, and $8.00 elsewhere.

Even before the orders appeared, the employers on the boards tried to trip up the operation by presenting questions on the constitutionality of the law to the state attorney general. These he had ducked. Almost immediately after the commission's order appeared, a shoe manufacturer of Winona sought an injunction from the state district court in Ramsey County to prevent the operation of the law. With the law challenged in the courts, the attorney general's office had to act. The assistant attorney general, John C. Nethaway, tried to avoid the constitutional issue: Did the law deprive persons of their liberty and/or property in violation of the Fourteenth Amendment? He defended the legislature's right to its legislative judgment, hoping to convince the court not to substitute its opinion on the appropriateness of the law for that of the legislature. The judge refused to take up this argument. With Ryan present in court, he granted the injunction that prevented the commission from enforcing its order. The law, he said, was an unconstitutional delegation of legislative power; and it abridged the right of individuals to make free contracts, a right protected by the Fourteenth Amendment. Lochner v. New York won over Muller v. Oregon. Ryan spoke for the progressive forces when he promised an immediate appeal to a higher court, an appeal from "Philip drunk to Philip sober." The Minnesota Supreme Court confirmed his faith in its sobriety: it reversed the decision of the lower court, and the law went into effect.[20]

[20] Ryan, "The Tasks of Minimum Wage Boards in Minnesota," *Survey*, Nov. 14, 1914, pp. 171–172; Minnesota *Union Advocate*, Jan. 30, Oct. 30, Nov. 20, 27, 1914; Ryan, *Social Doctrine in Action*, pp. 120–123; Ryan, "The Minimum Wage Law in Minnesota," Wisconsin State Conference of Charities and Correction, *Proceedings* (1913), pp. 27–37.

Ryan was jubilant, and regarded the victory as the beginning of a new era of social legislation on the state level. He looked forward to the 1915 session with renewed excitement. But in 1915 nothing happened; progressive enthusiasm faltered. Men were less venturesome, Ryan mourned, more timid. Actually the mood was national in scope. The reform movement had lost its momentum in the states, and even in Washington, President Woodrow Wilson told a colleague that the progressive movement had completed its mission; a "time of healing" lay ahead.[21] In Minnesota an inane debate over liquor, which caused paralysis in the legislature, concealed this nationwide sag. Ryan assumed that the debate over local option had stifled further reform.[22] More likely what he saw as cause was actually result: because the reform movement had sagged, the state could engage in the luxury of a debate over local option. Though reformers liked to think of the previous decade as the beginning of a new era, actually 1915 closed an era. Except for a brilliant flash of legislation in 1916, when Wilson was bidding for progressive support in the Presidential election, reform had made its maximum gains, and reformers were to lose much ground before they gained any more.

The minimum wage fight enhanced Ryan's reputation among reformers. His phrase "living wage" had shown up in quotation marks in the platform of the Progressive Party in 1912. In the fight for state legislation, no name was more common than his. He was on the committee of the National Consumers' League that drew up the model bill on which many state laws were based. In Wisconsin he shared honors with Professor Commons, the author of the bill. In Oregon, his student, Father O'Hara, a prime mover of the law, soon became chairman of Oregon's Industrial Welfare Commission. In Ohio, Thomas D. Farrell, who pushed a minimum wage provision through the Ohio State Constitutional Convention in 1912, was said to have "derived the idea from the writings" of Father Ryan.[23] In Minnesota, Ryan's notable contribution prompted the Executive Council of the Minnesota Federation of Labor to refer to the minimum wage bill quite explicitly as "the bill of Rev. John A. Ryan."[24] The Minneapolis *Tribune* reported the opinion that Ryan and Brandeis

[21] Arthur S. Link, *Woodrow Wilson and the Progressive Era, 1910–1917* (New York, 1954), p. 79.

[22] Ryan, "Minnesota's Social Legislation Halted by Liquor Debates," *Survey*, May 8, 1915, p. 145.

[23] National Consumers' League, *Thirteenth Annual Report* (New York, 1912), p. 42.

[24] *Proceedings of the 31st Convention of the Minnesota State Federation of Labor* (Minneapolis, 1913), p. 67.

were the two leading social reformers in the United States.[25] The Minnesota theologian was acquainted with some of the great names in the nonpolitical aspects of the reform movement: Florence Kelley, Brandeis, and Holcombe through the Consumers' League; Lindsay and Rabbi Stephen S. Wise from the National Conference of Charities and Correction. Because so few Catholics joined these groups, Father Ryan stood out all the more prominently. These years were his years in a special sense. The small troop of middle-class reformers who knew him were a strategic group, flushed with victory and close to the seats of power.

Ryan hoped to parlay this prestige into an appointment to the Commission on Industrial Relations authorized by Congress in 1912. In September the St. Paul professor, assuming that only one Catholic would be appointed, asked Kenkel to get the executive committee of the Central Verein to propose his name to President William Howard Taft. He knew that he had been favorably considered by the committee that had drafted the law authorizing the commission.[26] Actually, Ryan had no chance, for Taft nominated a commission studded with solid conservatives. Ryan prodded Kenkel again. These appointees, indeed any names that Taft might select, were "far from satisfactory." He wanted Kenkel to get the Central Verein's societies to write to Senator William E. Borah, of Idaho, asking him to use his influence in the Senate to prevent confirmation.[27] Borah needed no urging. In any case, the Democratic-dominated Senate sat on Taft's appointments, knowing that its failure to confirm would save the appointments for Taft's successor, Woodrow Wilson.

When Wilson came to office, Ryan's name cropped up again. Lindsay, Ryan's associate in the NCCC, urged the President to appoint Ryan. The Minnesota priest, he said, was very widely known for his studies of industrial questions. "He has, furthermore, the ear and can greatly influence the church organization that he represents, which has a far-reaching relation to the labor problem."[28] All in vain. The "Catholic appointment" went to Frank P. Walsh, a prominent attorney from Kansas City known for his interest in labor causes. Ryan endorsed this appointment and the commission in general; the quality of the appointments gave "concrete

[25] Minneapolis *Tribune*, April 29, 1912.
[26] Ryan to Frederick P. Kenkel, Sept. 19, 1912, Frederick P. Kenkel Papers, University of Notre Dame Archives. I am indebted to Philip Gleason for these references in the Kenkel Papers.
[27] Ryan to Kenkel, Feb. 13, 1913.
[28] Samuel McC. Lindsay to Woodrow Wilson, April 22, 1913, Commerce Department file, Archives of the United States. I am indebted to Leonard Rapport for this reference.

and eloquent testimony to the advance . . . toward social justice in the last few years."[29] Walsh saw this comment, and thanked Ryan for his "intelligent and sympathetic" attitude. He expressed the hope that the commission would call on Ryan for aid.[30] The call never came.

Meanwhile Ryan was attracting public notice by taking on Morris Hillquit for a sustained debate in *Everybody's Magazine* on the merits of socialism. Monsignor Joseph H. McMahon, of New York, whom Ryan knew through the National Conference of Catholic Charities, had asked Dr. Kerby at Catholic University to do the series. When Kerby demurred, McMahon turned to Ryan and would not take "No" for an answer. Ryan finally took on the job, for it offered a superb forum for getting Catholic views on socialism and social reform before the American people. Cutting his outside appointments to the minimum, and avoiding any premature publicity, he spent four months working over his seven exchanges with Hillquit. The debate was carefully designed to guarantee a real clash on real issues and to avoid the advantage of catching the opponent off balance. Hillquit wrote his first article, then sent it to Ryan. Ryan prepared his reply and returned both articles to Hillquit. Then each wrote a brief statement in rebuttal. This procedure went on for a series of seven. Each was permitted to revise his original statement in view of his opponent's argument, an arrangement that lost Hillquit a large advantage on at least one occasion. At one point Ryan gave Hillquit a superb opening by saying that even if socialism divided the total national wealth among all people equally, the poor would still not have a decent share. Socialism thus offered nothing more than the present system. Hillquit leaped eagerly at this opening. He pointed out that under socialism, production would mount because of the elimination of unproductive work and of duplication in competition. "I was particularly satisfied with this piece of writing," Hillquit has recalled. "My argument seemed to me quite convincing. But so it apparently also seemed to my candid opponent. When he read my reply he quietly eliminated the whole point in controversy from his manuscript and I was regretfully compelled to follow suit."[31]

A mood of mutual respect and courteous combat cushioned the con-

[29] Ryan, "Personnel of the Industrial Relations Commission," *Catholic World*, November, 1913, pp. 221–224.
[30] Frank P. Walsh to Ryan, Nov. 18, 1913.
[31] Morris Hillquit, *Loose Leaves from a Busy Life* (New York, 1934), pp. 88–89.

88

test. Midway through the debate Hillquit wrote intriguingly from Switzerland that Ryan had just put him in an awkward predicament, for Ryan's reply to Hillquit's fourth article was "one of the very strongest arguments that can be made against Marxian socialism." Ryan in turn was not to be outdone in courtesy. He noted in his last article that the debate had demonstrated that "it is possible for men to differ as widely as the poles and yet carry on a protracted argument with fairness and without bitterness, and conclude it with both self-respect and mutual respect unimpaired."[32]

Few readers could believe that the two men were poles apart. Hillquit, of course, started from a philosophical base in materialism and ended with the abolition of private ownership of the means of production. Ryan did not follow him to these extremes. Yet both agreed on the evils of industrial capitalist society. Both accepted a wide range of intervention by the state. Ryan repeated the substance of the "Programme of Social Reform by Legislation" from the *Catholic World* in 1909, and, having read Hilaire Belloc's *Servile State* (1912) in the interim, now added the idea that workers share in the ownership of industry. The St. Paul priest yielded nothing to Hillquit on the scope of his own program for social reform. Hillquit made the distinction that socialists wanted comprehensive reform, while mere social reformers tried to set terminal points. Ryan turned the argument back on Hillquit: utopians such as the socialists set a limit once they created the socialist state, while reformers, recognizing the evolutionary development of society, wanted to leave the door open to constant readjustments. Ryan's argument, neat if not wholly convincing, put him in the position of arguing that socialists were too little prone to true reform. In the course of the debate, the argument unexpectedly turned to an attack on the Catholic Church as a bulwark of capitalism. Ryan demurred from this characterization, and for the better part of two articles the Church replaced socialism as the main topic.

As a clash of ideas, the articles were a splendid success. Hillquit regarded Ryan as "probably the most formidable and at the same time the most gratifying opponent it was ever my good fortune to meet in public debate, well informed, painstaking, broadminded, and scrupulously fair."[33] Their contest "remains today the most intelligent debate on Socialism in print," Hillquit's biographer has written. "Ryan wasn't merely a foil for

[32] Hillquit to Ryan, June 30, 1913; Ryan, "Socialism: Promise or Menace," *Everybody's Magazine*, April, 1914, p. 535.
[33] Hillquit, *Loose Leaves from a Busy Life*, p. 89.

Hillquit's lawyer-logic, and both sides were presented fairly and completely. There was interplay, refutation, rebuttal and a very careful consideration of all issues raised. . . ."[34] Some of Ryan's correspondents at the time put their finger quite accurately on the significance of the series. A priest at the Holy Cross Seminary near Catholic University pointed out that not the least of Ryan's accomplishments was to get from a competent authority an accurate statement of the American socialist position. Frank J. Walsh told Ryan that Catholics were enthusiastic about Ryan's skill in handling the issues with such an able contestant. This enthusiasm took a special form for an Ohio lawyer: he was having great fun telling his Catholic friends that he was as much of a socialist as John A. Ryan. When the articles appeared in book form as *Socialism: Promise or Menace?* (1914), the *Catholic Fortnightly Review* reported a widespread Catholic opinion that Ryan had conceded too much. William E. Walling, a prominent socialist publicist writing for the *American Journal of Sociology*, came up with the intriguing judgment that Ryan won all the economic points, Hillquit all the religious ones.[35]

By the time of the Hillquit debate, Ryan was growing restive in St. Paul. His schedule at the seminary confined him, and he needed the flexibility of a university, free from the localism of a diocesan post, to pursue the outside activities that now consumed so much of his interest.[36] He wanted to go east, closer to the publishing world and to the centers of reform. He wanted to edit a magazine devoted to Catholic social doctrine. As early as 1910 he envisaged such a periodical as the house organ for the National Conference of Catholic Charities. Since New York seemed to be the appropriate headquarters for such a journal, he tried to interest John Cardinal Farley, Archbishop of New York, but without success.[37]

Then Catholic University beckoned. Cardinal Gibbons wanted Ryan to come. John J. Keane, former rector and now Archbishop of Dubuque, was anxious. Two other Midwestern bishops spoke enthusiastically: James McGolrick, of Duluth, Minnesota, and James O'Reilly, of Fargo, North

34 Robert W. Iversen, "Morris Hillquit: American Social Democrat," Ph.D. dissertation, State University of Iowa (1951), p. 75.
35 J. A. Burns to Ryan, April 12, 1914; Walsh to Ryan, *loc. cit.*; H. H. Haines to Ryan, Oct. 24, 1913; *Catholic Fortnightly Review*, June 15, 1914, p. 359; *American Journal of Sociology*, January, 1915, pp. 534–536.
36 For a contrary view, see John S. Cronin, *Catholic Social Principles* (Milwaukee, 1950), p. 626.
37 Ryan, *Social Doctrine in Action*, p. 96n.

Dakota.[38] At the university itself, his old sociology professor, Father Kerby, wanted him on the faculty. In the summer of 1914, Ryan served on the staff of the university's branch summer school at Dubuque, where a large roster of friendly professors from Washington spent the summer together. The matter probably came up more than once during the clerics' six weeks together. Just that spring Ryan had published his thoughtful treatise about the morality of interest on capital in the *Catholic University Bulletin*. They were scholarly in the classic style—the history of the question, the traditional authorities, the present state of the controversy, and finally the formally constructed argument. The technique and the quality of the articles invited the comment: Here's a good man in St. Paul. Not just a popularizer. We ought to have him here.

Archbishop Ireland was the stumbling block. He did not want to lose a good man, even to Catholic University. Already two of his professors had gone that route—Thomas E. Shields and William Turner. He did not propose to make his seminary a mere stepping-stone to Washington. Even proddings from Gibbons did not help. Ryan has reported that when he told Ireland of Gibbons' desire to have him at the university, Ireland replied curtly, "You may tell the Cardinal to mind his own business."[39] It was his business, of course, for the Archbishop of Baltimore was *ex officio* chancellor of the university. But Ireland did not welcome Gibbons' tending his business at the expense of St. Paul Seminary.

Yet in June, 1915, Ireland finally released Ryan. The knowledge that Ireland's Republican friends and some well-to-do members of his flock would weep no tears at the professor's departure may have made the final decision easier. Ireland knew of Ryan's long-standing desire to go; it may have been that when the archbishop succeeded in getting a satisfactory replacement, he finally yielded to the combination of pressures, especially from Ryan and from friends of both Ryan and the university in the hierarchy. Even to the end the decision seemed grudging. The diocesan paper, the *Catholic Bulletin*, announced simply that the Reverend John Waldron, a graduate of St. Patrick's College, Maynooth, Ireland, had been appointed to succeed Dr. Ryan. No explanation, no review of Ryan's impressive career, no editorial comment. Three weeks later the paper noted that Ryan had left to fill his appointment as professor of political science at Catholic University. It was a less than gracious send-

[38] *Ibid.*, p. 128.
[39] *Ibid.*, p. 129n.

off. The appointment of the considerably younger Father Lawrence Ryan as city missioner was given about equal play.[40]

Ryan took with him the manuscript of *Distributive Justice: The Right and Wrong of Our Present Distribution of Wealth*. Although published in 1916, after he had left St. Paul, the work belonged to the earlier period. A fresh study, not a compilation of previous writings, it drew together in 430 pages of closely reasoned text the main lines of Dr. Ryan's ethical teachings on economic institutions.[41] It ranged well beyond *A Living Wage*, covering the moral position not only of workers, but of land-owners, capitalists, and entrepreneurs as well. Like the earlier book, it synthesized the research of moralists and economists, but with greater depth. The theological passages drew from the great names all the way back to St. Thomas, and for his economic data he referred to English, German, French, and American authorities with the sure mastery gained in a decade of study.

Distributive justice governs the proper "distribution of the products of industry among the classes that have taken part in the making of these products." Each of the four agents of production—landowner, capitalist, entrepreneur, worker—had a claim on the finished product, Ryan said, because each contributed an element without which production could not be carried on. At generous length the theologian considered the claims of each. Those familiar with his writings found no surprises, but nowhere else had he set forth in one forceful consecutive account his compre-hensive ethical critique of existing economic institutions. Aware of the density of the material, he made his own brief summary of the argument, indicating the confident clarity that he felt he had at last achieved:

The landowner has a right to all the economic rent, modified by the right of his tenants and employés to a decent livelihood, and by the right of the State to levy taxes which do not substantially lower the value of the land. The capitalist has a right to the prevailing rate of interest, modified by the right of his employés to the "equitable minimum" of wages. The busi-ness man in competitive conditions has a right to all the profits that he can obtain, but corporations possessing a monopoly have no right to unusual gains except those due to unusual efficiency. The labourer has a right to living wages, and to as much more as he can get by competition with the other agents of production and with his fellow labourers.

40 *Catholic Bulletin*, Sept. 4, June 12, Sept. 25, 1915.
41 The best analysis of Ryan's ethical principles is the chapter "Principles of Social Ethics" in Patrick W. Gearty, *The Economic Thought of Monsignor John A. Ryan*, pp. 100–127.

The book was generally well received. The *Nation* found it useful as a résumé of economic reforms, but as a philosophical inquiry, "curious rather than interesting." Alvin S. Johnson, reviewing the book for the *New Republic* in February, 1917, noted that Ryan professed a Catholic ethic, "therefore conservative"; this fact "makes it all the more significant that Dr. Ryan's book should be worthy of adoption as a manual of radical economic reform." The Catholic press was, on the whole, favorable. The *Irish Theological Quarterly* was thorough and thoughtfully quarrelsome. In replying to the comment from Ireland, Ryan especially valued one point the *Quarterly* had made: "It is consoling to be assured that one is leaning toward conservatism rather than radicalism."[42] All the more consoling, no doubt, because it happened so infrequently.

With the publication of *Distributive Justice*, the basic frame of Father Ryan's program for social justice was set. In other areas—the relations between church and state, and international relations—he would have new things to say. But in the field of industrial ethics on which his reputation finally rested, he had had his say by 1916. What came thereafter was important: his career in popularizing his ideas was probably the more important part of his life. Yet ironically, when he moved from St. Paul Seminary to the Catholic University of America, he left scholarship behind. Like the college professor who fights his way to the top by publishing and once there does the things he always wanted to do, Ryan spent the major part of his career after 1916 in the active apostolate for social justice. No major scholarly work followed. He published collections of articles, books of readings (one with an extended commentary), and an autobiography which was itself largely a pastiche of his former writings, but no major work such as *A Living Wage* or *Distributive Justice*. The seedtime of his career had combined scholarship and the active apostolate in remarkable fashion. The minimum wage fight, the Hillquit debate, and *Distributive Justice* showed a remarkably varied productivity. Many more minimum wage fights would follow, and quite a few more Hillquit debates, though the adversary would more likely be the National Association of Manufacturers or the Republican Party. But not again a *Distributive Justice*.

[42] *New Republic*, Feb. 17, 1917, pp. 79, 81, 83; *Nation*, Sept. 6, 1917, p. 269; Ryan, "Social Justice: A Rejoinder," *Irish Theological Quarterly*, July, 1918, p. 219.

Committing the Hierarchy

THIRTEEN YEARS after the first invitation, Father Ryan finally joined the faculty at the Catholic University of America in 1915. He was forty-six, a little stockier, a good deal balder. The pince-nez acquired in St. Paul made him carry his head stiffly, giving him a stern air. Rumpled clothes were almost his trademark now—a new set of friends would have to grow used to them. A large quantity of books and his battered typewriter made the trip with him. He was ready to start work.

The university had changed since 1902. Several new buildings had gone up: two new residence buildings, Gibbons and Graduate Halls, and an engineering building with a "practical mechanics building" directly behind. The campus was still out in the country, and a couple of years after Ryan's arrival cows were still grazing on the pasture where the National Shrine of the Immaculate Conception now stands. Undergraduates were more numerous, and indeed the university had taken on more of the tone of a college. The major difference between Catholic University and its secular counterparts was the number and variety of clerical garbs that were apparent on the campus paths.

Old friends had stayed on from Ryan's student days. Father Kerby and Father Pace were still active. Bishop Shahan was the rector. Ryan's predecessors, Fathers Shields and Turner, who had made the transit from St. Paul, were still teaching. Most of them lived as the faculty community in Caldwell Hall, which henceforth became the center of Ryan's activities. He lived in a two-room apartment on the third floor, lectured in one of the west rooms on the first floor, ate in the refectory nearby. Each morning he celebrated mass in the chapel opposite his classroom. An occasional tennis game on the university courts helped to keep his weight under control.

Ryan's appointment to a post in political science rather than to the School of Sacred Sciences suggests that he was in demand as a person rather than needed as a moral theologian. No one doubted, however, that he would eventually move over into theology; for the academic year 1915–1916 both he and the university were simply holding onto each other with an eye to the future. At the beginning of the second year Ryan made the change to associate professor of moral theology, and immediately the faculty of the School of Sacred Sciences (sometimes loosely called the School of Theology) recommended that he be promoted. A full professor the following year, he was named secretary of the school (an appointment that reduced the school's minutes almost to illegibility), and was also elected to the Academic Senate for one year. Reelected to the Senate in 1918, Dr. Ryan found himself appointed dean of his school for a two-year term starting in September, 1919. Over the next decade and a half he moved in and out of this office. Routine administration did not interest him, so he did not care for this job, nor did he work at it.[1]

Ryan taught from an imposing podium. Though he sat at a desk, he towered over his graduate students, for the platform was raised considerably above the floor of the classroom. Still not regarded as a good teacher even by his warmest partisans, Ryan appeared to those less well disposed as dull, dry, phlegmatic, even listless, and to one critic as the "worst teacher" he had ever had. Ryan also taught a course in economics, and later one in political science, at Trinity College, a girls' college down Michigan Avenue a few blocks from the university. (The undergraduates at the university spoke of Trinity as "an institution for the higher education of CU students.") Father Ryan took occasional part in the social life

---

[1] "Acta Facultatis Theologicae Universitatis Catholicae Americae," Oct. 2, 1916; Jan. 22, 1917; Jan. 25, 1918. Some of these entries appear in the parallel record "Minutes of the Meeting of the Faculty of Theology," Catholic University Archives.

of both colleges. He made a few remarks at the first pep rally of the 1916 football season at CU. He was on hand in 1918 when Trinity gave a reception to its cardinal-patron, James Gibbons. In general, however, college life was not his milieu, and as his friendships among his colleagues and in the city grew, he avoided undergraduate social life.

A year after his arrival in Washington, Ryan finally achieved his ambition to edit a magazine devoted to Catholic social reform. In January, 1917, the first issue of the *Catholic Charities Review* appeared, the house organ, in theory at least, for the National Conference of Catholic Charities. For four or five years the *Review* was almost a one-man chore, Ryan serving not only as editor but also as business manager, editorial writer, and author of most of the articles. As a result he contributed less to other journals. In 1917, for example, he submitted only three articles to magazines other than his own. Then he brought in Father John O'Grady, one of the liveliest spirits in Catholic charitable work, as managing editor. Gradually he disentangled himself from the monthly duty of filling the journal's pages, but continued to contribute articles frequently.

Then new books began to appear, either compilations of his own articles or volumes of readings that he helped to edit. The parade started with *The Church and Socialism and Other Essays* (1919), a collection of his magazine and newspaper articles dating back to 1904. The next year he and Father Joseph Husslein, S.J., edited *The Church and Labor* (1920), documents on industrial relations drawn from popes, prelates, and other Catholic authorities. Ryan added his own brief statements on "A Living Wage" and on "The Reconciliation of Capital and Labor." In this same year Macmillan brought out a condensed version of *A Living Wage*.

Ryan kept his interest in labor problems up to date. In 1915 the National Association of Manufacturers had set up an Industrial Betterment Committee which soon proved to its own satisfaction that a minimum wage by legislation was impractical. Ryan noted that the conclusion owed more to the *a priori* views of NAM members than to the overpowering evidence from Australia and England. For him the Brandeis brief in the Oregon case was still unanswerable; the "ambiguities and obscurities" of Brandeis' opponents still had not improved. He was impatient with the committee's pious determination that sweatshops must go. The piety was commendable only if the committee figured out what to do about insufficient wages during the two generations needed to destroy sweatshops.[2]

2 Ryan, editorial note, *Survey*, Sept. 4, 1915, p. 519.

Ryan kept an eye alert for vulnerable targets. A favorite argument against the minimum wage was that employers would be forced to pay an employee more than she earned. This he regarded as a "high class pun" —a play on the meaning of the word "earn." His view was simple: if a worker was not worth the price paid for her labor, she could be fired. If her worth was determined by the amount previously paid to her, then of course a minimum wage was higher than her worth. But—and here was the crux of Ryan's argument—the employer's argument was irrelevant, for the idea that supply and demand determined the morality of wages was out of date.[3] At the fourth National Conference of Catholic Charities in 1916, McSweeney, Ryan's old adversary from Boston, called Ryan's view a "fabric of moonshine glistening off on the horizon." If the conference looked to Ryan for a repetition of his blast at McSweeney three years earlier, his reply disappointed them. Father O'Grady and Charles P. O'Neill carried much of the burden, leaving Ryan to add mildly that though the Church had made no formal statement on the minimum wage, "I think that implicit authorization of State intervention is contained in the Encyclical [*Rerum novarum*] in view of actual social conditions."[4] Wrath had not turned McSweeney away, nor was a soft word more successful.

Ryan's views on a minimum wage led him to support immigrant restriction. In January, 1915, President Wilson vetoed a bill that imposed a literacy test on immigrants; Grover Cleveland and William Howard Taft had rejected similar bills. In 1917 Wilson again vetoed the bill, but it became law over his veto. In the intervening two years Ryan held his nose and joined the agitation in favor of the bill. He knew that racial bigots were agitating for the bill, and he disliked aiding their cause.[5] Yet he took the stand that the bill was objectively good or bad, regardless of its adherents. If it was good, he would not stand aloof simply because of the scent of racial bigotry. Its essential goodness he did not doubt. Wilson vetoed the first bill because he refused to accept literacy as a test of character. Ryan agreed. He did not regard the literacy test as a test of character; it was simply a device to keep down the oversupply of un-

[3] Ryan, "Earning the Minimum Wage," *Survey*, Nov. 6, 1915, p. 150.
[4] *Proceedings of the Fourth National Conference of Catholic Charities*, 1916, pp. 325–334.
[5] Barbara Miller Solomon, *Ancestors and Immigrants* (Cambridge, 1956), *passim*, especially pp. 195–209.

skilled labor, probably a very effective administrative device. The Catholic press expressed nearly unanimous opposition to the 1917 bill, leaving Ryan unwontedly isolated on this issue.[6] Nonetheless, he argued vigorously. In a strongly worded letter to his diocesan paper in St. Paul, he wrote, "I believe that if the immigration of persons who possess no special industrial training could be entirely prohibited for ten years, the question of the living wage and of minimum wage legislation would have become relatively easy of solution." Organized labor had had much the same view, having favored immigrant restriction for over a generation. When the outbreak of war in Europe in 1914 cut off the avalanche of immigrants—1,000,000 had entered the previous year—wages did rise sharply, increasing labor's anxiety not to permit the flow to resume. Ryan credited the rise in wages in late 1915 and early 1916 to the absence of new immigrant competition, and he warned against assuming too placidly that the United States could absorb new labor indefinitely. Throwing in a Catholic hook, he asked the *Bulletin* if it were sure that the Church could absorb so many immigrants; about 7,000,000 Catholics had come in since 1899, he said (with considerable exaggeration), and not all were now accounted for in the *Catholic Directory*.[7]

The literacy test of 1917 was a distinct gain for labor; it opened an era of immigrant restriction that included the more drastic legislation of 1921 and 1924. The passage of the Owen-Keating Child Labor Law in 1916 was a comparable gain, but it led down a blind alley of unconstitutionality.

The Keating-Owen Act forbade the shipment in interstate commerce of goods made by child labor. In United States *v.* E. C. Knight (1895), the Supreme Court had held that manufacturing, as an operation local in character, fell outside Congress's regulatory power. Ignoring the drastic inroads made on this ruling by subsequent decisions, especially United States *v.* Swift (1905), the Court, in Hammer *v.* Dagenhart (1918), returned to the earlier distinction between commerce, over which "the regulatory power of Congress is ample," and manufacturing, which was "a matter of local regulation." The court, therefore, overturned the Child Labor Act as a patent invasion of the states' power.[8] Oliver Wendell Holmes spoke for the four-man minority. In a decision that made Holmes

[6] Edward Greaves Roddy, Jr., "The Catholic Newspaper Press and the Quest for Social Justice, 1912–1920," Ph.D. dissertation, Georgetown University (1961), p. 190.
[7] *Catholic Bulletin*, June 10, 1916.
[8] Hammer *v.* Dagenhart, 247 U.S. 251.

one of Ryan's enduring heroes, the justice argued that Congress's power to regulate trade extended to prohibition if necessary, and he cited previous occasions—Champion v. Ames (1903) and McCray v. United States (1904)—on which the Court ignored the ultimate consequences of an act of Congress and concentrated on its immediate effects.[9]

Ryan's reaction to the majority's decision was restrained, considering the blow the Court had delivered to a specially favored measure. Writing in the *Catholic World*, he said he knew of many states and many manufacturers who would welcome regulation of wages and labor practices in order to protect themselves from the competition of sweat shops. The problem was national. Progressive states needed protection from backward states. Yet he affirmed that honest and competent men could disagree on the meaning of key constitutional passages. Holmes convinced him that by citing parallel cases or by looking freshly at the plenary power contained in the commerce clause, the Supreme Court could have sustained the legislation. Still, Ryan conceded that this use of the commerce power would have done violence to the letter of the Constitution. He wondered, however, if the spirit of the Constitution did not demand interpretation in harmony with the needs of the day, not with a social philosophy 125 years old. In this sense Holmes' argument supplied a basis for hope for the future. The social thought of the time and the "whole logic of events" were on his side, and the power of Holmes' opinion itself would strengthen the movement for a change: "For clear and incisive thinking; for synthetic grasp and application of essential principles; for keen distinctions between things that superficially seem to be alike; for broad and humane conceptions of legal policy and social welfare; for progressive views of the nature and function of the Constitution; for overwhelming logic; and for conciseness, irony and simple eloquence—that document has few parallels in the annals of our highest and ablest judicial body."[10] Ryan thus joined in the idolatry of Holmes that was part of the progressive's catalog of loyalties in this period.

Part of the "logic of events" leading to social reform was the Seventeenth Amendment, which gave women the right to vote. Father Ryan looked upon it with neither fear nor great hope. Many of the crucial votes for the ratification in New York may have come from socialists,

[9] The opinion is reprinted in Max Lerner, ed. *The Mind and Faith of Justice Holmes* (New York, 1943), pp. 168-171.

[10] Ryan, "The Supreme Court and Child Labor," *Catholic World*, November, 1918, pp. 212-223.

but Ryan had no fear that women would turn to socialism. Women generally were conservative, Catholic women most of all. He noted that Belgian socialists opposed women's suffrage on just this ground. Though many women did not want the vote, Ryan told them bluntly in *America* that it was now a responsibility they could not shirk: they must study and vote wisely. Because of their social instincts, developed in the home, they must see the need for social legislation, and work for it. Catholic men had done little except oppose wrong views and measures; they had done "little or nothing" for constructive reform. "The Catholic women . . . have a splendid opportunity to put the men to shame."[11] Ryan had learned at meetings of social workers of the eagerness and potential of young socially dedicated Catholic women. They were for him a new breed.

On one other reform, prohibition, a topic that would command a good deal of his attention later on, Ryan had only a brief word. Writing as a "Catholic economist and theologian" in the *Fortnightly Review*, which had many German–American readers, he approved of prohibition whenever it could be reasonably, that is, 75 percent, enforced. No one's moral rights were violated, he said. Rights were not ends in themselves, but means to an end, the general welfare. The right to drink was less important to human welfare than some other rights, and it was therefore licit to submerge the right to drink in the greater social good that might be effected by the abolition of the right. Ryan saw an even firmer argument in economics—the utility of liquor did not balance its "disutility." Though not a total abstainer himself, he believed that the overwhelming majority of Americans would be better off without liquor. One of his students has recalled Ryan's speaking quite bluntly in class and after class in favor of prohibition. At the same time, Ryan had "nothing but detestation and contempt" for "the motives, the undemocratic spirit, and the false philosophy of the professional prohibitionists and the Anti-Saloon Leaguers. . . ."[12]

This was about as strong language as Ryan ever used in public. The move to the university seems to have given restraint to the theologian's language, as if the position itself called for a less aggressive posture. He

[11] Ryan, "Women and the Vote," *America*, Dec. 15, 1917, pp. 231–233; "Suffrage and Women's Responsibility," *ibid.*, Dec. 22, 1917, pp. 260–261.
[12] Ryan, "A Catholic Economist and Theologian on Prohibition," *Fortnightly Review*, April 1, 1916, pp. 100–101. Interview with Nicholas J. Berg, April 30, 1958.

did not shy away from strong positions, but he flanked them with moderate words—the taunt, the threat, the barb came less frequently.

The outbreak of the World War in 1914 left Americans feeling remote from its blind fury unless some personal or professional connection pressed the war on their attention. Wilson's campaign against neutral violations by Germany and by the Allies, especially England, commanded general notice; the sinkings themselves, general horror. But the mood of the nation clearly supported the slogan forced on Wilson in 1916, "He kept us out of war." And despite the thundering from Theodore Roosevelt, the Republicans tried to sound just as peaceful. In the winter of 1916–1917, Wilson allowed himself to climb way out on the limb of neutral rights; German submarines, authorized to sink neutral vessels without restriction after February 1, 1917, shot off the limb. America was at war.

For Americans of German and of Irish extraction, the war created characteristic conflicts in loyalty. European news, filtered through English censors, created a picture of Germany that German-Americans knew to be wrong. Wilson's policy of neutrality had impressed them as hollow pretense, and his enforcement of neutral rights against Germany when England's violations had been more numerous (though less drastic), had been so clearly partisan that they took him for a British hireling. When war came, most rallied to their adopted flag, but not without soul-searching and remorse. For the Irish, the issue was simpler: England was the traditional enemy; beyond that, the politics of Europe were remote and obscure. Irish-Americans had no reason to be pro-German; but their anti-British feeling made it hard for them to favor the Allies.[13]

Many German-Americans and most Irish-Americans were Catholic. Hence their divided national loyalties became problems for the Church itself, especially because of traditional nativist suspicion of the Church's connections with Europe. The Church, under the leadership of Cardinal Gibbons, met the problem with a total commitment to the American war effort, promising President Wilson every appropriate cooperation. In August, 1917, Gibbons named a committee of the hierarchy, called the National Catholic War Council, to be its liaison group with the national government.[14] Policy as well as loyalty dictated so overt a move. There

[13] John Higham, *Strangers in the Land* (New Brunswick, N.J., 1955), pp. 194–222; Carl Wittke, *The Irish in America* (Baton Rouge, La., 1956), pp. 273–285.
[14] John Tracy Ellis, *The Life of James Cardinal Gibbons*, II, 242–243.

was no question of Gibbons' unselfish devotion to the United States, nor
was there occasion to question the loyalty and genuine concern of the rest
of the hierarchy for the successful prosecution of the war. At the same
time, the rallying to the national effort provided two very concrete advantages to the Catholic Church, one positive, one negative. First, it permitted the Church, which had so often been suspected of foreign attach-
ments, to affirm in a most ringing and unanimous voice that it was as
American as its non-Catholic neighbors. Second, it dealt with the possibility that social and religious activities for the Armed Forces might
become a Protestant monopoly of the Young Men's Christian Association.[15]

Ryan's reaction was less prompt. America was at war almost a year
before he found his tongue. Intensely interested in domestic problems, he
was remarkably ignorant of foreign affairs. He had studied little history,
and that little was economic history. His trips to Europe had widened
the range of his experience, but he had gone abroad with the simple
wonder of a literate tourist who saw, compressed, and commented without really looking for the roots of what he had seen. On a trip to Paris in
1911, he saw the statue of Strasbourg shrouded to recall the humiliation
by Germany in 1871 and he caught the accents of French determination,
but he acquired little knowledge of the issues involved. His knowledge of
the past being fuzzy, his knowledge of the present was shallow until he
had lived long enough to have subjected a substantial number of years to
his critical contemporary judgment. As a result he was as ready as most
other Americans to absorb the image of the Hun whose unjust action in
"beginning an unnecessary and aggressive war" typified a political and
military oligarchy that threw morals to the winds. Ryan had no doubt
that the cause of democracy and of Christian civilization required that
the German ideology be utterly crushed. At the same time, he welcomed
Wilson's maneuvers to separate the German people from their Prussian
government and deal with them with essential justice. This involved, to
be sure, very extensive reparations and individual trials for those guilty of
atrocities, but not a permanent crippling of Germany by territorial or
economic restrictions. These latter stood condemned by morality, history,
and common sense.[16]

15 Michael Williams, *American Catholics in the War* (New York, 1921), pp. 88–
175.
16 Ryan, "A Democratic or a Prussian Peace," *America*, Nov. 9, 1918, pp. 103–104;
Nov. 16, 1918, pp. 125–127.

Meanwhile, in three different Catholic publications, Ryan was direct-ing his attention to questions within his more familiar ken. In the *Ecclesiastical Review* for February, 1918, he called for a living wage for the parochial clergy, hard hit by wartime prices and fixed income.[17] In the *Catholic World* he defended the government's policy of limiting free speech. Drawing on Leo XIII's *Libertas praestantissimum*, Ryan said that man has no right to utter an untruth or an unreasonable statement. He affirmed that efficient democratic government depended on the criticism that free speech encouraged. Yet moderation, always appropriate, was urgent in wartime. Criticism should not hinder the war effort. Ryan be-lieved that it was all right for him to criticize the excess-profits tax as inadequate, but wrong for someone else to utter bald falsehoods such as the assertion that Congress and the President had plunged the country into war at the behest of financial interests. Recalling that "the presump-tion of right is always in favor of the civil authority," those who dis-approve might be silent; if they spoke they had to be prepared to be martyrs to their convictions. Writing even after the federal courts had sustained the postmaster of New York in excluding the *Masses* from the mails, Ryan asserted that the federal government had behaved well. Some governors and many newspapers had gone too far in harassing critics of the war; the federal government had not.[18]

The America created by the war was in many ways an unlovely spectacle. Writing for the Irish publication *Studies*, Ryan was discour-aged at the evidence of greed that ran through all classes: ". . . has laissez-faire perverted our sense of values so much that we place the economic life beyond ethical judgments?" Despite government inter-vention, corporation profits were unparalleled; prices soared, leaving labor no better off than before. Yet there were notes of hope. Ryan felt that even though federal housing projects would come to a halt after the war, the example might stimulate cities and states. The national employ-ment service would undoubtedly continue its useful role. The railroads, taken over by the government as a war measure, would probably not return to private hands; Ryan regarded this prospect as the greatest eco-nomic gain from the war. The soldiers' and sailors' insurance laws would stimulate sickness and accident insurance for civilians. Finally, after the

[17] Ryan, "Increased Prices Affecting the Clergy," *Ecclesiastical Review*, February, 1918, pp. 210–211.

[18] Zechariah Chafee, Jr., *Free Speech in the United States* (Cambridge, 1946), pp. 42–50; Ryan, "Freedom of Speech in Wartime," *Catholic World*, February, 1918, pp. 577–588.

war, interest on the national debt and "inevitable" government enterprises would keep taxes high. This would be welcomed by the lovers of a Christian social order, for "social justice was not consistent with enormous profits and the retention of enormous incomes."[19]

As the war drew to a successful close—indeed, the week it ended— Ryan told the readers of *America* that Wilson was serving the causes of enduring peace and of Christian charity by his attempts to secure an armistice before Germany fell into the disorders of Bolshevism. The "diluted Prussianism" of some Americans called for a more vindictive peace, Ryan said, but Wilson's "calm impartiality" would not tolerate that. Continuing a five-week series in *America*, Ryan insisted that the League of Nations was possible and desirable: possible because the war had created a mood of sincerity and willingness to avert war; desirable because the League could settle disputes with weapons short of gunfire.[20] When Wilson returned from Paris for two weeks in the winter of 1919, Ryan renewed his appeal. Minor changes were perhaps desirable—an advisory representative assembly, a larger executive council. But Ryan saw no crippling objection to the League itself; "lessened sovereignty," a favorite cry of the League's opponents led by Senator Henry Cabot Lodge of Massachusetts, Ryan dismissed as an epithet like "Bolshevism." He observed the clear line between League proponents and opponents: all the diluted Prussians and Tories against, "practically all the progressives, the democratic-minded and justice-loving elements" in favor. Old selfish national interests belonged to the past. "Those who fear that the League will fail because the selfish interests and purposes of the nations will impel them to disregard its obligations forget that peoples will henceforth be the makers of national policies and the interpreters of national interests, and they will conceive national interests in terms of popular welfare, not in terms of national power, conquest, and economic advantage for a few special groups in the nation. In other words, national interests will hereafter be interpreted as bound up with peace and international justice. The rulers of states will not in the future bring the nations to the verge of war over a dispute in Morocco." Though this sounded like pure Wilson, Ryan claimed he was following Pope Benedict XV's peace appeal. He was glad to quote the pope "at a time when a disgraceful and detestable campaign

[19] Ryan, "Social Aspects of America in the War," *Studies*, March, 1918, pp. 80–93.
[20] Ryan, "Crippling Germany Forever," *America*, Dec. 14, 1918, pp. 233–235; "Militarism for the United States," *ibid.*, Nov. 30, 1918, pp. 175–177; "A Substitute for Militarism," *ibid.*, Dec. 7, 1918, pp. 209–211.

of abuse, misrepresentation and disparagement is directed against the President by hirelings of plutocracy, backward-looking bourbons and players of peanut politics."[21]

This call to Catholic America to rally behind Wilson, lost in the din of the larger fight over the League, died out when Wilson's voice failed. Knowing that he was not reaching most American Catholics, Ryan addressed his most urgent appeals to editors and bishops, who might give leadership on the issue. He needled both groups. Despite the dictum of Benedict XV, the Catholic press was never more than "spasmodic and half-hearted" in applying principles of Catholic political ethics to international questions, he said. They were as defective on this issue as on social questions. He addressed the hierarchy less directly. Noting Catholics' special obligation because of the pope's words, Ryan observed that in addition to the silence of the Catholic press, "no sympathetic voice has been raised in any more authoritative circle"[22]—a conspicuous nudge to the hierarchy.

Yet despite his best efforts, he fought a losing battle to the indifference and to the hostility Wilson had aroused among German-Americans because of the war, among Irish-Americans because of the failure of Ireland to win its independence from England, and among Italian-Americans because of Fiume. Americans generally were not ready to support Wilson's internationalism more than passively; Catholics felt no pressure to feel any differently, much less to lead the way. The bishops' pastoral letter in 1919 reminded Catholics of Benedict XV's hope for an international organization that would establish peace for the world on a solid foundation, and they added their voices to his.[23] But the pastoral did not succeed in arousing Catholic opinion on this issue.

On domestic social questions, the hierarchy fared better. Aware that other groups, religious and lay, were making pronouncements on postwar reconstruction, the Administrative Committee of the National Catholic War Council, headed by Bishop Muldoon, thrashed about for one of its own. It turned to Father O'Grady, secretary of its Committee on Reconstruction. O'Grady had already asked Ryan to prepare such a document, but Ryan had refused. O'Grady went back to him again. Meanwhile Ryan

21 Ryan, "The League of Nations and Its Opponents," MS of speech, 1919.
22 Editorial note, *Catholic Charities Review*, May, 1919, pp. 131–134; Ryan, "A Substitute for Militarism," *loc. cit.*, p. 211.
23 Peter Guilday, ed., *The National Pastorals of the American Hierarchy* (Washington, 1923), pp. 330–331.

had written a few notes on postwar reconstruction for a speech in Louis-ville, Kentucky, but, dissatisfied with it, he had laid it aside in favor of a speech on the League of Nations. O'Grady saw the unfinished fragment on Ryan's desk. Nothing more promising was likely to come along. He insisted on Ryan's finishing it. O'Grady was in such a hurry that Ryan pounded out the final version "during a five-hour session of dictating it to a typewriter."[24] The final product was a jungle of disorganization, betraying the hasty composition and inadequate editing. But O'Grady literally snatched it off Ryan's desk, and the committee issued it forthwith as their own view. It appeared as the "Bishops' Program for Social Re-construction." It was perhaps the most forward-looking social document ever to have come from an official Catholic agency in the United States.[25]

In a foreword, the bishops, warning that social justice and a contented people were the only safeguards to peace, linked their program to Chris-tian ethics: "Its practical applications are of course subject to discussion, but all its essential declarations are based upon the principles of charity and justice that have always been held and taught by the Catholic Church, while its practical proposals are merely an adaptation of those principles and that traditional teaching to the social and industrial needs of our time."

Then followed the specific recommendations. The bishops urged the government to maintain some of the services that had been created as emergency wartime measures, especially the United States Employment Service, which had operated a national system of clearinghouses for labor, and the National War Labor Board, which had made "a definite and far-reaching gain for social justice" by holding to the principles of the familial living wage, the right of labor to organize and to bargain collec-tively, and the prohibition of coercion of nonunion members by unions. They endorsed the proposal of the Secretary of the Interior, Franklin K. Lane, to find employment and perhaps a permanent livelihood for return-ing servicemen by lending them money to establish themselves as farm owners, or at least as tenants with long leases. Generously undertaken, such a program could "easily become one of the most beneficial reform measures that has ever been attempted."

The bishops accepted as "extremely probable" and "highly desirable"

24 Ryan to Sister Mary John, May 12, 1919, in Sister Mary John's possession; Ellis, *Documents of American Catholic History*, p. 611.

25 The entire statement is reprinted in Ellis, *Documents of American Catholic History*, pp. 611–629. A recent discussion appears in Aaron I. Abell, "The Bishops' 1919 Program," *Social Order*, March, 1962, pp. 109–118.

the private ownership of capital. But to break the private power of the few, they called for "prevention of monopolistic control of commodities, adequate government regulation of such public service monopolies as will remain under private operation, and heavy taxation of incomes, excess profits and inheritances." If antitrust laws proved ineffective, they were willing to endorse direct governmental competition with private industry. The program noted approvingly a wider distribution of the ownership of stock by workers and of shop committees of workers who shared in the management of industry. Cooperatives were approved as a way of eliminating the multiple exactions of middlemen and of engaging the talent of private individuals without the bureaucratic machinery of government. At the same time, the bishops demanded an expansion of vocational training with due safeguards against the creation of a permanent labor class and urged the elimination of child labor through the federal taxing power. Women workers should not hold jobs inappropriate to their sex, like driving streetcars and cleaning locomotives, they said, and, in general, women should remain out of heavy industry, and indeed out of all industry as much as possible. Yet those who remain were entitled to equal pay for work equal to that done by men.

The committee endorsed labor's attempt to resist general wage reductions, for, with certain exceptions in war industries, the wartime increases still fell short of the measure of justice due to workers. A living wage, the statement recalled, was not the full measure of justice; it was only the *minimum* of justice. Both good morals and sound economics demanded that workers be paid above this level. The bishops noted with approval that "there is no longer any serious objection urged by impartial persons against the legal minimum wage." States should therefore enact minimum wage laws, gradually raising the level of pay so that individuals could protect their families against sickness, accidents, invalidism, and old age. At the same time, the states should undertake housing projects and comprehensive insurance programs for their citizens, and cities should make themselves responsible for health clinics.

Finally, the bishops echoed the call of Leo XIII to return to Christian principles, laborers recognizing their obligation to perform an honest day's work for a fair wage, employers learning "the long-forgotten truth that wealth is stewardship. . . ."

The bishops' statement caused quite a stir, alarming or delighting according to the views of the reader. The president of the National Association of Manufacturers complained to Cardinal Gibbons that the document was "partisan, pro-labor union socialistic propaganda," and the editor of the *National Civic Federation Review* said the bishops had been deceived by radicals whose programs "would overthrow our present institutions and inaugurate a reign of chaos." Liberals, Catholic and non-Catholic, were delighted. Frank P. Walsh, now joint chairman of the War Labor Board, announced: "With a new enthusiasm we can go among our associates and say proudly 'I am a Catholic.'" Raymond Swing, writing in the *Nation,* commented on the striking social vision of the prelates "within the institution which, rightly or wrongly, has been reputed to be the most conservative." Even the socialist Upton Sinclair was amazed at the radicalism of the program; he called it a "Catholic miracle."[26]

The Bishops' Program, along with a bewildering number of similar manifestoes issued about the same time, reflected the wartime feeling that only a reconstituted society based on social justice could redeem the four years of carnage. Tactically, the times seemed right. The increase in governmental activity incident to the war gave reformers their chance: the problem was not to force government into unwonted areas, but to hold existing ground against abrupt withdrawal, to catch public favor at a time of decision, and to bed down favored reforms in the moment of victory. The reformers hoped in vain. In the skein of influences that create policy in the United States, it is not possible to weigh the force of these manifestoes, much less the force of any one of them. But in general, the legislative and industrial record of the 1920's gave liberal reformers little reason to think that their statements had yielded anything.

Within the Church itself, however, the Bishops' Program gave authoritative sanction to reforms for which Ryan had long struggled. The bishops appeared as spokesmen for the whole American hierarchy. The statement lacked any formal legislative or disciplinary significance within the Church, Ryan said in a series of lectures at Fordham University that later appeared as a book, *Social Reconstruction* (1920). Yet when no bishop publicly spoke against it and several spoke enthusiastically in its favor, it meant as a practical matter that these advanced views were, at the very least, "not out of harmony with the doctrines of the Church."[27] As soon as it appeared, it met with "instantaneous, wholehearted approval on the part of the Catholic press."[28] For Father Ryan's purposes, it

[26] Stephen C. Mason to James Cardinal Gibbons, quoted in Ellis, *Documents of American Catholic History,* p. 611; Ralph M. Easley, "Radicals Mislead Churches About Labor," *National Civic Federation Review,* March 25, 1919, p. 7; other statements quoted in Ryan, *Social Reconstruction* (New York, 1920), pp. 12, 15, 13.

[27] Ryan, *Social Reconstruction,* pp. 10–11.

[28] Roddy, "The Catholic Newspaper Press and the Quest for Social Justice, 1912–1920," p. 237.

created another standard to set beside *Rerum novarum* when he appealed to the conscience of Catholic America.

In a letter to Sister Mary John, Ryan made no attempt to conceal his delight. His sister had apparently asked why the document had not gone out over Father John's signature, so obviously were the ideas his. John replied:

The Bishops' names are on the Reconstruction program because they made it their own, and we all want the authority that it derives from this fact. My name attached to it would defeat this purpose entirely. Most people who are acquainted with these matters know that I am sufficiently radical. What they did not realize is that such doctrines pass muster with the bishops. I think that this action of the four Bishops has given me more satisfaction than anything that has ever happened in relation to my work. It is a vindication of all the theories that my name has been associated with, and indirectly of all that I have done in this field. It is more than I had ever expected to get in the way of worth-while appreciation.[29]

The creation of the National Catholic Welfare Council (NCWC) strengthened Father Ryan's position even further. In February, 1919, at the celebration of Cardinal Gibbons' golden jubilee as a bishop, the hierarchy decided to ask Rome for permission to create a postwar replacement for the War Council. Benedict XV assenting, plans for a national council of Catholic affairs took shape during the summer under the general direction of Father John J. Burke, C.S.P., who had been an active executive of the War Council. As part of a committee under the chairmanship of Bishop Muldoon, Ryan helped draw up an elaborate scheme for a bureau of social service, "informative, directive, inspirational," to coordinate charitable activities and to stimulate legislative reform. It planned also to conduct Americanization classes in foreign neighborhoods, to stimulate the study of social problems in seminaries, to urge young men and women to enter social work. The committee suggested a yearly budget of $125,000. When the group met again in December for further planning, Muldoon noted in his diary how difficult it was to find the right men to staff the agency; the absence of trained leaders in social action among Catholics showed dramatically the urgency of the new work.[30]

[29] Ryan to Sister Mary John, *loc. cit.*

[30] Ellis, *Documents of American Catholic History*, p. 629; "Report of the Committee on Social Service to the Bishops' Committee of Catholic Interests and Affairs," July 22, 1919, copy in the Archives of the University of Notre Dame; "Diary of

In fact, when the National Catholic Welfare Council created its Department of Social Action, the scope was less ambitious. It opened two offices: the Chicago office was assigned to John A. Lapp, a layman active in social work; the Washington office to Father Ryan. Even at the end of almost a decade, the Social Action Department's budget did not rise to a third of the $125,000 suggested, and its agenda was pretty much what the directors decided to make it. Ryan was to give his job ample scope.

The Bishops' Program and Ryan's appointment to the SAD improved his position in the American Church. In 1917 he gave a speech at the Old South Meeting House Forum in Boston, obviously drawing on a well-thumbed copy of Wilfrid Ward's paper "The Conservative Genius of the Church" (1900). Ward had argued that the Catholic Church moved slowly in assimilating what was new: she resisted aggressive change, then adapted constructively. Borrowing from Cardinal Newman, Ward had said: "The first process, of resistance, is the work of authority; the second, of assimilation, is the work of individuals, authority only tolerating and not necessarily helping it, until it is so far tested that authority can more or less ratify what individuals have initiated."[31] For his mixed audience, Ryan stated the idea more simply: "The way in which any new social idea, or social application of an idea, or piece of philosophy becomes current in Catholic thought, is through the instrumentality of individuals here and there who take up these things and make the application. And after sufficient time has elapsed and these applications seem to have stood the test of time, it is commonly accepted that the idea is all right and that there is nothing in it contrary to Catholic theory." Then, perhaps thinking of Father Dietz, whose career as a social reformer had vanished in an eclipse of episcopal disfavor, he added: "Once in a while a person becomes too enthusiastic or too zealous about adapting and adopting these new ideas, and he gets into trouble."[32] The reinforcement of Ryan's position by the events of 1919 gave him security and renewed courage.

Dr. Ryan had no illusions about his advanced views; he knew they

Peter J. Muldoon," Dec. 28, 1919, Archives of the Diocese of Rockford, Ill. Some notion of the NCWC's activities may be gleaned from William F. Montavon, "The National Catholic Welfare Conference," in Leo R. Ward, *The American Apostolate*, pp. 241–277.

[31] Wilfrid Ward, "The Conservative Genius of the Church," pamphlet (London, 1900), p. 5.

[32] Ryan, "The Attitude of the Roman Catholic Church Towards Radical Social Reforms," *Community Forum*, n.d., p. 15.

110

were advanced. Sister Mary John suggested that maybe Father John
should have been in line for the vacancy in St. Paul when Archbishop
Ireland died in September, 1918. He said:

Thank you, I have no desire or hope of being chosen for that place.
Happily I have been identified with too many new doctrines to be ever
considered seriously for such an honor. After I have been dead some
years, and the things that I have stood for have become regarded as quite
safe, men who believe in them will not be regarded as unsafe for that
reason. But I may be mistaken as to the time that it will take for the
change to come, as things are moving very fast now. Bishop Russell said
to me the other day: "You are coming into your own now."[33]

William Hard, a free-lance journalist writing in *Metropolitan*, took a
look at Dr. Ryan at just about this time. Ryan, he said, was not introducing new ideas into Catholic medieval darkness:

He has been engaged rather in bringing medieval darkness to illumine
modernity with its light. He is a quiet-moving, quick-sighted, steady and
strong-striking man; modest in manner; abiding his time; rejecting the
easy fame of extremes; flattering neither to the Right nor to the Left; a
priest, learned, seeking more learning; living in a little room off his
office; teaching younger priests; editing the *Catholic Charities Review;*
going into the pages of *Everybody's Magazine* to debate Socialism against
Morris Hillquit; going to Johnstown in Pennsylvania at the height of the
steel strike to say that Mr. Gary's rejection of a meeting with representatives of employees was not a rejection of radicalism but a rejection
of the primary elementary first steps to a sound system of cooperative
economic life; saying his say about the prices of commodities; returning
to his office to climb to his top shelves to see again what the Catholic
writers of the sixteenth century said about "scarcity" as a proper moral
factor in the making of a price of a commodity; always a priest; always
hewing to the line, the old line, of Catholic doctrine.[34]

This was a picture of himself that Ryan responded to. Taking his
mandate as a spokesman for Catholic social action seriously, he refused to
see himself as a radical or a conservative. He looked for a knowledge of
principles and a knowledge of facts: a knowledge of Catholic social
teaching according to right reason, and a knowledge of the social and
industrial facts of the day. To this he added the virtue of prudence: "Is

[33] Ryan to Sister Mary John, *loc. cit.*
[34] William Hard, "The Catholic Church Accepts the Challenge," *Metropolitan,*
January, 1920, p. 27.

it wise and prudent to advocate this reform at this time?" He feared that Catholics were especially weak on their knowledge of facts. True, facts were hard to come by, especially all the relevant facts. Hence most generalizations had to be qualified—"probably," "it seems that." The more facts, the surer the generalization. Ryan told an audience at Fordham that when you learned right principles and located the facts, it did not take courage to speak, even when most people have not reached the same conclusion, "for one will have acquired the habit of envisaging the problem in an objective light, free from temporary considerations, and free from all thought of praise or blame. After all, truth and justice are the only important ends to seek in matters of social reform."[35]

This was not the comment of an introspective man, or of a modest man, for that matter. Yet it did much to explain the intensity of Ryan's next twenty-five years and the loftiness of the standard by which he tried to judge action.

[35] Ryan, *Social Reconstruction*, pp. 214, 215.

Fighting a
Conservative
Decade

ON THE NIGHT
before the election of 1920, Dr. Ryan was talking to a
group of college students about "The Obligations of Citizenship." Tomorrow Warren G. Harding would be elected
President, the most mediocre man to hold that office in
seventy-five years, Ryan said, a minion of reactionaries,
innocent of any conceptions of industry and society. To
give himself courage, Ryan whistled hopefully, perhaps not
seeing, perhaps reluctant to admit to the dark days banked
solidly ahead. A progressive Congress, he was sure, would
check a reactionary administration. The incipient reaction
against reaction would give impetus to progressive legislation. Well, at least the attempt to pervert patriotism into
support of repressive industrial policies had failed.[1] Rarely
has a crystal ball been so clouded. Ryan was wrong on all
three judgments.

The decade that followed Versailles mocked the high
progressive hopes of 1919; America never retrieved the
banner of reform that Wilson had dropped in his second

[1] Ryan, "The Obligations of Citizenship," MS of speech, undated
[Nov. 1, 1920].

term. Reform lost its vogue as the cry of "Bolshevik" and half a dozen other epithets gave conservatives useful terms of abuse. A frightened generation found dangerous ideas everywhere, and affronts to civil liberties created a murky haze of hysteria. The definition of 100 percent Americanism stretched to an immigration bill written in discriminatory racial and religious terms; to a concept of union organization, the "open shop" or "American system," that guaranteed ineffective bargaining; to a limitation of the term "American" to the white, Protestant, native-born majority. The courts converged on unions and neutralized regulatory laws, cutting away the ground that reformers had long since taken for granted. Even when Congress passed progressive acts, such as the McNary-Haugen bill and the child-labor amendment, they fell victim to the conservative mood of the White House, or of the nation at large.

When the New York State Legislature expelled five Socialist assemblymen, properly elected and seated, Ryan wrote a letter of congratulations to Morris Hillquit, their attorney, for "the very able and altogether magnificent fight that you have been making at Albany on behalf of fair play and representative government." Ryan went on: "You and your associates are combatting the most brazen and insidious political outrage that has been committed in this country since 1877. I agree with the social and political principles held by your five clients as little today as in the days when you and I crossed swords in the pages of *Everybody's Magazine*, but I hope I still believe in justice, in democracy, in the reign of law."[2]

The letter set off a small tempest. Hillquit released it to the public, having first assured Ryan gratefully that it was "clear-cut, highminded, courageous, and just what I should have expected from you."[3] But William D. Guthrie, a Catholic lawyer prominent in the Union League Club in New York, deplored Ryan's public demonstration of sympathy with the Socialists; it created misunderstandings about the attitude of the Catholic Church.[4] In reply, Ryan dryly affirmed that "the alternative to causing such false inferences was cowardly inaction." If fear of possible misunderstanding silenced him, nothing would ever get done. For a final judgment on his act he appealed from present hysteria to future calm: in

[2] Ryan to Morris Hillquit, Jan. 26, 1920, quoted in Ryan, "To Keep the Record Clear," *Catholic Charities Review*, May, 1920, p. 137.
[3] Hillquit to Ryan, Jan. 30, 1920.
[4] William D. Guthrie to Ryan, March 11, 1920.

ten years Guthrie might rejoice that the Assembly's action drew forth "at least one protest by a Catholic against injustice and autocracy," rejoice that some uninstructed persons interpreted Ryan's protest as "the voice of the Catholic Church."[5] The reply was a revealing one—Ryan as the lonely link between a sobered America and the Catholic minority. The notion of his role was not a modest one, nor, as the Baltimore *Catholic Review's* editorial, "Socialists Have Rights," soon demonstrated, an accurate one.[6] Ryan's voice was not so lonely as he thought.

Memories of the episode in the New York Assembly were still fresh when Ryan joined in the move to free dozens of political prisoners confined during the war for miscellaneous violations of the amended Espionage Act of 1917. Ryan enjoyed a real tactical asset in seeking presidential pardons for them, for he had favored the original indictments as an aid to the war effort. But the war was over, the occasion of danger gone. By 1922 all other nations had released their prisoners; only the United States lagged behind. Ryan joined William Allen White of the Emporia, Kansas, *Gazette,* and other liberals in an interview with President Harding. Soon thereafter Harding wrote to Ryan, promising to release the prisoners in the near future, but adding that he was reluctant to pardon "men with I.W.W. tendencies" during the great industrial strikes.[7] When two months passed without action, Ryan urged Michael J. Curley, who had been made Archbishop of Baltimore after Gibbons' death, to prod the President again.[8] Finally the last of the prisoners was released in time for Christmas, 1923.[9] The following year, when the new Attorney General, Harlan Fiske Stone, announced that his staff would help lawyers prepare defenses against government prosecutions that drew evidence from tainted sources, Ryan hailed the "end of hysteria," the return to sanity.[10]

All through the decade Ryan associated himself with the fight for civil liberties. In 1921 he joined the California committee of the American Civil Liberties Union in opposing that state's criminal syndicalist law,[11]

[5] Ryan to Guthrie, March 13, 1920, reprinted in Ryan, "To Keep the Record Clear," *loc. cit.,* p. 139.
[6] Baltimore *Catholic Review,* June 12, 1920.
[7] Washington *News,* Oct. 19, 1922.
[8] Ryan to Michael J. Curley, Dec. 20, 1922, Archives of the Archdiocese of Baltimore.
[9] H. C. Peterson and Gilbert C. Fite, *Opponents of War, 1917–1918* (Madison, 1957), pp. 265–284.
[10] Ryan, "The End to Hysteria," *N.C.W.C. Bulletin,* June 1924, pp. 24–25.
[11] California Committee, American Civil Liberties Union, "California Attacked by One of Her Own Laws," pamphlet, n.p., n.d., p. 1.

and five years later he urged a California priest, Father Robert E. Lucey, to help win the release of Anita Whitney, a prominent social worker convicted of sedition.[12] He joined the American Civil Liberties Union and became the only Catholic priest ever to serve on its national board.

In the course of the decade, Ryan joined dozens of committees, councils, boards, leagues, associations dedicated to one liberal cause or another. He found a prompt welcome. He was always well received as a person: gracious, bluntly witty, well informed, apt in argument, he added a good deal to a committee meeting just by his presence. More important, he represented, in a very special sense, a large constituency. He might sign himself simply "Dr. John A. Ryan, Washington, D.C.," yet everyone who cared knew he was Father Ryan of Catholic University and the NCWC. To a reforming group like the American Civil Liberties Union, he looked like a line to a conservative buoy. Non-Catholic reformers were happy to invoke, even in this oblique form, the favor of American Catholic opinion. Ryan understood the game, and he was willing to play it in causes that attracted him. Favoring the causes, he wanted Catholics to be part of them. Furthermore, a position on an executive board or council permitted him to influence a group toward Catholic social teaching—sometimes a spur to further action, sometimes a brake on a proposed action. Affiliation with some reforming groups put him in a delicate position. The Public Ownership League created no difficulties, for his ideas and its program were roughly congruent. Organizations that sought reforms incompatible with his own religious convictions, such as the Planned Parenthood Association, he simply never joined. But suppose the American Civil Liberties Union went too far on one issue? Did one stay, knowing that criticism within the Church would go beyond what that one issue justified? Did one go, knowing that such a resignation dissociated Catholics from the fight for civil liberties and removed Catholic restraint on the group? These were not easy questions; now and again, the virtues of prudence and courage fought racking battles within him.

Occasionally his good causes backfired. Like many other liberals then and later, Ryan was reluctant to withhold his consent if the prestige of his name furthered a good cause. Because a busy man could not regularly attend meetings, much less check constantly on these groups, his membership continued blindly until some public action, frequently an embar-

---

[12] Ryan to Robert E. Lucey, telegram, Oct. 22, 1925.

rassing action, revealed the misuse of his name. Sometimes he was not safe even when he thought he had resigned from a group. In June, 1925, William Green of the AFL wrote to Ryan in shocked dismay about the presence of the priest's name, together with a number of avowed Communists, on the letterhead of the Labor Defense Council. Ryan explained that he had been an officer of the council two years before, when it had been formed to defend William Z. Foster and Charles E. Ruthenberg against the Michigan antisyndicalist law, but had resigned when the council started to defend all Communists, the Workers' Party, and similar groups. Ryan said that the council was guilty of bad faith in not removing his name from their letterhead. But the damage was done. Green asked Ryan to let him have a copy of his letter of resignation to show around in labor circles, but Ryan could not locate it in his files.[13] So the whole matter remained under a cloud. Aware of the continuous danger of embarrassment, Ryan plunged in anyway, confident that a statement of the facts would rescue him when he got in too deep. Part of the man's greatness lay in his courage in facing up to criticism from many sides when he promoted causes that, in his view, served the general welfare. Inaction rarely draws criticism. Ryan acted.

An error here or there was unavoidable, for Father Ryan constantly ran from job to job. The job at the university was not exacting, nothing like his previous duties at the St. Paul Seminary. In the School of Sacred Sciences, he normally taught two half-year courses in moral theology, one each term, meeting three hours a week, and conducted a seminar, one hour a week, for more advanced students. One year, for example, his half-courses were "Virtues and Vices in General" and "Faith and Hope." They were taught to a mere handful of students. In the twenties, Ryan averaged six or seven students working for advanced degrees in moral theology, although of course he taught many more who were studying moral theology as a minor field. He never had more than two candidates receive their doctorate in sacred theology in any one year, and frequently he had none. Ryan's course in industrial ethics for the economics department, later for the sociology department, reached a somewhat larger group, perhaps twenty-five or thirty.[14]

[13] William Green to Ryan, June 5, 1925; Ryan to Green, June 9, 1925; Green to Ryan, June 10, 1925; Ryan to Green, June 11, 1925.
[14] *Catholic University of America Announcements, Yearbook* or *General Catalogue*, Washington, D.C., 1916–1940, *passim*.

His classes were still notoriously dull. As one of his most loyal students, Monsignor Francis J. Gilligan, has observed mildly, Dr. Ryan was "not greatly interested in classroom work." In his lecture courses, he droned on for an hour, stopped, picked up the next time, droned on, "dry as a stick."[15] A long seminary and university tradition of lecturing from a podium stood behind him, and he offered it no challenge. In seminar, he was somewhat more relaxed, pipe at hand, not really informal but not holding to his platform manner. Among candidates for advanced degrees in his own field, he was known as easy, indeed, very easy. Yet he prodded his students into ambitious and delicate tasks. "Have you the courage to take a topic that will be exceedingly difficult and on which there's not much written?" he asked Gilligan when the young St. Paul priest was thrashing about for a thesis subject in the mid-twenties. Ryan pushed him into a study that emerged as *The Morality of the Color Line*, a pioneer theological work. Unknown to Gilligan, Ryan tried to interest several commercial publishers in the book, but it finally appeared with the imprint of the Catholic University of America Press. Once started on their tasks, Ryan's students were on their own—he neither interfered nor helped.

At Trinity College, a somewhat different Dr. Ryan appeared. In the atmosphere created by the Sisters of Notre Dame de Namur, his daily coming and going, like that of his friend Dr. Kerby, was the occasion for gestures of respect, even when he was gruff and hurried. The Sisters set high standards of academic excellence in their own classes, and this made Dr. Ryan all the more welcome to the students. He varied from close adherence to the textbook, which bored his students, to interesting but undisciplined classes in which he told them what was really on his mind. An easy mark with young priests, he was a pushover in his Trinity classes. Assuming that female students were incapable of serious work, he watered down his political science to their presumed level. Frances Smith Adams, class of 1928, has recalled: "If we didn't get anything out of it, it was no less than he expected."[16] His tests were, typically, injunctions to repeat back what he had taught them—"Show that corruption hurts city government." To make sure that they did not falter, he reviewed the appropriate material in the class prior to the test.

The girls thought him rather a dear, his manner "ostentatiously

[15] Interview with Francis J. Gilligan, April 26, 1958, and with Raymond A. Mc-Gowan, winter, 1958.
[16] Interview with Frances Smith Adams, April 24, 1957.

118

plebeian," his appearance firm as a prizefighter.[17] In later years many of them asked him to officiate at their weddings and to baptize their children. A handful who caught the spark of social work as a career or whose families predisposed them to progressive economic and social ideas responded to Ryan in spite of himself; his ideas, even in drab form, carried their own excitement. The rest, only vaguely aware of his growing reputation, knew him as a pleasant relief from more exacting teachers and as an entertaining, thoroughly appreciated guest at teas given by the girls for the faculty.

In addition to his classes at the university and at Trinity, Ryan also lectured at the National Catholic School of Social Service (NCSSS) on Sixteenth Street. There he got a new view of women, for these young students were training themselves to be the capable shock troops of professional social work. Ryan respected them for their commitment. When he taught them industrial ethics, a compelling relevance gave his lectures significance—rather different from teaching Trinity girls state and local government. This sense of relevance did not improve Ryan's teaching manner. His staunchest admirers among the girls regarded his lectures as drudgery and his textbook (E. A. Ross's *Ethics*) as "dull beyond its weight."[18] Yet some of his most pleasant friendships came from that school, faculty and students, and a fitting climax prolonged the long association when he lived at the school for the final six years of his life.

His first year at the university and his courses in political science at Trinity led to another book, *The State and the Church* (1922), a volume that he edited with Moorhouse F. X. Millar, S.J., under the auspices of the NCWC's Social Action Department.[19] Father Millar and other Jesuits wrote the largest portion, and another quarter of the book reproduced papal and episcopal statements. Ryan's share, largely based on carefully prepared series of articles that had appeared the previous year in *America* and the *Catholic World*, explored the nature of the state. In an extended commentary on Leo XIII's encyclical letter *Immortale Dei* ("The Christian Constitution of States"), Ryan argues that a ruler's moral authority to govern comes as a necessary consequence of the nature and ends of human beings. "They cannot live right and reasonable lives without human society;

[17] Interview with Sister Joan Bland, July 8, 1960.
[18] Loretto R. Lawler, *Full Circle* (Washington, D.C., 1951), pp. 135–137.
[19] Ryan and Moorhouse F. X. Millar, *The State and the Church* (New York, 1922), *passim.*

civil society cannot function effectively without a governing authority; therefore, the latter, just like political society itself, is necessary for human welfare, and consequently sanctioned and ratified by the Creator and Governor of the human race." The supreme test of good government is the general welfare, he goes on; a government that does not work to that end loses its legitimacy and should be replaced. The state, as "the most important of the secular societies," has an obligation to make "a public profession of religion." Ryan acknowledges that this is a "hard saying" to the present generation, committed to the separation of church and state, but he argues that consideration of the ends of the state and of the citizen make any other conclusion illogical. He points to the American practice of exempting church property from taxation as one example of the public profession of faith, undertaken in spite of the First Amendment. In fact, "The State should officially recognize the Catholic religion as the religion of the Commonwealth," though it may permit other religions if there is no danger of scandal to the faithful. Ryan recognizes that "superficial champions of religious equality" would denounce this view as the "essence of intolerance." He agrees that the view is intolerant, but not therefore unreasonable. "Error has not the same rights as truth."

On the other hand, these propositions "have full application only to the completely Catholic state," that is, one almost exclusively made up of Catholics. Quoting Joseph Pohle, the German theologian formerly at Catholic University, Ryan observes that there is probably no state anywhere in the world that fits this category, not even Spain. In practice, "complete religious liberty" is justified, first, because of "rational expediency, inasmuch as the attempt to proscribe or hamper the peaceful activities of established religious groups would be productive of more harm than good"; and second, because of "the positive provisions of religious liberty found in the constitutions of most modern States." Ryan acknowledges that "constitutions can be changed, and non-Catholic sects may decline to such a point that the political proscription of them may become feasible and expedient." What protection would non-Catholic groups have against a Catholic state? "The latter could logically tolerate only such religious activities as were confined to the members of the dissenting group." Ryan included this passage with some hesitancy, knowing that it would excite resentment. Yet he felt that he would not be honest if he ignored this important section of *Immortale Dei*,[20] and he

[20] Ryan to Philip Burnham, April 1, 1941.

was confident that "no practical man" would let an event that might happen "some five thousand years hence" affect his attitude toward those who differed from him in religious faith. In any case, "we cannot yield up the principles of eternal and unchangeable truth in order to avoid the enmity of . . . unreasonable persons. Moreover, it would be a futile policy, for they would not think us sincere."

Ryan's commentary, both his analysis of *Immortale Dei* and his other essays, covered a number of topics, many of them repetitions of stands he had already taken in the public forum. The publication of this volume made him a leading Catholic voice in America on the role of the state. His book, adopted in many Catholic colleges, went through frequent reprintings until a revised edition appeared in 1940. When the book appeared in 1922, Ryan had no way of foreseeing that six years later it would figure prominently in public debate when Alfred E. Smith ran for the Presidency.

Four or five days a week, when he did not have classes at all three institutions, Ryan went downtown to 1312 Massachusetts Avenue, N.W., the headquarters of the National Catholic Welfare Conference (the word "Council" in the title was changed in 1923). Father Raymond A. McGowan, a former student of Ryan's, ran the Social Action Department's Washington office as a full-time assistant director. The separate office in Chicago functioned autonomously. Both operated under the episcopal chairman of the department, Bishop Muldoon, nominally in charge, actually rather remote in Rockford, Illinois, and under the NCWC's general secretary, Father Burke, who had been largely responsible for initiating the organization.

The function of the Social Action Department was primarily educative: at last Ryan had an officially sponsored forum for Catholic social ideas. Since 1917 he had been slipping this kind of material into the *Catholic Charities Review;* now, in the *N.C.W.C. Bulletin* (later called *Catholic Action*), he had regular space. In addition, Father McGowan put out a weekly news bulletin summarizing for Catholic papers and Catholic organizations current news in labor and in related fields. Pamphlets, finally adding up to a "Half-Inch Labor Book Shelf," began to appear, many by Father Ryan, such as "The Christian Doctrine of Property." In 1920 Ryan and McGowan both cooperated with Edward T. Devine of the Federal Council of Churches of Christ in America in reporting the bloody Denver tramway strike.[21] Two years later, Ryan

[21] Ryan *et al.,* "Denver Tramway Strike of 1920," pamphlet (Denver, 1921).

and McGowan joined with Protestant and Jewish confrères to urge President Harding to mediate the differences in the coal industry, in which the clash between labor and management was approaching violence.[22] In 1926 the department investigated the conditions of engineers on the Western Maryland Railroad; its probing helped force out the Rockefellers as the controlling group, but did little to settle the basic issue.[23] Archbishop Curley, who never took the Social Action Department as seriously as did Father Ryan, suggested wryly that Ryan begin his survey "by investigating the Washington officials of the N.C.W.C."[24]

Working through the National Council of Catholic Men and the National Council of Catholic Women, both NCWC agencies, the department hoped to serve lay study groups curious about social questions. "A Catechism of the Social Question" was prepared for these groups, but this part of the SAD's program never got off the ground. In 1922 the department arranged a national Catholic Conference on Industrial Problems in Chicago. After this beginning, it stimulated other diocesan and regional conferences, always under local responsibility but drawing on the resources of the NCWC for organization, publicity, and speakers. These meetings claimed to be informative only: no votes were taken, and both capital and labor were heard. In fact, however, the conferences usually hummed in chorus with Ryan and McGowan.[25]

Within the department, Father Edwin V. O'Hara created the Rural Life Bureau to clarify and implement Catholic thinking on the religious and economic problems of America's depressed farmers. The bureau was chronically short-changed in the annual budget. The SAD was always poor, and the Rural Life Bureau, allotted just over 10 percent of the funds for the whole department, felt like its country cousin. In most matters, O'Hara operated independently of Ryan. Indeed, without O'Hara the bureau would not have survived.[26]

In two hours a day, four or five days a week during the academic year—he was frequently away for three months in the summer—Ryan

[22] New York *Times*, June 20, 1922.
[23] Raymond B. Fosdick to Ryan, March 15, 1926; Ryan to Fosdick, March 29, 1926; John D. Rockefeller, Jr., to Thomas D. Koon, copy, March 10, 1926.
[24] Curley to Ryan, April 12, 1926.
[25] Two essays consider the work of the Social Action Department in some detail: Sylvia M. Batdorf, "The Work of the Social Action Department of the National Catholic Welfare Conference in All Phases of Industrial Relations," M.A. dissertation, Catholic University (1933); and William J. Lee, "The Work in Industrial Relations of the Social Action Department of the National Catholic Welfare Conference, 1933–1945," M.A. dissertation, Catholic University (1946).
[26] J. G. Shaw, *Edwin Vincent O'Hara* (New York, 1957), pp. 106–113; Ryan to O'Hara, Dec. 6, 1927.

did little more than answer his mail, dictate a lecture or an article, or consult briefly with someone from another department. Monsignor George G. Higgins, a later director of the SAD, has even observed that "much of what Monsignor Ryan did would have been done about as well and in much the same way if there had been no NCWC."[27] Still, as Ryan shuttled from the university to his office at the NCWC, he worked with interacting authority: the prestige of his academic position made it clear that he was more than the mere spokesman for the hierarchy's ideas; his official status in the NCWC, especially in the sensitive Social Action Department, gave authority beyond that normally accorded to college professors' remarks.

Father Ryan welcomed any opportunity to go to New York, partly because of the lure of the city, partly because of a growing corps of friends who opened their doors to him even when he was unannounced. Carlton J. H. Hayes, the Columbia historian, first came to know of Ryan when he reviewed *Distributive Justice* for the *Annals of the American Academy of Political and Social Science*. Shortly thereafter he and Mrs. Hayes invited Ryan to dinner, and from this amicable beginning a warm friendship developed. The Hayeses gave Ryan a standing invitation to visit them, and he took advantage of it several times a year. The Hayeses' Irish maids had a running battle with Ryan's rumpled suits: it was not fitting that a Catholic priest should be that disheveled, and they regularly connived to get his suits away from him long enough to press them.

Hayes introduced Ryan to Lindsay Rogers, also on the Columbia faculty, and the Rogers home offered an alternate refuge in New York. In the course of the twenties, Ryan also came to know James J. Hoey, a real-estate broker in New York, active in Democratic politics. Hoey's sister, Jane, a social worker, had been a student of Ryan's at Trinity. Ryan and Hoey found that they both played bridge, earnestly if not expertly. Among these three households, Ryan could always find a home in New York; indeed, the Hayses and the Hoeys each assumed that he almost always stayed with them.[28]

The summer months gave the professor respite from his obligations. In the summer of 1921, he lectured in Nova Scotia, learning much there about parish credit unions. In 1922 he went to Ireland and moved about in the educated elite of the new Free State. During his three weeks he

[27] Interview with George G. Higgins, March, 1958.
[28] Interviews with Carlton J. H. Hayes, May 8, 1958, and with Jane Hoey, n.d.

lived at a Dominican convent just outside Dublin, and the pleasant interval led him to join the Dominican Third Order, a devotional organization primarily of laymen but also of diocesan priests associated with the Order of Preachers.

He met Michael Collins, one of the principal revolutionary leaders, just before Collins' assassination. Ryan's sympathies were with the Free State advocates who wanted home rule within the empire, not with the Republicans who wanted full independence. He had only contempt for Eamon DeValera and his Republican terrorists whom he viewed as insurgents revolting against legitimate Irish authority, using immoral weapons. Their idealism, Ryan asserted, is "buncombe."[29]

After 1925, when he bought a Dodge and learned to drive, more or less, Ryan regularly packed the car with young priests headed for the Midwest after their year of study. On one of these trips, he took Father Gilligan out to St. Paul Seminary to meet the proper, formal rector, Father Humphrey Moynihan. "Got anything to smoke?" Ryan asked his dignified contemporary as they settled down in Moynihan's office. Moynihan offered him a cigar; he took four or five, lighted one, put his feet up on the desk. Ryan loved to needle Moynihan's taste for decorum, but the rector knew enough not to respond.[30]

Mrs. Ryan was living in St. Paul again. Her husband having died of a heart attack in 1917, she had lived for several years just off the CU campus, after which she had returned to St. Paul. Ryan headed there first; then, as often as not, went farther west to visit parts of the family in Oregon and California. Late in August, early in September, he came back to Washington.

In the summer of 1926, he took his mother, Sister Constance, and Sister Mary John on a jaunt that finally reached as far east as New York. Entering Canada at North Troy, Vermont, Ryan received a yellow customs slip that he was required to surrender on reentry. But he missed the customhouse on his return trip and totally forgot the yellow slip until one of his sisters reminded him of it two hundred miles later. Not having bought anything in Canada, he felt no obligation to turn back. Instead he reported to the customhouse at Rouse's Point, New York,

[29] Ryan, "Impressions of Ireland's Civil War," *America*, Aug. 19, 1922, pp. 415–417; "Moral Aspects of Irish Insurgency," *ibid.*, Sept. 23, 1922, pp. 533–535.
[30] Interview with Gilligan, *op. cit.*

124

for he noticed on the yellow slip a mention of a $100 fine for failing to report reentry. The Rouse's Point inspector looked at Ryan, at his carload of passengers, at the yellow slip, and fined him $100 for "willful neglect." Several times in the fall Ryan appealed to the Secretary of the Treasury for a refund. The Treasury apparently did not even bother to file his letters, much less return his $100.[31]

With Ryan at the wheel, riding was hazardous. On this point all his friends agree in doleful and sometimes unprintable terms. Father Lawrence's first experience came one Thanksgiving Day when John drove to Baltimore. John drove by habit in the center of the road, talking all the time, gesticulating and turning toward his passenger. Nervous at first, Lawrence relaxed fatalistically as his brother tried to pass every car on the road. When they reached Baltimore, Lawrence said simply: "Well, you got them all, didn't you?" "Nope," said John ruefully, "missed one."[32]

The car soon became Ryan's main recreation, strolling with a cane his second choice. Tennis he had abandoned soon after his return to Washington. When the university completed its gymnasium in 1920, Ryan had appeared fairly regularly for a swim at four-thirty, his exercise including backward somersaults off the diving board; by the fifth decade of his life these had degenerated into bellyflops. Then neuritis had forced him to give up swimming. The car got him around town easily—going to the Social Service School became less of a chore. He could drive down to 1312 Massachusetts Avenue and get back to Caldwell Hall quickly and conveniently. After dinner in the evening, he walked with Father John J. Rolbiecki, who listened, or with Father Joseph P. Christopher, who did not. The local scene provided plenty to talk about, for the jungle growth of faculty politics at CU made the faculty politics at many other universities seem like desert wastes.

Money, by the mid-1920's, ceased to be a problem: many jobs, many incomes. The university paid him $2,000 a year, the NCWC about the same. Trinity and the NCSSS accounted for another $300 or so—the amount varied because faculty members at the NCSSS frequently returned their salaries to the barely solvent school. His articles and lectures brought in more. He averaged $50 a lecture, and if he went to the Midwest he

[31] Interview with Sister Constance, April 28, 1958, and with Sister Mary John, April 23, 1958. No record of the letter shows up in the Treasury Department's files at the National Archives.
[32] Interview with Lawrence F. Ryan, April, 1958.

insisted on $100 and his expenses. Royalties from his books came in now and again, especially from *The State and the Church*, which was adopted as a textbook by many Catholic colleges. Ryan kept an eye on the dollar: he noted for a visiting scholar that *Commonweal*, the New York magazine edited by Catholic laymen, paid more than other Catholic journals.[33]

Father John's family saw him as lively and, as Sister Mary John has put it softly, "always self-confident."[34] His secretaries were in awe of this "truly great man who acts and talks as simply as any other human being."[35] Ryan viewed himself in seeming paradoxes: liberal, yet Catholic; a critic of great fortunes, yet refusing to coerce Americans into giving up their oil lands in Mexico; pro-Ally, but in favor of canceling reparations and war debts; active in behalf of political prisoners, whose views he abhorred; advanced in economic views, yet the product of James J. Hill's seminary; trained in moral theology, but best known as an authority on social questions. He reconciled these contradictions simply: He was fundamentally a moralist, especially interested in the law of justice. His favorite motto was: "I love justice and hate shams."[36]

Ryan's "love of justice" kept him continuingly attentive to the workers' position. As the "Bishops' Program of Social Reconstruction" had indicated, his ultimate goal was industrial democracy, a program to make workers active partners in the planning, management, and profits of industry. Implicit in the teaching of Leo XIII, the idea came to life again for Ryan after his assistant, Father McGowan, took a trip in Europe. Hilaire Belloc's critique of contemporary industrialism, *The Servile State*, became the campaign book for the idea. The idea has endured. Ryan stuck with it for the rest of his life. And in the 1940's and 1950's it emerged again, first as Philip A. Murray's industrial-council plan, and more recently in the statements of Walter Reuther.

In many ways Ryan's program for union-management cooperation sounded like an echo from the twenties, when both capital and labor spilled many honeyed words on the subject. What Ryan wanted, however, was something quite different. He had tremendous respect for Daniel Willard, president of the Baltimore and Ohio Railroad, who had worked out a genuine alliance with his union: workers participated in

[33] Ryan to Alfred O'Rahilly, Dec. 13, 1926.
[34] Interview with Sister Mary John, *op. cit.*
[35] Catherine Schaeffer to Ryan, June 22, 1927.
[36] Ryan to Sarah A. Morris, April 1, 1927.

actual managerial problems through committees of a strong union. This meant cooperation between equals, not a handout from employers that debilitated unions and that could be snatched away as arbitrarily as it had been granted.[37] Year by year Colonel Patrick H. Callahan reported the results of the profit-sharing plan that Callahan, guided by Ryan's writings, had worked out for his varnish company in Kentucky.[38] But these were exceptions. It was no secret during the period that the expansive benefits of welfare capitalism were regarded by their sponsors as bait to keep the workers away from unions. Ryan distrusted this insidious paternalism. At the end of 1928, he snapped out the comment that stock-diffusion among workers had a long way to go before it would create a "Capitalism of the Workers."[39] He wanted industrial democracy immediately, not a diffused capitalism sometime in the remote future.

For the 1920's his program had a strange remoteness from reality. The decade was an age of retreat when holding actions, limited counter-offensives, and prayer were the only recourse. The battle over the living wage, union recognition, labor injunctions, and child labor had to be fought all over again, and, for more than a decade, fought and lost. The War Labor Board had been a stronghold of the living wage; its successor for the railroad industry, the Railway Labor Board, dismissed the living wage as "a bit of mellifluous phraseology," deceiving the unthinking. By 1925 Ryan regarded the board as so hopelessly partial to capital that he opposed giving it legal power to enforce its decisions.[40] The judiciary added to the conservative advance. In 1922 the Supreme Court, in over-turning the second Child Labor Act (1919) in Bailey v. Drexel Furniture Company (1922), disallowed Congress's use of the taxing power to prevent child labor in the manufacture of goods entering interstate commerce. The following year, in Adkins v. Children's Hospital (1923), the Court, by a five-to-four decision, struck down the 1918 law providing for a minimum wage for women in the District of Columbia.[41] This last decision ramified far, for if a minimum wage law passed by Congress was unconstitutional under the Fifth Amendment, the minimum wage laws in twelve states were probably doomed under the Fourteenth Amendment.

[37] *Catholic Review*, Oct. 7, 1927.
[38] Patrick J. Callahan to Ryan, Jan. 26, 1926.
[39] Ryan to Just Haristoy, Nov. 13, 1928.
[40] Ryan to William Quilty, April 16, 1925.
[41] Bailey v. Drexel Furniture Company, 259 U.S. 20; Adkins v. Children's Hospital, 261 U.S. 525.

Disappointed though not surprised by the child-labor decision, Ryan argued temperately for a constitutional amendment giving Congress the power to regulate labor conditions, including wages.[42] When the decision on the minimum wage followed, he exploded with wrath. He immediately echoed the demand of Senator Borah that the court not declare a law unconstitutional unless seven of the nine justices agreed. By this decision, Ryan argued, the court had taken the concept of liberty, which had already been stretched to include freedom of contract, and pushed it further to include the freedom to coerce a woman into accepting less than a living wage. Taking a cue from the minority opinion, written by Chief Justice William Howard Taft, Ryan charged that Justice George Sutherland's majority opinion rested essentially, not on legal grounds, but on grounds of ethics, economics, and public policy that were no part of the judicial function. And what perverted ethics! Directly contrary to Leo's *Rerum novarum*. A triumph of the individualistic and anarchic over the social and organic view of society. Sutherland's opinion vindicated the liberty of the few and powerful to oppress their fellows, a liberty "dear to the thug, the sneak thief, and to every other anti-social malefactor." Leo XIII had shown the alternative: Consider men in the concrete, not in their ideal equality. The state was bound to protect the weak; the rich protected themselves. "This is realism, common sense, humanity, good morals."[43]

Ryan was learning about constitutional law, his instructors being Brooks Adams, Roscoe Pound, and the dissenters on the high Court. Taft's vigorous dissent in the Adkins case reminded the majority that it was not the function of the Court to strike down legislation that it believed to be unwise, a point frequently made by Justices Holmes and Brandeis as well. Adams' chapter on "American Courts as Legislative Chambers" in *The Theory of Social Revolutions* (1913) destroyed some of the mythology of judicial objectivity and revealed the process of decision-making as part of the organic growth of law. Pound's book, *The Spirit of the Common Law* (1921), and his influential article, "The Theory of Judicial Decision," enlightened Ryan on the inevitable law-

[42] Ryan, "Federal Child Labor Law Unconstitutional," *Catholic Charities Review*, June, 1922, pp. 189–190.
[43] Ryan, "The Minimum Wage and the Constitution," *N.C.W.C. Bulletin*, May, 1923, pp. 18–20; "The Basis of the Minimum Wage Decision," *America*, June 2, 1923, pp. 165–166; "Ethics and the Minimum Wage Decision," *ibid.*, June 9, 1923, pp. 173–174.

making function of the courts and their invariable appeal to some conception of natural law.

The obvious remedy was the better education of judges—a rather slow procedure—or the appointment of new judges—also a program that took time. An amendment to the Constitution seemed more promising. During the fall of 1923, Felix Frankfurter, professor of law at Harvard, worked out a new minimum wage law for the District of Columbia and, in preparation for a national conference on the minimum wage later in the year, sent Ryan a copy.[44] Shortly thereafter Senator Thomas J. Walsh, Democrat from Montana, assembled a group to work on a child-labor amendment. Ryan was among them, along with Florence Kelley of the National Consumers' League and Owen Lovejoy of the National Child Labor Committee, Grace Abbott of the Children's Bureau of the Department of Labor, and many others. After a carefully planned campaign on the Hill, Congress sent the proposed Twentieth Amendment to the states. Opinion on the amendment divided as would have been expected, the social reformers actively in favor, along with labor unions and numerous church groups. On the other side, the business community, headed by James A. Emery, general counsel of the National Association of Manufacturers, worked hard to pin a socialist label on the amendment and to reveal it as the opening wedge for federal control of education.

At first reticent because of Catholic sentiment against the amendment, Ryan finally took part in the hopeless struggle for ratification. In November, 1924, he advanced the strange argument that the opponents of the amendment were undemocratic in not permitting the amendment to pass and then opposing the law that would implement it. They were taking improper advantage of the "tyrannical and undemocratic" power that states had over a constitutional amendment.[45] Early the next year he saw little prospect of ratification because of the "mendacious and misleading propaganda, unrivaled outside war time," that had been directed against the amendment by powerful economic interests, "evidently selfish." He warned that the hope for child-labor laws in the several states was illusory; the National Child Labor Committee, of which he was a member, had tried for twenty years to push through local laws, always with negligible success. He regarded the statements by the NAM and the Chamber of Commerce in favor of local action as

[44] Felix Frankfurter to Ryan, Oct. 3, 1923.
[45] Ryan, "The Proposed Child Labor Amendment," *Catholic World*, November, 1924, pp. 166–174.

propaganda against the federal amendment, not as constructive steps toward real reform.[46] In the fall of 1925 he attended the convention of Organizations Associated for the Ratification of the Child Labor Amendment, prudently appearing as the representative of the National Consumers' League and refusing membership on the executive committee. (McGowan was less prudent—he accepted.) The fight went on, but made little headway. Mrs. Kelley, whom Ryan regarded as one of the uncanonized saints of the reform movement, complained when she encountered the NAM's program in 1927 that "the righteous can not worship the Lord because they are incessantly fighting the Devil."[47] The fight limped along for the rest of the decade. The Twentieth Amendment that was finally ratified made whiskey legal, not child labor illegal.

In the face of setbacks in the legislative and judicial fields, Ryan hoped all the more desperately that organized labor would lead the crusade for industrial democracy. He condemned the open shop, as practiced after 1919, as a fraud; under it workers were permitted to belong to a union, to be sure, but employers refused to deal collectively with that union, even as the bargaining agent for its members. For industrial purposes, the open-shop union was no more useful than a parish sodality. Ryan condemned the dishonesty of employers who concealed the true purpose of the open-shop campaign under pious slogans like "the American plan." At the same time, he was critical of unions. As an outsider without emotional attachment to the labor movement as represented by the AFL, he constantly called them to tasks they were unwilling to undertake. Yet while management was using the open-shop movement to break up unions, while private armies patrolled the coal fields, while utilities squeezed labor and drained consumers, he found it difficult to keep his mind on the faults of the unions.[48]

Ryan's performance at a meeting of the National Conference of Catholic Charities in 1920 was typical. Scheduled for a talk on "Some Questionable Trade Union Practices," he listed some of his usual complaints—restriction of output, jurisdictional strikes, disregard of the public

[46] Ryan, "Present Position of the Child Labor Amendment," *Catholic Charities Review*, February, 1925, pp. 56–60; March, 1925, pp. 97–100.

[47] Florence Kelley to Ryan, Oct. 22, 1927.

[48] Ryan's views are stated in a variety of places. See, e.g., NCWC–SAD news release, Feb. 8, 1921; "The Right and Wrong of the Labor Union," undated speech, c. 1921; "Labor Unions," speech, July 30, 1921; "The Open Shop Fraud," in *Declining Liberty and Other Papers* (New York, 1927), pp. 209–212.

welfare during strikes. Yet the tenor of the speech moved in the opposite direction: labor's faults would disappear if business did not abuse its power, if laborers had work guaranteed for so many days a year, or better yet, if they enjoyed the change in status that gave them a part in management, profits, and ownership.[49]

Ryan wanted more militancy: a missionary fervor to embrace the entire working class, then a concerted campaign for union participation in management. At a Labor Sunday Meeting in Carnegie Hall, New York, in September, 1926, he warned that unless labor became more combative, it would never succeed in even its modest demands. "So long as the majority of wage earners remain unorganized and therefore a continuous menace to the standards won by the organized workers, the union will have to maintain a militant atitude. No social group has ever improved its position without the willingness and the ability to assert itself against those social groups and forces that were antagonistic." Labor must not blunt its fighting edge on "the shallow and false theory that the interests of labor and capital are identical." Organized workers have become too satisfied, their leaders too lazy. Wages were tolerably satisfactory, hours were lower, welfare services substituted for suitable working conditions. As workers became satisfied, unions withered, leaving workers more and more dependent on the good will of their employers. This condition Ryan called a "benevolent serfdom" creating in the worker a "slave mind."[50]

Ryan's warning was well timed but not heeded. Leadership could come only from the comfortable crafts. Satisfied with their own gains, most crafts were not moved to militancy. Union membership declined in the decade, and the leadership of the AFL, which in 1924 fell from the hands of the conservative Samuel Gompers into the lap of the supine William Green, made no determined effort to reverse the trend after the failure of the steel strike in 1919. Coal and textile workers, moved to militancy, could gain next to nothing in depressed industries that sweated workers. Most workers were unorganized, not in a position to talk back to management even if they wanted to.[51]

Ryan remained well outside labor's inner councils; his relations with

[49] Ryan, "Some Questionable Trade Union Practices," National Conference of Catholic Charities, *Proceedings* (Milwaukee, 1921), pp. 31–37.

[50] Ryan, "A New Task for Labor Unions," *Declining Liberty and Other Papers*, pp. 213–223.

[51] Philip Taft, *The A. F. of L. From the Death of Gompers to the Merger* (New York, 1959), pp. 1–2, 15–20.

labor were amicable rather than cordial. He gave the support of the Social Action Department to an anti-yellow-dog-contract bill in Ohio and sent a copy to the Archbishop of Cincinnati, his old friend, the Dominican John T. McNicholas, to gain his support too. He knew John Fitzgerald, head of the AFL in Chicago, well enough to give him a letter of introduction to Edward F. Hoban, Auxiliary Bishop of Chicago. The Illinois Federation of Labor sent a small contribution to the SAD for several years. Ryan's sermon at the "Labor Mass" in Detroit during the 1926 AFL convention—Bishop Michael J. Gallagher arranged the event— was published in the *Proceedings* of the convention, a courteous act to a friend. In 1928 Ryan advised Green on the Shipstead anti-injunction bill, shared the platform with him when the AFL launched a full-scale campaign to push the bill through Congress, and later advised him on Senator Norris's variation on the anti-injunction bill.[52] Only with Edward Keating, editor of *Labor*, the magazine of the railway brotherhoods, was he really close; they shared an interest in the Child Labor Amendment.

Considering Ryan's position at the NCWC, his record with organized labor is sparse. A legislative reformer in an era when organized labor was quiescent, he had little of use to say to workers that they were ready to hear.

Dr. Ryan's interest in one labor problem, the minimum wage, led him into the maze of the railroad valuation, a topic on which he came to write with the air of an expert. Indignant that railroads enjoyed a guaranteed return on their investment but balked at paying a living wage, Ryan argued that if railroads could not earn profits except by reducing wages indecently, "not a single Catholic authority" on moral principles would concede the right to profits. Ryan blamed the Esch-Cummins Act of 1920 for part of the trouble: it promised capital a return of $5\frac{1}{2}$ percent without guaranteeing workers their living wage—"immoral discrimination" against the workers.[53] When the Railroad Labor Board chose the "unethical" principle of supply and demand over the "ethical" principle of a living wage in granting maintenance-of-way workers a

---

[52] Ryan to Francis DeSales Kershaw, Dec. 5, 1925; Ryan to John T. McNicholas, Feb. 21, 1927; Ryan to Edward F. Hoban, Nov. 17, 1925; see, e.g., V. A. Olander to the SAD, Aug. 5, 1926; Green to Ryan, July 5, 1928; Ryan to Green, July 14, 1928; *Catholic Review*, Feb. 10, 1928; Taft, *The A. F. of L. From the Death of Gompers to the Merger*, pp. 22–25.

[53] Ryan, "The Railroads Reject the Living Wage," *Catholic Charities Review*, September, 1921, pp. 224–225.

two-cent increase, Ryan observed that this type of decision served no one but the "flagrant types of incompetent Bourbons."[54]

Ryan soon recognized, probably on the basis of the opinions of Justice Brandeis, that the evaluation of railroad properties was the crux of the issue. The Esch-Cummins Act promised a return of 5½ percent. But 5½ percent of what? The original investment or the cost of reproduction? The Supreme Court had never clarified this issue. Ryan now supported rates based on original investment, reversing his stand of twenty years before, defending the reversal because it produced the most desirable result for the public.[55] If the railroads could set their rates on the basis of the cost of reproduction at a time when prices had advanced strikingly, their profits could be as much as 25 or 50 percent higher. Conversely, if their profits were pegged at 5½ percent of the original investment, there was greater possibility of wage increases and of lower prices to consumers. Not just railroads were involved. The same problems concerned all public bodies regulating public utilities, and similar principles were involved when a governmental unit purchased a public utility from private owners.

Ryan followed the writings of Donald Richberg, general counsel of the National Conference on the Valuation of Railroads, who all through the 1920's hammered at public opinion to alert it to the railroads' campaign to sell the Interstate Commerce Commission on the theory of reproduction costs. When the Supreme Court told the Indiana Public Service Commission to raise the rates granted to the Indianapolis Water Company in 1926, Ryan combined Richberg's deflation of reproduction costs and Brandeis' defense of actual investment to back up his own denunciation of this "new form of usury." Ryan conceded a small increase over the original investment because of the rise in the general price level. But no more. "Examining the question on purely ethical grounds, we see powerful reasons for rejecting reproduction costs and accepting actual costs. When men put money into any productive enterprise, they expect to receive a fair rate of interest on their investment. . . . [An investor] has no reasonable ground for expecting that his dividend rate will be increased through the operations of any mere valuation theory. . . . All the uses of property are subject to the moral law, to the precepts of charity and justice. . . . There is nothing in the Catholic teaching which

[54] Ryan, "The Strike That Nearly Occurred," *ibid.*, November, 1921, pp. 298–299.
[55] Ryan, "Fair Evaluation of Public Utilities," in *Declining Liberty and Other Papers*, pp. 271–272.

sanctions a rate of 32 percent on a non-competitive investment, even though the rate may be legally established through some hocus-pocus called valuation." Warning capitalists to avoid greed lest they incite men against capitalism, Ryan recalled the words of Leo XIII that "rapacious usury . . . under a different guise" was still being practiced by "covetous and grasping men."[56]

Ryan tried to sell his articles to the *Atlantic Monthly*, but Ellery Sedgwick, the editor, judged the subject too technical for his audience.[57] The three articles appeared, somewhat implausibly, in the *Catholic Charities Review*, nudging an article on unmarried mothers and one on play-camp supervision.[58] When Macmillan and Harcourt, Brace turned down his idea for a small book, the National Popular Government League published the articles under its imprint.

Ryan stayed active in the fight over valuation. In 1929, when Washington's streetcar operators tried to effect a $50,000,000 merger, an eight-column banner headline in the Washington *Herald* called attention to Ryan's view of reproduction costs as a "hocus-pocus theory of valuation."[59] When the District committee in the Senate rejected the proposed merger, the *Herald* and Ryan won a joint victory, and Ryan's views appeared in the Baltimore *Sun* and a variety of Catholic diocesan papers.[60]

Like Justice Brandeis, Ryan worried about the direction of federal policy that resulted from the O'Fallon railway case (1929).[61] There the Supreme Court insisted that the Interstate Commerce Commission consider reproduction costs in setting rates, but it failed to define a rule for weighing reproduction costs against other factors. Brandeis, no more anxious than any of his brethren to make rate-setting a judicial function, nevertheless objected to the persistently high basis for capitalization tolerated by the Court. Ryan urged Senator Walsh to have Congress define the rule left vague by the Supreme Court. The Court would overturn an act that gave no weight to reproduction costs, Ryan said, but if direct congressional action provided a specific formula, the Court might accept Congress' standard. At least it was worth a try. While the Court

[56] Ryan, "The Ethics of Public Utility Valuation," pamphlet (Washington, D.C., 1928), pp. 22–23, 32.
[57] "The Editor" of the *Atlantic Monthly* to Ryan, Jan. 14, 1927.
[58] Ryan, "A New Form of Usury," *Catholic Charities Review*, April–June, 1927, pp. 129–132, 168–173, 213–220.
[59] Washington *Herald*, Jan. 7, 1929.
[60] *Ibid.*, Jan. 10, 1929.
[61] Alpheus T. Mason, *Brandeis: A Free Man's Life* (New York, 1946), pp. 547–553.

remained vague and Congress stayed inactive, he said, the ICC was deprived of the authoritative guidance it required.[62] The following January the ICC itself asked for congressional guidance on its rate base. By 1932, probably influenced by Richberg, Ryan himself moved on to the theory of "prudent investment."[63] But no effective action came during the Hoover administration.

Father Ryan felt equally committed to progressive views on public power. As chairman of the Washington Power Committee, an inactive subsidiary of the nationwide Public Power Committee, he kept in touch with Senator George W. Norris, Republican from Nebraska, on Muscle Shoals and Boulder Canyon.[64] Deeply respecting the leading advocates of public power, Ryan stuck by their organizations when they were under fire. In the course of a heated battle in Wisconsin, he blistered a spokesman for the Wisconsin Power and Light Company who tried to pin a Communist label on the Public Ownership League.[65] Carl D. Thompson, the league's grateful secretary, wrote to Ryan: "We rejoice to know that there are men in the country who have the moral conviction to stand up for their principles in spite of all the vituperation and abuse that is heaped upon them."[66] In January, 1932, *Public Ownership*, the league's periodical, delightedly published Ryan's defense of the league against the charge of socialism.[67] The same month *Public Service Magazine*, representing the opposite camp, noted that Ryan was coauthor with Morris Hillquit of *Socialism: Promise or Menace?* "Contemptibly dishonest," Ryan observed, "apparently a kept magazine."[68] When the National Popular Government League sent out a stinging attack on the political propaganda of the utilities lobby, Ryan refused to join in the clamor against the league, even though part of the attack offended Catholic sensibilities. The importance of the league's pamphlet overrode trifling objections. Besides, Ryan viewed the league's director, Judson King, as a great progressive: "There are few, if any, men in the United States doing as much good work . . . with as little money."[69]

Ryan's view on valuation and on public power seemed routinely pro-

[62] Ryan to Thomas J. Walsh, Aug. 9, 1929.
[63] Ryan to R. C. Beckett, Nov. 12, 1932.
[64] Ryan to George W. Norris, Dec. 10, 1926; Norris to Ryan, Dec. 19, 1926.
[65] Ryan to A. A. Oldfield, Oct. 31, 1931.
[66] Carl D. Thompson to Ryan, Nov. 16, 1931.
[67] *Public Ownership*, January, 1932, p. 2.
[68] *Public Service Magazine*, December, 1931, p. 165; Ryan to Callahan, Jan. 9, 1932.
[69] Ryan to Philip Kates, April 7, 1932; Ryan to Bertha King, Feb. 20, 1930.

gressive next to the radicalism of his proposals for anthracite coal. Even the priest himself admitted that they appeared fantastic. He regarded the Kenyon bill, which proposed an adjudicating board for anthracite workers, as the "most just and most statesmanlike program" ever to appear in an American lawmaking body. When it did not pass, he threw his support to the United Mine Workers, who wanted public ownership and management of the mines. "A most constructive contribution to settling the problem," Ryan said. "It attacks causes, it is fundamental, and it is comprehensive."[70] It also died a-borning.

Probably many people saw more truth than typographical error in the Washington *Star*'s identification of Ryan as director of the "Socialist Action Committee" of the NCWC.[71]

One new crusade attracted Ryan in the 1920's—international peace through disarmament. This was a legacy from his interest in European and world problems dating from the war years. Because he was not historically literate, the problems that led to the war eluded him. But the war had created a new world, and merely by being well informed on matters within his own memory Ryan understood passably those European problems, especially in economics, to which he gave attention. On some major issues Ryan reversed earlier opinions. As early as 1922 he argued before a high-school audience in Baltimore that the German war debt was excessive, a burden beyond what the German people should have to bear, or indeed could bear, and a continuing threat to world peace.[72] On the basis of John Maynard Keynes' *Economic Consequences of the Peace* (1920) and Harold G. Moulton and Constantine E. McGuire's *Germany's Capacity to Pay*, he argued that German payment was impossible.[73] And after reading John F. Bass and Moulton's *America and the Balance Sheet of Europe,* he contended that American industrial leaders were just as stupid and insincere as the French when they clamored for repayment of Europe's debt to us. He followed Harry Elmer Barnes' revisionist studies of German war guilt closely, and by the mid-twenties he shared the view quite common among liberals that the hopes raised by the war had been "completely frustrated," that the United States had erred in entering a war which it did not understand and in

[70] Ryan, "Justice to the Anthracite Mine Owners," *America,* July 14, 1923, pp. 297–298; "Anthracite and Ethics," *Catholic World,* December, 1925, pp. 297–306.
[71] Washington *Star,* Nov. 8, 1931.
[72] *Catholic Review,* Feb. 25, 1922.
[73] Ryan, "Charity Among Nations," *Catholic World,* January, 1924, pp. 433–442.

136

which it had no real stake.[74] American nationals should have stayed off foreign ships, he wrote to the New York *Times*. He believed that "all the nations including our own would be better off today if we had not entered the conflict."[75] The urgent corollary of the war was to avoid a repetition.

Ryan's friends encouraged his new interest. Father McGowan nagged a bit; Carlton Hayes helped. Worth M. Tippy, Charles S. Macfarland, and especially Sidney L. Gulick, all of the Federal Council of Churches, and Frederick J. Libby, executive secretary of the National Council for the Prevention of War, never missed a chance to draw him into activities for peace. They all urged him into a territory that Catholics had not entered. The popes had spoken vigorously for peace; the bishops had echoed them. On his visit to Europe in 1922, Ryan had met Joseph Keating, S.J., the British peace advocate, and had followed his articles in *Month*, the English Catholic periodical. Ryan learned enough about England's Catholic Council for International Peace to want it to be a model for an American association.[76] But there the matter ended. He did not exaggerate in 1925 when he said he could tell the whole story of American Catholic peace sentiment in a fraction of the sixteen hundred words the *N.C.W.C. Bulletin* wanted him to write.[77]

In April, 1925, at the request of Father Francis J. Haas, a former student, Ryan did an article on peace for *Salesianum*. He knew from his membership on the executive board of the National Council for the Prevention of War that the peace movement would welcome the adherence of Catholics. Why wait? he asked. Were Catholics afraid someone would question their patriotism if they spoke for peace as against the clamor for standing armies and large fleets? Join a group, he said; much of what you hear will be impractical, but the important thing is to start talking peace in an organized way. Have an opinion one way or the other on the League of Nations and the World Court, he said. Back disarmament and the outlawry of war; both are in "exact accord" with Catholic teaching.[78]

From his editor's chair, Father Haas reported an exceptionally favor-

[74] Ryan, "Cancel War Debts and Reparations," *Annals of the American Academy of Political and Social Science*, July, 1925, pp. 62–64; Ryan, "The Patriotic Citizen," MS of undated speech, *c.* 1923.
[75] New York *Times*, March 12, 1927; Ryan to Frederick W. Peabody, Oct. 9, 1926.
[76] Ryan to Joseph Keating, May 19, 1925.
[77] Ryan to Hayes, May 9, 1925.
[78] Ryan, "American Catholics and the World Peace Movement," *Salesianum*, April 1925, pp. 1–8.

able response,[79] and from New York James T. Shotwell, a divisional director of the Carnegie Endowment for International Peace, wrote to Professor Hayes with delight over Ryan's article. Could Hayes get a solid movement going within the Church? "I cannot imagine anything more important at the present time than that the Church which has a claim to universal outlook and has the traditions which the Catholic Church unquestionably has, should line itself up, if not with the definite and specific proposal of the Protocol, at least in support of its fundamental principles." (The "Protocol" was the Protocol for the Pacific Settlement of International Disputes adopted by the Assembly of the League of Nations.) Besides, Shotwell added pointedly, the Protestants are already moving.[80] Pleased, Ryan wrote to Shotwell asking to use his letter for publicity purposes.[81]

Groups with strong Protestant backing, like the National Study Conference on the Church and World Peace, wanted to draw the NCWC in, but Bishop Muldoon warned Ryan to avoid the type of official cooperation with Protestant organizations that might draw a rebuke from Rome and would certainly outrage the more conservative American bishops.[82] The hierarchy even steered clear of the National Council for the Prevention of War, a group less intimately associated with Protestant churches as such. Ryan himself moved cautiously, for a tinge of pacifism surrounded the peace movement generally; he was always wary of extremist views because he was willing to support war measures under some circumstances.[83]

The hierarchy's reluctance to cooperate with others made a Catholic organization even more urgent. A small conference, called by the Social Action Department and the Department of Lay Organizations of the NCWC, met in Cleveland on October 6, 1926, to lay plans for a future group. A committee on organization of the Catholic Association for International Peace emerged, Ryan as chairman, Judge Martin Manton and Father Husslein, members. The committee decided to undertake no wide activity until its second year, leaving Ryan, as chairman of a subcommittee on international ethics, some leisure to prepare a working paper for discussion.[84] His final product, which drew substantially from the book of Franziskus Stratmann, O.P., *The Church and War*, became

[79] Francis J. Haas to Ryan, May 11, 1925.
[80] James T. Shotwell to Hayes, copy, May 6, 1925.
[81] Ryan to Shotwell, May 9, 1925.
[82] Peter J. Muldoon to Ryan, Oct. 17, 1925.
[83] Ryan to Sydney Strong, Dec. 8, 1926.
[84] *Catholic Review*, Oct. 8, 1926.

the principal manifesto of the new association when it was published in a pamphlet entitled "International Ethics" (1927). The report accepted the use of force in international relations, but warned of the need for caution in invoking force. It rejected the pacifist position, for "Righteousness would surely not be promoted if wicked men were permitted to have a monopoly of physical coercion." Yet it limited the characterization of a just war to those declared by sovereign authority with a right intention for a good cause (that is, necessary self-defense). The heart of the issue was the just cause. Only an actual or imminent violation of a nation's rights, creating an injury proportionate to the evils of war, justified re-course to war, and even then only if peaceful means have proved in-effective and if rulers held a well-grounded hope of bringing about better conditions by fighting.

With the problem of creating a Catholic group in mind, the committee noted: "Justice requires a state to promote peace for the sake of its own members, while charity obliges it to pursue the same ends for the welfare of both itself and other nations. These duties rest not only upon govern-ments, but upon peoples, particularly upon those persons and organi-zations which can exert influence upon public opinion and upon political rulers."[85]

Ryan was trying to create a pressure group in a hurry. Given Catholic apathy, he wanted to get people talking about world peace. Let them be for or against the League, the World Court, disarmament—just so long as they thought and talked about the issues. Who could object so far? Here would be a nucleus for an organization. The Catholic Association for International Peace provided the organization. No protest so far. Once the group had some strength in numbers, it could gradually pick up more unity in point of view from a study of the principles of inter-national ethics. And one day, without anyone being able to name which day, there would exist an American Catholic pressure group for inter-national peace, working alongside Protestant and secular groups and lobbying before congressional committees. To say that Ryan planned it this way is to make of him a calculating schemer. But to deny that this ever crossed his mind is to assume that he was unable to learn from his own experience.

Other liberal measures kept Ryan busy; they were so numerous that he lost track of them. As a Washington representative of the National

[85] Ryan et al., "International Ethics," pamphlet (New York, 1928), p. 22.

Consumers' League, he lobbied for legislation in behalf of women in the District. A vice president of the American Association for Old Age Security and a member of the executive board of the American Association for Labor Legislation, he was urged by the International Labor Office in Washington to intervene in the internecine bickering between the two groups. He spoke at a convention of the Indian Rights Association in Atlantic City in December, 1928, even though this group and John Collier's American Indian Defense Association, to which Ryan belonged, fought for the Indian partly by fighting each other. He was friendly with the cluster of reform-minded men and women who hailed the name of George W. Norris. He sat on the Committee of Cooperation with the Clergy of the American Eugenics Society; became a vice president of the Public Ownership League; worked with the national committee of the National World Court Committee; remained active with the National Child Labor Committee. "Fed up" by the list, certain that one-third the number of committees would get more work done, he turned down an invitation to join the League for Minority Rights: "My name already appears on too many mastheads of organizations in which I am inactive."[86]

Not himself a prime mover, Ryan was part of the creative squad of liberal reformers that in a period like the 1920's mourns the day. In such a time reformers bustle and plot, arranging conferences and committee meetings at which the like-minded ignore facts, smile bravely, and build for the future. Power lies elsewhere. Bold stands are mounted, move toward success, fail miserably, are chalked up to experience and to public education. An awkward charade, mouthing hopes unheard by the rest of America.

And from this talk comes the future.[87]

[86] Ryan to Robert Gray Taylor, Feb. 25, 1932.
[87] A stimulating view, differing from mine here, is Arthur S. Link, "What Happened to the Progressive Movement in the 1920's?" *American Historical Review*, July, 1959, pp. 844–851.

The Liberal
& the Church

FATHER JOHN A.
Ryan ran with his liberal friends without ever really joining them. When they shared common goals, he worked
with them eagerly, but when his sense of justice put him in
opposition, he spoke unhesitatingly, even if reluctantly.

The Scopes trial in Tennessee in 1925 vividly showed
how different routes led, for practical purposes, to the same
end. John Thomas Scopes, a biology instructor in the public
school in Dayton, deliberately violated a Tennessee statute
that forbade the teaching of "any theory which denies the
story of the Divine creation of man as taught in the Bible."
After Scopes was indicted, the American Civil Liberties
Union assembled its national board in New York. Ryan, as
a member of the board, went up to be in on the excitement.

The meeting turned out to be unexpectedly harmonious.
The board decided to help Scopes and to argue the unconstitutionality of Tennessee's law—unconstitutional as a
deprivation of liberty guaranteed by the Fourteenth Amendment. The group agreed to hire Clarence Darrow, the
famous criminal lawyer, as principal defense counsel. Nothing published in the New York *Times* the next day sug-

gested that Ryan dissociated himself from this action.[1] As a matter of fact, Roger Baldwin, formerly executive director of the ACLU, has recalled Ryan's saying: "I can't object to your going into a case like this. I don't care where the body comes from as long as the soul is recognized as the creation of God."[2] Tennessee associated William Jennings Bryan, three-time presidential candidate and prominent fundamentalist, with the prosecution. The contest was joined, and because of Tennessee's "monkey trial," Dayton became the news center of the nation for a week.

Ryan himself disapproved of Scopes' action. He contended that the law merely forbade teaching that the Biblical story of the creation of man was untrue. Quoting a Jesuit and a Dominican, St. Augustine and Leo XIII, he argued that Scopes could probably have taught "a mitigated form of the evolutionary hypothesis" without doing violence to science, religion, or the statutes of Tennessee. Those who defended the right to do what the law forbade were in effect repudiating the principle that the schools should be neutral on religious matters. It was wrong, Ryan said, to teach either fundamentalism or antifundamentalism.

At the same time, Ryan conceded that the law was foolish. He abhorred what he called "intolerance's share" in writing the act. He also disliked the antireligious influences that created a situation that the law tried to meet, and he disliked meeting this situation by law. He saw a parallel situation elsewhere: he detested industrial syndicalism, but still did not favor antisyndicalist laws. State laws were not the proper way to keep antireligious propaganda out of the public schools, he said. For one thing, offenses under the law come before juries not competent to judge —how could a random jury decide whether Scopes had actually contradicted the Bible when even the ablest scholars would be far from unanimous? Furthermore, one direct legislative intervention in the curriculum prepared the way for another. Would the legislature next forbid comments on cooperatives? If the state legislature prescribed what might not be taught, would the legislature next prescribe what must be taught? All in all, not a wise use of legislative power. Ryan preferred to have the problem handled administratively, through boards of education rather than through legislatures. Catholics should hope the law would be called unconstitutional, he said, because it created a precedent for tyrannical legislative interferences with public and private schools. Yet, unlike many of

[1] New York *Times,* June 9, 1925.
[2] Interview with Roger Baldwin, May 8, 1958.

his liberal friends, he could not really question the state legislature's right to regulate its schools.[3]

An odd footnote to this episode occurred when the Scopes conviction was upheld by the Tennessee Supreme Court in January, 1927. A concurring opinion, written by Justice A. W. Chambliss, argued that Scopes need not have violated the law while teaching evolution, for evolutionary theory was not incompatible with the Biblical description of creation. A shock of recognition led Ryan to write to Chambliss describing the opinion as "very well reasoned out and extremely convincing." Your opinion, he told Chambliss, confirmed my own. In his reply Chambliss explained that he had admired Ryan's comment in the New York *World* and had used it in writing his opinion.[4]

The Scopes trial aside, Ryan's membership on the national board of the ACLU astonished some Catholics, even scandalized a few, for the ACLU's persistent defense of free speech, even in all sorts of radical causes, and its cosmopolitan membership, including names like Clarence Darrow and Morris Hillquit, made it suspect among conservatives. Ryan had been brought into the ACLU by Roger Baldwin. They had known each other at various meetings over the years, especially the conferences of the National Association of Social Work, and during the war Baldwin had enlisted Ryan's help in dealing with a Catholic conscientious objector who had gone on a hunger strike. Though they shared few religious ideas, they took to each other from the start. Both liked blunt, honest talk. Both liked a good story. Both had a yen for social justice. They never let theological differences obtrude on their personal relationships. Ryan never went looking for matters to quarrel about, and except for an occasional voice of protest, the ACLU welcomed Ryan as a colleague, both for himself and for the conservative ballast his connection with the Church gave to the organization.

On occasions when Ryan felt that the ACLU went too far, Baldwin's artful cajolery kept Ryan from resigning. In 1931 Baldwin, in the name of the ACLU, defended before a congressional committee the right of a citizen to advocate murder and assassination. Elsewhere he made a

---

[3] Letters to the editor of the New York *World*, June 4 and June 12, 1925; Baltimore *Catholic Review*, July 11, 1925; Ryan's statement in American Civil Liberties Union, "Anti-Evolution Laws," pamphlet (New York, 1927), pp. 27–28; "The Teaching of Evolution in the Public Schools," in *Declining Liberty and Other Papers*, pp. 115–120.

[4] Ryan to A. W. Chambliss, Feb. 1, 1927; Chambliss to Ryan, Feb. 5, 1927; Ray Ginger, *Six Days or Forever?* (Boston, 1958), pp. 208–209, 227–228.

thoroughgoing defense of academic freedom, even to the extent of defending a professor's right to publish what many regarded as pornography. Ryan sent in his resignation, insisting that the right of free speech falls short of "the advocacy of assassination and the dissemination of rank obscenity." Baldwin argued the facts of the two cases, quibbled on the interpretation of the facts. Ryan weakened a bit, and finally Baldwin, pressing his advantage, held him on the board.[5] In each situation Ryan had to weigh the embarrassment of the single issue against the value of the organization's total program. Each was a prudential decision.

Once in a while this type of decision came easily. When Clarence Darrow, the great agnostic, invited Ryan to join the national council of a foundation named for Victor L. Berger, the well-known Socialist, Ryan had no difficulty in saying "No." It would, he said mildly, "subject me to misunderstanding."[6]

There was no blinking the difficulties that separated Catholics and liberals. The priest was most unhappy about T. V. Smith's pragmatic, materialist volume, *The American Philosophy of Equality:* it dismayed him to think that thousands of Catholics heard only this kind of philosophy in secular universities.[7] The "new morality" in books such as Walter Lippmann's *Preface to Morals* troubled him. The old morality had a standard outside itself: God's moral order. It combined observation and intuition, with an ultimate base in God Himself. The new morality was rootless and, Ryan added in a striking raid on the opposition, not really scientific.[8]

On one noisy occasion, the liberal Ryan railed at his liberal colleagues for their illiberal attitudes. In 1926 the Mexican government and the Catholic Church in Mexico engaged in a trial of strength over those parts of the Mexican constitution of 1917 that imposed restrictions on the Church, especially Articles 3, 5, 27, and 130. For nine years the provisions had been relatively unenforced. Then in June, 1926, President Plutarco Elías Calles announced a penal code, to become effective August 1st, that provided penalties for violations of the religious laws of the nation. Whether this was an overt act of aggression against the Church, or

[5] Ryan to Baldwin, Nov. 5, 1931; Baldwin to Ryan, Nov. 6, 1931; Ryan to Baldwin, Dec. 5, 1931.
[6] Ryan to Clarence Darrow, Feb. 4, 1931.
[7] Ryan, "Evolution and Equality," *Commonweal*, Dec. 5, 1928, pp. 125–127.
[8] Ryan, "The New Morality and Its Illusions," *Catholic World*, April, 1930, pp. 129–136.

defense of the state against clerical interference, is still a matter of debate.[9] In any case it opened hostilities.

In the United States the American bishops sided with their brothers in Mexico: the anti-Catholic measures of the Mexican government constituted "absolute denials of those principles upon which we, as Americans, believe that just government must be founded." Avoiding any suggestion of strong measures, the hierarchy called upon the American government "to use its good offices to see that justice is restored."[10] No such moderation guided the Catholic laymen in the Knights of Columbus. In a series of horror books and pamphlets, they assembled a catalog of outrages perpetrated by the Calles government, denounced the regime as Bolshevik, and demanded American intervention in the name of international morality. American oil interests, which had felt the blows of the Calles government, also hoped for armed defense of their wells.

Ryan, sympathetic to the economic reforms of the Mexican government, still regarded its attack on the Church as a blow to freedom, and he condemned it on liberal grounds—the right to freedom of religion for Mexican Catholics. In this view he received less support from American liberals than he expected. The liberals failed to condemn Calles' invasion of religious liberty because they were unwilling to impede economic reform in Mexico, he said, just as many American Catholics failed to condemn Benito Mussolini's assaults on Italian civil liberties because they approved of other items in his program. Behaving consistently, Ryan condemned both. He called upon liberals to do the same.[11] Not satisfied with the response, he complained that the American liberal, silent on the Mexican persecution, "denies in effect that civic and religious rights and freedoms are matters of universal principle; apparently, they are merely matters of policy." Among the offending liberals, Ryan singled out Walter Lippmann of the New York *World* for keeping silent on the persecutions; Oswald Garrison Villard of the *Nation* for failing to give an adequate statement of the Catholic view in the *Nation;* and Norman Thomas, then executive director of the League for Industrial Democracy, for arguing that "the long record of clerical opposition in Mexico to

[9] Sister Mary Elizabeth Ann Rice, *The Diplomatic Relations Between the United States and Mexico, as Affected by the Struggle for Religious Liberty in Mexico, 1925–1929* (Washington, D.C., 1959), pp. 62–68. For the liberal viewpoint, see Ernest Gruening, *Mexico and Its Heritage* (New York, 1928).

[10] Raphael M. Huber, *Our Bishops Speak* (Milwaukee, 1952), pp. 268–270.

[11] Ryan, "American Liberals and Mexican Tyranny," *N.C.W.C. Bulletin,* August, 1926, pp. 13–14.

religious, political and economic freedom" made it impossible to judge the Church conflicts in Mexico by American standards.[12]

Ryan gathered a bundle of these criticisms together in an article for the *N.C.W.C. Bulletin* and, having named Thomas as an offending liberal, sent him a copy. Thomas picked up the gauntlet courteously, and for six weeks letters passed back and forth.[13] Sardonically amused at "being lectured by any Roman Catholic, even yourself," on devotion to absolute principles of civil liberties, Thomas told Ryan that Catholic appeals to religious freedom, especially in Mexico, left him cold—it would be well for those who appeal to religious freedom to give evidence of it in their time of power as well as in their time of persecution. Furthermore, Thomas feared that Ryan's defense of the Church's position would play into the hands of the Knights of Columbus, who were advocating withdrawal of recognition as a step toward intervention. "I am not enough of an absolutist on this matter to want to fight for civil liberty in Mexico in a way that may aid the aggressions of oil magnates," Thomas said, slyly professing to have found justification for this prudential, relativist attitude in Ryan's own "excellent book on Church and State." The controversy continued inconclusively. Ryan complained that Thomas's reference to the illiberalism of the Mexican Church in its time of power reminded him of the farmer who exclaimed on having oxtail soup put before him for the first time, "I'd say that's going pretty far back for soup." Thomas finally shut off the correspondence with the observation that both of them disagreed on the facts of the situation, both had different authorities whom they trusted: "If my bias is somewhat anti-clerical, . . . yours is pro-clerical." For his part Ryan said that he would rather deal with an opponent who frankly wanted to destroy religion in Mexico than with someone like Thomas, whose "evasions" were so slippery.[14]

The Mexican issue upset Dr. Ryan's equilibrium. He generally kept himself under control in the controversies he entered. On this issue, however, his self-control faltered, and so did his sense of fair play. One incident involved Villard. Ryan wrote to him in March, 1926, protesting against misstatements in the *Nation* that Ryan had "good reason for holding" to

---

12 Ryan to Patrick H. Callahan, Feb. 8, 1927, in "Callahan Correspondence," n.d., and Ryan, "American Liberals and Mexican Tyranny," *N.C.W.C. Bulletin*, February, 1927, pp. 10–12. (Despite the identical titles, this is a different article from the one cited above.)

13 The entire correspondence is reprinted as "Liberalism and the Mexican Crisis of 1927: A Debate Between Norman Thomas and John A. Ryan," *Catholic Historical Review*, October, 1959, pp. 309–326.

14 Ryan to Frederick M. Kerby, Feb. 18, 1927.

be false. They argued back and forth for several months without reaching any agreement. In the course of this correspondence, Villard offered to publish a factual article on Mexico by a reliable "Catholic of standing," and he even went so far as to promise publication of an anonymous article, anonymous even to Villard, if Ryan would vouch personally for the author's reliability. Ryan was never able to supply this article. In June, Villard did publish Ryan's own moderate essay on "freedom and Mexico." The two never had a meeting of minds, but their differences did not prepare Villard for Ryan's denunciation of him in the "Callahan Correspondence," a private newssheet circulated irregularly by Colonel Callahan. Ryan, asking Callahan to publish the letter, charged that Villard refused equal space in the *Nation* to the Catholic viewpoint, that his denunciation of Mexican tyranny did not go beyond damning the restraint of the press, in which Villard had a "special and professional interest." Villard and most nominal liberals were really tories who, while demanding freedom for themselves, did not stand for the same freedom for other people. Villard's retort sputtered indignation. He resented Ryan's assertion that the *Nation* was interested only in freedoms that directly benefited it, but his principal rage was reserved for Ryan's failure to report that the *Nation* had published Ryan's own article and that it had been willing to open its pages to an unknown Catholic of Ryan's choice—a gesture "far beyond usual journalistic practice." Villard added that in simple justice his protest should appear in the "Callahan Correspondence," which had given currency to Ryan's charges. Ryan's defense limped awkwardly. He pointed out that the balance of the *Nation*'s articles did indeed tilt in favor of the Calles government. He admitted that "complete fairness might require" an account of Villard's efforts to get a pro-Church article. "In extenuation of that inadvertent omission," he pleaded that the letter was written in haste and with some feeling: "as a rule my emotions are relatively quiescent when I write anything; but to me religion is the dearest and most fundamental thing in my life."[15] This reply was grudging and ungracious, but Villard did not carry the matter further.

Ralph Hayes, a mutual friend of Ryan and Lippmann, called Lippmann's attention to Ryan's criticism in the *Nation* and in the "Callahan Correspondence." In passing Lippmann's mild and conciliatory reply on to his clerical friend, Hayes worked in a gentle rebuke: "I confess to a feeling

[15] Ryan to Oswald Garrison Villard, March 27, 1926; Villard to Ryan, telegram, Sept. 21, letter, Sept. 22, 1926; Ryan, "Liberty and the Roman Catholic Church I. The Catholic Position," *Nation*, June 16, 1926, pp. 660–661; Ryan to Callahan, Feb. 8, 1927; Villard to Ryan, Feb. 23, 1927; Ryan to Villard, Feb. 25, 1927.

that he [Lippmann] has fought too well and often against Klansmen, bigots and tories to have his motives impeached, and with so few liberal leaders who are comparable to you two, we younger fellows in the rear ranks can't afford to have our generals slinging rocks at each other instead of at the enemy."[16]

By the middle of 1927, the crisis dropped quietly into diplomatic channels and disappeared from Ryan's letters and published work. But the year-long controversy left a mark. Ryan's "disinclination to work unnecessarily with pseudo-liberals" later grew into "disgust and disillusionment over the cowardice and illiberalism of most American liberals." This view extended to prominent Protestants as well. Ryan felt that the National Council for the Prevention of War, which had strong Protestant backing, was dispensing propaganda for Calles under the guise of urging arbitration. Amazed, shocked, angered, he quit the council, sure that in the future he could not "again possess the feeling of certainty and trust which would be necessary for effective cooperation in the work of the Executive Board."[17]

Occasionally displeased by the liberals, Ryan also displeased liberals on occasion. It was splendid to have him on the ACLU board. It was heartening to have a Dr. Ryan around to answer an antidemocratic pamphlet, widely circulated among the Catholic clergy, called "An American Catechism on Democracy." It was comforting to have Ryan catch up even Jacques Maritain, the noted Catholic philosopher, on the limits of papal authority over the citizen as citizen, and to read his assurance that nothing in "The Christian Education of Youth," Pope Pius XI's recent encyclical, encouraged opposition to American public schools.[18] Yet on occasion the fissure that divided Ryan from his liberal friends opened up. Sometimes the priest did not realize how deep these divisions were; when he did, his honesty guarded against any temptation to conceal them.

A suggestive incident was the concordat between Italy and the Church in 1929. Settling an impasse dating back to Italian unification, the agreement established the Catholic Church as the only religion with official standing in Italy, accepted canon law as the basis for marriage, and pro-

16 Ralph Hayes to Ryan, Feb. 28, 1927.
17 Ryan to William Hard, Jan. 28, 1927; Ryan to Frederick J. Libby, May 11, 1927.
18 Ryan, "Assault Upon Democracy," *Catholic World*, March, 1929, pp. 641–647; review of Jacques Maritain, *The Things That Are Not Caesar's*, in *Commonweal*, May 13, 1931, pp. 50–51; "The Pope's Encyclical on Education," *Current History*, March, 1930, p. 1088.

vided for religious education in the schools. Ryan defended this "Lateran agreement." He pointed out that despite a genuine union of church and state, the agreement did not exclude full freedom for non-Catholic denominations in Italy—their right to worship and to propagate their views was in no way impaired. As for the regulation of marriage by canon law, these measures stabilized Italian families. The compulsory religious and moral teaching in the schools was conducive to social morality and genuine progress. This view, he pointed out, was accepted in Great Britain, Canada, and Germany. The agreement was reactionary, Ryan concluded, only in the sense of being a return to social sanity.[19]

This defense was far from satisfactory from the liberal point of view. The substantial practical difference between establishing the Catholic Church and tolerating other religions aside, liberals could not fail to decry the enforcement of canon law on marriage and divorce. Ryan's defense of this provision—social utility informed by the traditional teaching of the Catholic Church—struck liberals neither as self-evident, nor, indeed, as true. They opposed legislation in this area as an invasion of the individual's freedom of conscience. Count Carlo Sforza, the Italian liberal in exile from Mussolini's Italy, and Charles A. Marshall, a prominent New York lawyer, wasted no time in pointing out to Ryan, in a debate before the Foreign Policy Association in Boston, that he was flouting the democratic principles of society. The debate did not move Ryan from his position.[20]

The gap between Ryan and his liberal friends also widened dramatically on the issue of birth control. On this topic Ryan talked a language alien or irrelevant both to liberals and to advocates of birth control. If his liberal friends listened to his argument, they probably did not understand it; when they understood, they rejected it.

Within the Church Ryan took part in the continuing debate over the grounds on which artificial contraception should be condemned. He preferred to rely on the "perverted faculty" argument: that mechanical interference with the proper functioning of sexual organs thwarted the proper order of nature and thus was intrinsically wrong.[21] As often as Ryan commented on birth control, he almost invariably returned to this metaphysical argument:

[19] Boston *Globe*, Feb. 17, 1929.
[20] *Christian Science Monitor*, March 4, 1929.
[21] Ryan, "The 'Perverted Faculty' Argument Against Birth Prevention," *Ecclesiastical Review*, August, 1928, pp. 133–145.

Against contraception the Catholic Church speaks without hesitation and with logical consistency. She stigmatizes it as a perversion of nature (not merely as "unnatural"), an abuse of function, a frustration of faculty. The faculty is so used that it cannot attain its primary end. Neither age, nor time, nor any other circumstance of the persons, but the very *use* of the faculty produces this perverse result. The faculty is compelled to defeat itself. This is an inherent contradiction and makes the act intrinsically wrong. To be sure, this argument is metaphysical. To be sure, it does not persuade those who identify morality with short-sighted utility. The proposition that frustrative use of the sex faculty is intrinsically immoral, can no more be proved than the proposition that two plus two equals four.[22]

Other Americans did not share this Catholic metaphysical view. For the general public, therefore, Ryan based his case against contraception on adverse social consequences: the loss of mutual respect between husband and wife, the creation of an environment of selfishness and flabbiness of will for children, the diversion of energy from social reform, a declining national population. He used this line of argument when he appeared in May, 1932, before the subcommittee of the Senate Judiciary Committee that was considering the repeal of the federal ban against sending information on contraceptives through the United States mails.[23] Yet he was careful never to rest his case on the slippery empirical base of social consequences alone: the consequences did no more than confirm the intuitive and metaphysical judgment that current birth-control practices (other than the rhythm method) were evil in themselves. A similar metaphysical truth—the intrinsic sacredness of the human person—also led him to condemn, as Pius XI had done, eugenic sterilization by the state.[24]

This kind of argument was strange to reforming ears. In attacking contraception, Ryan was urging the continuance of a federal ban on spreading information on the subject—an affront to free speech as understood by liberals. In this era of social pragmatism, progressives tested reform by a formula of results that was well illustrated by Holmes' distrust of dominating orthodoxies and by the "Brandeis way" of hammering at limited problems, solving them by attention and work. Worried about an unprotected conveyor belt, who spoke of the nature of man? Who

[22] Ryan, "Is Birth Control Right? A Debate. II: The Wrong of It," *Forum*, July, 1927, pp. 18–19.
[23] NCWC Press Release, "Economic and Social Objections to Birth Control," May 19, 1932.
[24] Ryan, "The Moral Teaching of the Encyclical," *Ecclesiastical Review*, March, 1931, pp. 267–268.

150

indeed could any longer speak with confidence about the purpose of man's existence, or the intended end of the sexual act? This latter question Ryan answered by pointing to the teaching authority of the Church of Rome, divinely preserved against error when speaking on faith and morals. At this point Ryan was no longer in contact with the thought processes of the liberals. He was talking a language that they thought they had outgrown. And Ryan did not beckon them back.

Here was the difficulty for liberals. Judgments from Catholic theology entered social policy, and even the American Church's most outspoken progressive threw his weight against measures that liberals thought were properly matters of individual choice. In the course of the decade, Ryan came to oppose prohibition; he denounced it as Puritanism and toryism. Why was prohibition Puritanism and toryism, but Catholic pressure against the spread of information on birth control proper? a liberal might ask. Ryan's answer was easy: birth control through artificial devices was an intrinsic evil; drinking whiskey was not. Restricting access to information on condoms deprived people of information to which they had no moral right in the first place. Keeping them from alcoholic drink deprived them of pleasure for an insufficient reason, unjustified in ethics. Many Protestant groups, of course, reversed this judgment in both cases. Liberals rejected state action in both. They knew nothing of intrinsic evil. Their standard was individual freedom.

An editorial in the *Nation* entitled "A Moral Pestilence" gave Ryan a chance to work out a full-dress exposition of his position. In its final issue of 1929, the *Nation* picked up a phrase from Rafael Cardinal Merry del Val, Secretary of the Congregation of the Holy Office, who had spoken of "that moral pestilence known as liberalism," and concluded that Catholic doctrine "is unalterably opposed to very nearly every tenet of the liberal creed." Henry Raymond Massey, the managing editor, invited Ryan to comment. Ryan replied briefly and privately, and then six months later, sent off a more extended reply—the most important statement on liberalism during his entire career.[25]

The ambiguity of the word "liberal," he said, caused part of the difficulty. An all-embracing liberalism, which went beyond politics and economics to include philosophy and religion, was unacceptable to any believing Catholic. Cardinal Merry del Val condemned this type of omnivorous liberalism as a pestilence: it denied or minimized the authority of God and of the Church over human thought and human conduct. The Church

[25] Ryan, "Catholicism and Liberalism," *Nation*, Aug. 6, 1930, pp. 150–154.

could not compromise with this liberalism without committing "intellectual and moral suicide."

Having eliminated this extreme question, Ryan came to grips with the more pertinent issue. If the *Nation* meant by "liberal" those who wanted freedom of opinion, of teaching, of speech, of writing, it was undoubtedly right that the Catholic Church did reject "unlimited freedom" in all these spheres. She denied the moral right of men to profess false opinions or to propagate doctrines contrary to the moral law and therefore to human welfare, for the "intellect and vocal organs are as subject to the moral law as any other human faculty." Even modern governments did not admit unlimited freedom of expression. Look at "Justice Holmes himself" in the espionage cases. Admittedly, drawing a line between reasonable and unreasonable freedom was difficult in practice. As a matter of prudence, the toleration of error might be preferable to the suppression of error by people who, by exceeding their authority, might suppress opinions that they disliked. The question of free speech presented complicated issues. As a practical matter, "The way in which it has been answered in the constitutions and statutes of our federal and State governments is quite satisfactory to American Catholics. They are never conspicuous in the groups that appear before Congress and State legislatures seeking diminution of this class of liberties. They perceive no conflict between their Catholicism and the traditional American policy."

Ryan declined to see a conflict within a Catholic who accepted "absolutism" in religion and "relativity" in politics and economics: "There is no contradiction, because the realities covered by these two classes of thought are different and the appropriate methods and instruments of knowledge are different. To demand or expect identical judgments concerning the knowableness of different kinds of realities is quite unreasonable."

The *Nation* disturbed Ryan by saying that a logical liberal "cannot be other than anti-Catholic." Why? Ryan asked. He himself rejected the creed of Christian Science without being anti-Christian Science; its followers did not attack his moral or civil rights. On the other hand, he was anti-Puritan because Puritanism *did* impose legal prohibition and threatened other liberties. No such threat was offered by the Catholic Church to an American liberal who did not accept her authority. "Why should he scold Catholics merely because they accept what he regards as tyrannical authority? Why can he not permit us to involve ourselves in what seems to him intellectual stultification? Or, does this brand of liberalism insist on saving men against their will from foolish loyalties? This seems to be the essence of toryism."

The task of establishing wider industrial and political justice was formidable enough to command the united efforts of all liberals, Ryan said in conclusion. "This cause will not be served by lecturing, threatening, and antagonizing Catholic economic and political liberals merely because they refuse to accept the anti-church variety of liberalism." Remember what happened in Europe, where prominent Catholics, lay and clerical, were compelled to throw in with economic and political reactionaries to protect their religious interests against doctrinaire liberals. "Should a similar alignment take place in our own beloved country," Ryan warned, "the blame will surely rest upon those liberals who will not concede to Catholics the right to profess and practice in their own way the religious loyalties which they cherish above everything else in life."

The *Nation*'s readers—at least those who wrote letters—were, for the most part, impressed by Ryan's lucidity but not convinced by his argument. One called it "a masterpiece of diplomacy and evasion." Another turned to Shakespeare for a comment on Ryan's conservatism in religion and liberalism in economics:

> . . . hot ice and wondrous strange snow.
> How shall we find the concord of this discord?

A third said that Ryan's argument was refuted by the strong Catholic undercurrent of intense opposition to liberalism in all its forms, specifically in matters of birth control, liberal divorce laws, and child-labor laws: "I know that Father Ryan on the last-mentioned question fought his church single-handed."[26]

Ryan's liberal associates looked upon his errant views tolerantly. After all, he was a Catholic, a Catholic priest at that, so he had to say some things out of line with his liberal convictions because he had to skirt the authority of the conservative Church. Remember what happened to Father McGlynn, who got himself into all kinds of ecclesiastical trouble after he supported Henry George. Ryan, on the other hand, saw a direct line from the fundamental principles of moral theology to the practical reforms that he recommended, and he viewed his reforms as more firmly based because they were anchored to fundamental principles.

The reality was, of course, more complex. Ryan was more the child of his secular age than he would acknowledge, and his position in an authoritarian Church was less of a burden than his liberal friends assumed. Ryan's

[26] Maurice del Bourgo, Ochunvay De Veldt, John Day, letters to editor, *ibid.*, Sept. 10, 1930, pp. 271–272.

own scholarly works—*A Living Wage* and *Distributive Justice* primarily—
confirmed the legitimacy of reform in terms of traditional Catholic social
thought. In talking to his Catholic audience, he fell easily into the language
of moral principles. This habit of talking made Ryan forget the profound
impact of the Populist and Progressive eras on his youthful years. In dealing with non-Catholic reformers, Ryan was free to attach himself to any
program that did not violate religious principles. With this group Ryan
talked tactics on an agreed item—How shall we get a child-labor amendment ratified?—without exploring sociological or theological premises.
Roger Baldwin and Ryan remained close friends at least in part because
Baldwin realized how little they agreed on fundamentals and how little it
mattered for the purposes they immediately shared. Baldwin was so committed to freedom of opinion that he did not recoil from Ryan's most
orthodox ideas, even in the area of religion. With other reformers, the
issue rarely came up, partly because of prudence, partly because of time.
Hence Ryan appeared to be one of them on their own terms. When he
struck out in disagreement, they sensed the restraint of an authoritarian
Church, implicit if not direct. Actually, what was happening was that
previously concealed routes of argument, the steps to a conclusion, were
becoming exposed. For his part Ryan felt surprise at their surprise. He saw
an unpopular stand—unpopular with the reformers, that is—as the obvious
corollary of first principles, just as his popular stands were corollaries of
first principles. He did not recognize how closely he approached secular
reformers by adopting their vocabulary and symbols. Ryan was always
more the progressive than he realized, and more the moral theologian than
his progressive friends realized.

The Washington professor enjoyed his occasional differences from his
friends, for it gave uniqueness to his position. While he ran with the reforming pack, he was indistinguishable from them, however much he
stood out among Catholics not committed to reform. When he stood apart
from the reformers, however, he stood alone, or at least so nearly alone
that he was quite visible from all sides. He esteemed the prestige that such
a position gave him: "It sometimes pays to assert one's independence and
individuality of opinion. It prevents people from taking too much for
granted and assuming that because you agree with them in some things
you are with them in everything."[27] Ryan did not care to be lost in the
liberal crowd.

[27] Ryan to Hard, May 23, 1927.

Fortunately for the cause of economic reform, the basic differences bedeviled the easy alliance between Ryan and his liberal friends no more than occasionally. He withdrew from the American Eugenics Society when it supported legislation encouraging birth control; this was the extreme case. With most other groups, the alliance held. The controversy stayed buried in the pages of the *Nation* and *Commonweal*, while the reformers—liberal, clerical, liberal-clerical, and liberal-anticlerical—battled reaction for limited goals.

As stimulating and frequent as Ryan's contacts with liberal and Protestant reformers were, his principal stake was among Catholics, especially the Catholic clergy. For this purpose his wide acquaintance outside the Church carried both advantage and disadvantage. For some, his activity in the general arena made him suspect as a Catholic spokesman, particularly when he defended causes still not accepted by most Catholics or by the majority of all Americans. In the decade of the thirties, this suspicion led to the term "Ryan Catholic," which, when set against "Roman Catholic," hinted at a departure from orthodoxy. Already in the twenties this note appeared, most strikingly in the kind of casual chatter among priests that never finds its way into print. On the other hand, recognition outside the Church added volume to his voice when he spoke within. Each appearance of his name in the press—testimony before a congressional committee, a statement on the Scopes trial, a stand against birth control—made him a more familiar figure, not to be dealt with lightly. As long as a falling-out with Church authorities did not disqualify him, his standing outside the Church buttressed his prestige within the Church.

The discouragements of reaction and the attacks on his own orthodoxy by prominent Catholics, primarily laymen, took their toll, however. Fifty-four years old in 1923, twenty-five years a priest, what did he have to show for a quarter of a century of the social gospel? The reaction against reaction had failed to appear, and the program closely associated with his name appeared more remote than it had at any time since well before the initial success of the campaign for the minimum wage.

In Ryan's troubles, his old student, Father O'Hara, now a member of the Oregon Wage Board, gave him balm by writing in *America* a long note on Ryan's published work: The foremost interpreter to America of Leo XIII's mind, a most effective teacher of the application of moral principles to industrial society, Ryan "has been a pathfinder who has been content to work with those who followed so that the trail which he has blazed has become a broad highway for the convenience of multitudes."[28] *Tower*, the student newspaper at Catholic University, picked up the praise and gave it local currency.[29] Even more significantly, Ryan's diocesan superior, Austin Dowling, Archbishop of St. Paul, preached at Ryan's silver jubilee mass in the St. Paul Cathedral. This attention to Ryan was the more striking because Dowling shared few of Ryan's progressive social and economic ideas. Writing to thank Dowling, Ryan noted criticisms and suspicions of his advanced, "even dangerous," ideas. He could not pretend that he was indifferent to these remarks: "I am concerned about my standing among my brother priests and before the ecclesiastical authorities. . . . [But] When my own archbishop thus honors me in his cathedral, 'I should worry' over the criticisms and misunderstandings of small minds."[30]

By the next year, William Hard, writing in *Hearst's International*, found Ryan composed. Interviewing him in Caldwell 319, Hard spoke of Ryan as "the top of a large heap of Catholic priests" who have had a part in the revival of the Christian voice against economic injustice, the "largest and deepest happening in the last ten years." Ryan, Hard reported, sat in his desk chair and smoked for hours, revealing no more of himself than Calvin Coolidge would: "So attached, so attacking, so full of conflict, so calm." A friendly picture emerged: Ryan is "plump, healthy, reasonably florid, nose not menacing but patiently stubborn; his eyes don't send forth fire but only quiet humor and quiet certainty. He is orthodox and devout, not even interested in modernism. In truth he is as simply and wholly a Catholic as any unlettered peasant girl in Connemara."[31]

Hard's article appeared in July, 1924. By October, Ryan's calmness was considerably shattered by the battle over the child-labor amendment.

The amendment, prior to its passage, seemed to be in line with Catholic thought, all the more since its sponsor, Senator Thomas J. Walsh, of Montana, was an active Catholic. The "Bishops' Program of Social Reconstruction" had opposed the continuous employment of children under the age of sixteen, and though the national pastoral letter of 1919 had not mentioned child labor specifically, it had been alert to the social problems surrounding labor and had recognized federal legislation as an appropriate remedy. At the 1923 convention of the National Council of Catholic

[28] Edwin V. O'Hara, "The Works of Dr. John A. Ryan," *America*, Feb. 24, 1923, pp. 448–449.

[29] *Tower*, March 9, 1923.

[30] Ryan to Austin Dowling, Sept. 26, 1923.

[31] Hard, "Father Ryan on Bread and Butter Morals," *Hearst's International*, July, 1924, pp. 52–53, 143–145.

Women, an NCWC subsidiary, a resolution favoring an amendment went through. The executive secretary, Agnes G. Regan, joined Father Ryan and Father McGowan in testifying before the House Judiciary Committee in support of the Walsh amendment. No Catholic appeared in opposition. Reviewing the year's legislative activity in 1924, Bishop Edmund F. Gibbons, of Albany, the chairman of the NCWC's Laws and Legislation Department, told the hierarchy that "no legislation of an antagonistic nature" had been enacted—a negative endorsement of the amendment, or at least an assurance that it did not positively offend Catholic principles.[32]

Once the amendment was submitted to the states for ratification, however, a deep division of Catholic opinion became apparent. Journals close to Ryan—the *N.C.W.C. Bulletin,* the *Catholic Charities Review,* and *Salesianum,* edited by Father Haas—supported the measure, while *America,* many diocesan papers, and the Catholic Central Verein opposed it. The opponents of the amendment feared that regulation of child labor could lead to the regulation of education, and once that possibility was raised, a multitude of horrors paraded past the imagination. The Central Verein, fearing a curb to parental authority, wanted regulation to come from state governments, and it put a challenge directly to the NAM and the United States Chamber of Commerce to show the sincerity of their objections to the amendment by actively supporting state laws. James A. Emery, general counsel of the NAM, himself a Catholic, led the fight for his organization, raising the specter of socialism as his principal weapon and not helping conspicuously in passing state laws.

A storm within the Church was obviously brewing. Ryan, on Bishop Muldoon's advice, stayed on the sidelines. Unsigned editorials in the *N.C.W.C. Bulletin* and the *Catholic Charities Review* could be attributed to him or to Father McGowan, but nothing appeared over their own names. Then, on October 1, 1924, Cardinal O'Connell recommended to all the pastors in the Archdiocese of Boston that they point out to their flocks the dangers in the amendment and the urgency of registering so that they could vote "No" in the advisory referendum scheduled for the following November. As the campaign grew hot in Massachusetts, Ryan and McGowan finally wrote off newsletters "correcting the misstatements" of the opposition. When they reached Boston, the Cardinal sent his assistant, Monsignor Michael J. Splaine, to NCWC headquarters to raise a ruckus. When he arrived, he was able to talk faster than Agnes Regan, but Ryan

---

[32] Vincent A. McQuade, *The American Catholic Attitude on Child Labor Since 1891* (Washington, D.C., 1938), pp. 79–100.

told him bluntly that Splaine's own propaganda had been Ryan's target, specifically the charge that socialists had written the amendment.[33]

At the same time, the cardinal was mailing off letters of protest to episcopal chairmen and vice chairmen of appropriate NCWC committees. He condemned the "nefarious and bolshevik amendment," and he warned that unless something was done quickly to change the tune of those in Washington so close to the "dangerous influences at the Capitol," Rome would be asking for explanations. He suggested that proponents of the amendment in the NCWC were angling for jobs in the government.[34] O'Connell finally got around to writing to Archbishop Curley, the hand-written note of a riled man: It was time for Ryan to be restrained from his "public activities and irresponsible communications," he said. "Why are all these people busying themselves attending dinners, making dubious addresses, talking before Committees, etc. It is all wrong and all hurting the University and the Catholic position which is certainly not theirs. Something ought to be done soon. I know that Your Grace will not hesitate."[35] Curley replied immediately that he would look into the situation, then sent Ryan a copy of O'Connell's letter.

This was an unhappy turn in Ryan's contacts with the Archbishop of Boston. Three years before when O'Connell had issued a pastoral defending labor's right to organize, Ryan had offered his warm congratulations. In replying, the cardinal had paid tribute to Ryan's own valiant work in the labor field. Now the mutual admiration disappeared. Ryan promptly caught a train for Baltimore, taking along a copy of his 1921 letter of congratulations to show Curley that the current trouble was not of Ryan's making.

Before Curley could answer O'Connell fully, 100,000 reprints of *Labor*, the journal of the railway brotherhoods, appeared in Boston. The reprints, containing a pro-amendment article by Ryan, showed up on the streets just a week before the advisory referendum on the amendment in Massachusetts. By now the fires of episcopal temper were well stoked. O'Connell again wrote to Curley:

Yesterday this city was flooded with the nefarious and false views on the amendment supposed falsely to be in the interest of the child, sent out from Washington by sly methods in which he seems to be an expert, by Rev. J. A. Ryan, Professor in the University.

[33] Ryan to Peter J. Muldoon, Oct. 23, 1924.
[34] Edward F. Gibbons to James H. Ryan, copy, Oct. 23, 1924.
[35] William Cardinal O'Connell to Curley, copy, Oct. 24, 1924.

From this vicious propaganda it is made to appear that we Catholics who oppose this soviet legislation are incapable of reading plain English and making correct logical conclusions—a thing which it would appear is the special privilege of J. A. Ryan, Jane Addams and a few more socialistic teachers and writers.

These same views are again neatly summarized on a pink slip distributed broadcast among our people—again the queer crooked views of J. A. Ryan, who undoubtedly knew that his doctrines and radical point of view would be made use of to offset the position taken by me and all my priests here during these trying days before the voting.

Your Grace, there is only one thing left for us to do—either abandon weakly our duty and turn it over into the hands of the Ryans, the Kerbys and the Regans, who have undoubtedly been inoculated with the radical germ by too close affiliation with bureaucrats and jobbers there in Washington, or demand that these servants of the University and paid agents of the N.C.W.C. either cease their crooked and false activities or leave the University and the offices of the N.C.W.C.

For a long time this weak sort of thing, by which the authority of the hierarchy has been too liberally and unwarrantedly entrusted to hands and brains unfit to be entrusted with so sacred a duty as that of the hierarchy alone, has been all too evident. In the strongest possible terms I protest against it. Evidently the Rector is either powerless or supine. Else long ago this would have been put in its place. Therefore with the fullest confidence in Your Grace I now repeat my request that these professors and paid agents be firmly reminded of their duty as Catholics. I am Your Grace's humble servant, . . .[36]

A week went by before Curley made his reply. It sorted out responsibility—Miss Regan came under the authority of Archbishop Edward J. Hanna of San Francisco. It excused the less guilty—James Ryan and Kerby had always done good work. It denied the guilt of the more guilty—John Ryan never had a thought of merely being in opposition, especially to the senior American cardinal-archbishop; he had taken his stand before the campaign in Massachusetts had developed. Curley was defending no one, he said, but he wanted to set the issue in proper proportion, and of course "Your Eminence wants to be fair and just."[37]

While the smoke poured from Boston, Ryan wrote mournfully to his family of the possibility of being shipped off to a small parish in western Maryland. The fear was a rhetorical one, really: Curley was standing fast; anyway, if Ryan were fired from the NCWC, he would have returned to the jurisdiction of the Archdiocese of St. Paul.

[36] O'Connell to Curley, copy, Nov. 2, 1924.
[37] Curley to O'Connell, Nov. 10, 1924, Archives of the Archdiocese of Baltimore.

The election over, O'Connell let the matter drop. The amendment had lost overwhelmingly in Massachusetts. He wanted to be indulgent to the university, he said, yet he had no doubt that the professors should speak more discreetly. If the whole matter made them more circumspect, much would have been gained. As for Ryan: "There is also no doubt that Rev. J. A. Ryan is steering a slippery road. His whole trend is toward a socialistic tendency, and I think he takes himself too seriously."[38]

So the matter ended officially. Thereafter Ryan's name rarely appeared in the *Pilot*, Boston's diocesan paper, and for the next twenty years he spoke in the archdiocese only twice. When asked, he was not willing to apply for permission to enter the archdiocese as a priest.

Archbishop Curley's role in the controversy was decisive. He had sided enough with O'Connell so as not to turn the Boston cardinal against him too—that had happened to the rector, Bishop Shahan—but, as chancellor of the university, he had conceded nothing to outside pressure on the expression of views by professors. He issued no ringing statement. He appealed to no fundamental principles. Yet by tactical skill he parried a thrust until it lost its drive.

When the calm became noticeable, Curley spoke up. On February 19, 1925, he addressed the Washington chapter of the International Federation of Catholic Alumnae, and condemned the centralization of power implicit in the child-labor amendment. Speaking after Ryan had bid for their support, Curley adverted to his difference with Dr. Ryan as testimony of Catholic freedom of thought. He added his opinion that no one was better qualified than Ryan to speak on labor matters; Ryan's writings had brought more credit to Catholic University than those of anybody else. Ryan was at liberty to disagree on the matter of the amendment or on any other matter, Curley said; the archbishop was delighted to have such an opponent.[39] Blunt, curt, sharp-tongued, witty, Archbishop Curley used the prestige of his position as a primary defense of academic freedom at the university. Later on, he and John Ryan would have a falling-out, and Ryan would feel the point of Curley's rapier tongue. But until their deaths, and especially in their last years, gruff bluntness and affection for the workingman generally held them in rapport.

Ryan managed to stir Catholic indignation quite as readily by his peace activities as by his labor stands. He did not go looking for trouble. He had

[38] O'Connell to Curley, copy, Nov. 12, 1924, Archives of the Archdiocese of Baltimore.
[39] Baltimore *Catholic Review*, Feb. 28, 1925.

great sympathy for Senator Burton K. Wheeler's resolution in 1927 asking the Senate Foreign Relations Committee to investigate American capital holdings abroad, but he refused to give any public support to the measure. It would be going too far afield from the SAD's function, and he did not care to get involved personally.[40] Still, trouble came uninvited. When he appeared before the House Naval Affairs Committee in 1928 as a representative of the Church Peace Union, an interdenominational group, to oppose the construction of new capital ships, the Buffalo *Catholic Union and Times* demanded to know "How long, O! Lord!" would Catholics have to put up with "the intrusion of Father Burke and Dr. Ryan into political questions in the discussion of which they have no authority to speak except for their own ill-informed and ill-considered convictions?" On the basis of an article in *America* on April 7, 1928, the Dubuque *Daily Tribune* implied that British pacifists were "lavishly" financing Ryan's attempts to block any increase in the American Navy. The San Francisco *Leader* warned CU to watch its step—"The funds for its maintenance do not come from the First Lord of the Admiralty."[41]

Ryan reddened at these attacks, especially when they questioned his patriotism. He called the *America* article "irresponsible and reckless," its author a disgruntled former NCWC employee. He told the Dubuque *Tribune* that if its association with professional patriots and heresy hunters were not so serious, it would be "deliciously ironical"—a sly dig at the pro-German sentiment that had existed in the Archdiocese of Dubuque during the war.[42]

The battle for peace went on tirelessly. Curley continued to stand solidly behind Ryan's job at the university. An editorial in the Baltimore *Catholic Review* in 1926 had set the matter straight: Ryan spoke for himself, not for the university. "The Catholic University does not gag Dr. Ryan. Neither does the Catholic Church gag its members. They are at liberty to express their individual opinions on a million and one topics."[43] With this backing, Ryan continued his efforts for peace, organizing Catholics into groups, working with existing Protestant groups to sell the United States on disarmament and world cooperation for peace.

Despite widespread dissent from his views, Ryan never faced a real

---

[40] Ryan to Benjamin C. Marsh, Oct. 20, 1927.
[41] Buffalo *Catholic Union and Times*, March 1, 1928; Dubuque *Daily American Tribune*, April 11, 1928; San Francisco *Leader*, March 13, 1928.
[42] Ryan, letter to editor, *Daily American Tribune*, April 25, 1928.
[43] Editor's note, *Catholic Review*, Oct. 22, 1926.

challenge within the Church after the O'Connell incident. He could count on several layers of insulation. In general, the hierarchical structure of the Church protected priests from the protests of individual laymen. The Catholic pulpit enjoyed a special position vis-à-vis the pew, for a priest, given his assignment by the bishop of his diocese without consultation with the laity, felt an independence from congregational pressures not shared by Protestant and Jewish clergymen. At the university, where Ryan did not regularly come into contact with prominent wealthy laymen who objected to his views, he received additional insulation. When laymen—or clergymen—did attempt to bring financial pressure on the university to curb or to dismiss the professor of moral theology, Bishop Shahan and subsequent rectors, backed by the chancellor, steadfastly refused to buckle. At the NCWC, different forces were operating. The NCWC was an operating committee of the hierarchy, continuously responsible to it. A spokesman who contradicted the mind of the hierarchy could have been dismissed as readily as an attorney who failed to represent his client. Yet even when Ryan persisted in his public support of the child-labor amendment at a time when no bishop was taking a comparable public stand, he stayed on.

Several factors made Father Ryan's tenure at the Social Action Department secure. For one thing, Ryan was a less conspicuous figure than a full-length biography focused on him suggests. He was the director of one of six departments at the NCWC. Directly above him were the episcopal chairman and vice-chairman of his department. Above them was the administrative committee of bishops. Their agent, the general secretary, was also Ryan's superior. In this bureaucratic maze, Ryan did not readily stand out. As late as December, 1930, he conceded that plenty of graduates of Catholic colleges had never even heard of him. Less prominent than he appeared later, he made a less vulnerable target. Furthermore, the social principles that he propounded fell within the protection of *Rerum novarum*, if not explicitly, at least by arguable implication. Thus they stayed clear of censurable areas, and the consoling assurance of Canon Fleming in 1911 proved to be an accurate prophecy.

Ryan also avoided needless provocation by careful rhetoric. In his formal papers he used the traditional vocabulary of Catholic theologians, and in his speeches and articles he normally stayed clear of belligerent phrasing, confident that even an unpopular statement avoided giving offense if phrased precisely, moderately, courteously. An old student from St. Paul, Father P. A. Forde, of Lincoln, Nebraska, used to write to him once in a while—delightful, outrageous letters, full of strong views, clerical small talk, witty commentary, and especially rich in the gossipy, iconoclastic chatter that comes so easily to old friends. Ryan's replies went back as sober as Sunday-school sermons. He acknowledged his delight in Forde's indiscretion, but gave him none to repay it. Cautious in what he said, he also avoided forums likely to produce awkward situations. His exile from the Archdiocese of Boston was voluntary, not a decision of Cardinal O'Connell. In part Ryan's decision came from pride—he would not suffer a rebuff. In part, though, it came from prudence—every occasion would invite an incident, especially since it was non-Catholic groups that invited Ryan to appear. (Catholic groups, knowing the mind of the chancery, held off.) Everywhere else, he applied for episcopal permission before he made a public appearance in a diocese; in a delicate situation, he even cleared his engagement with the local pastor.

Actually, excessive caution was not necessary, for his relations with members of the hierarchy were quite friendly, friendlier with some than with others, to be sure, but generally cordial enough to avoid any preoccupation with averting their wrath. Archbishop McNicholas invariably asked Ryan to stay at the episcopal residence whenever he was in Cincinnati. Patrick Cardinal Hayes of New York was as cordial as Cardinal O'Connell was cool. Bishop Gibbons of Albany had especially warm regard for Ryan's work; Bishop Francis C. Kelly of Oklahoma City was friendly. Archbishop Sebastian G. Messner of Milwaukee invited Ryan to address the seminarians of his archdiocese, a revealing assignment because of the presumed receptiveness of seminarians. Bishop James A. Griffin of the Diocese of Springfield, Illinois, said that Ryan's presence at a diocesan industrial conference ensured its success. Far from feeling hostility from the bishops, Ryan felt substantial support, and especially from those who had the most intimate association with him: Curley and Shahan at the university, Muldoon and (to a lesser extent) Thomas F. Lillis of Kansas City at the NCWC, Dowling and later John G. Murray in St. Paul.

Dr. Ryan had one brush with Rome, but it was minor and harmless. It was caused not by something Ryan had said but by where he had said it. In December, 1926, Cardinal Merry del Val wrote to the Apostolic Delegate in Washington, Archbishop Pietro Fumasoni-Biondi, expressing "wonder and surprise" that Ryan had spoken at a forum of the Young Men's Christian Association in Brooklyn. At the time the YMCA was proselytizing in Italy, and its spokesmen used the occasion of Ryan's address to demonstrate the friendlier attitude toward the YMCA among Catholics in the United States. The delegate asked for an explanation. Ryan's explanation—that the meeting had been a forum and not a religious service and that his remarks in no way compromised Catholic principles—was forwarded to Rome through the appropriate channels.[44]

Again invited to a YMCA forum, Ryan consulted Curley, who in turn checked with Fumasoni-Biondi. The delegate counseled against the appearance, for the Holy Office had not yet received the explanation of Ryan's earlier appearance. In answering Curley, Fumasoni-Biondi affirmed his "very highest esteem and admiration" for Ryan's ability to explain the doctrines of the Church and for the "dignity" with which his apostolic work had been done. While consulting the delegate, Curley wrote back to Ryan, jokingly and seriously: Don't go to the YMCA affair now, not when you "have been fortunate enough to fall into the dreadful hands of the Holy Office." Misunderstanding in Rome might lead to a suspension, and there was no use looking for trouble. "It is bad enough to have the Cardinal of Boston against you," Curley went on. "He might one day prevent your being appointed Archbishop of St. Paul." Ryan had Curley's "congratulatory sympathy" for being the first of the staff at CU "to form connection with the Holy Office."[45]

Cardinal Merry del Val received Ryan's reply to the Holy Office "with pleasure and satisfaction," and the incident closed.[46] This was the only disciplinary "note of interrogation," as Curley phrased it, that was ever raised about Ryan.

However impatient Ryan may have been for the spread of liberal economic ideas among the higher churchmen, he certainly did not fear their wrath. Hard's article on Ryan in *Hearst's International* reviewed a stereotype familiar then and now:[47] ". . . while to many of my fellow-Protestants it somehow seems that Father Ryan must be engaged in some sort of heroic combat with his ecclesiastical superiors, the fact is that no such combat exists and that while there is no obligation upon any Catholic to swallow and believe every word got out by the Social Action Department of the National Catholic Welfare Conference there is equally a strong

[44] Pietro Fumasoni-Biondi to Ryan, Dec. 29, 1926; Ryan to Fumasoni-Biondi, Jan. 3, 1927.

[45] Curley to Fumasoni-Biondi, Jan. 19, 1927; Fumasoni-Biondi to Curley, Jan. 20, 1927, Archives of the Archdiocese of Baltimore; Curley to Ryan, Jan. 19, 1927.

[46] Fumasoni-Biondi to Ryan, March 7, 1927.

[47] See, e.g., Eric Goldman, *Rendezvous with Destiny* (New York, 1952), p. 111.

presumption that the teachings of the department are consistent with orthodoxy in so far as orthodoxy is understood by the body of the Roman Catholic bishops in the United States."[48] Ryan himself certainly felt no undue apprehension about his position.

Actually, a different danger was more real: the danger of talking always to the already converted. The tone of *Commonweal* appealed to people with views like Ryan's; the *Catholic Charities Review* went principally to clerical and lay social workers of various capacities and interests, but all were probably close enough to social problems to be familiar with Ryan's ideas; the people who read the SAD section of the *N.C.W.C. Bulletin* probably already agreed with it—the others did not bother to read it. People who attended the Catholic Conference on Industrial Problems, and the people who addressed them, were drawn from so much the same mold that occasionally a bishop complained. Yet, even the converted frequently lacked information: groups filled by a sense of social justice might still not be able to apply general principles to specific problems in the 1920's. Does a man's right to a living wage extend to a right to organize into unions? into a closed shop? using the boycott as a weapon? with violence? Ryan felt most strongly that adequate moral judgments depended upon knowledge of industrial conditions; they could not be deduced from first principles.[49] Learn through experience, he told the clergy; a single important labor dispute would teach the essentials. As Ryan made the rounds of public lectures, industrial seminars and conferences, diocesan social-action studies, he tried to bring this combination of first principles and specific knowledge of contemporary conditions into a new focus. He stood out among others doing similar work because of three interacting facts: His academic position and his own books permitted him to speak with the authority of knowledge. The NCWC opened up occasions for speaking with the prestige of an official spokesman. His own vigor let few opportunities pass.

A friend of liberal reformers, Protestant leaders, and American Catholics, Ryan ran the danger that each group might embarrass him with the others. His role, to say nothing of his peace of mind, depended on keeping all three groups on speaking terms. His relations with liberals had been badly charred in Mexican fires. His confidence in Protestants was shaken in the election of 1928.

[48] Hard, "Father Ryan on Bread and Butter Morals," *loc. cit.*
[49] Ryan, "Labor Day Reflections for Priests," *Ecclesiastical Review*, September, 1928, pp. 225–237.

Prohibition & the
Campaign of 1928

THE ELECTION OF
1928 bruised American Catholics by attacking their religion
and their civic loyalty. For Father Ryan the campaign
yielded bitterness and, the memory of the Mexican issue still
fresh, new distrusts. In the trouble over Mexico, liberals had
faltered. In the 1928 election, Protestant leaders, indeed
ministers of the gospel, effectively poisoned the minds of
their fellow citizens in order to defeat Governor Alfred E.
Smith, the Democratic candidate. Such was Ryan's view,
whatever were the facts. He came out of the campaign with
a sense of emptiness beyond partisan disappointment. Could
Protestant Americans ever again look squarely into the eyes
of their Catholic neighbors? Could Catholics ever again feel
comfortable among neighbors that had repudiated them?

Much of the oratory of the campaign dealt with two
issues, not intrinsically related: prohibition, and the relations
between church and state. Smith, both wet and Catholic,
could not avoid dealing with these issues. On both Ryan had
taken controversial public stands, and in the course of the
campaign, his ideas cropped up frequently.

Initially well disposed to regulating drinking, Ryan had

in 1916 approved of prohibition "whenever it can be reasonably enforced."[1] After the Anti-Saloon League lobbied the Eighteenth Amendment through Congress, Ryan had questioned the need for national legislation, condemning the "undemocratic paternalism" and "superior tyranny" implicit in forcing abstention on states that did not want it. Once the amendment was ratified in January, 1919, however, Ryan prepared himself to wait and see if it would work. Even though the Volstead Act forbade possession of liquor for personal use—"a pernicious mixture of impertinent paternalism and State omnipotence"—he held his peace, publicly at least.[2]

In 1922, after a year of the Volstead Act, Ryan dropped a hint worth filing away for future use. Without specific reference to prohibition, he noted that civil law normally binds man's conscience because of the moral authority of the state; but "when the majority of the people disregard the law to such an extent and in such a way that its observance by a minority becomes detrimental to the State, it ceases to bind the individual citizen."[3] This doctrine contained dry comfort for thirsty moralists, as Ryan showed in commenting on a "conscience case" in the April, 1924, *Ecclesiastical Review*. The question was: Are prohibition laws "purely penal"? (A "purely penal" law carries no moral weight beyond the willingness to pay the penalty set if one is caught violating the law.) Admitting that moralists differed, Ryan still insisted that the state's moral authority permitted the legislature to use discretion in choosing ways of promoting the common good. Once the state has acted, the burden of showing a clear balance of evil over good rested with those who challenged the statute. Ryan believed that the Volstead Act's main purpose—to abolish the commercial manufacture and sale of liquor—was morally valid, the provisions directed to this end morally binding. In Ryan's opinion, a bootlegger who refused to discontinue his trade could not receive the sacrament of penance. The following month, frankly scandalized by the flagrant violations of the act, with thousands of Catholics prominent as offenders, he laid out the same principles in blunt layman's language for the *N.C.W.C. Bulletin*.[4]

[1] Ryan, "A Catholic Economist and Theologian on Prohibition," *Fortnightly Review*, April 1, 1916, pp. 100–101.

[2] Editor, "Undemocratic Prohibition," *Catholic Charities Review*, April, 1918, pp. 101–103; Editor, "Prohibition Tyranny," *ibid.*, February, 1919, pp. 40–41.

[3] Ryan, *The State and the Church*, pp. 258–259.

[4] Ryan, "Are Our Prohibition Laws 'Purely Penal'?" *Ecclesiastical Review*, April, 1924, pp. 404–411; "Peacetime Patriotism and Law Observance," *N.C.W.C. Bulletin*, May, 1924, pp. 9–10.

A year later Dr. Ryan conceded in the *Catholic World* for November, 1925, that if the Volstead Act was more breached than observed, the duty to obey it lost force. Therefore, a decisive judgment on the morality of the act depended on the facts about its enforcement. Until facts were available, the Eighteenth Amendment enjoyed a presumption of validity. A disgruntled citizen should work to change it by due process of law, not stooping "to accomplish by indirection that which he has not the courage to do directly."[5]

Still the matter would not quit Ryan's mind. Annoyed first by the righteousness of the Anti-Saloon Leaguers and then by the moral nihilism of reckless wets, he wrote the lead article for the very next issue of the *Catholic World*. He wanted to open the whole subject for debate in the light of Catholic moral principles. He hoped for agreement if he was right, and "systematic and reasoned argument" if he was wrong. For his "sole concern" was to discover the truth. The truth as he saw it consoled neither side. The drys were told that the manufacture, possession, and transportation of liquor for private use were lawful in conscience, regardless of the tyrannical provisions of the Volstead Act. The wets were reminded that the prohibition of manufacture and transportation of liquor for sale was morally binding. In short, if you want liquor, you make it yourself or find a friend who will give it to you.[6]

The initial reaction to this article pleased him. Extremists on both sides, he told a Paulist in New Jersey a bit proudly, disliked it.[7] This report was probably based on clerical conversation in the refectory at Caldwell Hall, where extremists were not hard to come by, for the following month Ryan moaned to Father Philip H. Burkett, S.J., of Georgetown University, that the *Catholic World* had not received a single letter about his article from a priest—no one outraged, no one delighted. "This confirms the impression . . . that priests are not intellectually alive, or intellectually courageous on this subject," he added dejectedly. Ryan urged Burkett into the fight. Burkett was willing, and James M. Gillis, C.S.P., the editor of the *Catholic World*, was prepared to publish what Burkett wrote. But Burkett's superiors held him off the topic.[8] A jolly controversy never developed.

[5] Ryan, "Prohibition, Pro and Con," *Catholic World*, April, 1925, pp. 31–35.
[6] Ryan, "Do the Prohibition Laws Bind in Conscience?" *Catholic World*, May, 1925, pp. 145–157.
[7] Ryan to Robert A. Skinner, May 26, 1925.
[8] Ryan to Philip H. Burkett, June 9, 1925; Burkett to Ryan, April 5, 1927.

Ryan's argument offered little attraction to an opponent. For a layman it was densely theological, couched in the vocabulary of Ryan's profession. To others similarly trained, Ryan was a formidable opponent. Perhaps that would not have discouraged most other theologians: the disputes in the *Ecclesiastical Review* showed a taste for precision and for bickering. Yet few felt any special competence in this field. Any good moral theologian could handle principles, but no one could say for sure just which principles were relevant.

To those anxious to see, the facts proclaiming the failure of prohibition became overpowering by mid-decade. The Treasury agents appointed to enforce the law won their jobs through political influence. For every Izzy Einstein, the fabled master of disguise responsible for hundreds of convictions, there were, in the words of an assistant attorney general in charge of prohibition cases, hundreds "as devoid of honesty and integrity as the bootlegging fraternity." In the first four years of the Bureau of Prohibition, 141 agents were jailed for cooperating with the lawbreakers whom they were pursuing. With thousands of miles of coastline and border to patrol, even honest Treasury agents could not turn back the massive waves of liquor entering from Canada and Mexico, from the Atlantic and the Pacific. Inside the country moonshiners—at every level of society—made their own beverages. The failure of law enforcement was creating a national scandal. Bootleggers created their own empires, defying police, building up private armies, corrupting politics. Liquor, before 1919 a millstone of the workingman, now became an amusement of women and adolescents, and only a willing eye could see the speakeasy as an improvement over the saloon. The "era of clear thinking and clean living" so confidently promised by the Anti-Saloon Leaguers in New York became murky and dirty.[9]

For Ryan six years of the experiment were enough. By March, 1926, he predicted that the liquor traffic would get more and more out of hand until laws conformed to human nature and common sense.[10] Later that spring he backed away from his stand in the *Catholic World* the previous year: He was no longer convinced that regulation of the liquor traffic under the Volstead Act was morally valid. The state had a choice of means in accomplishing legitimate goals—true enough. Yet in choosing means, the state might err, and failures of enforcement supplied abundant evidence that the state had erred in dealing with the evil of drink by means

[9] Herbert Asbury, *The Great Illusion* (Garden City, 1950), pp. 154–155, 176–178.
[10] Ryan to William Frederick Bigelow, March 27, 1926.

of absolute prohibition. He looked forward to repeal, the sooner the better.[11] That fall, as Ryan worked over his *Catholic World* article for publication in *Declining Liberty and Other Papers*, a collection of his essays that appeared in 1927, he stripped the Volstead Act and even the Eighteenth Amendment itself of any shred of moral standing:

Six years of experience with the legislation have changed its moral aspect. There is now grave reason to doubt that the conditions necessary to justify this degree of interference with individual rights really existed. The degree of success which attended state and local prohibition prior to the national legislation, the degree of success achieved by the Quebec system [state-owned dispensaries], and the degree of failure which has characterized the attempt to enforce national prohibition, constitute sufficient evidence to warrant a reasonable and prudent man in holding that the Eighteenth Amendment was an unnecessary, unwise and unjust enactment.[12]

However much a failure, prohibition showed few signs of succumbing to repeal. Walter Lippmann suggested in *Harper's* that repeal could be accomplished by indirection and avoidance: perhaps a decision in the Supreme Court "by the proper reasoning" to find that states were not violating the Constitution even if they became most permissive in tolerating alcohol content in beverages made for sale, perhaps "orderly disobedience . . . open, frankly avowed, and in conformity with the general sense of what is reasonable."[13] The realist in Ryan led him to approve Lippmann's idea emphatically.[14] His rebuke to those who stooped to accomplish by indirection that which would not yield to direct political action had outlived its usefulness. The reversal in Ryan's views was the measure of how much he had changed in those two years.

Father Ryan, not the introspective sort aware of the complexity of motivation, least of all his own, had no difficulty in explaining the change. Two years earlier he had said that his position on prohibition might be questioned; now "subsequent deeper consideration and wider observation of the working of this legislation" led to a new view.[15]

Yet undoubtedly the eye that looked more deeply and widely was sensitive to flashes of evidence that showed prohibition to be a failure.

[11] Ryan to Norman B. Nash, May 20, 1926.
[12] Ryan, *Declining Liberty and Other Papers*, pp. 57–58.
[13] Walter Lippmann, "Our Predicament Under the Eighteenth Amendment," *Harper's*, December, 1926, p. 56.
[14] Ryan to Thomas F. Maher, March 19, 1927.
[15] Ryan to William L. Hornsby, Feb. 23, 1927.

For one thing, Ryan himself, though moderate in his drinking habits, was not a total abstainer. Furthermore, he felt a violent distaste for the drys. In repudiating the Eighteenth Amendment, Ryan was disengaging himself from an uncomfortable, awkward alliance with the Baptist and Methodist Churches, groups not traditionally well disposed toward Catholics. Finally, Ryan as theologian felt the urgency of reweighing both the Volstead Act and the Eighteenth Amendment. The extensive violation of the civil law created in the moral order a grave burden of sin, ranging from serious sin in the case of bootleggers who understood the moral implications of their act to venial sin for their occasional patron. To such an impressive quantity of sin Ryan as a priest could not be indifferent. The theologian could not attack the problem of guilt by denying that sin was really sin. Yet faced with numerous violations of the civil law, a responsible moral theologian had to be careful in assessing the moral guilt of specific civil violations. Catholics looked to their Church for authoritative guidance in making their decisions of conscience on moral questions. The moral limits of civil authority presented a problem for the moral theologian. Dr. Ryan was professor of moral theology at the Catholic University of America. His words carried weight, not decisive weight perhaps, but respect, owing to his training and position. Hence the pressure to speak responsibly and precisely.

A valid act should promote the general welfare, should ordinarily enjoy general assent, and should be susceptible of adequate enforcement. When, as Ryan saw it, prohibition failed on all three counts, his position demanded that he repudiate the law explicitly, whatever protest this judgment might provoke from prohibitionists.

Whatever the cause of Ryan's change of views, the fact of the change prepared him to share in the arguments of the election, for the liquor issue was front and center in the presidential campaign of 1928.[16]

Father Ryan's book, *The State and the Church*, warmly debated, then and now, by Catholics as well as by Protestants and others, also projected him into the 1928 campaign. To those who feared that Catholics wanted a union of the church and state in the United States, his commentary on Leo XIII's encyclical *Immortale Dei* conveyed the idea that the union of church and state was indeed sound Catholic doctrine. At best, the issue, bedded deeply in both moral theology and canon law, did not lend itself

[16] A substantial part of the remainder of this chapter appeared, in somewhat different form, as "When Last a Catholic Ran for President," in *Social Order*, May, 1960, pp. 198–210.

to glib discussion. As the campaign got under way, nice distinctions were lost in a political clamor far removed from the atmosphere of a theological seminar.

Ryan entered the debate in March, 1927, as a result of a speech by Albert C. Dieffenbach at the West Side Unitarian Church Forum in New York City. The editor of the Unitarian *Christian Register*, Dieffenbach used *The State and the Church* as his text to outline his concern over the "difficult and delicate political problem" created by the Catholic view of church and state. With the prospect of Governor Smith's nomination in mind, he expressed alarm over Ryan's statement that the Constitution could be changed and that " 'non-Catholic sects may decline to such a point that the political proscription of them may become possible and expedient.' "[17]

Ryan could not let Dieffenbach's comments pass unnoted, for the Boston editor had clearly scored some strong points. Yet, though strong, they were answerable, Ryan thought, if set in their proper context. His reply took the form of a letter to the New York *World*, largely statements from his book. In theory the state should officially recognize the true religion, he said. At the same time, the unconditional rigor of the principle of the union of church and state had application only to genuinely Catholic states. Certainly the principle "has nothing to do with our country." As for the proscription of Protestant sects, Ryan explained, that passage was written as "a possible extreme difficulty." He "wanted to state the Catholic doctrine in all its rigor in order to forestall the charge of minimizing." At the same time, Ryan added, both in his book and in his reply to Dieffenbach:

While all this is very true in logic and in theory, the event of its practical realization in any state or country is so remote in time and in probability that no practical man will let it disturb his equanimity or affect his attitude toward those who differ from him in religious faith.[18]

Shortly after this incident, Ryan noted that the *Christian Century*, the outstanding "undenominational" Protestant journal, observed in an editorial that it had no fear of a Catholic majority, partly because such a majority was not imminent, but even more because Catholic political action in modern times had proved more modern than Catholic:

[17] Albert C. Dieffenbach, "A Roman Catholic for President?" *Christian Register*, Jan. 20, 1927, pp. 45–49.
[18] New York *World*, March 28, 1927.

All the Protestant opposition to the election of Catholics to high office will never be half such an insurmountable obstacle to the realization of such a program of intolerance as Father Ryan outlines as the resistance of Catholics to it if they ever got completely into power. Let the church declare what she will about the program of proscription which she would put into operation if she could—she can't, and she never can. And the chief reason is that American Catholics themselves would never stand for it. Father Ryan himself would not.[19]

Pleased to see the *Christian Century* adopt this commonsense approach, Ryan wrote to one of the editors of the journal, pressing his claim from Father Pohle and citing the additional authority of Viktor Cathrein and of Cardinal Newman's "Letter to the Duke of Norfolk," a reply to William E. Gladstone's attack upon the Church after the Vatican Council.[20]

The issue reached a larger audience soon thereafter. Writing in the April, 1927, *Atlantic Monthly*, Charles C. Marshall, a prominent New York lawyer, addressed "An Open Letter to the Honorable Alfred E. Smith." The letter covered a multitude of issues—the Church in Mexico, annulment and divorce, education—but finally came to the point where it asked how Smith could square his Catholic—Roman Catholic, Marshall always called it—allegiance with the obligations he sought to undertake as President under the United States Constitution. How could Smith live at once with the Constitution's prohibition of an established religion, its insistence on holding in equal favor different kinds of religion or no religion, with the statement of Leo XIII: "It is not lawful for the State, any more than for the individual, either to disregard all religious duties or to hold in equal favor different kinds of religion"?

Marshall did not deny Catholics the right to hold these views. Let them hold to their convictions, he said. "We are satisfied if they will but concede that these claims, unless modified and historically redressed, precipitate an inevitable conflict between the Roman Catholic Church and the American State irreconcilable with domestic peace." Smith had an alternative course: he might enter a disclaimer of these views imputed to the Church; nothing would be "of greater satisfaction to those of your fellow citizens who hesitate in their endorsement of your candidacy because of the religious issues involved. . . ."[21]

[19] Editorial, *Christian Century*, April 14, 1927, pp. 456–457.
[20] Ryan to Paul Hutchinson, April 11, 1927.
[21] Charles C. Marshall, "An Open Letter to the Honorable Alfred E. Smith," *Atlantic Monthly*, April, 1927, pp. 540–549.

Smith took up the challenge with considerable reluctance. He knew little of canon law, less of dogmatic theology, and he feared that any explanation would look to Catholics like an apology. All he knew was that he was as American as the Fulton Fish Market and as Catholic as Cardinal Hayes. For the rest, his whole record as a public servant supplied the answer to Marshall's conundrum. But silence would not do. Franklin D. Roosevelt warned him from Warm Springs Georgia, that the challenge, unanswered, would crop up elsewhere and press insistently for a reply: ". . . the boldest, and, therefore, the most effective way" was for Smith to answer the charge himself. Smith's closest political advisers, Belle Moskowitz and Judge Joseph H. Proskauer, agreed. So Smith took on the distasteful job, with a substantial assist from Judge Proskauer and from Father Francis P. Duffy, the World War I chaplain of the 165th infantry.[22]

Smith replied with simple eloquence which Ellery Sedgwick of the *Atlantic* naïvely hoped would silence the "whispering and innuendoes, shruggings and hunchings" in the campaign.[23] He pointed to his own record—his policies, appointments, public statements—and to the two Catholic Chief Justices, Roger B. Taney and Edward D. White, as sufficient evidence of the civil loyalty of Catholics. Smith declined to accept responsibility for every statement in every encyclical letter: "these encyclicals are not articles of our faith. . . . So little are these matters of the essence of my faith that I, a devout Catholic from childhood, never heard of them until I read your letter."

Smith descended to specific points. Marshall had charged that Catholics believed that other religions in the United States should be tolerated only as a matter of favor and that there should be an established church. In reply, Smith quoted Ryan's *The State and the Church:* This proposition has full application only to the completely Catholic state, not even to states as Catholic as Spain. Ryan quoting Pohle, and Smith quoting Ryan, came up with this flat declaration: "If religious freedom has been accepted and sworn to as a fundamental law in a constitution, the obligation to show this tolerance is binding in conscience." Smith quoted Ryan further: "Pope Pius IX . . . more than once expressed his satisfaction with the arrangements obtaining in the United States." On the respective functions of church and state, Smith pointed to his public life as the exemplification of

[22] Edmund A. Moore, *A Catholic Runs for President* (New York, 1956), pp. 71–73; Oscar Handlin, *Al Smith and His America* (Boston, 1958), pp. 112–136; James H. Smylie, "The Roman Catholic Church, the State and Al Smith," *Church History,* September, 1960, pp. 321–343.
[23] Editor's note, *Atlantic Monthly,* May, 1927, p. 721.

the "complete separation of Church from State which is the faith of American Catholics today." Ryan was at hand for support: "The Catholic doctrine concedes, nay, maintains, that the State is coordinate with the Church and equally independent and supreme in its own distinct sphere." Thus the answer continued, point by point, leading finally to Smith's concluding prayer that "never again in this land will any public servant be challenged because of the faith in which he has tried to walk humbly with his God."[24]

Back at the university, *Tower,* noting that the United Press carried the name of Catholic University in all its reports on Smith's reply, purred sedately: "It is pleasing to find that we have under our shadows a man whose writings are of such importance as to cause our name to be carried all over the United States and possibly Europe."[25]

Even before Smith's reply was published, Ryan had entered the fight on his own. When Marshall's article appeared, Ryan sent off a reply, but Sedgwick returned it, saying that he had an answer coming directly from Smith, and urging Ryan to publish his article elsewhere.[26] Ryan sent his detailed, point-by-point rebuttal to *Commonweal,* and it appeared in the April 27, 1927, issue. Blunt and occasionally barbed, it leaned heavily on *The State and the Church,* especially the quotations from Pohle and from Leo XIII.[27]

Ryan's crisp rebuttal might carry weight with those willing to go back to the citations of page and column in Marshall's essay; as an effective reply to Marshall it fell far short of the moving personal authority of Smith's remarks. Smith may have drawn on Ryan's article, for Ryan had sent him a copy of it, as well as a copy of his reply to Dieffenbach.[28] If Smith did use them, he and his advisers clothed them in more appealing form. Ryan thought Smith's reply was "very well done indeed," though he did say he would have dealt differently with certain points.[29] He did not specify which points, but—to mention only one—he undoubtedly would not have lightly dismissed the problem of papal authority with a comment on the limits of infallibility.[30]

---

[24] "Catholic and Patriot: Governor Smith Replies," *ibid.,* pp. 721–728.
[25] *Tower,* April 27, 1927.
[26] Ellery Sedgwick to Ryan, April 7, 1927.
[27] Ryan, "Church, State, and Constitution," *Commonweal,* April 27, 1927, pp. 680–682.
[28] Ryan to Alfred E. Smith, March 30, 1927.
[29] Ryan to Joseph Schmidt, Nov. 28, 1927.
[30] Ryan to Wilfrid Parsons, March 23, 1928.

After the *Atlantic* debate, Smith made no further comment until after his nomination, but the debate went on without him. Senator J. Thomas Heflin, Democrat from Alabama, was always ready on the floor of the Senate with a few ill-chosen words: his fears of a secret Catholic party recurred so often that his colleagues, weary of replying, left him to wallow in his own oratory. The presence of Senator Walsh, a prominent dry and a Catholic, among the candidates for the Democratic nomination kept the Catholic issue around so that it could be picked up during oratorical lulls.

For about a year after the *Atlantic* debate, Ryan said nothing in print, that is, until a full-scale attack on the idea of a Catholic President was scheduled to appear in *Current History*, the magazine of the New York *Times*. Charles Hillman Fountain, a Baptist Fundamentalist, argued at some length that the case against a Catholic in the White House rested, not on religious bigotry, but on the conflict between the Church and democratic principles. Fountain held that under papal encyclicals like *Pascendi Dominici Gregis* and papal decrees like *Lamentabili*, the Catholic clergy throughout the world was bound to condemn "modernism." Under papal definitions, Fountain asserted, this policy included "open opposition to the modern and American principle of the separation of Church and State." To this dogma Fountain attached the weight of papal infallibility. He went on to document from papal sources Rome's "condemnation" of religious freedom, its distaste for the condition of the Church in the United States, its status as a civil power, its view of the "illegality" of other churches. Taking eight topics from the *Syllabus of Errors* of Pius IX (1864), he argued that all these violated the American political creed and that all were binding on American Catholics. Fountain's conclusion was that the voters should keep Catholics not only out of the Presidency but out of all political offices, for every successful Catholic politician contributed to the prestige and power and influence of the Church and thereby brought that much nearer the day when Catholics would subject the state to their Church. "We should never oppose a candidate for political office under our flag because of his religion," he said, *"unless that religion contains a political element that is inimical to our democratic institutions. The religion of Rome contains this political element."*[31]

When Father Duffy declined to enter the controversy,[32] *Current*

---

[31] Charles Hillman Fountain, "The Case for the Opposition to a Catholic President," *Current History*, March, 1928, pp. 767–778.
[32] George W. Ochs-Oakes to Ryan, Nov. 26, 1927.

History turned to Ryan, who was now ready to fight every attacker. He conceded two points: (1) He revealed his embarrassment over the *Manual of Christian Doctrine* (a Catholic textbook for elementary schools to which Fountain had referred). The *Manual*, he said, stated the traditional doctrine on the union of church and state in "an extreme and indeed repellent form" without adequate qualification for non-Catholic states. Though the text was widely used, he went on, "there is no evidence that the section on the relations of Church and State has been taken seriously by the average teacher, or that any pupil has gotten from it the notion that we ought to have a union between the Catholic Church and the American State. . . ." (If Fountain accepted this explanation, he was more charitable than Ryan had a right to expect.) (2) Ryan admitted that "five hundred or five thousand or fifty thousand years hence" the majority of Americans might be Catholics and might then try to change the Constitution so as to bring about the union of church and state. This was the only "real danger" Fountain could produce, and indeed it was the "one and only" contribution that Fountain made to the discussion.

Except for these concessions, Ryan had little good to say of Fountain's argument, or, for that matter, of Fountain. He challenged the latter's use of terms, such as "democracy," as slippery devices for introducing whatever content he needed from time to time, and he attacked Fountain's extractions from context. His principal assault was on the Baptist leader's misunderstanding of rules of interpretation, especially in connection with the *Syllabus of Errors*. Fountain failed to note, Ryan said, that the *Syllabus* was an index of proscribed doctrines discussed more fully in encyclicals, allocutions, apostolic letters, and the like. Any given proposition—"The Church ought to be separated from the State, and the State from the Church"—could be understood only in the fully developed argument from which it was abstracted. Furthermore—and Ryan regarded this as the least excusable error of interpretation—Fountain substituted abbreviated and inexact forms of expression for the exact language of the condemned proposition. Finally, Ryan said that Fountain, in common with many others, assumed that the true doctrine on the subject affected by the condemnation was contained in the contrary of the condemned proposition. Actually it was contained in the contradictory proposition. For example:

Proposition: Every man is named Johnson.

Contrary: No man is named Johnson.

Contradictory: It is not true that every man is named Johnson. Or, using one of Fountain's examples:

Proposition: The church ought to be separated from the state, and the state from the church.

Contrary: Church and state should be united.

Contradictory: It is not true that the church ought to be separated from the state, and the state from the church. Ryan argued that these errors of interpretation vitiated much of Fountain's argument; he hoped that "men of good will and average intelligence" would hesitate before expressing themselves in a similarly dogmatic and uninformed manner. Canon law, like civil law, was a science with its own rules of interpretation. (Ryan, heeding his own warning, had had his reply to Fountain checked by Monsignor Filippo Bernardini, dean of the School of Canon Law at the university.)[33] "If this caution is kept in mind by the well-disposed and the competent, we can bear with the dishonesties of the malevolent and the futilities of amateur canonists like Mr. Fountain." Smith had concluded his reply to Marshall with a prayer that no public servant would ever again be challenged because of the faith in which he walked humbly with his God, Ryan recalled. "I do not think we have a right to expect such a large-scale miracle," he went on. "My prayer goes no further than this, that Almighty God may grant Mr. Fountain the grace to become, at a not too distant date, thoroughly ashamed of his performance in this magazine."[34]

Even as Ryan was answering Fountain, Marshall turned out a book-length indictment, *The Roman Catholic Church in the Modern State* (1928), an extensive examination of papal claims to authority. If Marshall's letter to Smith could pass as a polite inquiry about certain difficulties that Smith's non-Catholic friends faced in supporting his candidacy, his book left no doubt that he had in mind a full-scale attack on the authority of the Papacy and on what he regarded as the Catholic Church's impertinent interference with the sovereignty of the modern state. One heated chapter was devoted exclusively to Ryan's defense of Catholic doctrine on church and state, which Marshall described as "the political sovereignty of the Church of Rome" facing "the political sovereignty of the modern State" the authority of which derived from "the Civic Primacy of Peoples." Quoting extensively from Ryan's *The State and the Church*, Marshall argued that "Roman Catholic doctrine is irreconcilable, in objective truth,

[33] Ryan to W. Frank Kirkpatrick, Oct. 15, 1929.
[34] Ryan, "The Catholic Reply to the Opposition," *Current History*, March, 1928, 778–785.

with the principles of religious liberty as proclaimed in the modern state." Furthermore, since Catholics were in all conscience bound to their principles, and since Ryan did not waver from them, the modern state had to protect itself by "resisting the political aggressions of Roman Catholics against the secular state." Ryan's candor in not "minimizing" correct doctrine gave Marshall a clearly defined target, while his bluntness spurred Marshall's indignation. He affirmed his confidence in Ryan's "best intentions and highest motives," but that did not lessen the danger from a Church that did not acknowledge as a basic right the religious freedom guaranteed by the modern state. The fact that the Catholic doctrine in its full vigor applied only to Catholic states did not appease Marshall; that merely meant that Catholics granted religious toleration to their non-Catholic neighbors only as a matter of expediency or temporary favor. When conditions changed, when there was no call for expediency, that toleration might be withdrawn, for "a Roman Catholic majority in the modern state is under no obligation to recognize those moral rights as legal rights, although it may do so by favor or out of expediency." In the meantime Marshall was unwilling to have the state's sovereignty "challenged by the action of an independent religious sovereignty commanding a part of its citizens in virtue of a compulsory religious obedience." Marshall did not think that the history of the "[Roman] Catholic Church" warranted confidence in its custody of the morals of Christendom.[35]

Forum paid Ryan ten dollars to review Marshall's book. Once again Ryan wearily repeated his familiar arguments. Marshall could not point *"in all the years since the Constitution was adopted"* to an occasion when the claims of the Pope had brought the Church into conflict with American law, Ryan said. The remote contingency of a "Catholic state" was as remote as ever, and even should it come to pass, "American Catholics might not want to change the Constitution in this matter any more than the present Catholic majorities in many states show such a disposition"—an interesting echo of the *Christian Century*'s argument. Meanwhile Ryan was not so happy about the "curious modern Leviathan" that Marshall was creating: "this omnipotent political power" called the "Civic Primacy of the People."[36]

Privately, to Colonel Callaghan, Ryan blasted Protestant doctrine on the role of the state. Protestants had no doctrine of personal liberty except

[35] Marshall, *The Roman Catholic Church in the Modern State* (New York, 1928), especially Chap. VII.
[36] Ryan, "Vatican and White House," *Forum,* June, 1928, pp. xvi–xviii.

private interpretation of the Bible, he said. Neither Luther nor Calvin nor Henry VIII believed in liberty against the state. As a result, Protestants sooner or later handed over all authority to the state and gave up the idea of imposing obligatory moral rules on their followers. Hence it was natural for Methodists, Baptists, and Presbyterians to call upon the state to enforce moral conduct. Catholics, on the other hand, held the state to the minimum action necessary for the public good; therefore, they generally opposed prohibition because it was contrary to individual rights and to the public good. They also opposed it intuitively, Ryan told his Catholic friend truculently, because its strongest support came from Protestant groups that did not believe in individual liberty and looked upon the consumption of liquor as morally wrong.[37]

Just as Marshall's book appeared, Ryan attempted in *The Catholic Church and the Citizen* (1928), a short volume in Hilaire Belloc's Calvert Series, to allay non-Catholic fears of Catholic statements, not the least his own remark in *The State and the Church*. "The American hierarchy," he wrote,

is not only well satisfied with the kind of separation which exists in this country but would oppose any suggestion of union between the two powers. No Pope has expressed the wish for a change in the present relations between Church and state in America, nor is any Pope likely to do so within any period that is of practical interest to this generation.[38]

These comments proved useful to the New York *World*, but they had no noticeable impact elsewhere.

Father Forde, Ryan's boisterous friend in Nebraska, thought the whole discussion was getting too grim: "I have often wondered how you have managed to keep your personal humor out of your writings," he wrote to Ryan. "As I remember you in St. Paul nobody would have had you in mind in reciting the indignant query of the bard;

> 'Why leave the gaiety
> All to the laity—
> Why can't the clergy be Irishmen too?' "[39]

After Smith's nomination at Houston in June, many issues contributed to the campaign: prosperity, farm relief, development of water power, prohibition, imperialism in Latin America, labor injunctions, immigration.

[37] Ryan to Patrick H. Callahan, April 17, 1928.
[38] Ryan, *The Catholic Church and the Citizen* (New York, 1928), p. 31.
[39] P. A. Forde to Ryan, July 11, 1928.

Ryan's active decade made him aware of these issues; as a matter of fact, he noted in August, 1928, that a strong statement on water power would do more to win over the progressive vote than anything else Smith could say.[40] Yet it was the "campaign within a campaign," that curious blend of prohibition and religious and social snobbery, that commanded what little time was left over from Ryan's regular duties. In July he spoke of cutting down on his activity for the next few months; the toll of an illness in the late spring was still being paid. Thus Ryan reacted to the campaign rather than acted in it.

The campaign within the campaign stirred his ire considerably. Persistent underground whispers reported the imminence of the Pope's arrival in the United States; Smith was reported drunk on a number of occasions, his unsteadiness increasing with each retelling; his—and his wife's—reputed social ineptness formed the core of dozens of anecdotes that the socially self-confident passed among themselves. Even a nationally respected editor like William Allen White identified Smith as a legislative friend of gambling and prostitution, and the charge was sensationalistically repeated by John Roach Straton, a Baptist minister in New York City. A more famous clerical opponent of Smith was Bishop James E. Cannon, Jr., of the Methodist Episcopal Church, South, who, despite the protest of a majority of the bishops of his church, organized southern churchmen, clerical and lay, into battalions against Smith. The overt target was the danger to prohibition, but around it clustered a host of other fears. "Broadly speaking," a recent historian of the campaign has observed, "what was believed to be in danger was 'Anglo-Saxon civilization.' It was assumed that Protestantism was a mainstay of that undefined way of life. Roman Catholicism was regarded as belonging to an alien way, inimical to the preservation of the best in the American past."[41] From this view sprang full-fledged discussion of the Catholic issue, high-level debate of the genuine issues for those who had a taste for it, loose statement trailing off into scurrilous calumny and libel for the rest. The Ku Klux Klan, still active, did not waste time on high-level debate.

The Republican high command was not indifferent to the political advantage of this inner campaign. Herbert Hoover on occasion denounced the introduction of religious issues into the campaign, but his subordinates did not take his words to heart. White's charges—and even his nonretracting retraction—were exploited for all they were worth. Even more effec-

[40] Ryan to James J. Hoey, Aug. 2, 1928.
[41] Moore, *A Catholic Runs for President*, p. 163.

tive was the stump tour of Mabel Walker Willebrandt, an assistant attorney general in the Hoover administration, whose assigned task was the enforcement of prohibition. Mrs. Willebrandt made a specialty of appearing before church groups, and her appeal to the members of the Ohio Methodist Conference in Springfield, Ohio, on September 7th to organize their congregations for prohibition and for Hoover appeared to Democrats, and to Catholics, as an appeal for a religious crusade against Democrats, drunks, and sinners. While she never specifically averted to Catholicism, her appealing dance around related issues convinced Smith of the necessity of bringing the religious issue out into the open by making it a topic for a major speech in Oklahoma City on September 20th. Still she kept on, alternately with and without the blessing of the national party. In October, when criticism of her activities was at a peak, she played a trump card: a letter from Ryan's old friend, Colonel Callahan, a Catholic, dry and Republican, assuring her that he could find nothing in her speeches that criticized the Catholic Church or referred to Smith's religion. The assurance was perhaps correct, but it neatly evaded the Democratic-Catholic charges against her.[42]

Ryan stayed on the sidelines, increasingly dismayed at what he saw. He refused to join a group of Protestant divines in questioning presidential candidates on ethical issues; it smacked too much of "Church interference with politics on a large scale."[43] (What is more, it would undoubtedly have hurt Smith, for the issues of prohibition and of law enforcement would almost certainly have emerged in an embarrassing way.) He helped the cause in minor ways. In August he recommended a former student to James J. Hoey for Democratic political work in New York.[44] Writing to the continuingly hospitable *World*, he challenged Marshall to cite one recorded conflict between an American Catholic's religion and his civic duty. As for Marshall's assumption that Smith had reconciled his Americanism and his Catholicism only by rejecting his duty to obey the authority of the Church, Ryan chuckled that Marshall would have to wait a long time before the Pope would denounce Smith. He went further and turned the Protestants' criticism of the Catholic Church back on them: actually Protestant critics were themselves intolerant in insisting that a Catholic accept their indifferentism in dogma in order to be eligible politically; this, Ryan said in a striking riposte, was a "thinly disguised" demand

[42] *Ibid.*, pp. 107–194.
[43] Ryan to Hubert C. Herring, April 14, 1928.
[44] Ryan to Hoey, July 17, 1928.

182

for the practical union of church and state.[45] Later on, he sent a batch of scurrilous anti-Smith pamphlets to Lippmann at the pro-Smith *World;* Lippmann replied that so much of the stuff came to his desk that he was at a loss to know how to use it wisely.[46] When Lewis S. Gannett of the *Nation* asked for help in answering a patron worried about a future Catholic majority, Ryan replied that anyone afraid of that danger must also fear the dangers of riding in a subway.[47]

Ryan was subjected to some criticism within the Church for his public defense of the Catholic position. Many Catholics thought that prudence demanded silence. The Catholic clergy and the diocesan press had little to say; the Baltimore *Catholic Review* printed hardly a word about the campaign, though *America* and *Commonweal* were more outspoken, as befitted journals of opinion and affairs. When the Fountain-Ryan controversy appeared in *Current History*, the Philadelphia *Catholic Standard and Times* expressed astonishment that a Catholic had been found to dignify Fountain's strictures with a rebuttal. Even the Brooklyn *Tablet*, published by Ryan's friend, Patrick F. Scanlan, picked up the *Standard's* comment.[48] Ryan resented this rebuke a good deal. In a letter to *America*, which had backed him up, he acknowledged that Fountain could not be moved from his views. But others could be, and Ryan felt the responsibility to give a fair-minded person the opportunity to compare the two sides. His view of Fountain "alternated between contempt for his intellectual processes and resentment at his stupid prejudices and occasional unfairness of method." He felt that an example should be made of the man, "that the egregious presumption which impelled him to attempt a task so far beyond his powers needed to be adequately stigmatized."[49] Ryan seemed to feel equally strongly about his critic in the *Catholic Standard and Times*, for in a personal letter to Father Wilfrid Parsons, S.J., editor of *America*, Ryan said that it had been a long while since he had been so eager to get a communication published. "While I try to be reasonably indifferent to adverse criticism which I regard as unfair," he said, "I confess that I felt considerably hurt at the cavalier, superior but fundamentally ignorant attitude" of the editorial writer in the Philadelphia paper.[50]

[45] *World,* Aug. 25, 1928.
[46] Lippmann to Ryan, Oct. 22, 1928.
[47] Ryan to Lewis S. Gannett, Sept. 24, 1928.
[48] The article from the Philadelphia *Catholic Standard and Times* is fully reprinted in the Brooklyn *Tablet*, March 10, 1928.
[49] Ryan, letter to editor, *America*, March 24, 1928, pp. 591–592.
[50] Ryan to Parsons, March 23, 1928.

By September Ryan felt that the prejudices of the campaign had over-extended themselves so far that they would provoke a reaction toward tolerance and fair-mindedness, still fundamental characteristics of the American people.[51] But the next month he was not so sure. Bishop Cannon's crusade made Ryan mourn over the "paragraph after paragraph calculated to light the fires of denominational hatred and abounding in mendacious and misleading assertions."[52] (Ryan's capsule summary, made the previous February, still had point: "Cannon is a bad actor, a dishonest performer and a skunk. Aside from that he is all right.")[53] About the same time, he saw a note of social and religious snobbery in the *Christian Century*. This journal, in a statement that one historian calls "representative of the anti-Catholicism of the recognized Protestant press," took this position: "The increase of Catholic influence in American society threatens certain institutions which are integral to our American system." Therefore, a voter "declines to assist in its extension by helping to put its representative at the head of the government."[54] This was the same *Christian Century* that Ryan had praised the year before. Ryan found this attitude incomprehensible; that it should have appeared in this magazine he regarded as more discouraging than anything else in the campaign. After the election when the *Century*'s editor said he disagreed with those who would vote against Smith because of religion, Ryan dismissed him as a liar and a hypocrite.[55]

Even Colonel Callahan did not escape. Ryan was appalled when Callahan did his best to make Mrs. Willebrandt respectable. How could he let himself be used to extract her chestnuts from the fire? The Kentuckian had exonerated her from faults few had charged against her; the result was a fraud perpetrated on the public, which had been led to believe that Catholics did not resent the unspoken innuendoes of her campaign.[56] Bad enough to have Protestants attacking the Church, Ryan thought, without having Catholics making it easier for them.

When the election was over, Smith had lost decisively, even his own New York rejecting him. Whatever else contributed to Smith's defeat, prosperity undoubtedly had the most influence. The fear of a rocking boat

51 Ryan to Harold Marshall, Oct. 2, 1928.
52 Ryan to John W. Carter, Jr., Oct. 30, 1928.
53 Ryan to L. A. Rowen, Nov. 2, 1928.
54 Quoted from Robert Moats Miller, *American Protestantism and Social Issues, 1919–1939* (Chapel Hill, 1958), pp. 61–62.
55 Ryan to John A. MacCallum, Dec. 5, 1928.
56 Ryan to William J. Meininger, Nov. 21, 1928; Ryan to Callahan, Oct. 26, 1928.

has elected more than one President, and the promise of continued Republican prosperity meant at least as much as in 1924 and 1926. The burden of proof was on the opposition party—Why *should* the Republicans be turned out, especially when in Herbert Hoover they offered a candidate of impressive stature? Prosperity and Republican candidate aside, was Smith the man to beat the Republicans? Many voters were repelled by Smith's Eastern urban immigrant background and his debt to Tammany Hall, especially since he was candid enough not to disclaim any part of his heritage. When to these handicaps were added his wetness, which for some voters affronted divine law, and his Catholicism, which, for all its advantage among Catholic voters, ran up against an anti-Catholic tradition of long standing in the United States, his defeat appears less surprising.[57] In fact, Smith's achievement in defeat puts his loss in proper perspective: he recovered a substantial share of the popular vote that had been lost by John W. Davis in 1924, bringing the Democrats within the range of possible victory in 1932, and he restored unity and new strength to the Democratic Party, awakening some ethnic groups previously silent, converting other ethnic groups previously committed to the Republicans, and getting the ear of large urban concentrations. "He lost a campaign that had to be lost, but in such a way as to restore his party as an effective opposition and to pave the way for the victories of F.D.R."[58]

Dr. Ryan did not share this view. Writing his official public verdict two days after the election, he asserted bitterly that without the religious factor Smith would not have been defeated. He saw the religious factor operating at three levels: (1) the "chamber of horrors," the gutter campaign of pamphlets, cartoons, fly-by-night newspapers, and the word-of-mouth scurrility that passed so rapidly from willing person to willing person; (2) the next level up, Bishop Cannon's misquotations and false history; (3) the able journals like *Christian Century* which, in making respectable the Protestant case to vote against Smith as a Catholic, gave permission to its readers to indulge their prejudices.

He found some cause for rejoicing: Some fine Americans had spoken out against the tone of the campaign. The Church itself had behaved with restraint. He quoted Ellery Sedgwick's letter to the New York *Sun* on October 20th: "May I be allowed to bear public and admiring testimony

---

[57] Michael Williams, *The Shadow of the Pope* (New York, 1932), pp. 292–298, takes a similar view. So does Moore.

[58] Samuel Lubell, *The Future of American Politics* (New York, 1952), pp. 34–41; Richard Hofstadter, "Could a Protestant Have Beaten Hoover in 1928?" *Reporter*, March 17, 1960, p. 33.

to the dignity, the forebearance and the good citizenship of the Roman Catholic clergy in America? I doubt indeed whether our history affords an instance of a large and cohesive body of men who, under the bitterest provocation, have better kept their self-control and self-respect. . . . Had the Catholic clergy thrown themselves into the hurly-burly after the pattern of their Methodist brothers the Republic would have rocked on its foundations." Finally, Ryan rejoiced that the one argument "which enjoys any real plausibility"—the danger latent in a Catholic majority that might work toward a union of church and state—received little attention. Possibly, he said in a spate of wishful thinking, this "fantastic and remote 'menace'" was not exploited because even the intolerant retained a modicum of common sense.

His total view of the outcome of the election was one of dismay: "As a Catholic, I cannot be expected to rejoice that some millions of my countrymen would put upon me and my co-religionists the brand of civic inferiority. As an American, I cannot feel proud that the spirit of the Sixth Amendment to the Constitution [that is, the Sixth Article, forbidding a religious test for public office] is thus flouted and violated. As a believer in personal freedom and political honesty, I cannot feel cheerful over the prospect of four more years of the arrogant, despotic and hypocritical domination from which we are suffering by the grace of the Anti-Saloon League. As a democrat and a lover of justice, I cannot look with complacency upon a President-elect who, judged by his campaign addresses, believes that the economic welfare of the masses should be confided, practically without reservation, to the care of corporate business, in the naïve faith that corporate business will dispense and hand down universal justice. This is industrial feudalism. Possibly it may turn out to be benevolent. In any case it will do violence to the most fundamental and valuable traditions of the America we have known and loved."[59]

[59] Ryan, "A Catholic View of the Election," *Current History*, December, 1928, pp. 377–381.

The Hoover Era

THE HURT RE-mained, for Catholics were seared by the reminder of civic inferiority. They reacted to the pain differently. The bishops continued the silence they had maintained during the campaign. Some diocesan papers, the Baltimore *Catholic Review* for example, reprinted Ryan's article from *Current History* without comment.[1] Father Peter Guilday, professor of church history at the university, said that Catholics, after a campaign of "damnable, obscene and calumnious lies," were "through with cooperating."[2] But Colonel Callahan warned against sullen indignation: where prejudice existed, social contacts and attention to social questions would help; a separatist policy was "fatal to the last degree."[3] The Archbishop of Cincinnati wanted sober stock-taking, ideally, a private conference in the library at Catholic University at which a small group of prelates, priests, and laymen could explore the idea that "we have not approached public

[1] Baltimore *Catholic Review*, Dec. 7, 1928.
[2] Quoted in Patrick H. Callahan, "Politics and Prejudices: The 1928 Campaign," *Fortnightly Review*, Jan. 15, 1929, p. 25.
[3] *Ibid.*, pp. 26–27.

opinion in an altogether sound way."[4] Ryan was invited, and he accepted; but the meeting did not take place. Many Catholics wanted to
forget quickly, to accept the decision of the 1928 campaign, even to
accept prohibition.

For a moment Ryan sagged, a heavy sadness settling over him. Then
he rallied; from the depths the only way was up. He wanted Catholics to
face frankly the bias exhibited in the election, not ignoring rampant prejudice, he said, but also not feeding their already severe inferiority complex.
Certain that the opposition would respect Catholics more if they stuck to
their principles, he deplored the widespread disposition "to feel subdued,
humiliated and beaten, to submit to things as they are and show an attitude
of complete conformity."[5] Nothing was to be gained by "exhibiting ourselves as good little boys who know when they are licked."[6]

President Hoover's inaugural gave Ryan an occasion to reopen hostilities. Speaking on the prohibition issue, Hoover observed that disregard for
one law destroyed respect for all law and that citizens who opposed the
Eighteenth Amendment should work for repeal, at the same time discouraging violations of the law.

These innocuous clichés Ryan chose to use as a target. The Volstead
Act did not impose a legal duty to discourage violation of the law, Ryan
asserted, and only a doubtful moral duty in view of the failure of enforcement generally. Pointing to the "blue laws" as a parallel, he hinted at a
possible route for the wets: "When the forces of fanaticism made formal
repeal impossible, the mass of the citizens repealed these obnoxious statutes
by indirection, that is, by persistently disobeying them. Thus they created
a custom contrary to the law, and customary law of this sort is quite as
valid as formally enacted statutes." Launching into his familiar denunciation of the tory character of the Eighteenth Amendment, he stated confidently that those who fought prohibition would "rightfully feel that they
are engaged in a great crusade for fundamental liberties."[7]

Ryan dashed off this deliberate provocation without second thoughts.
He wanted to buck up Catholic morale and perhaps even to compel the
respect of the President by manly Catholic resistance. Perhaps if Hoover
had alternate support, Ryan thought, he could break with the Anti-Saloon
League and "all its allies in the fields of bigotry and intolerance." As long
as prohibition and intolerance were "definitely and closely linked," it was

---

[4] James Hugh Ryan to Ryan, Jan. 8, 1929.
[5] Ryan to Bernard J. Mahoney, May 9, 1929.
[6] Ryan to Thomas R. Lynch, May 2, 1929.
[7] Ryan, "Who Shall Obey the Law?" *Commonweal*, April 3, 1929, pp. 616–618.

accurate to say that "in exact proportion as the prohibition cause succeeds, the position and the interests of Catholics in this country would suffer." Ryan looked forward to the scrap: "For myself, I feel more eager to fight these forces than I ever have felt with regard to any other issue or conflict. It seems to me that the forces of reason, liberty, democracy are all on our side. . . . Even if the cause in which we believe . . . should ultimately fail, we shall have the satisfaction of having fought on the right side and, incidentally, having got a good deal of fun out of it."[8]

The angler in the White House snapped at Ryan's bait. Speaking to the Associated Press in New York City later the same month, the President said: "No individual has the right to determine what law shall be obeyed and what law shall not be enforced. If a law is wrong, its rigid enforcement is the surest guaranty of its repeal. If it is right, its enforcement is the quickest method of compelling respect for it. I have seen statements published within a few days encouraging citizens to defy the law because that particular journal did not approve of the law itself. I leave comment on such an attitude to any citizen with a sense of responsibility to his country."[9]

Quickly identifying Hoover's target, the New York *Herald Tribune* telegraphed Ryan for a comment. Answering promptly, Ryan pointed out in passing that thirteen thinly populated states could always thwart the will of a great majority anxious for repeal. He saved his main attack for the President's ethics. Pouncing on Hoover's denial that an individual might morally elect not to obey a law, Ryan asked:

What about the right of the individual conscience? Must a man obey a civil law which he believes to be wrong? Apparently the President would not only deny the moral supremacy of conscience but cast opprobrium upon those honored names of men and women who in every country and in every age have dared to put their conceptions of right above their fear of political penalties. President Hoover aligns himself in effect with those who hold that the State can do no wrong. He bids us bow our knees before the Omnipotent State. This is neither good ethics nor good Americanism.[10]

Bishop Cannon promptly showed that he too was pretty handy with a *reductio ad absurdum*: He said that Ryan taught that people "were not

[8] Ryan to Michael Williams, March 9, 1929.
[9] "Address of President Hoover at the Annual Luncheon of the Associated Press in New York City," pamphlet (Washington, D.C., 1929), p. 2.
[10] New York *Herald Tribune,* April 3, 1929, quoted in Ryan, *Questions of the Day* (Boston, 1931), p. 11.

under obligation to obey a law in which they did not believe."[11] Ryan picked this one up for reply—morally, "the citizen is not obliged to obey a law which he believed to be wrong."[12] There was a difference. Meanwhile, Hoover let the issue die.

Senator Heflin resumed the fight after a disturbance at a speech in Brockton, Massachusetts. He reported on the floor of the Senate that he had been combating Ryan's "raw Roman doctrine flaunted in the face of the American flag and the Constitution." As he was leaving the hall, a group of Catholics hissed at him, he said, and then he had been "assaulted by one of the group who sought to assassinate me."[13] At the same time, The *Congregationalist* came reluctantly to the conclusion that Ryan was "an encourager of the lawless elements of this country and a booster for booze."[14]

The stir delighted Ryan; the influence of his article went far beyond his expectations. *Commonweal*, the young and far from affluent vehicle of Catholic laymen in New York, had never been so widely quoted. Arthur Brisbane, columnist for the Hearst papers, took Hoover's side, but H. L. Mencken, famous for his acid view of the "bluenoses" who supported prohibition, told Ryan he wished he had had the article for the *American Mercury*.[15]

For Father Ryan, the incident aptly synthesized statism, prohibition, anti-Catholic prejudice, the Anti-Saloon League, and the humiliation of 1928 in the person of Herbert Hoover. Harding had been affable, and Coolidge only blind. Hoover was impossible. If Hoover could be discredited, Ryan thought, the forces that had won together in 1928 would collapse together.

Warming to the fight, he reached out for his customary allies among liberal and religious leaders. Anger subsided, issues passed, and new struggles uncovered common ground. He noticed that not all liberals had offended in 1927, nor had all Protestants, nor even most Protestants, been at fault in 1928. The Mexican government and the Church reconciled their differences in 1929, easing the pressure from that issue. Early in 1929 Charles S. Macfarland, general secretary of the Federal Council of Churches, took the first step toward resuming friendly relations with the SAD. The NCWC and the Federal Council ought to stay above the

[11] Norfolk *Virginian Pilot*, May 17, 1929.
[12] Ryan to editor, *Virginian Pilot*, May 21, 1929.
[13] *Congressional Record*, 71st Cong. 1st Sess., Vol. 71, Part 1, pp. 352–360.
[14] *Congregationalist*, April 25, 1929, pp. 533–534.
[15] H. L. Mencken to Ryan, June 3, 1929.

190

bigoted slashes that Catholics and Protestants were making at each other,
he said. Responding to this dignified opportunity for reconciliation, Ryan
affirmed his confidence in the FCC and its officers. He noted, however,
that he would henceforth avoid Protestant groups that accepted Bishop
Cannon. Macfarland correctly interpreted this grudging reply as a re-
newal of relations. Men of religion had more important things to do than
to nurture unhappy memories.[16]

On occasion Ryan took the initiative. When William Allen White
caused a flurry of comment in 1930 with a gentle, affectionate gesture to
an aged Negro in Haiti, Ryan told him that "that action was generous,
courageous, chivalrous, spontaneous and entirely worthy of a Christian
gentleman"; the act erased the memory of things that White had said
during the campaign. White accepted the reconciliation eagerly. He had
honored Ryan for thirty years, and, adverting to more recent events, he
said, "No one views in perspective the bitterness of the last campaign
more sadly than I."[17]

The present needed unity among progressives, Ryan thought. Let the
past live by itself.

The depression that spread over the land after the stock market collapse in 1929 made that cooperation doubly urgent. The faltering economy
overshadowed difficulties among progressives. As unemployment mounted,
the economic issue predominated for Father Ryan.

Ryan had sensed the problem of unemployment even before the crash.
As early as November, 1928, he had told the Consumers' League of Ohio
that the general impression that unemployment was negligible ignored
facts. "A real problem exists and it will not be solved by letting things
take their course, no matter what Mr. Coolidge and Mr. Hoover may say
to reassure us."[18] The following February Ryan had pushed his analysis
further for a wider audience, first in the *Catholic World* and then, by
courtesy of Senator David I. Walsh (Democrat from Massachusetts), in
the *Congressional Record*. Accepting three million unemployed as a fair
estimate, Ryan pointed to the notoriously depressed soft-coal industry and
the troubled textile industry as special danger spots. How real was Republican prosperity when America tried to solve its basic problem, over-

[16] Charles S. Macfarland to Ryan, Jan. 8, 1929; Ryan to Macfarland, Jan. 10, 1929;
Macfarland to Ryan, Jan. 16, 1929.
[17] Ryan to William Allen White, March 4, 1930; White to Ryan, March 13, 1930;
Walter Johnson, *William Allen White's America* (New York, 1947), p. 421.
[18] Ryan to Elizabeth Magee, Nov. 13, 1928.

production, with elaborate advertising and comfortable bromides about "religion in business"? The real solution was an adequate spread of purchasing power. If the Supreme Court blocked obvious solutions, there were still things to be done: government employment exchanges, the wartime device which the "Bishops' Program of Social Reconstruction" had so urgently wanted continued after the war; unemployment insurance, perhaps on the Wisconsin model, which placed the burden directly on industry; and most important of all, public works programs.[19]

Ryan's hope for productive industrial reform shriveled quickly when the stock market crash in October, 1929, spread despair throughout the economy. On the crash itself Ryan said little in print. Money and banking were admitted blind spots in his knowledge, and he despaired of mastering their intricacy. Mounting unemployment was a different matter. No one knew just how much there was. The President and his official family made officially confident statements; the periodic catches in the market's decline made confidence plausible. Summoned to Washington, business leaders promised to hold wages up and to keep their workers on during the temporary snag.

Meanwhile Ryan went home as usual at Christmastime. This time he went, not to join in the usual festivities, but to be with his mother at her death. After returning to St. Paul in 1923, Mrs. Ryan had spent her last six years at St. Joseph's Hospital, where Sister Constance was the pharmacist. She died early on New Year's Day, 1930. At the funeral mass sung by Father John, Archbishop Dowling of St. Paul unexpectedly mounted the pulpit to pay tribute to the deceased: "We have had no great apostle [in the United States]. . . . If you wish to find the explanation of the Catholic Church in America, there it is, there lies an apostle; there lies one responsible for the planting of the faith; there lies an example of Christian virtue; there is patience; there is silence and sanctity."[20]

By the time Ryan returned to Washington, Congress was in session. The scope of the depression was still not clear. After Hoover's message on the state of the Union, Ryan praised Hoover unstintingly for the business conferences: the recognition of high wages as a weapon against the business crisis removed from public discussion the old fallacy of reducing wages to reduce costs. At the same time, he regretted that in the talk of reduced

[19] Ryan, "Unemployment: Causes and Remedies," *Catholic World*, February, 1929, pp. 535–542.
[20] "Words of His Grace, Archbishop Dowling . . ." typescript, Jan. 4, 1930.

taxes, Hoover unearthed the "dreary sophistries in some of his campaign speeches."[21]

Winter passed. The spring of 1930 brought the news from the Bureau of Labor Statistics that employment had declined 10 per cent in the past year, that in every month since November, 1929, things had grown worse. A parish priest in New York reported in *Commonweal:*

I do know, and so do most other pastors in New York, that not for many years have there been so many people out of work, and in such keen distress because of unemployment: Through my reception rooms last week there passed nearly two hundred of my parishioners; each one begging for help to secure a job; or a job for Jimmy or Jane, or Mary or Bob, thrown out of work without fault of their own. . . . Moreover, there is discontent; there is sullen anger, in addition to bewilderment and distress. The poor are asking why they should suffer, when the rich multiply; and not only is it the very poor who ask that difficult question; for hundreds of families that generally would not be classed among the poor—respectable people, usually quite safe and fairly prosperous—are now sinking down among the indigent class. And upon these smoldering sparks of sullen anger, of justifiable discontent, are being blown the winds of the revolutionary spirit. The soil is rich for the seeds of Bolshevist agitation. And they are being scattered lavishly. . . . I believe that if to-day or to-morrow there appeared a man of magnetic personality, an apostle of social revolt, fires would soon flame up in many places; possibly to meet in some great conflagration.[22]

The sag became a slump. Ryan was impatient with optimistic talk and with futile remedies like "stabilization," that is, spreading a factory's work over a whole year to avoid lean months. Talk created no new jobs, rationalizations were useless to persons who lacked money to buy the necessities of life. In April the National Unemployment League had suggested a $3,000,000,000 program of public works, but no one in Washington (much less in industry) seemed interested. Ryan was already playing the game so popular since: comparing presidential statements of hope with the hopeless facts of deepening depression. In May, 1930, Hoover told the United States Chamber of Commerce: "We have now passed the worst." Two days later the stock exchange broke sharply downward. "Our industrial resources and powers are undoubtedly sufficient to produce the

[21] Ryan, "Economic and Social Topics in the President's Message," *Catholic Charities Review,* February, 1930, pp. 9–11.
[22] Quoted in Ryan, "Unemployment: A Failure in Leadership," *Catholic World,* July, 1930, p. 386.

goods adequate to a decent living for all our people and a considerable surplus for a large proportion," Ryan said impatiently. "If this possibility cannot be realized through the existing system then this system is not worth preserving."[23]

By September, 1930, more were unemployed and there was still no action. The ever hospitable *Commonweal* gave Ryan a forum for an attack on Hoover. The depression was Hoover's bad luck, not his fault, Ryan wrote, but his paralysis since November, 1929, has exploded his reputation as a great economist, a courageous and effective leader, and a master of fundamental principles, the "inflated popular estimate . . . deliberately and systematically created by journalistic and political propagandists." Hoover wanted to lower the federal income tax by $160,000,000: a perfect example of the topsy-turvy economic world that Ryan deplored, for the uncollected tax would remain principally in the hands of the rich, who did not need it for consumption. Meanwhile federal departments, cutting down their payrolls to meet reduced appropriations, let part of their staff go, thus adding to unemployment. Hoover never got beyond the "ridiculous Coolidge-Mellon theory" of leaving capital to businessmen for expansion, Ryan said, and he persisted in this remedy at a time when business could not sell what it was already producing.[24]

The *Catholic Universe Bulletin* of Cleveland noted sarcastically that it was fun to see David go after Goliath, especially since David's remarks were "so free of acrimony and partisan criticism." The Chicago *Journal of Commerce* had a simpler view: Ryan was just mouthing "shallow radicalism."[25] For what it was worth, Ryan had the consolation of knowing that he was not the only one thought to be radical: the 1929 convention of the American Legion had asked for a Senate investigation of the Federal Council of Churches.[26]

To Leo XIII and Hobson, Ryan now was adding the idea of public spending as a major element of his economic ideology. Leo supplied the moral obligation of the state to intervene when, in an industrial world, the worker failed to get reasonable and frugal comfort from his wage. Hobson added the theory of underconsumption, and in March, 1931, Ryan com-

[23] *Ibid.*, pp. 385–393.
[24] Ryan, "Mr. Hoover and National Welfare," *Commonweal*, Sept. 10, 1930, pp. 457–459.
[25] Cleveland *Catholic Universe Bulletin*, Sept. 11, 1930; Chicago *Journal of Commerce*, Sept. 11, 1930.
[26] Robert Moats Miller, *American Protestantism and Social Issues, 1919–1939*, p. 148.

194

mented to Hobson on the satisfaction Hobson must feel to see his fear of oversaving "pretty widely if somewhat grudgingly accepted by the economists."[27] The idea of public spending for public works came to Ryan directly from *The Road to Plenty* by William T. Foster and Waddill Catchings, a lucid, palatable text in fictional form, not overweighted with the fiscal analysis that Ryan regarded as inexplicable, and therefore unimportant. The book enjoyed quite a vogue,[28] but promiscuous spending was not favored policy for a President who set fiscal responsibility as a prime goal.

In January of that winter of 1930–1931, the concerted voices of organized American religion determined to make themselves heard, Ryan for the NCWC together with his alter egos in the FCC and the Social Justice Commission of the Central Conference of American Rabbis. Compassion for their equally ill-fed flocks led the three groups to call a Conference on Permanent Preventatives of Unemployment in Washington. Everybody gave his expected word. George Soule of the *New Republic* wanted a national economic council to plan American industrial development. Darwin J. Meserole of the National Unemployment League asked for public works. Professor Commons of Wisconsin spoke up for unemployment insurance; John E. Edgerton, president of the National Association of Manufacturers, spoke against it. Ryan gave a treatise on justice so technical that with a new introduction, it appeared in the *Ecclesiastical Review*. Then as everyone finished, Rabbi Edward L. Israel, Ryan's opposite number in the Central Conference of American Rabbis, cut loose on the NAM's president.

Edgerton, speaking as a "citizen and a churchman," had warned against hasty expedients, for "Man's extremity is not only God's opportunity, but the devil's as well." Thoughtful, careful, prayerful study had led Edgerton to think that unemployment insurance was un-American, unconstitutional, impractical, immoral. It hurt religion: "What need, it may be asked, have the people for a God and the church when human government is undertaking to do everything for them that both God and the church promise?" He spoke for a golden mean between "false gods of materialism ever beckoning us to worship at their shrines of selfishness" and "equally false

[27] Ryan to John A. Hobson, March 5, 1931. See also George G. Higgins, "The Underconsumption Theory in the Writings of Monsignor John A. Ryan," M.A. dissertation, Catholic University (1942).
[28] Arthur M. Schlesinger, Jr., *The Crisis of the Old Order* (*The Age of Roosevelt*, I) (Boston, 1957), pp. 134–136, 186–191.

gods of unanchored sentimentalism luring us towards their tents of casuistry."

Rabbi Israel observed bitingly that the speaker who had used "God" and "religion" most often was the "most anti-social person who came before us." Then he warmed up: "It is high time for the die to be cast. It is high time for us to serve notice that this type of conscience cannot dare to mouth sanctimonious words in the name of religion, and that we are not organized as churches to level, by charity, the ills of competition. Religion must declare unequivocally that an economic order, which, by its unbridled wastefulness and shortsightedness under the guise of 'competition' and 'rugged individualism' brings misery to millions, cannot endure with our sanction and without our protest." His protest caught the spirit of the religious reformer in the crisis of the depression better than any public statement of Ryan:

We sound the voice of social protest against the raising of a sanctimonious cry of "Americanism" and "the Constitution," whenever any fundamental social change is being projected. We must maintain, in unequivocal terms, that our government, our democracy, founded in an age when political freedom was the cry of the moment, now finds itself, due to a changing civilization, in a new age where not political freedom but social and industrial freedom is the most insistent cry; and unless that democracy of ours is flexible enough to adapt itself to the demands of the justice and morality of the new day and the new age, then its future security is indeed dark with foreboding.[29]

It was not in Ryan to speak out with this fervor. His distaste for show, his reserve, his guard never let him warm up to a public performance of this kind. Even when he recited Edgar Allan Poe's "The Bells" as a rhetorical performance, it lacked the full man: there was range in his voice, and even music, but not the vibrant freedom that loses a man in his own eloquence and lets form and substance merge as an unselfconscious whole. Ryan could not speak as Jeremiah. He was too much John Hobson and not enough Ignatius Donnelly. Yet in this outburst Rabbi Israel, nearly thirty years junior to his colleague, spoke Father Ryan's thoughts as well as his own.

Ryan's urge for basic reform received authoritative support in May, 1931, when Pope Pius XI unexpectedly turned a fortieth-anniversary ob-

[29] "Permanent Preventatives of Unemployment," pamphlet (Baltimore, 1931), *passim.*

servance of *Rerum novarum* into a substantive restatement of Catholic thought on social justice. For several months the Catholic press had been enthusiastically reviewing Leo XIII's epochal statement. No one was more enthusiastic than Father Ryan.[30] Then in the midst of this self-congratulation, *Quadragesimo anno* reinforced the earlier document and went beyond it on some specific points. Father Ryan went to the office of the New York *Times* in New York to hear the encyclical firsthand by short wave from the Vatican. At first the encyclical seemed a perfunctory recollection of what Leo had already said. Even that would have been worthwhile, for it would have brought up to date ideas that, after all, were geared to a world that had changed considerably. As the broadcast continued, however, it became apparent that the Pope was saying new things as well. He spoke of "social justice" several times, implying that measure of "distributive justice" that had been the burden of Ryan's own book. For the worker's right to "reasonable and frugal comfort," the Pope now spoke of "ample sufficiency," enough to maintain a worker and his family in decency. This was the "familial living wage" toward which Ryan had groped in *A Living Wage*. The encyclical implicitly dismissed compulsory economic poverty as an asset in the spiritual life. In its section on "reconstructing the social order," it urged cooperation among workers and masters in a guild system in which each industry governed itself under restraint by the state to prevent oppression of either the worker or the consumer. As if to distinguish this from the fascist corporations of Mussolini, the Pope warned the state against usurping private initiative or imposing an excessively bureaucratic domination.[31] With nervous excitement Ryan listened through the static, and when he returned to Washington he had no reason to question the verdict of Bishop Shahan, rector emeritus of the university: "Well, this is a great vindication for John Ryan."[32]

All through the year 1931 Father Ryan urged the government to take action, preferably a $5,000,000,000 public-works program, but at least some plan for extensive benefits for the unemployed. Passing through Denver in July on his way from the Pacific Coast back to St. Paul, he gave an interview to the Denver *Post*, talking "less like a churchman than [like] a hard-headed, straight-thinking businessman." Unemployment was critical, he told the reporter: "Relief through natural causes which we hoped

[30] Ryan, "Some Effects of Rerum Novarum," *America*, April 25, 1931, pp. 58–60.
[31] The encyclical is expounded at length in Oswald von Nell-Breuning, *Reorganization of Social Economy* (New York, 1936).
[32] Ryan, *Social Doctrine in Action*, p. 242.

the summer would bring has not materialized. September may bring an upturn in business, but this may again prove merely seasonal. Unless prompt, adequate relief is afforded, the winter threatens to bring such conditions of hardship and suffering as this country has never known." He proposed to pay the interest on the $5,000,000,000 bond issue by increasing taxes on incomes in excess of $10,000.[33] Time enough to worry about retiring the bonds when the country got back on its feet.

For Ryan, the administration was so beyond hope that he stopped abusing Hoover. When the Social Action Department attached itself to a group interviewing the President, Ryan sent his assistant, Father McGowan. Ryan had already had his say. Anyway, Hoover alone was not to blame. The Senate turned down the La Follette–Costigan bill, which provided $375,000,000 for relief. Senator Robert M. La Follette, Jr., Republican from Wisconsin, warned his colleagues not to be so blind as the Bourbons before the French Revolution. Senator Royal S. Copeland, Democrat from New York, saw enough in one weekend in New York City to say: "There are thousands upon thousands, and I suppose literally millions of men, women, and children in the country who are not getting enough to eat, whose clothing is rapidly falling into rags, and many of whom are dispossessed from their homes."[34] La Follette tried a $5,500,000,000 public-works bill—very close to what Ryan wanted. It died quickly, and its mild successor, the Wagner-Garner bill, was killed by a veto. Ryan watched with dismay, begging La Follette "and a few others who have been keeping your heads" to defeat "the disastrous measures [like the Emergency Relief bill] that at the present moment are in danger of becoming enacted into law."[35]

In January, 1932, the central committees of the three major religious groups raised a common voice, their first joint statement since their attack on the twelve-hour day in the steel industry in 1919. They pointed to the specter of unemployment that had haunted the nation for three years. Current measures were said to be "grossly inadequate to prevent tragic demoralization of individual and family life." Deploring the timid inaction of the national government, they called for an immediate large-scale program of public works.[36] The statement showed the hand of McGowan, Israel, and the Reverend James Myers of the Federal Council of Churches;

[33] Denver *Post*, July 28, 1931.
[34] Quoted in Ryan, "Relief for the Unemployed—Whose Responsibility?" *Catholic Charities Review*, March, 1932, pp. 67–70.
[35] Ryan to Robert M. La Follette, Jr., April 22, 1932.
[36] New York *Times*, Jan. 5, 1932.

their views had remarkable unanimity. But the statement carried less weight than might have been expected, for while the three groups spoke in the name of their constituencies, there was abundant evidence that they did not necessarily speak for all, or even most, of their memberships.

Ryan carried his messages to meetings in various cities. In May, 1932, at Baltimore, he warned of the "imminent danger of violent resentment and uprising unless adequate relief is soon forthcoming." Parishes could not carry the load—many were on the verge of bankruptcy. He cited the warning of Edward F. McGrady, the AFL's legislative representative, to the Senate: "If nothing is done by government and starvation increases, the doors of revolt will be thrown open and the leaders cannot close them." Ryan was ready for extreme measures: "If an adequate public works program cannot be financed by either an issue of bonds or of paper money, there is nothing left but government operation and control of such basic industries as are necessary to provide the destitute millions with the means of decent human existence. To shrink from this last alternative is to confess intellectual and economic bankruptcy."[37] By October of the same year Ryan carried his program further before a group in Providence, Rhode Island. Drawing heavily on *Quadragesimo anno*, Ryan called for reorganization of American capitalism into occupational groups, in which workers and managers, cooperating with consumers and the state, manage industry for the general welfare. For the current "mixture of industrial anarchy and industrial despotism," he wanted a "guild State" equipped for adequate economic planning. Capitalism in the sense of private ownership would be retained. But its evils would be removed by making it responsive to the needs of the whole society through economic planning cooperatively arrived at by all interested parties. The goal was simply "the common good of society."[38]

Primarily concerned with industrial recovery, Ryan gave only passing attention to the farm problem. He saw through the futility of the Federal Farm Board's attempt to sop up grain surpluses, but his own offhand approval of scrapping farm machinery in 1931 was hardly better.[39] No longer the free silverite of 1896, he had little patience with currency tinkering. When John D. Black of Harvard came up with a domestic allotment plan, however, Ryan perked up. Black, along with a dozen other

[37] The speech, "Catholic Principles and the Present Crisis," is reprinted in Ryan, *Seven Troubled Years* (Ann Arbor, 1937), pp. 66–72.
[38] Ryan, "A New Social Order," *Catholic Action*, October, 1932, pp. 15, 18, 31.
[39] Ryan to Simon J. Lubin, Aug. 18, 1931.

farm economists, was thinking of limiting production and giving farmers who cooperated benefit payments collected by a fee charged at the point of processing. As a free trader, Ryan admitted to a prejudice against this kind of device, but farmers deserved better than unrestrained competition was giving them.[40]

Ryan knew that fundamental reform would not occur until Hoover left the White House. A balanced budget, a Federal Farm Board to absorb the presumably temporary glut of farm goods, and a Reconstruction Finance Corporation to tide shaky firms over the lean days—these were the administration's prescriptions.[41] The most one could hope for was relief to meet immediate hunger and public works to redistribute purchasing power. The buoyant hopes of the Hoover administration that the brief upturn in mid-1932 foreshadowed the end of the depression made even these modest demands visionary.

Until a more favorable administration should come into office, Ryan went back to his familiar role of educating Catholics to progressive ideas. Never had the battle been less lonely. In the depression years the voices of the faithful chorus of progressive social thinkers in both clergy and laity gained depth and breadth.

The atmosphere in the Church had changed considerably, partly because of the liberal posture on economic issues taken by the NCWC and in the bishops' joint pastorals, partly because of the depression, and now partly because of the new encyclical. There was no conceivable danger of a rebuke to Ryan for the radicalism of his views. Samuel A. Stritch, Archbishop of Milwaukee, probably expressed the norm: The constructive criticisms and proposals in Ryan's writings were a very great service to the Church. Even when Stritch disagreed with Ryan, "it has always been abundantly clear" that Ryan was "always safe within the range of sound principles."[42]

Still, it was one thing to avoid difficulties, another to spread social doctrine. Over the years Ryan had inoculated several hundred priests, not all successfully, to be sure, but enough to add volume to the call for social reform. Father O'Hara, Ryan's old cofighter on the minimum wage, became Bishop of Kansas City; Father McGowan stayed on in the SAD

---

[40] Ryan to W. L. Stockton, May 27, 1932.

[41] Hoover's policies are deftly sketched in Schlesinger, *The Crisis of the Old Order*, pp. 224–242, and more fully developed in Harris Gaylord Warren, *Herbert Hoover and the Great Depression* (New York, 1959).

[42] Samuel A. Stritch to Ryan, April 19, 1932.

office. Father Gilligan was back in St. Paul, working closely with labor leaders of all faiths, and losing caste with many of his brethren for such unorthodox activities. Father John W. R. Maguire, C.S.V., was embarked upon his career as a troubleshooter for labor. No one can measure this element of Ryan's influence accurately, but it had the effect—at least—of making liberal ideas familiar. Even more striking was the SAD's impact on the annual bishops' pastorals. These were prepared in committee, little debated on the floor. Yet, because the episcopal leadership of the NCWC was consistently weighted on the progressive side, these statements rarely fell far behind Ryan's own views. The joint Jewish-Protestant-Catholic statement on unemployment reflected Ryan's own views quite closely. It went out with the authority of the NCWC's administrative committee, and therefore, in the mind of the general public, in the name of the Catholic Church of the United States. A statement like this had a double force: it brought pressure on Congress to heed the voice of churchgoing Americans, and it set the standard by which churchgoers could measure their own tolerance for reform.

The Catholic Conferences on Industrial Problems carried the gospel to the diocesan level. Initiated by the SAD, but conducted under the auspices of the local bishop, these conferences were normally dominated by social reformers, like Ryan and McGowan, who enjoyed featured positions on the programs. The secular press, and even more, the religious press, gave them substantial coverage. Meanwhile the National Conference of Catholic Charities was still functioning, and its perennial speakers, like Father John O'Grady, were saying many of the same things.

No longer could Ryan complain of a dearth of Catholic magazines to carry the social message. *Commonweal* was constantly open; the *Catholic Charities Review* was available. Father Gillis of the *Catholic World* was delighted with Ryan's attack on the "American's Catechism on Democracy." He lamented that the Church lacked an Ireland, Gibbons, or Keane "to perform periodically the defense of the democratic ideal," and he welcomed Ryan's effort to fill that need.[43] With the advent of Father Parsons as editor of *America*, Ryan ended a five-year absence from that magazine dating back to differences in the child-labor fight. Parsons lauded Ryan's statements to the La Follette committee in 1931; Ryan was enthusiastic about *America*'s publicity for *Rerum novarum* on the fortieth anniversary. As long as Father Kerby edited the *Ecclesiastical Review*, he

[43] James M. Gillis to Ryan, Jan. 11, 1929.

could always find room for an article like Ryan's "The Priest's Concern with Unemployment" in 1931.

And yet, if much was done, much still needed doing. Two years into the depression Ryan had to acknowledge that the overwhelming majority of the American Catholic clergy still lacked competence in the economic field. About all that could be said as the Hoover administration trickled out was that Catholic social teaching was spreading, that the official pronouncements of the Church backed Ryan up, and that the despair of the depression years had given point and urgency to his criticisms.

More definite concern developed at the university, where periodic pressure from affluent benefactors, or potential benefactors, drew attention to the radicalism of the professor of moral theology. The individuals involved, the amounts involved, the occasions—all are subject of countless word-of-mouth anecdotes, none of sufficient authority to record as fact. The names vary with the telling, but the most persistent story was of a million dollars that one contributor made contingent on Ryan's departure from the university. The real event was undoubtedly less naked. The chancellor, Archbishop Curley, and the rectors, first Bishop Shahan and later Monsignor James H. Ryan, refused to buckle to any pressure to temper John Ryan's public statements on economic questions. Curley made his view clear in a letter to the rector: "A lot of people with money, like his [John Ryan's] namesake of the fallen copper industry, do not like some of the ideas put forth by Dr. Ryan. However, if they do not like Dr. Ryan's attitude, I am sure that they will not have much use for the attitude of our Holy Father."[44] The reference was to Thomas Fortune Ryan, industrialist and financier, whose benefactions to Catholic causes, reaching an estimated $20,000,000, did not include any substantial gift to the Catholic University of America.

The university felt pressure as a result of some articles on Ireland that Ryan wrote after a trip to Europe in the summer of 1932. On the way to the International Eucharistic Congress in Dublin, Ryan spoke to the Catholic Social Guild in London, the great predecessor to which he felt the Social Action Department and indeed all America owed much inspiration. After the congress, he went on to Rome for a private audience with Pope Pius XI, and on his way back he delivered a paper at the International Conference on Social Work in Frankfurt, Germany.

[44] Michael J. Curley to James Ryan, May 26, 1932, Archives of the Archdiocese of Baltimore.

The trip was the kind of relaxing occasion that Ryan rarely experienced. Originally planning to go over on the *SS Samaria*, he changed to the *SS De Grasse* to avoid unpleasantness when a friendly monsignor warned him that a "certain eminent gentleman" would be on the *Samaria*.[45] Ryan had had a recent reminder of his lack of favor with Cardinal O'Connell. When he was preparing *Questions of the Day* (1931), a collection of his papers, for a Boston publisher, he sent his manuscript to the censor of books for the Archdiocese of Boston for a routine *imprimatur*, that is, permission of the bishop to publish. In the friendliest possible way, the censor returned it with the assurance that the cardinal would never approve. Just the week before, the cardinal had condemned those who criticized the President in the troubled times of depression, and Ryan in his book had included some of his most stinging public remarks about Hoover.[46] Unconcerned, Ryan shipped the manuscript out to his own diocese and received the *imprimatur* forthwith. The incident was enough to remind him of his strained relations with Boston, and he wanted to avoid embarrassment on either side.

So he found himself on the *De Grasse*. Remote, not looking for company and finding little except for an occasional bridge game, he roamed the decks or settled into a deck chair while the convivial ark made its way to the congress. Because of the destination, the passengers were themselves overwhelmingly of Irish extraction, and the trip was a fine Irish stew of religious fervor and patriotic remembrance. The passengers were appropriately awed by their scholarly mate, so Dr. Ryan was left to his own routine; that is, until the next-to-last night, the traditional occasion for the ship's farewell party. Then even he was recruited, and an eyewitness has reported that he was equal to the demand. There was enough Irish left in him to associate courage, the faith, and the old country in just the right proportions to bring tears to Irish-American eyes. His old elocution piece, Joseph C. Clarke's ballad of the Spanish-American War, "The Fighting Irish"—"Kelly and Burke and Shea"—was just right, and an audience that had never heard of his speaking on anything more frivolous than unemployment insurance, wept openly:

> "Read out the names!" and Burke sat back
> And Kelly dropped his head
> While Shea—they called him Scholar Jack—
> Went down the list of dead. . . .

[45] Charles F. Shay to Ryan, April 6, 1932.
[46] Patrick J. Waters to Ryan, April 27, 1930.

"We're all in that dead man's list, by Cripe!
Kelly and Burke and Shea."
"Well, here's to the *Maine*, and I'm sorry for Spain,"
Said Kelly and Burke and Shea.

All his lessons in declamation came back to him as he intoned:

"Oh, the fighting races don't die out,
If they seldom die in bed,
For love is first in their hearts, no doubt,"
Said Burke; then Kelly said:

—and Ryan, caught up in his own Irish mist, let his voice soar—

"When Michael, the Irish Archangel, stands
The Angel with the sword,
And the battle dead from a hundred lands
Are ranged in one big horde,
Our line, that for Gabriel's trumpet waits,
Will stretch three deep that day
From Jehosaphat to the Golden Gates—
Kelly and Burke and Shea."
"Well, here's thank God for the race and the sod!"
Said Kelly and Burke and Shea.

A reporter was there to catch the spirit. "Father Ryan put his whole heart and soul into the declamation. We saw a new Father Ryan. We saw a Father Ryan proud of his lineage, proud of his Faith, putting everything his Irish heart could draw upon into that poem. One knew that his heart-strings were being played upon by himself, for he was thinking of his heritage and what his ancestors in the Faith had suffered and accomplished."[47]

The party arrived in Ireland just after Eamon De Valera had taken over the government from William T. Cosgrave. Almost immediately De Valera kicked up a great controversy by suspending "land annuities," the yearly payments to the British Treasury for the land that the British government had taken over in 1891 to distribute to Irish peasants. The issue was legal, technical, and almost literally charged with gunpowder. The British regarded the payments as their legal due. Though Irishmen were divided on the issue, many regarded the land annuities as the hang-over from generations of plunder and persecution. Legal correctness con-

[47] *Catholic Review*, July 8, 1932; Joseph C. Clarke, "The Fighting Irish," in *The Fighting Race and Other Verses and Ballads* (New York, 1911), pp. 13–15.

firmed the debt; Irish memory despised it. Characteristically. Irish-Americans responded to their emotions, memory winning over legal correctness.

As Irish as the rest of them, Ryan plunged into the controversy for *Commonweal* as if he knew all about it. The case for discontinuing the payments was weak legally, he said, though morally the argument was equivocal enough to warrant arbitration. He regretted the stubbornness on both sides. He obviously thought the recent change of government, De Valera replacing Cosgrave, unwise, but he felt confident that Cosgrave would "eventually pull Ireland out of the mess" De Valera was creating.[48] *Commonweal*, barely keeping afloat during the depression, less sure than its contributor that nothing was more fun than a good clean fight, felt no mission to enrage it readers. All but visibly holding its breath, it tried to cushion Ryan's dynamite in a bed of soft words. Ryan had made a careful study, "weighing impartially" the opposing arguments, an editor's note said, and anyway the editors might differ with his conclusions.[49]

For a while there was a calm; then *Commonweal*'s mail started coming in. A priest snorted at Ryan's "swagger" in announcing himself as an authority on the question; Ryan was "presumptuous" in writing on the topic at all. A lawyer thought that Ryan was basically ignorant of the governmental structure of Ireland and England. In the *Sign* and *Ave Maria*, more indignation was aired. Ryan fought back, holding his own fairly well. On moral grounds few were better prepared to argue than he. Taking the unpopular side, he had the advantage of claiming to be disinterested, or even better, interested only in justice. Commenting on the charge that he was playing England's game, he remarked pointedly that if the charge applied to all who opposed De Valera on the annuities, then "the players in the game are so numerous and crowded that they must be stepping on each other's toes."[50]

The controversy echoed at the university. A Cleveland priest wrote to the rector that having boosted the university for thirty years, he now had a helpful suggestion: "Get rid of that meddlesome Rev. John A. Ryan." Ryan had offended every Irishman by his stand; his bias leaves him "discredited and contemptible." The priest threatened that the Irish societies in the United States would condemn Ryan by name and "will

[48] Ryan, "Irish Land Annuities," *Commonweal*, Sept. 28, 1932, pp. 502–505; Oct. 5, 1932, pp. 530–532.
[49] Editor's note, *ibid.*, Sept. 28, 1932, p. 502.
[50] John Cullen, letter to editor, *ibid.*, Oct. 26, 1932, pp. 618–619; John F. Finerty, letter to editor, *ibid.*, Nov. 2, 1932, pp. 19–20; Ryan, letter to editor, *ibid.*, Nov. 2, 1932, pp. 21–22; Ryan to Thomas Woods, Nov. 25, 1932.

boycott the Catholic University until Ryan is driven from the staff."
The rector, James Ryan, replied mollifyingly, pointing out that the
university was not any one of its professors and that academic freedom
protected the staff in its public statements. The rector sent a copy of
the letter along to Curley, adding sadly that he had had several others
like it. But to John Ryan he gave no reproving word.[51]

A nasty intramural fight caused John Ryan more heartache than the
wealthy and the Irish.[52] After James Ryan became rector of the university
in late 1928, he undertook a general reorganization of the university,
hoping to make it resemble other American universities rather than the
Continental models on which originally it had been based. He hoped also
that reorganization would have the collateral effect of raising standards;
the trustees had come to believe that Bishop Shahan had not been sufficiently insistent upon academic excellence. As part of his reform, he
hoped to let ten or fifteen full professors go.

The reform covered the entire university, but James Ryan's special
nettle was the School of Theology. With relatively few students, its
overloaded roster of professors offered an obvious spot for pruning.
Furthermore, the trustees heard persistent reports that many bishops,
dissatisfied with the professional adequacy of the faculty of Sacred
Sciences, were sending their priests abroad for advanced work. Some
of the staff recklessly cut classes, diluting even further the already inadequate training. And finally, the school blocked new appointments
that the rector tried to make, offering candidates of its own who were
unacceptable because of inappropriate training. On the other side, the
School of Sacred Sciences felt that the new rector was unduly centraliz-
ing authority in his own hands. Behind him the school saw the gray

[51] The letter, Dec. 14, 1932, James Ryan's reply, Dec. 17, 1932, and his covering
letter to Curley, Dec. 17, 1932, are in the Archives of the Archdiocese of Baltimore.
[52] My account of this dispute is based on a survey of the *Catholic University
Catalogue*, 1928–1935; the letters of Curley and James Ryan in the Archives of the
Archdiocese of Baltimore and in the James Hugh Ryan Papers in the Archives of
the Archdiocese of Omaha (especially a long "Aide Memoire," dated Jan. 8, 1932,
sent by James Ryan to Monsignor Filippo Bernardini in Rome—this item in Omaha);
the correspondence between Archbishop John T. McNicholas and John Ryan in
the Archives of the Archdiocese of Cincinnati and in the Ryan papers at Catholic
University; the minutes of the Board of Trustees of the Catholic University of
America in the University Archives; miscellaneous correspondence in the John Ryan
papers; Roy J. Deferrari, "Memoirs of the Catholic University of America, 1918–
1958," MS in Mr. Deferrari's possession; and interviews with a number of men
whose memories go back to the dispute. No attempt has been made to describe this
incident exhaustively.

shadow of the dean of the Graduate School of Arts and Sciences, Roy J. Deferrari, a layman intimate with the rector.

The main tug of war was between James Ryan and two members of the theological faculty, Franz J. Coeln, dean of the school, and Henry Schumacher, professor of New Testament Scripture. He wanted them dismissed, partly for incompetence, partly for other reasons. For more than a year, the rector tried negotiation, but by October, 1930, he decided after a conference with them that "These people are determined to have war."[53]

John Ryan was both apart and involved. If his principal job was at the university, his principal interest was elsewhere—his department at the NCWC. Though Ryan lived in Caldwell Hall, Deferrari routed routine mail on university business to him at the NCWC office on Massachusetts Avenue. For all his years at the university, Ryan was not in close touch with its operation; he did not even know whether geology was taught there. There was plenty in the America of the early 1930's to occupy his mind without making a career of faculty politics. However, although he was not particularly friendly with Coeln and Schumacher, he felt that the school deserved his loyalty. When the rector dismissed Father Rolbiecki, associate professor of philosophy and one of Ryan's regular walking companions, the school's image of the new rector took on new vitality for John Ryan. The ouster, engineered by Deferrari, had been an arbitrary decision arising from a querulous resolution offered in a faculty meeting, and it was eventually reversed in Rome. Wrong in this act, was James Ryan also wrong in others? In an atmosphere that grew dense with mutual suspicion, it was easy to believe so. The faculty dining hall divided into cautious blocks, each noting and reporting the words of the other. John Ryan no longer had a wave or a friendly nod for his friend Father Maurice S. Sheehy when it became apparent that Sheehy was in the rector's camp.

To some extent John Ryan himself fell within the scope of the rector's complaints. He had attempted to have one of his own students, Father Haas, appointed for the theological faculty even though Haas's degree was in philosophy and not in sacred theology. (Coeln, the school's dean, also did not hold a doctor's degree in theology.) It was true, furthermore, that Ryan himself produced little in the particular field of his professorship. Since *Distributive Justice*, largely completed before his arrival at the university, he had produced no major work. He thought

[53] James Ryan to Curley, Oct. 27, 1930, Archives of the Archdiocese of Baltimore.

off and on of doing a textbook on ethics, but he wisely warned a friend not to wait for it. Some of his specialized articles for the *Ecclesiastical Review* were all right in their way, but less than could be expected from a university professor. However serviceable for the Church as a whole, Ryan's work outside the university actually weakened the department's reputation in one sense, for Ryan's expert knowledge on the virtue of justice left a substantial area of moral theology less adequately covered. As the rector wrote to a friendly monsignor in Rome who had the ear of the Sacred Congregation, "the University needs someone who will devote *all* his time to the promotion of Moral Theology understood in the common acceptance of the word, and not mere Moral Theology as applied to modern industrial problems." And finally, there *were* absences, not excessive in Father Ryan's case, perhaps, but enough to make him sensitive and to give substance to the rector's complaint.

The untidy episode dragged on for almost four years, and even then it was not ended completely. The rector enjoyed the support of Curley as chancellor, while the rebels, mainly through John Ryan, had a friend in Archbishop McNicholas of Cincinnati, who in turn was thought to have the ear of the Apostolic Delegate in Washington. When Coeln and Schumacher resigned at the end of 1931, the greatest sources of friction were gone, and John Ryan then succeeded Coeln as dean. Some unresolved problems remained. A new apostolic constitution for theological faculties, *Deus Scientiarum Dominus*, issued by Pope Pius XI on May 24, 1931, forbade members of theological faculties from teaching in other areas. When this mandate seemed to eliminate Ryan from his popular and influential course in industrial ethics in the School of Philosophy, a new avalanche of correspondents—James Ryan, John Ryan, Curley, McNicholas, and Archbishop John G. Murray of St. Paul—exchanged views before John Ryan got a mandate to continue his course. Not the least of the problems facing the rector and the new dean was the revivification of the School of Sacred Sciences. Though the depression left dioceses ill equipped to pay for graduate training for their priests, John Ryan personally urged bishops to send their brightest young men. In three years he brought enrollment up substantially. Several new appointments were made; these coincided with some retirements. The effect was to remake the school. To avoid cause for unfavorable comment, Father Ryan also became more circumspect about cutting his classes for outside engagements.

The trouble was nasty, painful to all concerned. It left Ryan unrumpled, largely because it was peripheral to his main interest. Once Coeln and Schumacher were gone, Ryan's own courses were settled, and the school began to grow, the controversy—John Ryan's share in it, at least —ended, and Ryan returned to public affairs with his customary verve.

The great issue in 1932, of course, was the election. As the depression grew worse without effective action from the White House, Ryan finally stopped pecking at President Hoover. There was a limit after three years, and besides there were better projects, like picking a new President. As Ryan surveyed the potential candidates for the Presidency, they seemed unpromising. Hoover, of course, was out, and, after the nominating convention, the whole Republican party as well. Ryan ruled the Socialists out too, after a somewhat greater effort. Socialists were more eligible than they had ever been before. Ryan noted that the Labour Party in England was "probably little, if any, more anti-religious than the other political parties in Great Britain." Before the election Ryan could not bring himself to say anything about the propriety of voting for Norman Thomas.[54] He hoped that Newton D. Baker would be the nominee: "You have abundant ability, you realize the gravity of the situation, you are persuaded, I think, that the old formulas will not get us out of this crisis, you have the courage to utilize such new methods as are necessary, and you retain a sufficient belief in sane liberalism to impel you to identify the common good with the welfare of the masses rather than with that of the powerful classes."[55] Then, while Ryan was in Ireland, the Democratic Convention in Chicago nominated Governor Franklin D. Roosevelt of New York, and a new era opened.

Ryan viewed Roosevelt without enthusiasm. Four years before, Governor Roosevelt had written in great confidence to ask for Ryan's view of a prospective appointee. Neither knew the other except by reputation. In September, 1932, Roosevelt wrote to him again, notifying him that Raymond Moley was now heading a staff of advisers. Would Ryan send Moley his views from time to time and give Moley whatever specific help he might ask for? Ryan replied quite generally that he would be glad to respond to requests from Roosevelt or Moley.[56] For Roosevelt it was

[54] Ryan to A. J. Beck, Sept. 29, 1932; Ryan, "American Catholics and American Socialism," *Ecclesiastical Review*, December, 1932, pp. 584–592.

[55] Ryan to Newton D. Baker, June 10, 1932.

[56] Franklin D. Roosevelt to Ryan, Dec. 8, 1928; Sept. 1, 1932; Ryan to Roosevelt, Sept. 7, 1932.

an inexpensive fishing expedition, and he got no better than the bait was was worth.

Roosevelt's campaign gave Ryan little basis for enthusiasm. The governor's speeches emerged from the tensions of three group of speech writers.[57] As Roosevelt shuffled from his liberal to his conservative to his moderate teams, who was to know which was the real Roosevelt? When Roosevelt rapped Hoover for excessive spending and an unbalanced budget, where was Father Ryan, he of the $5,000,000,000 public-works program, to go? Just before the election, Ryan put his argument for increasing purchasing power into the *Catholic World* as "National Responsibility in the Present Crisis."[58] Did Roosevelt stand for this, Roosevelt who said at Pittsburgh that Hoover's four years of spending was "the most reckless and extravagant past that I have been able to discover in the statistical record of any peacetime government anywhere, any time"? He then promised to reduce the cost of current governmental operations by 25 per cent.[59]

Right after the election, Father McGowan read Ryan's lecture on "The Present Emergency" to the Catholic Conference on Industrial Problems in Albany, New York. Again no mention of FDR; praise for *The Abolition of Unemployment* by Frank D. Graham of Princeton, but not a word about the President-elect.[60] In the course of his article on American socialism for the *Ecclesiastical Review*, written that same month, Ryan observed that neither of the old parties appeared willing or able to move toward the practical political instrument for achieving social justice. Would Catholics thus have to organize a new party?

At the same time, Dr. Ryan was throwing out lines to the people around Roosevelt, perhaps trying to ingratiate himself, more likely adding to the liberal pressure aimed at pulling Roosevelt to an active program of government intervention. Without much real excuse, he wrote a note off to Moley praising FDR for ridding the White House of Hoover and for committing himself in his Commonwealth Club speech to adequate distribution of purchasing power. In January, 1933, he had a kind word for a recent speech by Rexford Tugwell, another braintruster. Tugwell had outlined a fairly active governmental policy, and the notion easily

[57] Frank Freidel, *Franklin D. Roosevelt: The Triumph* (Boston, 1956), pp. 261–274, 323–337.
[58] Ryan, "National Responsibility in the Present Crisis," *Catholic World*, November, 1932, pp. 169–174.
[59] Freidel, *Franklin D. Roosevelt: The Triumph*, p. 363.
[60] Ryan, "The Present Emergency," reprinted in *Seven Troubled Years*, pp. 81–85.

210

spread that he was throwing up trial balloons for the President-elect himself.[61] Was there to be some new vision after all? As Ryan crouched beside his radio that cool fourth day of March, 1933, he was ready to hear a message of hope.

[61] Ryan to Raymond Moley, Nov. 29, 1932; Ryan to Rexford B. Tugwell, Jan. 31, 1933.

Right Reverend
New Dealer

THREE DAYS BE-
fore the inauguration of Franklin D. Roosevelt, a student
reporter caught Dr. Ryan at Caldwell Hall. The situation,
the stocky priest told him grimly, was not merely critical
but desperate. "The great obstacles are the greed of the
few who will still enjoy an abundance of comforts, the
timidity of the many who have never learned to think
courageously." Will the government take the necessary
action? That depends on the incoming President. "We should
all earnestly pray God to give him the vision and courage
that he will surely need in the stupendous task of leading
the American people out of the valley of indecision and
despondency."[1]

With a keener feel for alliteration than for the sense
of the interview, *Tower* reported: "F.D." POSSESSES PANIC
PANACEA. The headline, prophetic of Ryan's later judgment,
was premature in early March. For the first few weeks,
Ryan, ill in bed, said little. Roosevelt's inaugural address
moved him: its bold confidence, its sense of the seriousness
of the crisis, its promise of an active government. Did Roose-

[1] *Tower*, March 2, 1933.

velt's bold words have magic denied to Hoover's tired litany of confidence?

The new faces in Washington were strangers to Ryan. Surprising enough, he had never even met Frances Perkins, the Secretary of Labor, although she had been active in social reform since the early days of the National Consumers' League. Before the inauguration Ryan had, rather formally, worked on James A. Farley, chairman of the Democratic National Committee and Postmaster-General-Designate, to appoint Maurice Ryan, John's younger brother, chief inspector of the department.[2] Then after FDR went into office, Ryan wrote to the President in the hope of getting Judson King appointed to the Federal Power Commission.[3] That same month the administrative board of the NCWC instructed its staff to stay out of the patronage scramble.[4] Ryan did not interpret the ruling as applying to his brother, for his pressure on Farley ended only in 1938 when Maurice was appointed Inspector-in-Charge in St. Paul.

Ryan watched as legislation went into the congressional hopper. Representative John W. McCormack, Democrat from Massachusetts, sent him for criticism a bill giving relief to homeowners; Ryan returned it with favorable comment.[5] Senator Hugo L. Black, Democrat from Alabama, spoke in favor of a bill limiting work to thirty hours a week, defending it by a loose construction of the interstate commerce clause. The speech was an "astonishing achievement," Ryan told Black; though he regarded himself as quite an authority on the Constitution, he had "no idea that such a good case could be made."[6] The Economy Act, passed in mid-March, was discouraging: in reducing salaries of government employees and lowering veterans' benefits, Roosevelt was cutting off purchasing power, just as Hoover had done. Ryan had no particular enthusiasm for the currency manipulation involved in the Emergency Banking Act—it did not put more money into the hands of the people who could spend it, and that was the important thing.[7] When Professor Edwin W. Kemmerer of Princeton denounced the processing tax in the proposed Agricultural Adjustment Act, Ryan hastily defended it in the

[2] Ryan to Maurice I. Ryan, Jan. 17, 1933.
[3] Ryan to Franklin D. Roosevelt, April 5, 1933.
[4] Ryan to Fred J. Collins, Jan. 12, 1934.
[5] John W. McCormack to Ryan, April 1, 1933; Ryan to McCormack, April 5, 1933.
[6] Ryan to Hugo L. Black, April 7, 1933.
[7] Ryan to M. S. Rukeyser, May 16, 1933.

New York *Times*. The device created difficulties perhaps insoluble, but, as the President said, bold experimentation offered the only way out of the present intolerable conditions.[8] Certain that large governmental expenditures provided the real test of Roosevelt's success, Ryan had doubts about the $3,300,000,000 public-works provision attached to the National Industrial Recovery bill (NIRA). Inadequate to give impetus to business, it might well discredit public spending to prime the industrial pump. Furthermore, momentum was important, and the NIRA lacked the necessary sense of urgency. Ryan approved the industrial-agreements proposed, but not as a substitute for a statutory thirty-hour week and minimum wage.[9]

In the early months of the new administration, Ryan moved in closer to the New Dealers. At the request of the White House, Miss Perkins sent Ryan a form letter inviting him to a conference on labor problems in late March.[10] The atmosphere at the Labor Department typified the change in Washington. Headed by an old social worker, excited by the prospect of new vigor in the American economy, the department proclaimed the promise of the New Deal. The reformers, no longer mourning the day and cursing the blight, now had power. Plans long deferred, dreams half believed, now showed up on legislative dockets. The White House listened, often, though not always, with approval. Ryan, catching the mood, smothered his doubts about FDR and the New Deal. Writing for the Dublin *Studies* for May, 1933, he noted that the laws enacted or in immediate prospect—relief for the unemployed, banking reform, Agricultural Adjustment Act, NIRA, Tennessee Valley Authority—were epochal. "Taken together, they constitute a more comprehensive and fundamental program of legislation than all the enactments of Congress during the preceding ten years."[11] When the President visited Catholic University in June to receive an honorary degree, no smile—with the exception of Roosevelt's, of course—was broader than John A. Ryan's.[12]

During the next six months the administration called upon his services. In July the public relations office of the NRA asked him to help prepare a letter for the President's signature enlisting the support of each American

[8] New York *Times*, April 9, 1933.

[9] Ryan to William M. Leiserson, March 23, 1933.

[10] Letter, undated, undirected; acknowledged by Ryan to Frances Perkins, March 29, 1933.

[11] Ryan, "President Roosevelt's Economic Program," Dublin *Studies*, June, 1933, pp. 194–204.

[12] *Catholic University Bulletin*, July, 1933, cover.

clergyman for the NRA codes.[13] Later that month Miss Perkins asked him to join the advisory council of the United States Employment Service.[14] Ryan accepted, and the following year he became chairman of the group, a post "merely honorary," he said honestly.[15] In September, Harold Ickes, Secretary of the Interior, appointed him to the National Advisory Committee of the Subsistence Homesteads Division.[16] In November, 1933, the Department of Labor asked Ryan to submit a comprehensive agenda of labor legislation.[17] By this time, however, he was caught up in the excitement of an ecclesiastical honor; there is no record of his having replied.

In September, 1933, the Apostolic Delegate in Washington announced that Pope Pius XI had named Father Ryan a domestic prelate. Now Father Ryan became the Right Reverend John A. Ryan, his somber black cassock replaced by the purple dress robes of a monsignor. The new rank, above a priest and below a bishop, was honorary, carrying with it no additional responsibility.

Bishop Ryan, the rector at Catholic University, had initiated the process.[18] Just at graduation time, the rector sent Father Sheehy to sound out John Ryan. Not fond of either the rector or his intermediary, Ryan uttered a vulgar phrase that he saved for conversations among men. He had always stood on his own feet, never seeking favor, never particularly wanting it. He made a show of annoyance that anyone should think he cared. Sheehy pointed out mollifyingly that, aside from the personal honor, the promotion would reinforce Ryan's teaching authority, announcing to all that in Rome Dr. Ryan was not thought unorthodox or radical. This was what the rector had in mind, Sheehy explained soothingly. (The rector also thought privately that the honor might smooth over the hard feelings created by his own squabbles with the School of Theology, and increase the prestige of the school among the American clergy.[19]) Put this way, the offer gave Ryan a graceful way to reconsider. Having "emulated Caesar—but only a little way,"[20] he accepted. The

13 Ryan to William E. Sweet, July 18, 1933.
14 Perkins to Ryan, Aug. 5, 1933.
15 Ryan to J. M. Deem, Sept. 12, 1934.
16 Harold L. Ickes to Ryan, Sept. 22, 1933.
17 Boris Stern to Ryan, Nov. 4, 1933.
18 Interview with Maurice S. Sheehy, April 19, 1958; Ryan to John T. Mc-Nicholas, Sept. 20, 1933.
19 James Ryan to Michael J. Curley, June 15, 1933, Archives of the Archdiocese of Baltimore.
20 Ryan to Mary Spencer, Oct. 5, 1933.

machinery moved swiftly. In September, the rector frantically hunted for Father Ryan on the New Jersey coast to report that the official word had come through from the Holy See.

The new monsignor replied to the flood of congratulatory mail with characteristic variety. To the bishops, he was proper and, unless he knew them very well, formal. From Boston congratulations came from Francis J. Spellman, auxiliary bishop. Father Ryan was "sincerely grateful." Even to a former student, Bishop Louis D. Kucera of Lincoln, Nebraska, he remained stiff. But to brother priests and old friends, a jocular Ryan replied. He warned an older priest to be "mindful of the proprieties." To those who saw this as the first step to higher ranks within the Church, he was happily prepared to "admit with you that I ought to be Pope"; he would even accept a cardinal's red hat if he did not have to live in Rome. But he did not want a bishopric, thank you, because that means work and trouble—unfortunate both for him and for a diocese. (Father McGowan, down at the SAD office, would not quarrel with that.) For one of his correspondents who thought that his new rank entitled him to wear an episcopal ring, he promised to get a large iron ring with a correspondingly oversize iron knob. He assured another that if anything cramped his style at their next party together, it would be his faulty digestion, not his purple trimmings. One warm greeting noted that the recognition was overdue; to this Ryan replied: "My well known modesty would tempt me to disagree with you in this judgment were it not for the fact that several bishops . . . have said the same thing."[21] When Harry Earl Woolever, an old opponent from the campaign of 1928, hinted that the honor rewarded Ryan's fight against prohibition, the new monsignor chuckled to a friend that the Pope should have waited until the thirty-sixth state ratified the Twentieth Amendment (repealing the Eighteenth).[22]

Behind his jocularity, however, was ample understanding of the honor: the recognition and the implied approval of his teaching and activities.

On December 8, 1933, in the National Shrine of the Immaculate Conception on the university grounds, Archbishop Curley invested the monsignor with the purple robes of his rank. At an elaborate banquet that evening in the Willard Hotel, the rector presided, and a parade of speakers reviewed Ryan's contributions to American social thought and action. His teacher, Father Kerby, and his student, Father Haas; Miss Perkins;

[21] The letters are all in Ryan Writings, 1909–1935: Congratulations.
[22] Ryan to Russell J. Clinchy, Oct. 4, 1933.

Senator Norris, an old ally; Senator Henrick Shipstead, a fellow Min-
nesotan; Edward Keating, editor of *Labor*—all spoke their appointed pieces,
recalling Ryan's career almost as if it were over. In reply, Ryan reviewed
the years and acknowledged his long-standing debt to the academic freedom that the university had guaranteed to him. Part of Miss Perkins'
speech and all of Monsignor Ryan's speech were broadcast, and up at
Trinity College, Ryan's two sisters, Sister Constance and Sister Mary
John, close by the radio, shared their brother's great moment.[23] For the
month surrounding the event Ryan thought of little else, and when he
went to St. Paul for the Christmas vacation, the rounds of congratulations
started all over again.

When he returned in January, his mind went back to social questions.
The situation in his own office was the nation in microcosm: not enough
money to pay the salaries of the three priests and six women on the SAD's
office staff. Several men were being dropped from the NCWC, and
Ryan tried to place some of them elsewhere.[24] But thousands of executives
all over the country were trying to do exactly the same thing. The nation
needed a general upturn to absorb excess executives as well as excess
workers.

For that upturn the new monsignor looked to FDR. Writing in *Commonweal* in April, 1934, on the "New Deal and Social Justice," Ryan
came within a hair of equating the two. The individual measures, especially
the NRA and the heavy tax on large incomes, conformed well to Catholic
social thinking. More than that: the New Deal "implies an economic
system that is neither individualism nor socalism," he said. "It assures
the abolition of the anarchy and manifold injustices of the former and
avoids the political despotism and economic inefficiency of the latter. It
would provide the maximum attainable measure of self-government by
the industries themselves. If it gives labor full participation in the codes
it will ensure the maximum of industrial democracy. It would reserve to
the state the functions which, in the words of Pope Pius XI 'the state
alone can perform,' namely, 'directing, watching, stimulating and restraining as circumstances suggest or necessity demands.' " In a word, this new
social order would provide "a *via media*, perhaps the only possible *via
media* between capitalism and Communism."[25] Ryan was confident that

[23] Ryan, *Social Doctrine in Action*, pp. 263–265.
[24] Thomas F. Lillis to Ryan, Feb. 20, 1934.
[25] Ryan, "The New Deal and Social Justice," *Commonweal*, April 13, 1934, pp.
657–659.

the administration was going as far as practicable, and seemed "willing to go further when the time is ripe."[26]

Father Ryan was making a conscious, deliberate verdict for the Roosevelt administration. Now almost sixty-five, he would scarcely know any other President. If Roosevelt remained two terms, those eight years would carry Ryan past his Scriptural threescore and ten, certainly past the time of great new activity. It was now or never. In the ferment that followed the spectacular "hundred days," Ryan decided against pettifogging quibbles on detail. If progressive hopes shriveled as they had in 1915, the nation might never get moving again. A social reformer had to support an administration more committed to social change than any other in American history. Monsignor Ryan never regretted this decision.

Through the spring of 1934, Ryan busily prepared two summer courses at the University of Wisconsin. Invited by Edwin E. Witte, chairman of the department of economics and an old Washington associate on the preliminary advisory board for social security, Ryan, who had taught only at Catholic institutions, accepted with delight, even though the fame of Madison's summer heat had reached his ears. He stayed at a nearby Dominican sisters' convent—as a member of the Third Order of St. Dominic, he was sort of a member of the family—and between his professorial duties and the social life of Madison, he had a busy and thoroughly enjoyable six weeks.[27] His schedule include a little extra-curricular fighting for good causes. He told a local group of the National Conference of Christians and Jews, meeting at a Catholic church in Madison, that much as he deplored the violence of labor in strikes, he regretted even more the tactics of employers in labeling strikers as communists. The communist bugaboo, he said, was the figment of too eager imaginations. Communists were pestiferous and irritating, but their influence, even in the labor movement, was negligible.[28]

Before Ryan returned from Madison, General Hugh S. Johnson, administrator of the NRA, appointed the priest-professor to a three-man Industrial Appeals Board to hear the complaints of the small manufacturers who felt unduly burdened by NRA codes. A presidential board, headed by Clarence Darrow, had recently charged that the codes were encouraging the growth of monopoly and cartels. Widely publicized, the report appealed to the powerful sympathy—of Americans generally and of progressives in particular—for the small businessman, and stimulated the critics of the NRA into renewed activity.

Johnson appointed the Industrial Appeals Board to allay this outcry —"to fill the gap recently left by the dissolution of the independent Darrow Review Board," the Washington *Post* observed.[29] Ryan's appointment came on the recommendation of Father Sheehy,[30] who was maneuvering into the position of Catholic liaison man with the administration. To his two full-time jobs and two part-time jobs, Ryan now added one more full-time job, at a salary of $6,000 a year.

Conscientious about his new duties, Ryan never missed a hearing in the board's ten-month life. The board heard a total of sixty-nine cases, and while the three members averaged only about twenty hours a month in the hearing room on Sixteenth Street, they spent almost as much time in conference, and perhaps as much again in writing their decisions. Almost all the cases involved an appeal for relief by a small producer who could not make ends meet when he lived up to code requirements on wages and hours. Fearful of the demoralizing effect of exceptions, the Industrial Appeals Board frostily turned down the appeals. As the board said in one decision, "It is not the purpose of the National Industrial Recovery Act to penalize efficient production units by granting compensatory exemptions to their less efficient competitors."[31] If small-scale producers could not meet the minimum standards, Ryan told a group of Catholic women in Baltimore, then "let the small businessman perish."[32] Holding to this line, the IAB was reversed by its superiors only once.

Ryan's job ended abruptly in May, 1935, when the Supreme Court overturned the NRA.[33] Ryan had known right along that the NRA would probably not pass muster with the Supreme Court. Yet when the court sustained the Minnesota Moratorium Law in 1934, liberal observers had detected tolerance for emergency legislation that might extend to the NRA. Now dismayed, Ryan gave out a press release: "Some other way must be found, now the NRA has been declared unconstitutional, to subordinate wealth and business to the common welfare of the country. . . . Destroying the NRA opens the doors to a general lowering of a

[29] Washington *Post*, July 17, 1934.
[30] Sheehy to Ryan, June 28, 1934; Ryan to Sheehy, July 3, 1934.
[31] National Recovery Administration, Industrial Appeals Board, Decision on the Appeal of J. F. Wieder, April 12, 1935, Archives of the United States.
[32] Ryan, "Present Outlook for Business Recovery," MS of speech, Jan. 20, 1935.
[33] Schechter *v.* United States, 295 U.S. 495.

standard of living which is already too low. Employers who do not wish to cut wages and lengthen hours will find it hard to resist the competition of those who will hasten to reduce their wage costs. It is a time, too, for the greater growth of union membership so as to establish general wage and hours contracts."[34] Justice Brandeis' assent to the decision toned down Ryan's rebuke considerably.

The year 1934–1935 had been exhausting. The enrollment in the School of Sacred Sciences had risen sharply, though it was still below what the trustees regarded as a full-time load. Ryan continued at Trinity and at the Social Service School. The SAD bore the brunt of his job with the NRA. He still put in his regular two hours a day, but Father McGowan had to handle the regular work even more than usual. Ryan also found time for a reduced schedule of outside lectures to lay groups. The monsignor carried his years well, but by June he was worn out. So a week with his niece, Mary Quinn, and her family at Seaside Park, New Jersey, where the days were crowded only with Atlantic breezes, relaxed the tensions built up by the year-long fidgety circuit in Washington.

The year had also been discouraging: the demise of the NRA and, even more dismaying for the long run, the New Deal's loss of its dynamic thrust. Ryan now saw that social security legislation would pass, to be sure, and he could rejoice in his share, rather a small share, in hammering out the details as a member of Frank P. Graham's general advisory council.[35] But the President's public-works program, inadequate to restore purchasing power, faced a terminal date, July, 1936. Ryan feared that Roosevelt, with ill-informed optimism, expected the depression to end by that date. The New Deal was faltering because of halfhearted measures. Ryan heard echoes of Hoover when the administration emphasized production and credit instead of consumption. No wonder the lunatic fringe commanded an audience, he said: the Townsend plan for $200 a month to all persons over sixty-five, Senator Huey P. Long's "share the wealth" program, quack remedies for complete federal control of currency and banks "which are week by week advocated over the radio" (a reference to Father Charles E. Coughlin, the "radio priest" from Royal Oak, Michigan).[36]

[34] NCWC–SAD press release, May 29, 1935.
[35] Paul H. Douglas, *Social Security in the United States* (New York, 1936), pp. 26–68; Witte to author, *loc. cit.*
[36] Ryan, "Quack Remedies for the Depression Malady," *Catholic Charities Review*, April, 1935, pp. 104–107; "The Present Industrial Outlook," speech, May, 1935, in *Seven Troubled Years*, pp. 192–195.

The summer months put the national welfare in a new light, however, for a busy Congress extended the horizons of the New Deal. The Wagner-Connery Act (1935) rescued Section 7a from the NRA and set up a National Labor Relations Board to encourage unionization of workers—"probably the most just, beneficent, and far-reaching piece of labor legislation ever enacted in the United States," Ryan said later on. The Social Security Act provided unemployment and old-age insurance. Less than two years before, Ryan dared not hope that Congress would enter this latter field, and even fifteen months before, when he served on the advisory board that helped prepare the act, congressional approval seemed remote. Yet the fact was that the Social Security legislation passed. The Holding Company Act broke open the device through which public utilities concealed their affairs from effective public regulation. The Guffey Act created a code for the sick bituminous coal industry. And finally the Revenue Act contained a startling schedule of progressive taxes on personal and corporate income. The New Deal caravan, stalled in April and May, now raced with these "conspicuous and far-reaching" acts.[37]

If much was done, much still needed doing. Returning to Washington in the fall, Ryan wrote a long letter to the President, urging him to new efforts. "I have rejoiced over practically all the legislation enacted since you assumed the high office of President of the United States," he told Roosevelt. But, he went on, "I do not believe that the legislative program or the New Deal is yet substantially complete." Nor could it be without a huge program of useful public works supplemented by relief or work relief for two or three years. The essentials of the NRA, especially on wages and hours, had to be reestablished, by a constitutional amendment if necessary. An appeal to the amending process, Ryan said, will become "absolutely necessary and probably reasonably feasible" if the Supreme Court overturns the AAA, the Guffey Coal Act, the Wagner Labor Act, and some others.[38]

During the summer Father McGowan had worked on a draft statement of Catholic principles relevant to the present crisis. Ryan now took the draft, revised it, and helped circulate it among prominent Catholics, lay and clerical, for their signatures. As finally issued, it carried 133 names. Two bishops, Robert E. Lucey of Amarillo, Texas, and Aloisius J.

[37] Ryan, "Social Justice in the 1935 Congress," *Catholic Action*, September, 1935, pp. 7–9.
[38] Ryan to Roosevelt, Sept. 24, 1935.

Muench of Fargo, North Dakota, signed, but their signatures were blacked out to avoid embarrassment to them or to many other bishops who were not asked to sign. The statement, entitled "Organized Social Justice," acknowledged the need for a reform of public morality to end greed as an obstacle to social reform, then gave principal emphasis to occupational groups. Looking back ruefully at the NRA, the Catholic group warned that only a comparable arrangement could save America from fascism or communism. In ten years the NRA could have led to a national system; even now, it could be reestablished in five years by a constitutional amendment.[39]

Roosevelt showed no inclination to fight for a new NRA, however; indeed, the impression was widespread that his public protests at the Schechter decision masked private relief at the clean quick death blow for the NRA. Without FDR's support, the NRA would not return.[40] No matter. Ryan had fought losing battles for most of his life. He was used to advocating the momentarily unpopular. His approval of Roosevelt did not hinge on this one measure.

As the result of the 1935 Congress, Ryan regained his early fervor for the New Deal: "Not one of these measures violates any legal or moral right of any individual. Not one of them is socialistic or unpatriotic or un-American. Every one of them is in accordance with humanity, Christianity, and social justice. The only liberty that they interfere with is the liberty of the economically strong to oppress the economically weak."[41]

This judgment did not, by any means, command the assent of all Catholics. The *Catholic World*, under Father Gillis, an old and respected ally—"a sincere, valiant and effective champion of social justice," Ryan called him—went against Roosevelt in February, 1936. Gillis feared the mounting national debt and the New Dealers' careless disregard of the Constitution.[42] Ryan tried to argue Gillis back into the fold. He cited the authority of O. M. W. Sprague, a Harvard economist who left the New Deal because of disagreement over fiscal policy, to show that the debt could safely rise $10,000,000,000 (to $40,000,000,000). He also appealed

[39] Ryan *et al.*, "Organized Social Justice," pamphlet (Washington, D.C., 1935).
[40] Arthur M. Schlesinger, Jr., *The Politics of Upheaval: The Age of Roosevelt, III* (Boston, 1960), pp. 289–290.
[41] Ryan, "Americanism: The Counterfeit and the Genuine," speech, February, 1936, in *Seven Troubled Years*, pp. 223–228.
[42] James M. Gillis, "Our Unconventional President," *Catholic World*, February, 1936, pp. 513–523.

to Professor Edward S. Corwin, the Princeton authority on constitutional law, who had argued brilliantly in *The Twilight of the Supreme Court* (1934) that in confronting New Deal legislation the Court had virtually unfettered freedom of choice to sustain or upset an extension of federal power. The Court could simply draw on either of two sets of precedents, one favorable, one unfavorable. Ryan went even further on this latter point: "In considering legislation of supreme importance to a very great industry [the soft coal industry], with its hundreds of thousands of employees and thousands of employer capitalists, both the President and Congress were in duty bound to disregard constitutional doubts, even if the chance were ten to one against constitutionality." He closed with a vigorous warning:

Let us not deceive ourselves. Let us honestly face the inevitable alternative. If Roosevelt is defeated the victors will not be men who have either the desire or competence to provide a more perfct program of social justice. If Roosevelt is defeated it is the Bourbons who will triumph. Just as the Harding administration brought the country back to "normalcy," so will the triumphant Bourbons return the government and industry to that type of *laissez faire* which brought on the great depression. Only, the new depression will be incomparably more disastrous than that which followed the policies and practices of the delirious 1920's.[43]

Gillis remained unconvinced, and henceforth remained in the ranks of Roosevelt's opponents.

Ryan's open support of Roosevelt finally reached its climax in a famous radio speech, "Roosevelt Safeguards America," delivered three weeks before the 1936 election. Ostensibly a denial of the slander that FDR was a communist or a communist dupe, the speech was unmistakably intended as a rebuttal to Father Coughlin.

Father Coughlin and Monsignor Ryan had been building up to a clash for a long time. Neither wanted the public spectacle of two Catholic priests at each other's throat, yet neither was willing to let the other's statements stand unchallenged as the teaching of the Catholic Church, and polite argument finally gave way to public brawl.

Father Coughlin, as a young parish priest in Royal Oak, Michigan, began broadcasting his Sunday sermons in the early 1930's, and in the course of the depression these sermons moved into social and economic

[43] Ryan, "An Open Letter to the Editor," *ibid.*, April, 1936, pp. 22-26.

policy. An early supporter of Roosevelt, the radio priest warmly applauded the social reforms of the "hundred days." Some time in 1934, however, Coughlin turned on Roosevelt and proposed a program that, to the extent that it was specific, looked to fiscal reform.[44] The primary targets of Coughlin's barbs were Wall Street and the Federal Reserve Board. By 1936 Coughlin managed to tie the New Deal, Roosevelt, communism, and Jewish domination into a tidy bundle for a radio audience, not by any means wholly Catholic, that regularly numbered millions. In August, 1936, *Social Justice*, the newspaper of Coughlin's National Union for Social Justice, printed as "facts no one can deny" that Bernard Baruch, the financier, was in truth "Acting President of the United States" and that the "communist philosophy" of Felix Frankfurter held a "dominating influence" in the New Deal.[45] The following month, less than seven weeks before the election, Coughlin set the issue for November clearly: "Christ against chaos and Christianity against communism."[46]

At first Ryan looked upon Coughlin benignly. In December, 1933, at the end of a prepared speech in Detroit, Coughlin's backyard, Ryan was asked what he thought of his clerical associate. He would come to regret his reply: "As between those who are fighting for social justice and those who are fighting against it, Father Coughlin is on the side of the angels. Even though he makes mistakes, he is stirring up the animals, and that had to be done by somebody."[47] The statement got Ryan into trouble immediately, for Coughlin's followers did not like being called "animals," but Ryan meant no conscious offense; he was using what he thought was a familiar colloquialism—he knew it was familiar to one old farm boy at least—and he regretted the offense he had given.[48] Ryan knew that he and Coughlin differed on the means to recovery, but this awareness did not trouble him. Actually, temperate clashes of opinion among the clergy in the public press were not a bad thing, he said: "Such differences show that there is more freedom of speech in the Church than non-Catholics assume."[49]

[44] Coughlin's break with Roosevelt is explored in James P. Shenton, "The Coughlin Movement and the New Deal," *Political Science Quarterly*, September, 1958, pp. 352–373. Coughlin's sixteen-point platform is reprinted in Donald R. McCoy, *Angry Voices: Left-of-Center Politics in the New Deal Era* (Lawrence, Kan., 1958), pp. 119–121.

[45] *Social Justice*, Aug. 31, 1936.

[46] *Ibid.*, Sept. 21, 1936.

[47] Quoted in Ryan to Lloyd M. Cosgrove, Oct. 15, 1936, and in *Social Justice*, Oct. 19, 1936.

[48] Ryan to John L. Richards, Dec. 13, 1933.

[49] Ryan to Louis F. Mesiner, Dec. 13, 1933.

Then, after Coughlin turned savagely on FDR, Ryan reversed his earlier opinion. In February, 1935, his judgment was that Coughlin "is proposing no constructive measure of social justice. He is merely denouncing social injustice and most of the time in an intemperate and extreme manner."[50]

By this time Ryan had felt the impact of Coughlin's power. In January, 1935, a comfortable majority of the Senate supported the proposed adherence of the United States to the World Court. But since a two-thirds vote was required, the opposing forces put on a last-minute radio appeal for popular pressure on the senators. Ryan joined Mrs. Roosevelt and others in speaking for the Court. Coughlin, opposing the measure, spoke on the radio with characteristic forcefulness: "Are you in sympathy with the United States Senators, two thirds of whom are prepared to sign on the dotted line thereby casting America into the very thraldom of communistic atheism,—of European non-Americanism?"[51] The measure failed by seven votes to carry two-thirds of the Senate. Senatorial supporters of the Court spoke freely of Coughlin's pivotal role in defeating the measure, and Ryan agreed that Coughlin had supplied the margin necessary to sway the vote.[52]

Exasperated, angry, Ryan nevertheless kept his head. He refused to agree with a correspondent who wanted the Church to suppress Coughlin: "Freedom of speech is more important than the preaching of Father Coughlin."[53]

When Commonweal and America printed articles sharply critical of Coughlin shortly thereafter, the public was given notice that Father Coughlin did not speak for the Church, despite the public support that he enjoyed from his bishop, Michael J. Gallagher of Detroit. The point was made even more dramatically the following December when the University of Notre Dame gave President Roosevelt an honorary degree. George Cardinal Mundelein, Archbishop of Chicago, surprised everyone, including the President, by using the occasion to endorse the President's policies. Cardinal Mundelein rarely ventured into politics, and Arthur Krock of the New York Times interpreted the remarks as a direct rebuke to Coughlin and as a reprimand to the Knights of Columbus, a group also lukewarm to the New Deal.[54]

[50] Ryan to Sister Barbara [sic], Feb. 26, 1935.
[51] Charles E. Coughlin, "The World Court," pamphlet (Royal Oak, Michigan, 1935), p. 7.
[52] Ryan to George N. Shuster, Feb. 2, 1935.
[53] Ryan to Michael Williams, April 13, 1935.
[54] New York Times, Dec. 13, 1935.

With some difficulty Ryan avoided public comment on Coughlin for most of 1936. It was uncomfortable to have this newcomer usurp the term "social justice" and win a national audience with reckless "blathering about the money question."[55] Coughlin was a brilliant orator, as Ryan was not. He had a national audience, could sway senatorial votes. Ryan did not deceive himself that he wielded comparable immediate influence, however much his doctrines affected American Catholic social thought, perhaps even American social thought, in the long run. He was not willing to compete on Coughlin's terms, which were simply demagoguery, spreading hate for injustice instead of love of justice, denouncing instead of constructing, allying with pie-in-the-sky advocates like Townsend, Gerald L. K. Smith, and the man known in *Social Justice* as the "martyred Huey Long."[56] Furthermore, Ryan did not relish an unseemly dogfight between priests: it harmed the Church without accomplishing any concrete good. So he held his peace.

As the election approached, the Democratic National Committee prodded him. The previous year Farley had learned from a private poll that Huey Long could easily pull three or four million votes as a third-party candidate, perhaps enough to swing some pivotal states like New York.[57] Now Long was dead, but the same lunatic fringe—Townsend, Smith, Coughlin—might throw the election into the House of Representatives. The fear now seems chimerical, but elections are won by running scared, and the Democrats were anxious to counteract the "communist" charge leveled at the President and his administration. Senator Joseph O'Mahoney of Wyoming, a member of the Democratic subcommittee worrying about the Coughlin problem, reached Ryan through James Hoey, who had become Collector of Internal Revenue in New York. Unenthusiastic for a passing moment, Ryan soon consented and wrote his speech. At the Biltmore Hotel in New York, Hoey and O'Mahoney tinkered with it, then brought in Charles E. Michelson, the Democrats' publicity chairman. The first draft contained an explicit reference to Father Coughlin. Then it was edited out. Then it went back in, reportedly at the direction of the President. Finally, on October 8th, Ryan went on the air.[58]

Ryan cast a wide net. Some might call it a political speech, he said, but it was not that. "It is mainly a discussion of certain political events

[55] Ryan to Alice S. Duffy, May 8, 1936.
[56] *Social Justice*, June 29, 1936.
[57] James A. Farley, *Behind the Ballots* (New York, 1938), pp. 249–250.
[58] James J. Hoey to Ryan, Sept. 25, 1936; Ryan to Hoey, Sept. 26, 1936; Hoey to Ryan, Oct. 2, 1936; Ryan to Hoey, Oct. 5, 1936.

in the light of the moral law, specifically, the Eighth Commandment, which forbade bearing false witness against one's neighbor." Ryan denied that the President, or his principal advisers like Frankfurter and Tugwell, or his supporters in the labor movement, like Sidney Hillman and David Dubinsky, were communists. He asserted that anyone who had damaged their reputations by calling them communists were bound in conscience to restore their good names insofar as he could. He scoffed at the communist danger in the United States. "Those timid Tories who see Communism just around the corner—where, by the way, prosperity was lurking from 1929 to 1933—are quite as mistaken as those frightened liberals who think that Father Coughlin is going to set up a Fascist state the day after the election." Ryan personally repudiated all kinds of totalitarianism, but added frankly his preference for Italian fascism over Russian communism: fascism, less comprehensively despotic, showed consideration for "humanity's dearest possession, that is, religion." Ryan argued that one of Roosevelt's great achievements was to check the spread of communism and other destructive radicalism in the United States. If he were defeated, communism would grow here rapidly.

Talking directly to wage earners, Ryan drew on the authority of forty-five years of publishing articles on economic questions, which carried him back to the year Father Coughlin was born. "In the light of this experience, I say deliberately to the laboring men and women of America that Father Coughlin's explanation of our economic maladies is at least 50 per cent wrong, and that his monetary remedies are at least 90 per cent wrong. If the latter were enacted into law they would prove disastrous to the great majority of the American people, particularly to the wage earners. Moreover, Father Coughlin's monetary theories and proposals find no support on the encyclicals of either Pope Leo XIII or Pope Pius XI. I think I know something about these encyclicals myself." He begged the "toilers of America" not to abandon Roosevelt and others who were "your tried and competent champions in public life."[59]

In his excitement Ryan spoke rapidly, his voice firm and flat. Indeed, he spoke so rapidly that he ran out of text before he ran out of time, and a studio pianist had to fill in with a Chopin nocturne to round out the half-hour. The deed done, Ryan caught the train back to Washington and was in bed in 319 Caldwell Hall by 2:00 A.M.[60]

[59] The speech is reprinted in Ryan, *Seven Troubled Years*, pp. 295–299.
[60] Pittsburgh *Catholic*, Oct. 15, 1936.

He woke up to headlines. The Associated Press carried the story nationally; the Washington *Post* gave him a three-column banner on page one; and the New York *Times* carried a detailed account of the speech under a double-column headline on the top of page one. The following day the *Times* reported that Church officials were visibly embarrassed by the squabble, and speculated on the possibility that Eugenio Cardinal Pacelli, Papal Secretary of State, was in the United States to try to get the Church out of politics. The *Times* made no editorial comment, but the *Post* joyously approved Ryan's speech, pausing only to inquire where Ryan had found even 10 per cent of truth in "Coughlin's monetary twaddle."[61]

The next Sunday Father Coughlin made his reply. In an interview before his broadcast he praised Ryan as "a good priest, a noble priest" who was fighting for social justice when few other priests were in the field. That afternoon in his regular Sunday broadcast, Coughlin abandoned politeness. Taunting the "Right Reverend spokesman for the New Deal" for appearing under the auspices of the Democratic National Committee, Coughlin challenged Ryan to put his own monetary theories down in writing next to Coughlin's. Then America could compare and choose. He renewed his charge of "Communist tendencies." Pointing to the Public Works Emergency Leasing Corporation, "conceived in Washington and executed in Delaware," he quoted its charter to show "paragraphs which prepared the way for the Commissars of Communism to acquire in 'any manner' any industry and trade name which exists in America." Coughlin quoted Ryan as saying that he had been writing articles on economics the year Coughlin was born; was it then a "heinous crime" to be young? the radio priest asked piteously. On and on the talk went, Coughlin's rich voice heaping sarcasm on the "Right Reverend Democratic Politician." Why had Ryan been silent about the AAA which had been guilty of immorally destroying God's gifts to man? An impressive performance, it delighted Coughlin's supporters. Even Ryan managed to smile, a bit lamely perhaps, over the "Right Reverend New Dealer."[62]

The Catholic press split in commenting on the exchange. The Omaha *True Voice*, pointing to Ryan's expert knowledge of the encyclicals and competence in social and economic questions, observed that his opinion carried great weight. The paper agreed with *America* that Coughlin's intemperateness had set the cause of social justice back twenty-five

---

[61] *Times*, Oct. 9, 10, 1936; *Post*, Oct. 9, 10, 1936.
[62] *Social Justice*, Oct. 19, 1936.

years.[63] From Baltimore came a very different reaction. In a stinging front-page editorial entitled "Two Political Priests," the *Catholic Review* suggested that both, having made spectacles of themselves, go back to their priestly business. "If both the Reverend Gentlemen would retire for some time to the Carthusian Order where perpetual silence is observed, they would do a great favor to the Church and to the Country at large."[64]

Around Catholic University the general opinion among the faculty was that Curley had written the editorial himself. Ryan certainly believed that at first, and he thought he understood why the Archbishop had done it: "It is not that he loves me less but that he hates Roosevelt more."[65] Actually, Curley did not write the item, but he saw it before publication and raised no objection. The warm friendship between Curley and Ryan went into eclipse, and Baltimore joined Boston on the list of places in which Ryan was unwilling to appear.

Twelve hundred letters poured in on Ryan, only twenty-five of them, by his own estimate, expressed in courteous language. The milder letters referred to his "sanctimonious game," or charged him with "munch[ing] at the Democratic pie-counter," or with yearning "to bask in the sunshine of a hypocritical smile." Most of the rest were "intolerant, intemperate and discourteous, many of them being abusive, insulting, and some of them worse," Ryan said. "It is very saddening to realize what Father Coughlin has done to the minds and emotions of his followers."[66] These letters were balanced, however, by notes commending his action. Hugh C. Boyle, Bishop of Pittsburgh, was quoted as saying that the address would do much good, and this view showed up in the Pittsburgh *Catholic*. George Sarton, the historian of science who edited *Isis*, praised Ryan without meaning to tempt him into speaking often: the country needs "political thinkers who are *not* politicians, and who do not speak except occasionally." Many members of the Ryan family rallied round; Maurice hit a sensitive spot by calling the performance "the best political speech given so far in this campaign." Frank P. Walsh, now chairman of the executive committee of the Progressive National Committee for Franklin D. Roosevelt, observed with characteristic relish: "The three outstanding blessings for which I thank Almighty God this beautiful day: That I am a Catholic; that I know you; that in my small way I am supporting

[63] Omaha *True Voice*, Oct. 16, 1936.

[64] *Catholic Review*, Oct. 16, 1936.

[65] Ryan to Paul Kiniery, Oct. 28, 1936.

[66] Ryan to Mary Rita Dowling, Oct. 21, 1936. The file of abusive letters is in the Ryan Papers; see also Shenton, "The Coughlin Movement and the New Deal," pp. 366–370.

Roosevelt." The administration added its gratitude. Homer S. Cummings, Attorney General, found the talk "admirable in every way." Farley noted that he knew of no more effective address made during the campaign.[67] After an interval of three weeks, after Hoey prodded Farley and Farley prodded Roosevelt, the President telegraphed Ryan to say how much he appreciated the "magnificent" speech.[68]

Ryan ran into a varied reaction to his performance as he went from job to job. The bulk of opinion in the refectory at Caldwell Hall was probably against him; even those who favored Roosevelt and felt keen distaste for Father Coughlin were uncomfortable at the notoriety for the university. Most of Trinity's clientele came from Republican families not hungry for four more years of Roosevelt, but it was deliciously exciting to see Ryan on the front page of the *Post* one day and at the front of the classroom the next. At the Social Service School, the girls' affection was increased by the ethics professor's latest adventure, especially since it was not hard to pull him off the day's lecture onto commentary on the Coughlin affair. At the NCWC, there was unmistakable administrative uneasiness: Would there be repercussions when the bishops met?

Monsignor Ryan had no apologies and no regrets. When *Commonweal* wrote a strong editorial praising his speech, he used it as an occasion to rebut the *Catholic Review*. No longer did Roosevelt's defeat seem possible. But at the time of the speech Ryan feared what America would think if a Catholic priest, leading a large group of voters to Lemke, caused Roosevelt's defeat. "The bad effects of that conclusion would not have been easy to live down, particularly in those regions of the United States where the Catholic population is small," Ryan wrote. Furthermore, both Protestants and Catholics have now been reassured that "Father Coughlin's economic theories and proposals have no positive support in the encyclicals of Leo and Pius or in any other authoritative Catholic source." These gains made the speech worth while: "I am glad I made that radio speech. I regard it as one of the most effective and beneficial acts that I have ever performed in the interests of my religion and my country."[69]

When Roosevelt invited Ryan to give the benediction at the 1937

[67] M. Luella Sauer to Ryan, Oct. 21, 1936; George Sarton to Ryan, Oct. 21, 1936; Maurice Ryan to Ryan, Oct. 9, 1936; Frank P. Walsh to Ryan, Oct. 9, 1936; Homer S. Cummings to Ryan, Oct. 9, 1936; Farley to Ryan, Oct. 31, 1936.

[68] Hoey to Farley, Oct. 28, 1936; Farley to Roosevelt, Oct. 31, 1936; in "Selected Materials from the Papers of Franklin D. Roosevelt Concerning Roman Catholic Church Matters," microfilm, Mullen Library, Catholic University; Roosevelt to Ryan, telegram, Nov. 1, 1936.

[69] Ryan, letter to the editor, *Commonweal*, Nov. 6, 1936, pp. 44–45.

inaugural, Ryan's critics were quick to see a payoff for the radio speech the previous October. "Perhaps they were right," he commented in his autobiography. "If so, I have no reason to be ashamed nor is the honor thereby diminished." The benediction was short, but it managed to include a generous appreciation of Roosevelt's role: "Do Thou bless abundantly our Chief Magistrate. Inspire his leadership. Grant him, O God of infinite wisdom and power, the light and the strength to carry through the great work he has so well begun, and to pursue untiringly his magnificent vision of social peace and social justice. Through Christ, Our Lord. Amen."[70]

As the second administration began in 1937, the shadow of the Supreme Court still hung over the New Deal. The NRA, AAA, Guffey Coal Act had already been struck down. The TVA had slipped by, but the fate of the National Labor Relations Act was very much in doubt. The conservative five held the balance, and neither death nor resignation had given Roosevelt a chance to change the mood of the Court. The President tried to break through the impasse with a drastic proposal to appoint up to six extra justices—an ill-concealed attempt to reverse the present majority. While not without precedent, it cut across the popular idea of separation of powers and did violence to the aura of Olympian detachment that surrounded the Court in the popular imagination.

Monsignor Ryan, unhesitant in taking up Roosevelt's cause, did not waste time on Roosevelt's clumsy subterfuge that the proposal would increase the efficiency of a court hampered by the age of many of its members. The argument did not appeal to a man nearly seventy who still managed to juggle three or four different jobs, and it was a stinging affront to Justice Brandeis, the eldest of the "nine old men." Ryan went right to the heart of the problem in a speech to the Manchester, New Hampshire, City Club a fortnight after Roosevelt dropped his bombshell. Ryan reminded his audience of Corwin's sets of alternate precedents. With characteristic disdain for sham, Ryan said he wanted "new judicial legislation for old."[71]

Manchester survived the speech easily. The explosion came in Baltimore. Ryan was back in Caldwell Hall only two days when a front-page editorial in the *Catholic Review* denounced his "Fascist, dictatorial mind."

[70] Ryan, *Social Doctrine in Action*, p. 271.
[71] Ryan, "Industrial Legislation and the Constitution," MS of speech, Manchester, N.H., Feb. 22, 1937.

He would make "pikers" of Stalin, Mussolini, Hitler. The *Review* complained that unless you agreed with Ryan, he regarded you as an ignoramus or as hostile to the poor. Noting that Ryan had held a "number of positions under President Roosevelt," the *Review* implied coldly that he had lost his independence of judgment.[72] The attack stung Ryan, but he held his peace, refusing the Washington *Times-Herald*'s invitation to comment.[73] The tempest spread rapidly to *Social Justice* and to the Brooklyn *Tablet*, both of which gleefully reprinted the *Review*'s attack.[74] But Ryan found his defenders as well. The Buffalo *Echo* was appalled that the Catholic University professor had been "wantonly assailed" in diocesan papers, and the *Catholic Telegraph* of Cincinnati asked urgently if Catholic critics of Ryan were "set on driving him out of the field where he has been rendering such splendid service." That had happened to Father Dietz; was it to happen again?[75]

The embattled monsignor made no public retraction or defense. He did not question Curley's private denial of prior knowledge of the offending editorial in the *Review*. Of Scanlan, the managing editor of the *Tablet*, he observed that anyone who could reprint the *Review*'s editorial must have the "soul of a thug." He feared, a bit sanctimoniously, that Scanlan's and Curley's hatred of Roosevelt was searing and demoralizing their characters.[76]

Ryan worried more about the reactionary public image created for the Church by the extravagances of the *Review*, the *Tablet*, and *Social Justice*. In the April, 1937, *Forum*, this fear was vividly presented in an anonymous article, "A Priest Warns the Church." Regardless of its occasional public pronouncements, this writer said, the Church had identified itself with every reactionary force in American society, preparing for the American Church the catastrophic fate of the Church in nineteenth-century Europe.[77] Ryan, who saw the article before it was published, thought that it exaggerated considerably the Church's coolness to Roosevelt. At the University, he thought, twenty-five of the thirty professors he knew best were for Roosevelt. (This was less of a random sample than Ryan imagined.) And in the Church generally he guessed that 75 per cent of

---

[72] *Catholic Review*, Feb. 26, 1937.
[73] Washington *Times-Herald*, March 1, 1937.
[74] *Social Justice*, March 15, 1937; Brooklyn *Tablet*, March 6, 1937.
[75] Buffalo *Echo*, March 11, 1937; Cincinnati *Catholic Telegraph*, March 11, 1937.
[76] Ryan to John D. Moore, March 10, 1937.
[77] Peter Whiffin [pseud.], "A Priest Warns the Church," *Forum*, April, 1937, pp. 195–201.

the priests and 70 per cent of the sisters voted for Roosevelt.[78] These statistics were generally in line with the guess of Father Sheehy, who, in a cross-country trip as a volunteer liaison man between the Church and the Democrats, got the impression that most Catholic bishops supported Roosevelt in the 1936 election.[79]

At the same time, Monsignor Ryan did worry about the volume of conservative impressions created by prominent Catholics. Writing to Bishop Lucey, he warned that the Church's renewed opposition to child-labor legislation was antagonizing even Catholic labor leaders.[80] When Bishop John F. Noll, of Fort Wayne, Indiana, published a pamphlet entitled "It Is Happening Here," Ryan shuddered. Noll exercised a wide influence in Catholic journalism because *Our Sunday Visitor*, which he had once edited, came from his diocese and spread, through local editions, all over the nation. The pamphlet was a swashbuckling attack on the Roosevelt reforms, and especially on the Court plan. Ryan thought it "the most superficial and unreliable thing ever gotten out by a bishop in this country."[81] Yet for every Noll, there was an O'Hara and a Lucey. For every Curley there was a Mundelein, for every Coughlin, a Ryan. Ryan's reputation allowed him to contribute substantially to a liberal image of the Church. His position was authoritative and influential, as he himself recognized. He never claimed to be an official exponent of the social teachings of the popes, he told the San Francisco *News* in July, 1938. But he was "something more than an average private interpreter," and probably had more authority than any of his critics. "So long as the hierarchy of the United States maintains me as director of the department of social action of the N.C.W.C., I will continue to interpret the Catholic social thinking as I understand it, with the help of God and subject to correction by my superiors."[82] No rebuke ever came, nor did the composition of the NCWC's administrative board make one seem likely or imminent. The influential Archbishop McNicholas wished "we had a hundred John A. Ryans in the country to speak for the Church and for human beings."[83]

[78] Ryan to Henry Goddard Leach, March 19, 1937.
[79] Sheehy to Marguerite Le Hand, April 10, 1937, "Selected Materials from the Papers of Franklin D. Roosevelt Concerning Roman Catholic Church Matters," *loc. cit.*
[80] Ryan to Robert E. Lucey, March 10, 1937.
[81] Ryan to Duffy, April 26, 1937.
[82] San Francisco *News*, July 23, 1936.
[83] John T. McNicholas to Ryan, Oct. 21, 1934.

The question was: Which image of the Church, Noll's or Ryan's, could make the most sustained impact on the public mind? The answer had to come in terms of specific issues. And issues abounded: The appointment of Senator Black to the Supreme Court; the emergence of the Congress of Industrial Organizations; the Spanish Civil War; civil liberties in Jersey City, New Jersey, under Mayor Frank Hague.

Following the resignation of Willis Van Devanter from the Supreme Court, Roosevelt appointed Senator Black to the vacancy. Suddenly, when it became known that Black had been a member of the Ku Klux Klan for a brief period years before, a great outcry went up, not the least in the Catholic press.

Ryan condemned the outcry. In an interview in the *Indiana Catholic*, he argued that Black's present repudiation of the Klan left the way clear to judge him by his total career. Scoffing at critics of Senator Black who feared him as a partisan lacking judicial temperament, the monsignor dismissed "temperament" as too vague a criterion of judicial character; the same charge had greeted Brandeis' appointment in 1916. As for partisanship, Ryan had a frank, if unorthodox, defense: "When it comes to deciding as to the constitutionality of economic legislation, he will do as all the other justices do, vote according to his own economic philosophy."[84] This was hardly a defense calculated to help Black's cause, but it was honest and candid.

Ryan feared a wave of anti-Catholic feeling if Catholics spearheaded the campaign to reject an outspoken progressive like Black. To reject a man of that caliber for a major post simply because of pique at a repudiated association was unwarranted, unjust—and unwise.[85] Ryan rejoiced to see the appointment confirmed.

Ryan showed up in quite different company when he joined 174 other Catholic laymen and clergymen to defend the American Church's support of the insurgents in the Spanish Civil War. The Catholic statement insisted on the right of revolution against a government that made persecution of the Church an integral part of its program.[86] Ryan had little doubt that "Communistic elements" dominated the Negrín government. He conceded that he found Francisco Franco and his band pretty unattractive too. Still, he "had no apologies to make" for signing the letter, and he

[84] Reprinted in *Catholic Review*, Oct. 1, 1937.
[85] Ryan to Francis J. Gilligan, Sept. 27, 1937.
[86] *Times*, Oct. 14, 1937.

ridiculed the notion that orders to issue it had come from the American bishops or from Rome. Ryan had no affection for fascism, but Eugene Lyons' *Assignment in Utopia* made anything seem preferable to communism. Ryan felt that the coming struggle in Europe would be between communism and democracy rather than between democracy and fascism. Therefore, he feared fascism less than communism. That this view set him off from most liberal opinion in America was unfortunate, but he reminded himself comfortingly that where religion was involved, liberals were likely to be "muddleheaded."[87]

Ryan did not let his distaste for real communists affect his support of the Committee for Industrial Organizations (later, the Congress of Industrial Organizations). The CIO's great challenge to the major unorganized industries, steel and automobile, led to a skillfully planted popular opinion that communists, who had undoubtedly infiltrated the CIO, actually controlled the organization.[88] The charge was probably nowhere so explicit and extreme as in the pages of *Social Justice*, no longer under Father Coughlin's personal direction, but widely viewed (especially among his followers in the National Union for Social Justice) as reflecting his views. The CIO, the paper said, was "red in its conception, in its method, in its objective, and in its effective personnel."[89]

Though Ryan dealt seriously with the communist charge in his public addresses, his private view was that the fears, especially as expressed in *Social Justice*, *Our Sunday Visitor*, the *Tablet*, and *Truth*, the organ of Father Edward L. Curran's International Catholic Truth Society, were actually "shallow and trivial." He believed that "America is in far less danger from the preachings of communists than from certain professedly anti-Communist propaganda, which is in reality directed against social justice." In the pressure in 1937 for a public statement by the hierarchy against the CIO, Ryan saw a parallel with the pressure fifty years before to have Rome condemn the Knights of Labor. Now, as then, Ryan said, the condemnation would be unjust and would alienate thousands who were members of both the Church and the union.[90] Always the example of Europe came to his mind: the Church had lost the workingman when it failed to identify itself with his legitimate aspirations.

[87] Ryan to Carl D. Thompson, Nov. 16, 1937; Ryan to Daniel M. Welch, Oct. 25, 1937.
[88] Arthur S. Goldberg, *AFL–CIO: Labor United* (New York, 1956), pp. 173–177.
[89] *Social Justice*, Nov. 1, 1937.
[90] Ryan to Daniel P. Clancy, Oct. 22, 1937.

Long reproachful of the AFL for its smug, unenterprising defense of the skilled crafts, Ryan saw in the CIO a major instrument for raising the living standards of significantly large groups of people: "I have no hesitation in saying my sympathies have been with the CIO. I am not interested in the aristocracy of labor generally. I am interested in the human being who works. . . . The CIO is doing a job the AFL did not do." As for communism: "We pay too much attention to the dangers of Communism when we would be much better off to work harder to offset conditions that foster Communism." Communists had joined local unions, he conceded, perhaps even controlled twenty-five locals; but on the national level they had made no headway, nor had they succeeded in controlling the leadership in any state.[91]

Right along, Ryan's position gained considerable strength from a public statement made in September, 1937, by Archbishop Edward F. Mooney of Detroit, chairman of the NCWC administrative committee and (since the death of Bishop Gallagher) Father Coughlin's ordinary. Mooney flatly stated his opinion that the communists in the CIO were insufficiently numerous or influential to taint the entire organization. The following year he sent Ryan some searching questions on the CIO and on the communist threat for presentation to the annual bishops' meeting. In reply, Ryan drew on his own experience with reforming groups, weaving in references to manuals of moral theology and to prior statements on communism prepared under the bishops' authority.[92]

The progressives' hold on the machinery of the American Church was rarely more vividly illustrated. The NCWC, originally the creature of the liberal wing of the hierarchy, drew onto its executive board those bishops sufficiently sympathetic to take on the added chore of being episcopal heads of departments. This sifted group then appointed congenial directors for the several departments: Bishop Muldoon as episcopal head of the Social Action Department, Dr. Ryan as director—the arrangement was the perfect illustration. Then from this staff came the raw material on which the annual public statements were based. In some cases, such as the famous "Bishops' Program for Social Reconstruction," the actual text came up from below. Now Ryan used these statements as arguments in preparing a new progressive brief for the whole body of bishops, and the bishops in turn issued their statement on "Industrial and

[91] Minneapolis *Tribune,* June 30, 1938.
[92] Michael J. Ready to Ryan, Sept. 21, 1938; Ryan to Ready, undated.

Social Peace" without a hint of the dangers of communist infiltration.[93] To the conservatives this must have been a frustrating process. But the liberals had the votes, so they controlled the Administrative Board. By the simple process of "handing the jobs around among ourselves," as one eminent participant has described it,[94] they kept the tone of the national body almost as progressive as John A. Ryan.

Many threats were tangled into an awkward skein when Mayor Frank Hague of Jersey City, a Catholic, prevented CIO organizers from entering the city, then blocked an attempt by Norman Thomas to speak there in protest. Ryan had no doubt that Hague was "unreasonable, tyrannical, and contemptible."[95] Yet it was one of those occasions for prudent silence. He knew that the NCWC high command was reluctant to offend the Archbishop of Newark or the prominent priests who sat on Hague's platform when he defended his conduct.[96] New difficulties would be felt in the NCWC, and specifically in the Social Action Department. Just the year before, Archbishop Curley had abruptly assigned Father McGowan to a rural Maryland pastorate, and, though Ryan had succeeded in getting McGowan back to a full-time job in the SAD, Curley was still disgruntled about having him in the archdiocese at all.[97] Curley's impatience with Ryan's public posture was no secret anywhere. Even Ryan's praise for Roosevelt in the benediction at the inaugural led Curley to observe with his usual bite: "Here is 'the old man' from Minnesota at it again. I wonder if he will not throw off the purple soon and put on a red shirt. It would be a little going up in color anyhow."[98] Ryan did not know of this quip, but he knew how he stood on North Charles Street, Baltimore. There were enough good causes without taking on this prickly one in Jersey City.

Yet as July approached, Ryan could not let the Fourth pass without a blanket denunciation of fascism, nazism, communism, and Mayor Hague. Local groups devoted to civil liberties, the Catholic League for Democracy and the Citizens Committee for American Democracy, invited

[93] NCWC Administrative Board, "Industrial and Social Peace," in Raphael Huber, *Our Bishops Speak*, pp. 320–321.

[94] In an off-the-record interview. The same conclusion may be reached by a close inspection of the roster of successive administrative committees in Huber, *Our Bishops Speak*, pp. 383–394.

[95] Ryan to Paul L. Blakely, Jan. 18, 1938.

[96] Ryan to Edward Murphy, Jan. 13, 1938.

[97] Curley to Ryan, March 17, 1938, Archives of the Archdiocese of Baltimore.

[98] Curley to Joseph M. Corrigan, Jan. 26, 1938, Rector's File, Archives of the Catholic University of America.

him to speak in Jersey City on the Fourth, or anytime. Ryan refused, pleading a prior engagement in Duluth, Minnesota, with B'nai B'rith, the Jewish laymen's organization.[99] A little remote to smack of temerity, the location was not beyond the wires of the Associated Press, and Ryan knew that his remarks would travel east. Denouncing Hague's acts as "illegal and arbitrary," Ryan lamented Catholic gullibility: Catholics were taken in by the charges of atheism and communism leveled against those who insisted on the CIO's right to organize and on every American's right to speak in their defense. "The real conflict," he insisted, "was between American civil rights as against the subserviency of city officials to selfish employers who seek to prevent the organization of labor." The *Catholic Review* reported Ryan's remarks without comment.[100]

The year 1937 had been one of holding actions: disarming the Catholic campaign against Black, fighting the enemies of the CIO so that the CIO could attend to its proper work, opposing a non-Catholic attack on Catholic sympathies in Spain, resisting a new invasion of civil liberties. What was worse, the New Deal again seemed to have lost its forward thrust.

The Court-packing battle had consumed Congress' energy, and Roosevelt's decisive defeat destroyed the momentum built up by his overwhelming victory the previous November. Even so, two measures in which Ryan had a tangential interest were enacted. Ryan had had a token membership in Secretary Henry A. Wallace's Committee on Farm Tenancy. Partly as the result of the deliberations of this group, the Bankhead-Jones Act set up the Farm Security Administration to encourage the purchase of farms by tenants, sharecroppers, and farm laborers. The National Housing Act (Wagner-Steagall Act), authorized federal loans to local governments willing to clear out slums. Good in itself, the measure fell so far short of the need for low-cost housing that Ryan helped organize the National Housing Committee, incorporated in November, 1937, to lobby for more effective legislation. The committee produced an extensive pamphlet literature, and Ryan, as chairman, tried to lobby through the House of Representatives a resolution to investigate the high price of materials used in the construction of homes. But he was

[99] Ryan to J. Owen Grundy, June 10, 1938; Felix E. Tumulty to Ryan, May 31, 1938; Ryan to Tumulty, June 1, 1938.
[100] *Catholic Review,* July 8, 1938.

not an experienced lobbyist, and his committee dissolved within a year, quite in debt.[101]

While the New Deal lost its momentum, the nation drifted into a new recession. Ryan thought that Roosevelt was allowing talk of "confidence" to dominate the public forum in a way strikingly reminiscent of 1929–1933. He believed that new vigor was needed to avoid acquiescence in a permanent pool of 6,000,000 unemployed.[102] "Roosevelt recession" threatened to become a label as adhesive as "Hoover depression."

The White House, also worried, regathered its forces for a new surge in 1938. In February, Congress passed the new AAA, which provided payments to farmers without using the processing tax that had fallen afoul of the Supreme Court. Then President Roosevelt called upon Congress to expand the Work Projects Administration and the relief programs, to prime the pump of spending through liberalized Reconstruction Finance Corporation loans. The spending included not merely the direct outlay on public works but also a $1,000,000,000 bill to expand the Navy to two-ocean strength. From an economic point of view, naval expansion provided jobs as fully as public works. Ryan was delighted: "The whole scene is thrilling. And I think the Miracle Worker in the White House is about to reestablish himself, mainly through his big programs of public spending."[103] The 1938 Congress then went on to enact two more important laws. One was tentative and promising rather than a real accomplishment: the creation of the Temporary National Economic Committee, a joint executive-legislative study group under Senator O'Mahoney to recommend legislation to reverse the growing concentration of economic power in relatively few large corporations. The other measure was more spectacular: the Fair Labor Standards Act, passed in June, 1938. For businesses engaged in interstate commerce, the act provided a minimum wage of forty cents an hour and a maximum work week of forty hours. Many occupations were exempted from the provisions of the law; the minimum wage was low; and the maximum work week was ten hours in excess of Ryan's ideal. But the act did establish federal standards on wages and hours, and that was the important thing.

The act was a triumphant laurel on a lifetime of struggle. No single measure was more central to Monsignor Ryan's social philosophy than a

[101] See folder, "National Housing Committee," in Ryan papers.
[102] Ryan, "The Church, the State, and Unemployment," MS of speech, April 24, 1938.
[103] Ryan to Williams, April 18, 1938.

living wage guaranteed by legislative enactment. The struggle for state laws in the second decade of the century had done more than anything else to establish his national reputation. Now in the autumn of his life, a federal law, applying to men as well as to women, committed national policy to the maintenance of the minimum standard of living necessary for health, efficiency, and general well-being of workers. No matter that the standards were too low, or that even this minimum standard would not be attained for another six years. Ryan had been around Washington long enough to know that "as soon as improvement becomes politically feasible the wage rates can be raised by Congress."[104] The principle was the important thing. Ryan was confident that the law would pass the scrutiny of the Supreme Court, especially if Roosevelt had the opportunity to appoint some more of the justices. When the Court did sustain the law in U.S. *v.* Darby (1941), Ryan noted contentedly, "Time moves on."[105]

Time, having moved on, caught up with Dr. Ryan. Having propagandized for social justice for thirty-five years, he now within his lifetime saw substantial fulfillment.

Just after the passage of the Fair Labor Standards Act, Ryan sailed for Europe, primarily to give a paper at the Catholic International Peace Congress at The Hague in August. On the way he stopped in Ireland; for a change his visit did not set off tempests in Irish-American teapots. He dined with the papal nuncio, Archbishop Pascal Robinson, O.F.M., a former colleague at Catholic University, received more than routine hospitality at the National University of Ireland (which had given him an honorary degree in 1930), and, surprisingly enough, attended a lavish Irish banquet as the guest of Eamon De Valera, the prime minister. Ryan, his Irish spirit reawakened, purred delightedly, for "in this splendid room, where for many centuries the lord lieutenants and their friends had dined as the ruling representatives of the English Crown, there were now seated Irish rebels and the sons and daughters of Irish rebels, presided over by the chief executive of a free Ireland."[106] Ryan made his peace with De Valera, confessing to the *Irish Press* that he thought De Valera "has done wonderfully for the country in the last few years."[107] He ran into

104 Ryan, *Social Doctrine in Action,* p. 260.
105 *Ibid.,* p. 226; 310 U.S. 10.
106 Ryan, *Social Doctrine in Action,* p. 206.
107 *Irish Press,* Aug. 13, 1938.

his cousin, Desmond Ryan, leaving him with a charming compliment: In an unsettled world, Ireland was among the half-dozen countries where life is still tolerable and wholesome. Not to be outdone in courtesy, Desmond gave the readers of the London *Daily Herald* a summary view of the American monsignor who was now reaching for seventy after a turbulent career:

He does not even go in for being lean and worn and pale, with hawk nose and eagle eyes.

He is plump, healthy, and reasonably florid, with a nose that is not at all menacing, but only patiently stubborn, and with eyes that do not send forth fire but only quiet humor and quiet certainty.

His activities seem like a cyclone and his personal temper at the center of them seems such a pool of stillness.[108]

After returning to the United States in the fall of 1938, Monsignor Ryan had the great joy of speaking at the Harvard Law School at the unveiling of a portrait of Justice Brandeis. (Ryan represented the "laity" —as distinguished from the "bar.") Nothing less than such an occasion would have led Ryan to ask the Boston chancery for permission to make a public appearance within its jurisdiction, and even for this occasion, he hesitated. Yet he could not let pride win out over admiration for his old friend. For more than a decade Ryan had been a frequent visitor to the Brandeis home, and a regular guest on Thanksgiving Day each year.[109] The speech at Harvard, after excisions by Professor Frankfurter,[110] reviewed Brandeis' judicial opinions in the area of social legislation. If a layman's talking law to an audience of lawyers seemed presumptuous to his listeners, Ryan did not care, for he had thought for twenty years that he knew more about constitutional law than 95 percent of American lawyers anyway. The speech was long, quite dull, but it ended with the deeply felt statement that "Justice Brandeis is one of the two or three genuinely great Americans of our time." To this Ryan added in his autobiography:

Justice Brandeis has one of the keenest intellects that I have ever known. No man of my acquaintance possesses a finer sense of honor, honesty, and decency. In his conception of life values, his tastes, and his manner of

108 London *Daily Herald*, Aug. 27, 1938. Desmond Ryan was obviously familiar with William Hand's description in 1924. *See above*, p. 155.
109 Interview with Elizabeth Brandeis, April, 1958.
110 Felix Frankfurter to Ryan, Nov. 2, 1938.

living, he approaches the standards of an ascetic. His wide human sympathies, his faith in the capacities of ordinary men and women, are deep, and his eagerness to advise and assist those who seek his counsel is universally recognized. From personal association, as well as from his writings and his judicial opinions, I have derived not only stimulating knowledge but genuine inspiration.[111]

The valedictory for Brandeis came just as the New Deal was closing its books. For Ryan the one marked the passage of years, the other a record of great national accomplishment. His unequivocal defense of the New Deal, his attack on Father Coughlin during the 1936 campaign, his participation in the 1937 inaugural—all these, taken together with his long previous career of advocacy of social reforms, have given rise to the enduring myth in Catholic circles that John A. Ryan, as a confidant of Roosevelt's, inspired much of the New Deal program. Parts of the myth die hard. In 1959, twenty years after Ryan's departure, a priest living in Caldwell Hall could not be reached in an emergency because telephone service was discontinued at night. When he asked why, he was told that the suspension dated back to John A. Ryan. "He was always being called by the White House in the middle of the night, and those sleek black White House limousines would show up. . . ."[112] Actually, Ryan probably saw Roosevelt only four times during the days of the New Deal: at the university in 1933 when the President got his honorary degree, at the White House in February, 1936, at the second inaugural, and once in a private interview in 1937 at which FDR voiced his resentment of the Supreme Court. They corresponded perhaps half a dozen times, Roosevelt writing polite, noncommittal letters. Nor did Ryan have any contact inside the White House, as Sheehy did in Roosevelt's secretary, Marguerite Le Hand. Only with Miss Perkins was he close. Sixty-three when Roosevelt entered the White House, he was a little too old to be a prime mover; Corcoran and Tugwell and Frankfurter were men in their middle thirties to early fifties.

Ryan was more prominent as a Catholic than as a reformer. He was known in Catholic circles through the SAD, the Catholic Association for International Peace, or the Catholic Conferences on Industrial Problems, and in secular reforming groups as a distinguished Catholic spokesman. This reputation made him a valuable ally. Frank P. Graham has recalled that when Ryan worked on the preliminary committee for social security,

[111] Ryan, *Social Doctrine in Action*, pp. 272, 273–274.
[112] Interview with John T. Farrell, July 5, 1960.

242

he was valued as much for his status as for his knowledge. "Whenever Father Ryan sat on a committee, he automatically had a constituency."[113] All in all, Monsignor Ryan was more the New Deal's ambassador to Catholics than a Catholic legate to the New Deal. He helped create the social mood and the social program that the New Deal embraced. But his greatest service was in acclimating that program to Catholic Americans.

One of his former students, Father Russell Wilbur, reflecting on Ryan's function in American life, told him: "You, yourself, are predominantly and almost exclusively an *ethical*—a great ethical—personality."[114] The remark, not meant as a compliment, was remarkably apt. Ryan's preoccupation with the virtue of justice led him into pioneering work, but at the expense of the rest of moral theology and, indeed, of much else in religion. He was untouched by, perhaps even unaware of, the liturgical revival spreading afar from St. John's Abbey in Collegeville, Minnesota, just sixty miles from St. Paul. The great Benedictine liturgist, Dom Virgil Michel, believed that Ryan relied too much on legislation and on the state, that (in the words of Michel's biographer) Ryan made "too little insistence on the absolute need of the spiritual in social reform and on the need for a general spiritual revival for a complete program of Christian social regeneration."[115] In the record he left behind, Ryan revealed little of his views on the spiritual element in social reform, but Father Wilbur's comment did lead Ryan to say, picking up a clause from Wilbur's letter: "Of course I do not regard 'the supernatural order as a kind of second story built, as if by an afterthought, on top of the natural order,' but I confess that the assumption of no connection between the two except by elevator has always seemed to me rather logical and involving fewer difficulties than the opposite assumption. Best wishes."[116]

Ryan's disciples were quite prepared to exchange his blind spot for the brilliance of his performance as a "great ethical personality." Yet Ryan's insensitivity to other approaches—the liturgical movement, the Jesuit labor schools, and the Catholic Worker movement, to mention just three —led him, irked by a follower of Father Coughlin, to comment: "In fact it is not too much to say that the only adequate and effective leadership

[113] Interview with Frank P. Graham, Nov. 30, 1956.
[114] Russell Wilbur to Ryan, Oct. 4, 1935.
[115] Paul Marx, *The Life and Work of Virgil Michel* (Washington, D.C., 1957), pp. 216–217.
[116] Ryan to Wilbur, Oct. 7, 1935.

both in education and in social problems that exists in this country derives from the Catholic University."[117] Even in the context of a moment of irritation, the remark did him no credit. He did not need darkness all around in order to make visible the brilliant glow of his contribution to American social thought and to the Catholic Church in the United States.

[117] Ryan to Catharine T. O'Keefe, March 9, 1937.

The Final Years

AS MONSIGNOR Ryan's seventieth birthday approached in the spring of 1939, he suggested to Father McGowan that the event called for a small gathering of friends. McGowan caught the hint and drew on Father Sheehy's talent for organization. On May 25th, six hundred people from all walks of life appeared at the Willard Hotel in Washington. Felix Frankfurter, now Justice Frankfurter, an old friend, was there with Justice Black, a new friend, and together they brought along Justice William O. Douglas. Secretary Perkins, a close friend and sympathetic colleague, appeared for the administration and for herself. The university was represented by the new rector, Monsignor Joseph M. Corrigan, and the NCWC by its general secretary, Monsignor Michael J. Ready. More than a score of congressmen were present. From all the professions, especially those connected with social welfare, came enthusiastic admirers, as well as critics who recognized a great life even when they did not altogether approve of it. Father Lawrence and Maurice came on from St. Paul to share in the testimonial to their brother.

Many who did not come sent greetings: Ryan's superior,

Archbishop Murray of St. Paul; Archbishop Mooney of Detroit, chairman of the NCWC's administrative board; Archbishop Amleto G. Cicognani, the Apostolic Delegate to the United States. Even the Baltimore *Catholic Review* fell into line. From the White House, the President commended Ryan's perennially youthful spirit, his zest for service to his fellow men, and his modesty. "With voice and pen," Roosevelt said, "you have pleaded the cause of social justice and the right of the individual to happiness through economic security, a living wage, and an opportunity to share in the things that enrich and ennoble human life."[1]

Ryan made himself happily unaware of the detailed planning that lay behind the apparent spontaneity of the occasion: no need for him to know that the President's letter, like all such letters, had been carefully solicited well in advance.[2]

The speeches stretched past three hours until praise ran afoul of the law of diminishing returns. To Ryan the proceedings did not seem long. As he observed three years later, he appreciated expressions of regard "quite as well as the average person."[3] The evening, however tedious, testified to the position he had come to occupy. No quantity of maneuvering would have assembled distinguished people to pay their respects unless they were willing. In 1933 Ryan had gone through three senators before he found a speaker for the banquet following his investiture. Now, however, he was part of a triumphant alliance for social justice, his teachings and his reputation in the ascendant. The dinner, as Frankfurter observed, was to be remembered "as testimony of our gratitude and as proof of a life greatly lived."[4]

The triumph at the Willard was balanced by a bitter disappointment at the university. In April the trustees had set sixty-five as the normal retirement age for members of the faculty; professors might be invited to stay on, but in no case past the age of seventy.[5] Though expressed in general terms, the regulation applied only to Ryan in 1939, and, coming six weeks before his seventieth birthday, it appeared to be directed specifi-

[1] Ryan, *Social Doctrine in Action*, pp. 277–284; Baltimore *Catholic Review*, May 19, 1939.
[2] Sheehy to Marguerite Le Hand, April 29, May 8, 1939; Le Hand to Sheehy, May 9, 1939; "Selected Materials From the Papers of Franklin D. Roosevelt Concerning Roman Catholic Church Matters," *loc. cit.*
[3] Ryan to Sister Paulette [*sic*], Jan. 9, 1942.
[4] Felix Frankfurter, *Of Law and Men* (New York, 1956), p. 331.
[5] Catholic University of America, "Minutes of the Board of Trustees," April 19, 1939, Catholic University Archives.

cally against him. No more ready to retire than most active men, he hoped to have the regulation suspended in his case. Several years before, Monsignor Edward A. Pace, the vice-rector and professor of philosophy, had been kept on until he was seventy-four. By June, Ryan's hopes for an exception vanished. The trustees awarded the "retired professor" a pension, but no expression of regret at his departure accompanied it, no appointment to the honorific status of professor emeritus. The blow was doubled when an administrative order, later explicitly confirmed by the trustees, required him to give up his rooms in Caldwell Hall.[6]

When Father Lucien L. Lauerman, director of the National Catholic School of Social Service, heard of the trustees' ruling, he offered Ryan an apartment at the school. Hoping until the last minute that the university would change its decision, Ryan stayed on in Caldwell over the summer, and then in September he picked up his belongings and moved to the NCSSS without a word to anyone. Lauerman knew nothing of the change until he returned for the fall and found John Ryan already moved in.[7]

Living at the NCSSS had advantages. Father Lauerman and Father McGowan both had apartments at the school. With Lauerman, Ryan's contacts had always been professional rather than intimate, but McGowan was a close personal friend of many years' standing. Their ideas were congruent, and their personalities complementary. Ryan was gruff, quick to speak, blunt. McGowan was no less ready to speak out, but he was more soft-spoken, more gentle. Ryan made his presence immediately known with what Justice Frankfurter called his "almost coercive charm."[8] McGowan moved into a group inconspicuously; before long his strength broke through his quiet manner. When Ryan grew angry, his jaw dropped. McGowan's face never gave a comparable hint. From the beginning of the NCWC, they had worked as a team without losing mutual respect or affection.

The NCSSS housed some of its students, and Ryan moved happily in and out of this residential part of school life. A stern residence director, Clara V. Bradley, who, according to Father Lauerman, "could tell the winds which way to blow," kept her new boarder on a diet increasingly regulated by his doctors. He made unconvincing appearances at the school's softball games, donning a baseball cap and moving tentatively

[6] Joseph M. Corrigan to Ryan, Oct. 31, 1939; "Minutes of the Board of Trustees," Nov. 14, 1939, loc. cit.
[7] Interview with Lucien L. Lauerman, March 26, 1956.
[8] Frankfurter, Of Law and Men, p. 330.

toward a batting position. A cigar in hand and a black fedora nearby, however, made it clear that he knew he was no longer the first baseman at St. Thomas's. Many evenings Monsignor Ryan found his way to the library where, in a deep overstuffed chair, he became the center for a discussion of past and present, frequently his own past and present. He grew thin, wisps of white hair hanging around his ears and neck, his rimless glasses giving him the air of a quizzical Dickensian rector surrounded by his nephews' many grown-up daughters. He made a willing fourth at bridge if the girls stuck to playing and did not prattle. When he wearied of them, he withdrew to his own privileged area.[9]

Rabbi Edward L. Israel visited Ryan there one day: "Adorning an archway between his modest study and bedroom is a group of photographs of his 'children,' as he calls them. His nieces and nephews and their families, other young people with whom he has been in unusually close contact, all of them are represented in photographic replica on that archway. At the lower left-hand side is a picture of Dr. Ryan himself, in ecclesiastical garb, bestowing his blessing on his 'family.' And surmounting the circle of pictures is a sign on which are inscribed the words 'Peru urevu' in Hebrew letters. I drew the letters for Monsignor Ryan at his request. He gets great joy from showing his visitors the pictures and the Hebrew form of the biblical injunction, 'Be fruitful and multiply.' "[10]

There was time now for revisions and review. A new edition of *The State and the Church* appeared in 1940 as *Catholic Principles of Politics*. Ryan acquired a new collaborator, Father Francis J. Boland, C.S.C., of Notre Dame. In place of Father Millar's chapters and those of other Jesuit contributors, Ryan and Boland substituted new chapters on natural law, natural rights, and the origin and nature of the state. Mindful of Jersey City and similar areas, Ryan added a blunt statement: "In many of our cities, Catholic officials have been and still are conspicuous among the offenders against civil honesty and civic decency. It is not too much to say that they are sufficiently numerous and prominent to constitute a grave scandal."[11] Then the book went into an extended commentary on the duties of the citizen. The comments on international ethics were greatly expanded. Classical and Hegelian views of the omnipotent state surrendered space to criticisms of Nazi and communist ideologies.

The most striking change came in the famous sentences so much

[9] Interview with Lauerman, *loc. cit.*; Loretto R. Lawler, *Full Circle*, pp. 136–137.
[10] Edward L. Israel, "The Catholic Problem," *Reconstructionist*, May, 1941, p. 6.
[11] Ryan and Francis J. Boland, *Catholic Principles of Politics* (New York, 1940), p. 195.

quoted in the campaign of 1928: "But constitutions can be changed, and non-Catholic sects may decline to such a point that the political proscription of them may become feasible and expedient. What protection would they have against a Catholic state?" That passage now reads: "Suppose that the constitutional obstacle to proscription of non-Catholics has been legitimately removed and they themselves have become numerically insignificant: what then would be the proper course of action for a Catholic State?" The answer that followed was identical, except that Ryan began it with a softening word, "Apparently." His answer was still that in a state almost exclusively made up of Catholics, such sects could only be tolerated, with no right of propaganda, nor of exemption from taxation. Still, he insisted, that possibility was so remote—"some five thousand years hence"—as to be irrelevant for practical purposes in the United States.[12]

Criticized again for the passage, Ryan stolidly refused to alter it. He argued that a Protestant church did not have the same rights as the Catholic Church. He knew that Protestants found this view immensely distasteful. Nevertheless, "They are wrong; we are right. And error has not the same rights as truth."[13] Ryan's logic would not let him escape from this blunt statement, which most Americans—even Catholic Americans—undoubtedly regarded as extreme. He had no right to change the text, he thought, for the hard saying in his book was nonetheless the truth. Furthermore, since this teaching on church and state would have no practical effect in the United States for the next five thousand years, it presented no danger to existing American practice, including the free exercise of religion. Uncomfortable with the way in which he left the question, Ryan was glad when Philip Burnham at *Commonweal* planned to open up the whole topic of tolerance for extended treatment.[14] Ryan hoped for a fruitful discussion among competent people, just the sort, in fact, that has since taken place in the writings of Jacques Maritain, John Courtney Murray, S.J., and Francis J. Connell, C.SS.R, and a growing number of others.[15]

Soon after finishing work on *Catholic Principles of Politics*, Ryan felt a marked physical decline. When the Archdiocese of New Orleans organ-

[12] *Ibid.*, p. 320.
[13] Ryan to Daniel E. Lawler, Jan. 13, 1942.
[14] Philip Burnham to Ryan, March 28, 1941; Ryan to Burnham, April 1, 1941.
[15] This whole topic up to 1950 is discussed temperately in Anson Phelps Stokes, *Church and State in the United States* (3 vols., New York, 1950), III, 454–485, 638–640. See also A. F. Carrillo de Albornoz, *Roman Catholicism and Religious Liberty* (Geneva, 1959).

ized a social action conference in March, 1940, he begged off. It would disrupt his classes at Trinity and at the NCSSS, he told himself lamely, and with his salary at the university reduced to a pension, he felt poor. Though reluctant to admit it, he also felt tired, and long trips did not appeal to him. Never partial to airplanes, Ryan now disliked trains too, and an automobile trip to New Orleans was out of the question. Furthermore, a trip to California was coming up in April on the occasion of the first solemn mass of one of the sons of his brother James. Under pressure from Archbishop Joseph F. Rummell of New Orleans, however, Ryan finally went. Once there, he never missed a meeting.[16] Then he went on to the coast, returning across the country early in the summer.

The schedule was strenuous, and in July came the reckoning. Toward the middle of the month he was rushed to the Georgetown University Hospital for what was probably a kidney ailment. He received the last rites of the Church, and Father Lawrence was summoned from St. Paul.[17] The crisis passed quickly, by August the monsignor was back at work. But his days of great vigor were now over. In September a caller found him markedly fatigued, and throughout the fall he fell victim to colds quite easily. There were dizzy spells as well, and as a result, minor automobile accidents that warned him that the time had come to give up his car.

Returning to work at the NCWC in September, 1940, Ryan sensed some interest in his resignation. Fatigued by colds, he nevertheless made a frantic show of being on the job. At his desk every day, he avoided engagements away from Washington. He wanted to give no grounds for being eased out of the NCWC, not after the void in his life left by the compulsory retirement from the university. His relations with Monsignor Ready, the NCWC's general secretary, were correct rather than friendly, and the illness of the previous summer had called attention to his years. But Ryan was not ready to go to pasture. Besides, he had work to do, and he needed his office and secretary. He needed three months just to revise *Distributive Justice*, and then he wanted to go on to his autobiography. It was vital to avoid the appearance of slowing down. The stratagem worked. He stayed busily at his desk for about six months, and the crisis passed.

16 There is a rhythm in the sequence of this footnote: Linna E. Bresette to Ryan, telegram, March 19, 1940; Ryan to Bresette, telegram, March 19, 1940; Bresette to Ryan, March 19, 24, 28, 1940; Joseph F. Rummell to Ryan, telegram, March 25, 1940; Ryan to Rummell, telegram, March 26, 1940; Ryan to Bresette, April 3, 1940.
17 St. Paul *Catholic Bulletin*, July 20, 1940.

Ryan's explicit summary of his career came in his autobiography, *Social Doctrine in Action,* published in 1941. His record went beyond his own life to show the strength of the liberal wing of the Church since the founding of the NCWC. There was no comparable record elsewhere. The book dipped back into Minnesota for glimpses of Ignatius Donnelly and Archbishop Ireland, touched on the progressive ferment leading to state minimum wage laws, and carried the story down to 1941. The omissions were as significant as the inclusions. The trouble with Cardinal O'Connell was never mentioned, nor was the coolness in Baltimore after the Court-packing speech, nor was Father Coughlin. Father Lawrence inspired some of the omissions. As to Coughlin, for example, he urged his brother with great passion to "adopt the vehicle of silence" which would be "a thousand times more eloquent than all the words of a Shakespeare."[18] Having put in about six typewritten pages on Coughlin with some misgivings, Ryan took them out the same way, for he wanted a permanent public record of the fact that some priests had given "some badly needed opposition" to the radio priest. Only when Father John's editor at Harper approved the exclusion did Ryan fully reconcile himself to it.[19]

John rejected some of Lawrence's other suggestions. The younger priest objected to the extravagant praise of the Roosevelt administration and to the acid condemnation of Hitler: both were transient judgments, controversial and out of place in the permanent record of John's total career. But John would not delete a word from either. The justice of his strictures against Hitler, he believed, would become even clearer in twenty years, when prejudice blinded fewer people. "I have in mind particularly the bigoted Irish who obstinately refuse to consider the facts about Hitler but who will be compelled to do so within a few years."[20] On Roosevelt, he would not budge. Perhaps the President would go out of office completely discredited, John said, but "the things that I say about him will remain true as of today."[21]

One item did much to reveal the difference between John and Lawrence. Father Lawrence thought that the manuscript lacked adequate recognition of Father McGowan.[22] In the autobiography, John was acknowledging that McGowan had done the greater share of the planning

[18] Lawrence Ryan to Ryan, Dec. 3, 1940.
[19] Ryan to Lawrence Ryan, Dec. 7, 1940; Ryan to Ordway Tead, Dec. 6, 1940; Tead to Ryan, Dec. 9, 1940.
[20] Ryan to Lawrence Ryan, Nov. 20, 1940.
[21] *Ibid.,* Nov. 29, 1940.
[22] See the reference to this in Ryan to Lawrence Ryan, Dec. 7, 1940.

and execution of the work of the SAD; he had furnished most of the new ideas for the department. Ryan could not recall any important error in judgment. "So pleasant and amicable have been our personal relations that my recollection does not cover any occasion on which a word of blame, complaint or annoyance passed between us."[23] John's tribute was just but not gracious. It lacked warmth and spontaneous gratitude. It betrayed that halting formalism that insulated Ryan from everyone except his mother, Sister Mary John, and perhaps Father Lawrence. Lawrence's ready warmth called for sentences worthy of the ally who had been closer to John than four of his brothers. John did not have the warmth to give, not even to Father McGowan, which is what he usually called him.

In fact, such an intimate note would have appeared discordant all by itself in a stiff 290 pages, half of them extracts from articles and speeches. This formal tone was undoubtedly what the reviewer for the Catholic Book Club meant when he spoke of *Social Doctrine in Action* as "disappointing in a literary sense"—a remark, incidentally, that set Ryan off into a blustering huff.[24] Yet he knew it was not sprightly: "Bea, my book just lacked glamour," he said with a laugh to a cousin; "the kind that makes best sellers has to have a love interest, a glamorous one."[25]

Only in the last pages did Ryan reveal a bit of himself, his satisfaction at the increase in social action among Catholics and its recognition by those outside the Church, his own motivation deep in his religious faith. On the last page, he quoted Frankfurter's comment at the testimonial dinner: "Perhaps it will be permitted to one outside his faith to suggest that the practical pursuit of Monsignor Ryan's convictions has been strengthened by the thought that in promoting his conception of social justice, he was faithfully carrying out the commission his Church gave him to preach." And then Ryan's own final comment in his book, a testament of that "childlike simplicity"[26] that Bishop Haas saw as characteristic of his teacher: "My good friend of more than a quarter of a century was right. In fact, he could have made his statement stronger; for my efforts on behalf of social justice have not only been 'strengthened' but fundamentally motivated by the command to preach and expound the Gospel of Christ. In striving to fulfill this commission, to comply with this command, I have, indeed, concentrated upon that part of the Gospel which

---

[23] Ryan, *Social Doctrine in Action*, pp. 154–155.
[24] Ryan to Tead, June 30, 1941.
[25] Beatrice Rohan Burke to author, Dec. 22, 1958, in my possession.
[26] Francis J. Haas, sermon at Monsignor Ryan's funeral, in *Catholic Action*, October, 1945, p. 26.

applies to social and economic relations. My natural inclination thus to specialize was strongly reinforced by my realization that the number of priests who were laboring in this portion of the Lord's Vineyard was pitiably small. For whatever I have accomplished in this field, I humbly thank Almighty God, Who inspired me with the desire to preach His social gospel and Who has sustained and guided me through all the years of my life."[27]

His next major job, the revision of *Distributive Justice*, was most gratifying. Much had happened since the 1927 edition, and Ryan made some adjustments to take account of *Quadragesimo anno* and the New Deal. "Social justice" now had the explicit backing of both Papacy and Presidency, and the familial living wage had papal standing as a requirement of strict justice. No single revision gave Ryan greater satisfaction than that on wages and hours. The Fair Labor Standards Act, passed by the Congress and sustained by the courts, opened a new era, and the triumph of Ryan's career was epitomized by the changes in his basic text on the ethics of distribution.[28]

As a scholar he had one more job to do. From the earliest days of his productive life, he had deplored the failure of Catholic texts in moral theology to apply moral principles to contemporary practices. Finally, at seventy-five, he managed to get onto paper a long essay on the subject. Too short for a book, too dense for a popular pamphlet, "The Norm of Morality Defined and Applied to Particular Actions" was turned down by commercial publishers. It finally appeared in 1944 as a privately printed pamphlet, which still has a small but steady sale through the NCWC. The pamphlet gave Monsignor Ryan the sense of having tidied up a stack of ideas too long neglected.

During Ryan's final six years, questions of public policy, as usual, had first call on his time, especially the long debate over America's role in a world threatened by Axis aggression. Nowhere was this quarrel over foreign policy more bitter than among Catholics.

At the Catholic International Peace Congress at The Hague in August, 1938, Ryan had readily grouped Russia, Germany, and Italy as nations denying individual rights, but within that general criticism he made distinctions. If Russia transformed its ideology of world revolution into a nonviolent, noninternational collectivism, he said, other nations could safely maintain normal relations with the Soviets. Nazism was "clearly the

[27] Ryan, *Social Doctrine in Action*, pp. 287, 289–290.
[28] Ryan, *Distributive Justice* (New York, 1942), pp. 313–339.

most definite and the most formidable threat to international order and security," and Mussolini, though not a madman like Hitler, might in the face of economic insecurity attack a weaker nation.[29] On his return to the United States, Ryan continued his analysis in a pamphlet for the Paulist Press. Citing the marked resemblance between the race hatred of the Nazis and the class hatred of the communists, he condemned both as un-Christian and abhorrent to American principles. Both Nazis and communists threatened America. Moscow ran the American Communist Party, he said, and communist falsehood was a serious—and inadequately suspected—danger to many American groups, especially to labor leaders, youth groups, and peace organizations. He also feared the spread of Nazi ideology, specifically the anti-Semitism spewing forth from the German-American Bund.[30]

Anti-Semitism cropped up distressingly in a speech by Father Coughlin. In November, 1938, Coughlin used one of his Sunday broadcasts to express sympathy with the plight of the German Jews. From this promising beginning he then let the suggestion arise that the Jews' own conduct had provoked the persecution.[31] Cardinal Mundelein, horrified, explained in a public statement that Coughlin spoke on his own responsibility as an American citizen. "Nor does he represent the doctrines or sentiments of the Church," the prelate added.[32] Ryan, equally dismayed, replied to Coughlin on the radio. He traced Coughlin's sources, largely discredited them, and then wondered what the Detroit priest was up to. "The only adequate answer is that Father Coughlin is eager, or at least willing, to promote anti-Semitism in the United States." Ryan warned that Coughlin's weapons against the Jews were no different from what could be used in a future anti-Catholic campaign.[33] Yet he approved the decision of Archbishop Mooney not to silence his troublesome priest; Mooney was "pursuing the most sensible course available."[34] Ryan himself refrained from further public attack to avoid the appearance of "unnecessary and uncalled for persistence, if not persecution."[35]

Nazis, communists, anti-Semites—Ryan despised them all, but he was

[29] Ryan, "Political Causes of International Disorder," *Commonweal*, Oct. 21, 1938, pp. 667–669.
[30] Ryan, "American Democracy vs. Racism, Communism," pamphlet (New York, 1939).
[31] New York *Times*, Nov. 21, 1938.
[32] *Ibid.*, Dec. 12, 1938.
[33] Ryan, "Catholics and Anti-Semitism," *Current History*, February, 1939, pp. 25–26.
[34] Ryan to B. Storm, Nov. 30, 1938.
[35] Ryan to Daniel A. Lord, Feb. 20, 1939; Ryan to Gregory Feige, May 13, 1939.

not ready to silence them, for proscription of hateful ideas spreads swiftly to suppression of unpopular ideas. The better weapon was truth, exposure to the sunlight of public opinion.

By March, 1939, the impending war seemed ever closer. The Munich settlement collapsed when Hitler marched his troops into the sections of Czechoslovakia that had remained outside the Reich after the acquisition of the Sudetenland. Even Neville Chamberlain, British prime minister, knew that "peace in our time" would not last past the next German attempt to move eastward. Remote, and powerless to do more than raise his voice for peace, President Roosevelt urged Germany and Italy to give guarantees of peaceful intent for the next ten years.[36] Within a month, the NCWC's Administrative Committee commended the government's efforts to preserve peace.[37] Ryan was elated: the bishops' statement "ought to give pause to some of the Catholic snipers at the administration's attitude toward international affairs."[38]

As usual, Ryan had trouble keeping his committees and councils and leagues straight. Through a misunderstanding, he showed up as a member of the American Council Against Nazi Propaganda where, in the alphabetical listing on the stationery of the group, he was right next to Margaret Sanger, executive director of the Planned Parenthood Association.[39] He refused to work with the American Union for Concentrated Peace Efforts because of its tie with the procommunist American League for Peace and Democracy; but in the excitement of the German invasion of eastern Czechoslovakia, he became a sponsor of a "Stop Hitler" parade in New York City without realizing until the day of the parade that the American League for Peace and Democracy had helped to organize the parade.[40] The Brooklyn *Tablet*, carrying a report on the incident, noted that it had caused "disedification to Catholics and surprise to non-Catholics." The editors then went on to a well-placed rebuke: "The Monsignor's scholarship and service have often been recognized and extolled in THE TABLET. His ability to call names and to attack and his contempt for people who disagree with him are, likewise, well known. It is a pity that while he seems to be able to give it, he is unable to take it."[41]

[36] New York *Times*, April 16, 1939.
[37] NCWC Administrative Committee, "American Government's Efforts for a Peace Conference," in Raphael Huber, *Our Bishops Speak*, p. 322.
[38] Ryan to Joseph A. Conry, April 23, 1939.
[39] Ryan to Albert E. Kahn, April 19, 1939.
[40] Ryan to John J. A. O'Connor, April 29, 1939; Ryan to Louis Weil, March 25, 1939.
[41] Brooklyn *Tablet*, April 8, 1939.

Once the war started in September, America's relations with the belligerents became a prime political issue. The President proposed that Congress repeal the arms embargo to belligerents, so that the Allies could take
advantage of England's command of the sea lanes to buy American munitions. Ryan immediately supported this plan. He favored staying out of
the war, but he believed America "morally obliged to do all that it reasonably can to defeat Hitler and destroy Hitlerism." The Christian's duty, he
warned, was not to be the Levite passing on the other side while "paganism
and barbarism" triumphed over Christian civilization in Europe. "To permit the sale of munitions and other materials under a 'cash-and-carry'
system, would not cause an unreasonable inconvenience or grave risk. On
the contrary, it would help us to keep out of the war. Supplying Britain
and France with munitions would enable them to win a speedier victory
and to make the war shorter. The shorter the war the less likely are we to
be drawn into it."[42]

Yet his argument contained a real difficulty. If the overthrow of Hitler
was the prerequisite for a just peace, the nation could find itself making
an endless series of individual decisions, no one of which was a commitment to war but the end product of which was total involvement. This
series the noninterventionist sought to stop right at the beginning by maintaining the embargo. Ryan, denying the inevitability of an inexorable
series, justified each decision in its own right.

Under the sponsorship of the Non-Partisan Committee for Peace
Through Revision of the Neutrality Law, John Ryan broadcast his views
to reply to an attack on the President's proposal by Father Coughlin.[43]
So the donnybrook started all over again. The postman brought Ryan
another sack of scurrilous letters. One pictured Ryan and Cardinal O'Connell plotting with Roosevelt to trick America into the war—an intriguing
trio of conspirators. Another suggested a likely target for the first load of
shrapnel. To various correspondents Ryan was treasonous, drunk, jingo-
istic, bloodthirsty, a payroll patriot who had been feeding at the public
trough since 1934. Monsignor Fulton J. Sheen, who also opposed Ryan's
views on neutrality legislation, nevertheless gave him a consoling aphorism:
"No one can get ahead of you as long as they are kicking you in the
pants."[44]

The opposition to intervention was not by any means all demagoguery

---

[42] Ryan, "Shall the Embargo Be Lifted?" MS of speech, Oct. 24, 1939.
[43] New York *Times*, Oct. 16, 1939.
[44] Fulton J. Sheen to Ryan, Nov. 15, 1939.

and passion. The Buffalo *Union and Echo* saw the issues of the war as merely economic, and it doubted that either side had the will or capacity to pursue an extended struggle for power. The editor found himself unimpressed by the "difference between the Secularized Liberalism of the so-called Democratic Front and the paganized state absolutism of the Hitler Front."[45] To noninterventionists, repeal of the embargo looked like the first step toward war; and for a variety of motives as wide-ranging as those of their opponents, they fought against it.

In the spring of 1940, the invasion of Belgium and the Netherlands, and especially the fall of France, made the outlook distressing. England obviously could not do the job alone. William Allen White spoke for many influential Americans, including the one in the White House, when he viewed Great Britain as our barrier from destruction: behind the British fleet "we could have two years in which to prepare for the inevitable attack of the totalitarian powers upon our democracy, which must come unless Great Britain wins this war."[46] White promptly became head of the hastily formed Committee to Defend America by Aiding the Allies, a group *Social Justice* viewed as "the most dangerous fifth column that ever set foot upon neutral soil."[47] Bishop Lucey joined at once, and Monsignor Ryan was not far behind, not only accepting a position on the policy committee but enlisting other leading Catholics, lay and clerical. For the group as a whole, as well as for Ryan, the primary goal became the defeat of Hitler. The members bridled when dubbed a pressure group for war. Yet, faced with the alternatives of war and a Nazi victory, a substantial number of them would have unhesitatingly chosen war.

The deepening crisis abroad overshadowed, even for Monsignor Ryan, the 1940 statement by the American bishops on "The Church and the Social Order," which endorsed every major reform (except the child-labor amendment) that the Social Action Department had supported for almost two decades. Reaffirming the right to private property, the bishops nevertheless stressed the obligation of the civil authority to regulate the concentration of wealth and the "anonymous character" of wealth which impaired its responsibility toward society. They warned that industry's abuse of power, not the excessive claims of labor, constituted the most immediate problem in labor relations, and they acknowledged the legitimacy of unions and even of strikes as instruments for redressing the balance be-

---

[45] Buffalo *Union and Echo*, Nov. 16, 1939.
[46] Johnson, *William Allen White's America*, p. 524.
[47] *Ibid.*, p. 525.

tween capital and labor. They insisted that industry, acting in tandem with government, should provide "not merely a living wage for the moment but also a saving wage for the future against sickness, old age, death, and unemployment." A "saving wage" constituted "an essential part" of the definition of a living wage, they went on, and, in a conspicuous endorsement of the New Deal, they commented: "Heartening indeed are the beginnings toward the greater security of the people that have already been made through legislative enactment and public policy." Between the extremes of socialism and individualism, they pointed to the "via media," a system of vocational groups "which will bind men together in society according to their respective occupations, thus creating a moral unity."[48]

Reporting on the platform, Ryan noted in the *Catholic Charities Review* that "all American Catholics can point with pride and satisfaction to the episcopal statement."[49] He omitted any mention of his share in preparing it. When the administrative board of the NCWC had decided in January, 1940, to issue a Catholic code of social ethics, Archbishop O'Hara had turned the job over to his old professor, asking him to enlist the help of Haas and McGowan, two other pupils of Dr. Ryan.[50] "Organized Social Justice" had been the statement of individuals within the Church; "The Church and the Social Order" carried the official prestige of the American hierarchy. Ryan had no hesitancy in speaking of it as "the most important pronouncement made by the Catholic Church in the United States on labor and economic issues."[51]

During the presidential election of 1940, Ryan, with some difficulty, kept silent. The law had been laid down by Monsignor Ready: stay clear of partisan politics.[52] As the arm of Catholic action for the whole American Church, the NCWC dared not identify itself with either political party. This restraint had to extend to Ryan, for he could not divest himself of his public identity as an official of the NCWC. If he were free, he said, he would unquestionably speak for Roosevelt. He smarted under his enforced silence, especially after Monsignor Sheen, Father Gillis, and *Social Justice* endorsed Wendell Willkie, the Republican nominee. Father Sheehy toyed with the idea of a public statement to balance this barrage,

[48] NCWC Administrative Board, "The Church and Social Order," in Huber, *Our Bishops Speak*, pp. 324–343.
[49] Ryan, "Recent Episcopal Statement: The Church and Social Order," *Catholic Charities Review*, March, 1940, pp. 68–69.
[50] Edwin V. O'Hara to Ryan, Jan. 30, 1940.
[51] Ryan to John R. McCurdy, July 14, 1941.
[52] Michael J. Ready to Ryan, Feb. 13, 1940.

Ryan told an angry pro-Roosevelt priest in the Midwest, but, following advice from the Archdiocese of New York, from Catholic University, and from the White House, Sheehy too adopted a "policy of silence."[53] Ryan was not convinced that the situation was urgent. In 1936 he had spoken out only when he feared that Roosevelt might lose. Now he had no such fear: in an office pool, he predicted that the President would carry thirty-nine states. (He carried thirty-eight.)

Ryan's silence did not extend to routine social issues, yet he avoided activities likely to vex his superiors into making an issue of his age. At the first convention of the Association of Catholic Trade Unionists, he took a firm stand against communist infiltration into executive jobs in trade unions. Progress in ousting communists from the United Automobile Workers pleased him, but he pointed to the lawyers' and newspapermen's guilds as danger spots.[54] He urged the House Committee on Interstate Migration in December, 1940, to encourage family-sized farms and to provide relief for displaced farmers.[55] Through the Social Action Department, he took the lead in organizing regional and diocesan celebrations of the fiftieth and tenth anniversaries of the great social encyclicals.

By the beginning of 1941, war was much closer. In February, 1941, Ryan went on the radio for the White Committee to win popular support for the Lend-Lease bill, which made credits available to Great Britain for the purchase of war materials in the United States. He denied that aid led necessarily to armed involvement. If Hitler won, America would have to defend itself sooner or later, he said; if America helped England enough, the United States need not enter the war as a belligerent. He conceded that a Nazi defeat might increase the threat of communism. Even if it did, he argued, isolationist critics would be hard pressed to show that communism would be worse than Nazism: "Frank avowal is easier to deal with than deceit."[56]

The heated national debate over each step in the program of aid to Britain, and later to Russia, set off an intensely bitter controversy, nowhere more heated than among Catholics. While Archbishop Mooney linked Pius XI and Roosevelt as workers for peace, Archbishop Francis J. L.

[53] Ryan to W. S. Flanagan, Nov. 28, 1940.
[54] Ryan, MS of sermon to the Association of Catholic Trade Unionists, Sept. 1, 1940.
[55] Washington *Evening Star*, Dec. 5, 1940.
[56] Ryan, "Wrong Attitudes Toward the European War," *Current Religious Thought*, April, 1941, pp. 25–29.

Beckman of Dubuque spoke of Roosevelt as a warmonger, and *America* and the *Catholic World* opposed American involvement in temperate language alien to *Social Justice*. In May, Bishop Joseph P. Hurley of St. Augustine, Florida, defended aid to England as a Christian duty and a necessary act of prudence. He spoke again in July, this time with a spirited attack on the tantrums of the isolationists: "Years ago they established the crank school of economics; latterly they have founded the tirade school of journalism; they are now engaged in popularizing the ostrich school of strategy." In rebuttal, Beckman took to the air with an impassioned plea to save American boys from the war which, however falsely represented, was essentially "an economic war based on greed, a vast struggle for power and possessions between two diametrically opposed systems of finance"; actually, "a war, not to end wars, forsooth, but, whether we know it or not, a war to make the world and particularly this beloved America safe for the new Bolshevism."[57]

While the hierarchy's feuds reminded old-timers of the days of Ireland and McQuaid, Ryan did not feel alone and exposed. *Social Justice* still favored him as its whipping boy. "This ecclesiastical Harold Ickes," the "New Deal's hatchet man," it called him.[58] But this abuse no longer took the form of a personal feud between Father Ryan and Father Coughlin, for Coughlin, now silent on public issues because of pressure from the Detroit chancery, had no overt connection with *Social Justice*. His only appearance in the paper in this period was a reprint of a moving sermon on the grandeur of the priesthood.[59] Ryan, for his part, tried to avoid direct personal controversy over the war issue. Privately he thought Beckman's radio speech was "contemptible,"[60] but in public he avoided rancor, and stayed on the issues.

Ryan, like the administration and indeed the nation itself, drifted toward the war. Giving the baccalaureate sermon at Trinity in June, 1941, he acknowledged that the navy and air force would before long be "directly involved in the conflict," though he did not expect American armies to go abroad "for a while."[61] Later that month when Germany invaded Russia, Ryan instantly supported lend-lease for the Russians,

[57] Joseph P. Hurley, mimeographed copy of radio address, July 6, 1941; Francis J. L. Beckman, "Congressmen: Be Warned," Pittsburgh *Catholic*, July 31, 1941.
[58] *Social Justice*, April 21, 1941.
[59] *Ibid.*, July 7, 1941.
[60] Ryan to John D. Collins, Aug. 1, 1941.
[61] Ryan, "Baccalaureate at Trinity College," in "Statements on the War and Hitler," mimeographed pamphlet, 1942.

though he drew the line at addressing a mass meeting sponsored by the American Council on Soviet Relations.[62] He was angry at Catholics who used papal condemnation of collaborating with communists as a reason for denying aid to Russia. He preferred the view expressed in London's *Catholic Times:* Russia's enemy is our enemy, but Russia's cause is not our cause.[63]

Thereafter Ryan was silent on the issue of peace and war, his silence not of his own choosing. Monsignor Ready constantly urged caution, once even objecting when Ryan quoted Hurley. Though not sympathetic to Ready personally, Ryan appreciated his superior's position. Ryan's activity was "necessarily though not reasonably" involving the NCWC. Even when he was invited to voice his support of the Free French, he refused, explaining that he could not "properly ignore the effect upon the NCWC of the strong objections and criticisms that would be aroused. . . ."[64]

Once war came, Ryan put together a mimeographed collection of his prewar statements. He had understood the menace of Hitler, he said, and he had seen America's obligation in international charity to oppose the Nazis even before they directly threatened the United States. His assertion that America was morally bound to do all it reasonably could to destroy Hitler always carried the "clear implication" that the nation would have to face the obligation of waging war. Ryan was setting the record straight —for himself as much as for anyone else. It was important to him to feel confident when the war came that he had understood what was involved in "this dreadful but glorious enterprise."[65]

The attack on Pearl Harbor having rallied the nation to war, the intense passions aroused by the debate over intervention subsided, and new issues arose. As in 1918, Ryan argued that no one had a right to hinder the prosecution of the war. By virtue of this principle, he thought that *Social Justice* should be denied mailing privileges. In April, 1942, under curious joint pressure from the Detroit chancery office and the Attorney General's office, *Social Justice* discontinued publication, and Father Coughlin withdrew to concentrate on a successful career as pastor of the Shrine of the Little Flower in Royal Oak. Ryan did not fear that the suppression of *Social Justice* would set off a hysterical proscription of journals that dared to be critical. Confident of Attorney General Francis Biddle's discretion,

[62] Ryan to American Council on Soviet Relations, telegram, June 30, 1941.
[63] Edith [Duncan] to Ryan, Aug. 11, 1941.
[64] Ryan to Selma M. Borchardt, Nov. 11, 1941.
[65] Ryan, "Statements on the War and Hitler," foreword.

he foresaw action against less than six journals. The *Tablet* and the *Catholic World* were not included in this list.[66] The *Tablet*, although not enthusiastic about the war, soon fell into step loyally or kept silent on war issues. Ryan, who had read the *Tablet* regularly before Pearl Harbor "mainly in order to assure myself that I was keeping alive my capacity for indignation," found in March, 1943—almost wistfully—that the *Tablet* had become "very tame."[67]

The resentment he had once felt against the *Tablet* he redirected toward Irish-Americans. When the war broke out in Europe, they had allowed hatred for England to form their opinions about the war, he charged. He regarded the need for the American Irish Defense Association, a sort of small-scale Committee to Defend America by Aiding the Allies, as tragic testimony that something was wanting in the patriotism of Irish-Americans. Ryan viewed his compatriots who "denounced or ridiculed or sniped at" lend-lease and armed merchant ships as unpatriotic and disloyal. Even after the United States entered the war, they were less fervent than they should have been, he said; gratitude to America and Christian forgiveness for England both dictated more loyal support of the war. Ryan noted that the Irish at home did forgive; their cousins in America look at their ancient grievances "through the distorting fog of oral tradition, plus too much imagination."[68] Ryan was not alone in this sentiment. His namesake, James Hugh Ryan, the Bishop of Omaha, was saying at just this time: "As for myself, I am ashamed of the Irish. They are shortsighted, selfish, dominated by old hatreds, with little or no conception of their duty toward *Western Civilization*."[69] Clearly this was an explosive topic, divisive, embittering. Monsignor Ryan avoided open reference to it lest it become a public scandal. Yet it never ceased to hurt him. Midway into 1943, Ryan was still concerned enough to ask the *Catholic News*, the newspaper of the Archdiocese of New York, plaintively if nothing could be done about the "unpatriotic and unChristian attitude of Catholics of Irish birth or extraction in greater New York."[70]

Ryan did not comment on the conduct of the war. Once Americans

[66] Ryan to Burnham, March 30, 1942. Many details of the story of the discontinuance of *Social Justice*, now unavailable, are in the chancery office of the Archdiocese of Detroit.
[67] Ryan to Edward Skillin, Jr., March 8, 1943.
[68] Ryan, "Ireland Today, and Her Sons in America," MS of speech, March 17, 1942; Ryan to Michael Monaghan, March 23, 1944.
[69] James Hugh Ryan to J. B. MacLean, March 5, 1942, James Hugh Ryan Papers, Archdiocese of Omaha Archives.
[70] Ryan to Richard Reid, June 10, 1943.

were committed to halting Nazism, he had little to add. He did not allow the American alliance with Russia to trip him into extravagant friendliness toward the Soviets, and he grew increasingly cool to Franco. Never a partisan of the Spanish dictator, Ryan had seen him only as the lesser of two evils. Now in 1942 he was "almost tempted to think" Franco the greater evil, especially because of Franco's indifference to "Hitler's crucifixion of the Catholic religion" and his disbelief in any form of political democracy.[71]

Domestic policy, on the other hand, engaged the monsignor's attention as much as ever. During the war years he acquired a new cause: Negro rights. In his seminary days, Ryan had thought momentarily of joining the Josephite Fathers as a missionary to the American Negro.[72] Years later he had coaxed Father Gilligan into a doctoral dissertation on *The Morality of the Color Line*. The dramatic migration of Negroes from the South in the mid-1930's had led him to try, unsuccessfully, to get a Negro settlement house started in southwest Washington. Then again a long, surprisingly indifferent silence punctuated only by gingerly mediation between rival factions of Negro Catholics. In 1939 he had joined in sponsoring Marian Anderson's famous concert in front of the Lincoln Memorial after the Daughters of the American Revolution had refused her access to Constitution Hall.[73] Once America was at war, he favored an integrated army.

When Howard University invited him to lecture in 1943, he showed how little fresh and original matter he had to offer. J. Saunders Redding's *No Day of Triumph* gave him a hasty background for the talk, and Father Gilligan's book some of the moral principles. He regarded economic discrimination as the basic problem, and spoke of the need for a vigilant, active leadership. At the same time, he urged his Negro audience to practice patience, to avoid violence, and to encourage assistance from men of goodwill in the dominant white group. The talk was platitudinous and unconsciously patronizing. Later the same year Ryan spoke at the first presentation of the James J. Hoey Awards for Interracial Justice, prizes named for Ryan's late friend who had been active with Father John La Farge, S.J., in creating the Catholic Interracial Councils. He criticized Catholics for indifference to the obligation of charity to Negroes; narrow-

[71] Ryan to Lawrence Ryan, Dec. 10, 1942.
[72] Sister Constance to author, *loc. cit.*
[73] Caroline O'Day to Ryan, telegram, April 1, 1939, with Ryan's penciled notes.

ness or thoughtlessness held them aloof.[74] He also accepted membership on the executive committee of the National Council for a Permanent Fair Employment Practices Committee. The total record was meager, for the problem was outside his normal scope and he lacked information, the starting point for all sensible judgments.

On the more conventional "social question," Ryan continued to speak with vigor. He saw some progress toward the occupational group system. At the CIO convention in 1941, Philip Murray, the head of the CIO, proposed steps toward joint labor-employer "industry councils" for the management of major aspects of industry. Ryan quickly approved Murray's idea as "the most constructive thing yet offered to speed up production."[75] When John C. Cort pointed out in *Commonweal* the resemblances between Murray's proposals and Pope Pius XI's encyclicals,[76] Ryan saw how readily one could lead to the other.[77] Even more encouraging was the War Production Board, an industrial triad of labor, management, and public, that was directing the nation's total war industry.

Little in wartime America encouraged Ryan to see a progressive future. Many liberals feared that the President, by concentrating on the war, had surrendered his role as reform leader. While "Dr. Win-the-War" pondered his worldwide strategy, "Dr. New Deal" had lost his practice to sharp practitioners who liked the medicines of an earlier generation.[78] The congressional election of 1942, producing a sharp turn toward conservatism in the House of Representatives, suggested that the people were losing their reforming urge. Ryan brooded for six weeks after the election, and then erupted at the convention of the American Catholic Sociological Society in Cleveland. He warned that the NAM, most metropolitan newspapers, and the most powerful farm organizations were combining to recover all the ground lost to labor in the previous decade. These groups, sharing the reactionary mood of the recently elected Congress, were the "authentic Bourbons" of our times—"They had learned nothing and forgotten nothing." The recent election was frightening, he said, for the

[74] Ryan, "The Place of the Negro in American Society," *Catholic Mind*, July, 1943, pp. 13–22.

[75] *Michigan Catholic*, Jan. 8, 1942.

[76] John C. Cort, "Are We Missing a Bus?" *Commonweal*, Aug. 14, 1942, pp. 392–394.

[77] Ryan, "Catholic Social Teaching," MS of speech, Aug. 25, 1942. The resemblance is explored at some length in Leonard A. Williams, "The C.I.O.'s Industry Council Plan as an Approximation to Pius XI's 'Industries and Professions,'" M.A. dissertation, Catholic University (1950).

[78] Eric Goldman, *Rendezvous with Destiny*, p. 386.

composition of the House of Representatives left only the unsure barrier of the Senate as a block to hostile legislation. Ryan felt confident that social justice was safe while Roosevelt remained in the White House. But what of the future, especially the postwar world? Returning soldiers would demand more than honeyed promises of an automatic prosperity. Ryan foresaw a need for a gigantic public-works program continuing until business learned to spread purchasing power, a program such as the ambitious reconversion plan of Alvin H. Hansen of the National Resources Planning Board. To gain a hearing for this program, Ryan said, Americans educated by the 1930's would have to battle the "enormous power of the plutocracy with its retainers in politics, economics, and education." In the meantime, "the middle class must liberate itself from the blabbering of their daily papers and acquire economic intelligence, or they will deliver us by votes to the champions of free enterprise."[79]

The New York *Times* teased the monsignor about his Bourbons. It noted that the original Bourbons were a mere handful that lorded over 25,000,000 Frenchmen. "But when you get the Bourbon manufacturers, and the Bourbon metropolitan newspapers, and the farmers, and a majority of the House of Representatives—who by themselves should be theoretically representing a majority of the American people—and add, from a preceding paragraph in Monsignor Ryan's speech, the whole American middle class, you get an awful lot of Bourbons of our time. It almost suggests a variation on Winston Churchill: Never before in history were so few Americans so badly oppressed by so many."[80] The Tucson (Arizona) *Daily Star* was less amused. It was confident that Earl Browder, the American Communist leader, would approve every word that Ryan had said.[81]

But from the White House came the congratulations of President Roosevelt, who had not seen Ryan since the late winter of 1937. "In troubled times it is reassuring to hear so clear a call to duty and to know that you are still on the firing line," the President said.[82] Ryan's old student, Father E. Harold Smith, welcomed the speech as a platform from which Catholic liberals could toss their own "little slings and pebbles."[83] To publicize the platform, Senator Joseph F. Guffey of Pennsylvania had

[79] Ryan, "Labor and Economic Reconstruction After the War," *Vital Speeches,* Feb. 15, 1943, pp. 266–269.
[80] New York *Times*, Jan. 3, 1943.
[81] Quoted in San Francisco *Leader*, Feb. 6, 1943.
[82] Roosevelt to Ryan, Dec. 30, 1942.
[83] E. Harold Smith to Ryan, n.d.

it reprinted in the *Congressional Record*.[84] *PM*, the New York tabloid, did a feature story. Ryan, boyishly delighted, sent an annotated copy to Sister Mary John, a large question mark in the margin of the paragraph that described him as "modest."[85] And when Alfred A. Knopf, the publisher, saw the speech, he wrote to ask if Ryan had a new book in mind.[86] Any one of these compliments would have pleased the monsignor. Taken together, they reinforced his pride in being still active in public affairs.

Ryan's speech led easily to a new chapter in his running dialogue with liberals. In March, 1943, George P. West, a California newspaperman, wrote with a sense of urgency in the *New Republic* about Catholic "aggression" on public issues dating from resentment over the election of 1928. Ever since that election, and in large part because of it, West argued, the Catholic Church has been extending its power, imposing its standards on others in such issues as birth control, supporting reactionary business interests consistently. Ryan, as usual, was noted as the exception, and his December attack on the NAM was praised as a model of progressive vigor. His loyalty to the Church had kept him silent on Spain, to be sure, yet he had "the flaming spirit of the true American democrat."[87]

Ryan paused to digest the article, then replied. He found the theory of aggression since 1928 "interesting," but without "substantial basis in fact." On issues such as birth control, he pointed out that Catholics were merely opposing repeal of legislation already on the books, and he insisted on the right of both sides to propagandize openly. He found the discussion of the Spanish Civil War as oversimplified in West's essay as it had been in the Catholic press, and he recalled his own support of Franco despite a distaste for Spanish—or any other kind of—fascism. As for the association of Catholics with reactionary business interests, the charge had less substance than it had had in the previous fifty-five years, he said. He knew this from his own experience. For official confirmation, he turned proudly to the hierarchy's statement, "The Church and Social Order," issued three years before.

The monsignor maneuvered to attack. The danger of reactionary influences within the Church came not from anything indigenous to Catholic social doctrine, he said, but from "angry reaction and resentment against those socially illiterate persons who discredit social and economic

84 *Congressional Record Appendix*, 8th Cong., 1st Sess., Vol. 89, Part 9, A154.
85 *PM*, Dec. 31, 1942. Sister Mary John has the marked copy.
86 Alfred A. Knopf to Ryan, Jan. 11, 1943.
87 George P. West, "The Catholic Issue," *New Republic*, March 1, 1943, pp. 278–280.

reforms by identifying them with anti-Catholicism, or as they disingenuously and euphemistically call it, 'anti-clericalism.' " If liberal critics like West organized an open attack on reactionary Catholic pressures, Ryan warned, Catholic social reformers would find themselves alienated from current movements for progressive reform. Anti-Catholic intolerance would be matched by Catholic retaliation.[88]

The debate seesawed for several issues of the *New Republic*, and then John Haynes Holmes, minister of the New York Community Church, tried to close the contest. He regretted West's article, and urged liberals to respect the Catholic Church for the best in it. If it organized *against* progress, let liberals organize *for* progress, he went on. But "let us not whimper and whine, least of all preach suspicion and ill will, just because the Catholic Church is awake while we are asleep, and pushing zealously its faith while we have little or no faith at all."[89]

Ryan sympathized with many liberal criticisms of the Church. Marking up an editorial in the *New Republic* in June, Ryan wrote "good" next to criticism of Tammany Hall, of Hague, of anti-Semitism, and of Catholic boycotts of newspapers that criticized the Church, and an emphatic "Yes" when the *New Republic* noted that Ryan must blush for Catholic journalism.[90] Yet he was "greatly concerned over the danger of dissension in the ranks of believers in economic and social reforms, caused by the introduction of irrelevant considerations based upon religious differences."[91] A concerted attack, either by churchmen against liberals or by liberals against churchmen, poisoned the atmosphere both for liberal economic measures and for religious amity.

Gaetano Salvemini, Harvard lecturer in history and a refugee from Mussolini's Italy, did not think that the issue was so simple. The Catholic Church spoke of man's dignity, Salvemini said; it also taught that whoever did not conform to the teaching of the Church forfeited that dignity and that the secular government should prohibit the spread of doctrines condemned by the Church. Catholics "walk hand in hand with the liberals until some order descends on their heads from Rome," he said, and then "they leave the liberals out in the cold." The Catholic Church did teach

[88] Ryan, "Is There a Catholic Issue?" letter to editor, *ibid.*, April 12, 1943, pp. 477–478.
[89] John Haynes Holmes, "The Catholic Issue," letter to editor, *ibid.*, May 3, 1943, p. 596.
[90] Editorial, "Catholics and Liberals," *ibid.*, June 7, 1943, pp. 751–752. The marked copy is in the Ryan papers.
[91] Ryan to Bruce Bliven, March 22, 1943.

the dignity of the individual soul; it also had something else in the bag, Salvemini said. "It is this something else which would create a permanent rift betwen Catholics and liberals even if many, too many, Catholics did not indulge in reactionary activities."[92]

Ryan answered temperately. He drew a distinction between natural and supernatural dignity in man. Supernatural dignity was achieved normally through the instruments of grace administered by the Church; yet this grace, this dignity, was conferred upon all baptized persons, Catholic or non-Catholic. Natural dignity was not "equivalent to" the dignity of personality, as Salvemini had said; it was rather "the basis of" the dignity of personality. The human rights inherent in all men because of their natural dignity created a strong bond, not a barrier, between men. Catholics and "genuine liberals" both affirmed it, and this distinguished them from totalitarian views of the state. Furthermore, Ryan argued, Salvemini feared too much the Church's demands on the state. Actually, the secular government should prohibit the spread of ideas condemned by the Church "when and to the extent that this policy is conducive to civil order and the common good." As for proscribing erroneous doctrine, the state had that obligation only in an "*almost entirely* Catholic" state; religious freedom in Eire, for example, was fully protected. Ryan insisted that differences between Catholics and secular liberals need not spread to politics and economics. Straightforward cooperation, neither side attempting to divert the alliance to its own ends, worked. Liberals should welcome progressive Catholics. It was "neither fair, nor reasonable, nor wise" to reject their cooperation simply because they "have not yet been able to convert their reactionary co-religionists," he said. "I use the word 'convert' advisedly and with a moral connotation," he went on, "for most of the Catholic reactionaries, at least in the field of economics, are ignorant of or deliberately reject the principles or the clear implications of the social encyclicals promulgated by Popes Leo XIII and Pius XI."[93]

Even before the discussion in the *New Republic* had subsided, Ryan himself extended the area of debate. Turning to *America*, now in the congenial hands of Father John La Farge, Ryan speculated on postwar European regimes for the May 8, 1943, issue. The liberal press—specifically, the *Nation*, the *New Republic*, and *PM*—and prominent liberal journalists —such as Max Lerner, Freda Kirchwey, and I. F. Stone—found disquieting

[92] Gaetano Salvemini, "Catholics and Liberals," letter, *New Republic*, Aug. 2, 1943, p. 144.
[93] Ryan, letter to editor, *ibid.*, Sept. 20, 1943, pp. 395–397.

evidence that Roosevelt was leaning toward "postwar clerical-reactionary regimes" in Europe. Lerner wanted the President to support General Charles de Gaulle, who was in touch with French resistance forces, rather than General Henri Giraud, a recent convert from Vichy. Lerner feared that in orienting American policy toward Giraud, Roosevelt was inviting reactionary postwar governments more oriented toward, say, Marshal Pétain than toward Léon Blum.[94] Ryan was as suspicious as Lerner of reactionaries, and he made no exception for Catholic reactionaries. Christian democrats should "strive with all their might and with all their intelligence for postwar regimes which will be not only anti-Fascist and genuinely democratic in the strict political sense, but also in the economic and social spheres." Skeptical of the social views of diplomats, army officers, and high clergy ("I have not forgotten the lessons of France and the French Revolution"), he had "no hesitation in declaring that 'finance, big industry, and the large landowners' should be permitted to play only a minor role in the postwar political system." Ryan was talking to Catholics in a Catholic publication. "The Catholic who thinks of the post-war governments in Europe merely in terms of Catholic political philosophy versus secularist and revolutionary political philosophy, or of Catholicism versus 'Liberalism,' is handicapped by fundamental ignorance." The economic and social aspects of postwar reconstruction, he went on, were "of primary importance." He feared that a Catholic might "take his stand against democracy because the democratic cause has been temporarily usurped by the enemies of religion." This, he said, would be a disastrous mistake; he hoped and prayed that influential Catholics would avoid it.[95]

As for the liberal critique of Roosevelt's policy, however, Ryan doubted the wisdom of Lerner's advice to throw in with De Gaulle. His hunch was that the French underground did not represent the political spectrum of France, but rather the leftist segment of "Communists, near-Communists, and anti-clericals." He wanted the government to support Giraud in order to locate power in the hands of "Christian (not reactionary) forces" until after France could make its own decision in a free election after the war. "In defending this choice," he added belligerently, "I am just as good a democrat, even just as good a liberal, as Max Lerner."[96]

[94] These fears are discussed in Goldman, *Rendezvous with Destiny*, pp. 389–398.
[95] Ryan, "Thunder on the Left: Postwar Storm Brewing," *America*, May 8, 1943, pp. 117–119.
[96] Ryan, letter to editor, *ibid.*, June 12, 1943, p. 278.

The Christian Democratic line for Europe was hard to maintain. Attack came from right and left, the conservatives calling it socialism because of its progressive tone, the liberals viewing it as reactionary because of its religious base. Ryan feared both reactionaries and radicals, but not equally, for Roosevelt provided an effective barrier against reactionary domination of postwar European governments. The danger came from the other side: from liberals and radicals who called for reform in terms that threw out religion. With this group Ryan felt himself increasingly out of touch.

The extended dialogue was inconclusive, both in itself and in its impact on postwar Europe. Yet it may have had some value in permitting discourse to continue between Catholic progressives and other American liberals.

By the summer of 1943, Monsignor Ryan slackened his pace considerably. He told White the previous summer that he wished they saw each other more often, "especially since the time for such pleasant experiences is growing pretty short." Now he noted ruefully the "rather frequent reminders that have come to me lately of the fact that I belong to the generation of ancients."[97] When in Washington, he went to the office regularly, but increasingly spent a large part of his workday reminiscing and visiting old friends in other departments. On one such day he received a vivid reminder of how much work remained to be done in educating American Catholics on the social question. After a lifetime of expounding *Rerum novarum*, he heard one secretary at the NCWC observe that Monsignor Ryan must be a great movie fan, "for he is always talking about Ramon Navarro." The two hours a week at Trinity became burdensome when he gave up his car, but Washington taxis were inexpensive then, and he wanted to continue as a teacher. As his obligations lessened, he gave more attention to his appearance. His friends and family were enchanted to see him become something of a dandy. His suit was usually pressed, breaking the precedent of forty years. If there was any excuse for formality, his suit coat was exchanged for a Prince Albert, the long lines of which made him seem taller. He went out for dinner more often, with old students who happened to be passing through Washington, or with friends in town. Miss Perkins took him to the Sulgrave Club, and a dinner at Justice Black's gave Ryan his first chance to meet Justice Frank Murphy.

There was always family to visit. Ryan left Washington late in May,

[97] Ryan to White, July 29, 1942; Ryan to Joseph McSorley, Aug. 17, 1943.

1943, and did not return until mid-October. Once again he crossed the continent with no engagement more compelling than a visit to San Diego. He was perhaps the world's most useless uncle. Once in St. Paul when he was visiting his nephew Joseph, he came down the stairs half absorbed in a book and, seeing his nephew, said absently: "Maybe you better go upstairs. The baby is about to fall off the bed." Yet he was always a welcome guest. He regaled the family for hours with reminiscences. He liked especially to tell of the time in 1939 when he and some of the family in St. Paul were listening to a recording of one of his speeches. Joseph Ryan's daughter, Kathleen, came in, listening intently. When the recording ended, they asked her if she knew whose voice that had been. "Of course," she replied instantly. "It's Father Coughlin."[98]

Though Ryan avoided Baltimore in his later years, his relations with Archbishop Curley grew cordial once again. Curley appreciated the warm words in *Social Doctrine in Action* in which Ryan lauded the academic freedom at Catholic University, and he wrote an ingratiating note to the monsignor: "I feel you have done a great piece of work for Labor, and because for Labor, you have done a great work for the Church. When we get away from the laboring man, we stand to lose a great deal. If you have taught priests and members of the laity to go out to the laboring man rather than to wait to have him come to us, then you have accomplished a wonderful lot of good." Just after Ryan's Cleveland speech about "American Bourbons," Curley told Ryan: "There are certain features of your talk that I do not like and you know that I do not like them and I am glad that you know that I do not like them and I am still more glad that you go ahead and express them just the same. If you keep on, you might reach the White House."[99] Ryan recognized in the archbishop's rough banter an overture for reconciliation. Curley's affable notes to "my dear Father John of Minnesota" were a vast improvement over those front-page editorials in the *Catholic Review*.

In the spring of 1944, Columbia University honored Ryan, Rabbi Louis Finkelstein, president of the Jewish Theological Seminary, and Dr. George Arthur Buttrick, of the Madison Avenue Presbyterian Church, for promoting friendly relations among the three major faiths. Ryan took great satisfaction in this recognition, all the more so because he knew that some deft academic politicking had led to the substitution of his name for that

[98] Interview with Joseph M. Ryan, April 25, 1958.
[99] Curley to Ryan, June 21, 1941; Jan. 12, 1943; Jan. 15, 1943.

of another prelate loftier in rank but less deserving. Ryan had no part in this chicanery, but since the prelate was not one of his favorites, he mischievously savored the details.

A visit to Columbia also meant a stay at Corpus Christi Parish nearby, and few American rectories were as congenial as the home of his old student, E. Harold Smith, and of the pastor, Father George B. Ford. Many other households in New York were still anxious to welcome him anytime: the Hoeys and the Rogerses, to say nothing of former students from Trinity and the Social Service School. (The Hayeses were at the embassy in Madrid for most of this period.) All over the American landscape, from Seattle to Hartford, his girls had just the right tone of irreverent reverence for their old mentor to make him feel respected and loved.

As usual, there were tensions with some members of the hierarchy. Ryan and John Courtney Murray, S.J., were emphatically anxious to speak at the Institute for Religious Studies in New York City, but the chancery office of the archdiocese vetoed the idea, equally emphatically.[100] (One of Ryan's older friends commented dejectedly that "These people would have forbidden St. Paul to preach to the Areopagus.")[101] Ryan did not see eye to eye with Bishop Karl J. Alter of Toledo, Ohio, the episcopal head of the Social Action Department and Ryan's old boss at the NCSSS. And when Ryan spoke at a dinner celebrating Monsignor Ready's promotion from the NCWC to the See of Columbus, Ohio, he scarcely mentioned the guest of honor.[102] Bishop-Designate Ready must have wondered just what occasion was being celebrated.

Ryan's own seventy-fifth birthday celebration in May was a modest affair: just a hundred or so, mainly from Washington. Ryan was aware that "the shadow which follows me as I move toward the setting sun has greatly extended itself and I cannot expect to see many more birthday commemorations." He had no new thoughts. His voice was softer. His sentences had lost their clipped vigor. He had no regrets or complaints: "I have already lived a long life and through it all God has been very good to me." He reviewed his experience at St. Paul Seminary, at the university, at the NCWC. Ireland, Curley, the administrative board of the NCWC— none of them had hindered his free expression. "From long experience and

100 J. Francis A. McIntyre to Ryan, Sept. 22, 1943; Ryan to McIntyre, Oct. 8, 1943; John Courtney Murray to Ryan, Sept. 29, 1943.
101 The letter, dated Sept. 28, 1943, is in the Ryan papers.
102 Ryan, "Remarks," MS, Dec. 11, 1944.

observation I have derived the comforting conclusion that as long as a person, whether priest or layman, exercises a fair amount of prudence and discretion, he need have little fear of repression by the authorities of the Church, even though some timid and economically illiterate souls may call him 'radical.' Sometimes the prudence and discretion will be more important in how a thing is said than in *what* is said. After all, very few Catholics will be tempted to be more genuinely radical than Popes Leo and Pius in *Rerum novarum, Quadragesimo anno* and 'Atheistic Communism.' "[103]

He exercised an old man's prerogative to speak bluntly. A woman at a cocktail party asked him what he really thought of Hoover. Surprised by the question—"I thought everyone knew what I thought of Hoover"—Ryan replied with such graceless acidity that his questioner fled in embarrassed dismay. When his office staff reproved him the next day, he said waggishly: "Well, she asked me, didn't she? I had to tell the truth."[104]

The monsignor's appearances at Catholic gatherings, like the rounds of the family, turned to reminiscence. He was now a figure of inspiration to a younger generation. Not a vastly creative role, it was, nevertheless, a useful and a satisfying one.

On occasion some of the old fire returned. When Ryan looked to the future, he dreamed of a peaceful world and a prosperous, progressive America. Speaking at the AFL's Postwar Forum in New York in April, 1944, Ryan asserted that the moral law demanded an international organization of nations as indispensable for peace. It should have more scope than the League of Nations, each nation surrendering sovereignty without going to the extreme of a unitary superstate. Ryan disliked the idea of sovereignty, for he thought the concept as developed from Hobbes and Bodin to Rousseau and Austin led to idolatry of the state. Yet these were the terms of current discourse in political science, and he had to use them. He thought the new agency needed both a judiciary and a legislative-administrative body, and in addition, battleships and bombers for enforcement. Like any national government, the agency was obliged to promote the general welfare, not as the instrument of victors, but as the instrument of justice. One of its first chores would be the revision of tariffs that created the economic dislocations that led to war. Though the war with

[103] Ryan, "Remarks," MS, May 16, 1944; Washington *Times-Herald*, May 17, 1944.
[104] This anecdote came from a variety of interviews with Monsignor Ryan's friends.

Japan was still at a bitter stage as Ryan spoke—the bloody Marine assault on Tarawa was just behind, the invasion of the Marianas just ahead—Ryan reminded his audience that Japan might not have attacked the United States if it could have reached essential markets in any other way. Ryan spoke of replacing tariffs with subsidies wherever it was necessary in promoting "the common good and social justice."[105]

His postwar program had a steely side as well. He had no doubt of the justice of punishing war criminals. The peoples of Axis nations should be treated with brotherly love, Ryan wrote in *Liberty* in 1943, "but do not let irrational, weak-minded, and anti-social sentimentalism be adopted in the treatment of their responsible and guilty leaders, the international criminals."[106] Two years later he used more technical terms for *Catholic Action*. The state has no authority over the moral order as such; therefore, repairing the injury to the moral law and punishing the guilty may be left to God. If the common good of nations could be served by complete forgiveness of war criminals, they could be forgiven. But Ryan thought it "fantastic" to suggest that such was the case. He believed that the common good would be better served if war criminals, those morally responsible for beginning and continuing the war and those who committed unspeakable injustices against civilians, were "compelled to expiate their crimes, according to the canons of retributive justice."[107]

In a talk to the Catholic Economic Association late in 1944, Ryan turned to the rehabilitation of war-torn nations. The needs of Europe would be enormous, its coffers empty. World War I's inter-Allied debts suggested what to avoid; the success of lend-lease pointed to the alternative. In the two years after the war, the United States could easily spare $10,000,000,000 to provide food and clothing to avoid starvation and exposure. The project would help Europe; it would help provide full employment in the United States, serving as an alternative to public works. A Europe restored to prosperity could buy American goods. Uncomfortable with his own emphasis on dollars and cents, Monsignor Ryan hastened to point out Europe's moral claim on the United States in justice and in charity. The European's right to America's surplus took precedence over America's right to abundance. "Just as the common right of property is

105 Ryan, "Some Aspects of an International Postwar Organization," MS of speech, April 13, 1944.
106 Ryan, "Religion's Stand on Axis Punishment: A Catholic Speaks," *Liberty*, June 5, 1943, p. 32.
107 Ryan, "The Question of Punishment of War Criminals," *Catholic Action*, March, 1945, pp. 3–4.

morally superior to the private right; just as the social element in ownership takes precedence, in some situations, over the individual element; so
the common right of mankind to the natural resources of a particular
country is sometimes superior to the right of that country's inhabitants."
Ryan conceded that the application of this principle was difficult. But the
principle itself he regarded as incontestable. With this point, he added, the
Pope clearly agreed.[108] Ryan did not live to see this principle carried into
execution in the Marshall Plan in 1948 and reaffirmed in most explicit
terms in the papal encyclical *Mater et magistra*, issued by Pope John XXIII
in 1961.[109]

The domestic postwar economy also worried him. The hostility of
Congress and the President's unwillingness to take on any domestic fight
led Ryan to turn with unwonted enthusiasm to labor unions as the most
effective instruments of social reform, especially since Murray's endorsement of the industry council plan put him in the front rank of Ryan's progressive reformers. Ryan saw little chance to push legislation for full employment through Congress unless vigilant, aggressive labor organizations
took the lead, for the "middle class and professional classes are followers
not leaders in the struggle for social justice."[110]

As the election of 1944 approached, the abusive campaign launched
against the Political Action Committee of the CIO riled Ryan. The CIO
had learned from the disaster of 1942 that unless labor fought for friendly
candidates, a hostile majority appeared in Congress. The year 1944 was a
presidential year, and the CIO–PAC was using a substantial political fund
to get out the vote: doorbell ringing, block-by-block campaigns in critical
districts, national organization paralleling that of the major parties. The
threat of the CIO's success led its opponents, principally Republicans, to
howl, and in the heat of the campaign the CIO–PAC was continually denounced as a Communist front.[111] When Father Benjamin J. Masse, S.J.,
did a skillful rebuttal of the charge for *America*, Ryan welcomed a chance
to tell the editor, Father La Farge, how glad he was to see *America* widely
quoted on the issue.[112]

Ryan was delighted with the outcome of the 1944 election. Curley

[108] Ryan, "Some Economic Aspects of European Relief and Rehabilitation,"
Current Religious Thought, March, 1945, pp. 12–16.
[109] Pope John XXIII, *Mater et magistra*, pamphlet (New York, 1961), pp. 51–59.
[110] Ryan, "Labor's Role After Victory," *Catholic Mind*, March, 1944, pp. 156–159.
[111] Joseph G. Raybach, *A History of American Labor* (New York, 1959), pp.
385–387.
[112] Ryan to La Farge, Nov. 13, 1944.

twitted him for thinking that only one man could fill the Presidency.[113] Ryan did not care. As he wrote to Roosevelt after the election: "For twelve years you have filled [the Presidency] with conspicuous success from every sane viewpoint."[114] Shortly thereafter, the White House asked Ryan to give the benediction at the 1945 inaugural. He did so with as much enthusiasm as he had eight years earlier. For both men the end was nearing: Roosevelt would not survive the spring, nor Ryan the autumn.

Dizziness was becoming more of a problem. Late in 1944 Ryan collapsed on the New York Central platform in New York, and returned to Washington only after Father Higgins, later Ryan's successor at the SAD, came to fetch him. For several years his weight had been going down alarmingly, and urological troubles bothered him constantly. In January, 1945, he missed a Round Table dinner at the Cosmos Club and took to his bed. He snapped back quickly, and the next month he was off to Cleveland to speak at the Community Religious Hour on "America and the Rehabilitation of Europe" and to comment on newspaper clippings for a luncheon meeting of the National Council of Catholic Women. He came back to Washington feeling extremely well despite the strenuous days in Cleveland, but shortly thereafter he was rushed off again to Georgetown University Hospital with grippe, and there he stayed for six weeks. Ryan was impatient with the five different kinds of pills that were forced on him every morning, but his secretary told Sister Mary John that, despite his fretfulness, he loved all the attention. He spent most of his time reading detective stories—"terrible tripe and a waste of time."[115] He did not let the chance pass to pay tribute to Justice Black when Black received the Thomas Jefferson Award. Black's fidelity to the Jeffersonian ideals of political and social justice made him the ideal recipient of the prize, Ryan said, and at a time when the Bourbons were longing for laissez faire, the celebration was a "timely and important factor in the conflict between plutocracy and social justice."[116]

Ryan left the hospital just before Easter in 1945, weak but well out of danger. During April he regained his strength and planned for the future. He agreed to judge an essay contest in November, and made a speaking engagement in Boston for the following March—Cardinal O'Connell had died the previous April, and his successor, Archbishop Richard J. Cushing,

[113] Curley to Ryan, Jan. 15, 1943, Archives of the Archdiocese of Baltimore.
[114] Ryan to Roosevelt, Nov. 10, 1944.
[115] Ryan to Alice Carney, March 26, 1945.
[116] Ryan to Hugo L. Black, April 6, 1945.

was friendly. Ryan even planned a trip to the West Coast for the summer of 1946.

In May, however, flu hit him again, and in June he was back at the Georgetown Hospital for more "tinkering with my kidney and bladder" and more sulfa drugs. Twice he had to cancel reservations for home. Late in June, Father Higgins arranged a trip to St. Paul in a private plane, for Monsignor Ryan wanted to die at home.

There was still one more job to do. When Roosevelt died in April, Ryan had spoken feelingly of him as "a supremely great American, a supremely great President, a supremely sincere lover of his fellow men."[117] Now flat on his back, Ryan undertook a more extended appraisal for the *Review of Politics*. Measure by measure, Ryan reaffirmed his approval of the New Deal's program. The National Labor Relations Act, the Fair Labor Standards Act, and the Social Security Act "have done more to promote social justice than all the other federal legislation enacted since the adoption of the Constitution."[118] Appropriately enough, the article on "Roosevelt and Social Justice" was the last Ryan ever wrote.

Over the summer Monsignor Ryan held on from day to day in the hospital where Sister Constance had served for more years than either cared to remember. More detective stories were found. The old prelate said that he felt about his mystery stories like the drunk who thought that all that glare in Pittsburgh came from distilleries producing whiskey that he had to consume. His care was no longer a matter of recovery but of comfort, so his doctors raised no objection when Monsignor Ryan wanted to see his old home in Vermillion. Father Lawrence drove him out the eight miles. Father John looked without a word. They returned to St. Paul. It was now a matter of waiting. Father McGowan came on from Washington, almost a member of the family.

Early on the morning of September 16, 1945, Father McGowan was offering mass for the sick old priest. When he reached the gospel, word came of Monsignor Ryan's death. Pausing only a moment, Father McGowan continued the mass as a requiem for his friend.

[117] Ryan, "Tribute," MS of statement on the Catholic Hour broadcast, April 15, 1945.
[118] Ryan, "Roosevelt and Social Justice," *Review of Politics*, July, 1945, pp. 300, 305.

A Long &
Varied Experience

ONSIGNOR
Ryan's death brought forth tributes to his career from
people in all professions. Obituary notices and comments on
his life filled many pages of the oversized scrapbooks that
the old priest had used for clippings about his activities. At
the funeral mass, celebrated by Archbishop Murray of St.
Paul, Bishop Haas gave a final eulogy to Ryan's simplicity,
his faith, and his hunger for justice for his fellow men. In
Washington, President Harry S. Truman took note of
Ryan's death: "We shall all miss the wise counsel which he
gave so generously out of his long and varied experience."

If the experience was indeed varied, it nevertheless contained a unifying central principle: the application of the
canons of justice to social life in the twentieth century. By
associating himself with the social reformers of the era, Ryan
added his strength to the progressives who were reshaping
modern industrial practices. To the extent that progressive
reformers succeeded in the era of the New Deal, Ryan
shared their laurels. Yet this was not his peculiar contribution. His special role was to show Catholic America that
these progressive reforms were essential for achieving the

social justice to which their religion beckoned them. His basic texts, *A Living Wage* and *Distributive Justice*, argued this case in the traditional vocabulary of the moral theologian, argued, that is, in terms that indicated no break in Catholic tradition, but an application of tradition to the problems of the needy of his day. When the hierarchy of the Church in America accepted his views—in the "Bishops' Program of Social Reconstruction" (1919) and in "The Church and the Social Order" (1940)—the burden of argument shifted from progressives to conservatives within the Church. However conservative a bishop, priest, or layman might be in practice, the Church itself spoke officially with the voice of economic progressivism. Nor was the Church in America eccentric in this respect, for *Rerum novarum* (1891) had inspired the mood within the Church, and *Quadragesimo anno* (1941) had confirmed it. *Mater et magistra* (1961) gave Ryan's program a retroactive, posthumous endorsement. Ryan had little impact on the universal Church, but in America he was the peerless leader of progressive social thinkers who wooed the Church from individualistic fear of the state as the agent of encroaching socialism and won it back to an acceptance of the state as an instrument of the common good. Ryan served both his Church and his nation: his Church by acclimating its traditional theology to the norms of twentieth-century industrial society and to progressive attitudes toward social policy; his nation by galvanizing Catholic pressure on the modern state to deal effectively with social problems.

Even Monsignor Ryan's stand on church and state inadvertently helped to reconcile the Church to its American environment. When he stated the traditional teaching without compromising—without "minimizing," to use his own word—the clarity of his blunt statement, the embarrassment it created, paved the way for subsequent statements by the Administrative Committee of the NCWC and by the Apostolic Delegate that reduced non-Catholic fears by insisting that Catholic Americans were well satisfied and would remain well satisfied with the limitations that the Constitution imposed on the relations between state and church.

In many ways John A. Ryan was the child of good fortune. It was a happy accident that he should grow up and work under prelates like Archbishop Ireland and Archbishop Curley, both of whom defended his right to speak even when they disagreed with what he said. He was fortunate to work in academic and institutional environments relatively free from the pressures of the pew.

In other ways Father Ryan created his own security. He did not seek provocative situations. When they appeared, he dealt with them in moderate, normally conciliatory language. He skirted the more sensitive areas of modern controversy, such as the evolution of dogma. The modernist controversy held no real dangers for him. And he argued within the Catholic tradition: from St. Thomas ultimately, and from *Rerum novarum* and *Quadragesimo anno* proximately. From his confidence in the orthodoxy of his own views, he argued temperately, steadfastly, and at last successfully.

The triumph of Monsignor Ryan's career came from the skill with which he blended traditional Catholic principles and the American progressive tradition, from the recognition of his achievement both by the Church and by the nation, and from the translation of social justice into the law of the land during his own lifetime.

Bibliographical Note

The basis for a study of Monsignor Ryan, aside from his extensive published work, is the John A. Ryan Papers in the Manuscript Collection, Mullen Library, Catholic University of America. Disappointingly little material on his first fifty-five years survives: his journal as a seminarian, some letters to him, quite a few manuscripts of his sermons and public lectures, complete sets of notebooks containing the lectures for his courses at the St. Paul Seminary and at Catholic University. After about 1925, when Ryan's secretaries began to file incoming letters and to keep copies of outgoing letters, Ryan accumulated an abundantly full record of his work. Following his death in 1945, all his files at the Social Action Department of the National Catholic Welfare Conference were transferred to the university: they include not only material relevant to the NCWC but also his personal files and his correspondence as faculty member and dean of the School of Sacred Studies at the university, as well as six large scrapbooks of clippings about his career. There may be additional material in the NCWC's general files, but these are not yet open to scholars. The Archives of Catholic University contain other relevant material: "Academic Senate: Reports," "Acta Facultatis Theologicae Universitatis Catholicae Americae," "Catholic University of America, Faculty Records," *Yearbook of the Catholic University of America*, 1898–1902, and "Record of Students, 1896–1902," for Ryan's years as a graduate student; and "Annual Reports of the Rector," "Minutes of the Meetings of the Faculty of Theology," "Rector's Files, John A. Ryan," and "Minutes of the Board of Trustees" for the years of Ryan's return to the university as a professor. Surprisingly, neither the Thomas J.

Shahan Papers, recently transferred to the university, nor the Francis J. Haas Papers contains anything of direct relevance to Ryan.

Manuscript collections elsewhere yield a good deal of additional information. The Archives of the Archdiocese of Baltimore contain Ryan's correspondence with Archbishop Michael J. Curley as well as Curley's correspondence with successive rectors of the university. Since Curley candidly discussed the fight over the School of Theology in his correspondence with Bishop James Hugh Ryan, the Baltimore archives are particularly important at this point. The James Hugh Ryan Papers in the Archives of the Archdiocese of Omaha yield many items not available in Baltimore, the most prominent of which is James Ryan's long *aide-mémoire* to Monsignor Filippo Bernardini. The John T. McNicholas Papers in the Archives of the Archdiocese of Cincinnati have only a few items not available in John Ryan's own papers in Washington. The Archives of the Archdiocese of St. Paul yielded little, half a dozen letters, only two or three of which contribute to the narrative. Bishop Peter J. Muldoon's "Diary" is available on microfilm at the Catholic University; the original is in the Archives of the Diocese of Rockford, and this is the only useful item that turned up there. At the University of Notre Dame, the Frederick P. Kenkel Papers have a small group of letters not available in Ryan's own papers; Notre Dame also has a copy—not available elsewhere—of the "Report of the Committee on Social Service to the Bishops' Committee on Catholic Interests and Affairs." At St. Thomas College in St. Paul, the St. Thomas Seminary "Roll of Honor," 1891–1892, and at St. Paul Seminary, the *Library Journal*, 1895 ff., are the only archival items relevant to Ryan that have survived. John Ryan's brother, Monsignor Lawrence F. Ryan of St. Paul, and his sister, Sister Mary John, have a few additional items of importance. The files of the Industrial Appeals Board of the National Recovery Administration in the Archives of the United States illuminate Ryan's short-lived role as a governmental employee.

Ryan's published work—sixteen books, dozens of pamphlets, and hundreds of articles—has been skillfully compiled in Theodora E. McGill, "A Bio-Bibliography of Monsignor John A. Ryan," M.A. dissertation, Catholic University, 1952, a work of notable accuracy and completeness. Miss McGill has also included a brief sketch of Ryan's life and lists of articles about Ryan and of reviews of his books. The availability of this essay makes it superfluous to include here a bibliography of Monsignor Ryan's work. The only full-length study of Ryan's career is Patrick W. Gearty, *The Economic Thought of Monsignor John A. Ryan* (Washington, 1953), a work that illuminates the ethical basis for Ryan's ideas on economics. John Fitzpatrick, "A Study of John A. Ryan in Minnesota from Public Sources, 1869–1915," manuscript in Father Fitzpatrick's possession, reviews a wide array of material discriminatingly. George G. Higgins, "The Underconsumption Theory in the Writings of Monsignor John A. Ryan," M.A. dissertation, Catholic University, 1942, discusses Ryan's most distinctive economic idea. Both Sylvia M. Batdorf, "The Work of the Social Action Department of the National Catholic Welfare Conference in All Phases of Industrial Relations," M.A. dissertation, Catholic University, 1933, and William J. Lee, "The Work in Industrial Relations of the Social Action Department of the National Catholic Welfare Conference, 1933–1945," M.A. dissertation, Catholic University, 1946, deal obliquely with Monsignor Ryan. Karl H. Cerny, "Monsignor John A. Ryan and the Social Action Department," Ph.D. dissertation, Yale University, 1954, has some keen comments on the internal structure of the NCWC and a thoughtful analysis of the occupational group system.

In assessing Ryan's relation to the development of Catholic thought in the United States, the historian checks newspapers and magazines as a matter of course. This is necessarily a selective process, intensive at times of controversy, more random at other times. For the period before 1915, the *Northwestern Chronicle* and then the St. Paul *Catholic Bulletin* deserve continuous attention. For the period following Ryan's return to Washington, the Baltimore *Catholic Review* carries the fullest account of his activities. For the period of Ryan's editorship, every page of the *Catholic Charities Review* reveals his influence, and the *N.C.W.C. Bulletin*, later *Catholic Action*, gets special attention as the house organ of the bishops' organization. During the Roosevelt administration, Father Coughlin's *Social Justice* and the Brooklyn *Tablet* are important for comments adverse to Ryan's position. The *Catholic World*, *America*, and *Commonweal* are essential as journals of opinion, usually in agreement with Ryan, sometimes vigorously opposed.

The historical literature that leads to a better understanding of Monsignor Ryan must necessarily embrace a large part of the studies in American social and political history, especially in American Catholic history, that have appeared in the past quarter of a century. I cannot claim to have more than sampled that literature; the footnotes in the text are a mere suggestion of its range. For the literature on Catholic history, the annotated listings in John Tracy Ellis, *A Guide to American Catholic History* (Milwaukee, 1959), provide a useful start. The rich synthesis of recent scholarship contained in Robert D. Cross, *The Emergence of Liberal Catholicism in America* (Cambridge, 1958), explains the Church in the late nineteenth century with deft clarity and attractive prose. A comparable volume for the first half of the twentieth century would fill a real need. Two books on Protestant social thought and action—Paul A. Carter, *The Decline and Revival of the Social Gospel* (Ithaca, 1954), and Robert Moats Miller, *American Protestantism and Social Issues, 1919–1939* (Chapel Hill, 1958)—provide a valuable parallel to Ryan's experience: both the differences and the similarities are instructive. On the course of American liberal thought for this period, Eric Goldman, *Rendezvous with Destiny* (New York, 1952), strikes me as the most suggestive and useful guide, even though Goldman's judgments on Ryan go wide of the target. For a sensitive, informed, brilliant exposition of religious sociology in America, no work compares with Will Herberg, *Protestant–Catholic–Jew: An Essay in American Religious Sociology* (rev. ed., Garden City, 1960). I wonder if anyone can write in this field without cribbing, consciously and unconsciously, from this seminal work.

Index

Adams, Brooks, 80, 127
Adkins v. Children's Hospital, 126
American Civil Liberties Union, 114–115, 140–143
American Federation of Catholic Societies, 62
American Irish Defense Association, 261
Anti-Saloon League, 166–167, 168
anti-Semitism, 253
Ashley, William J., 33, 51
Associated Charities, St. Paul, 56, 66, 79
Association of Catholic Trade Unionists, 258

Bailey v. Drexel Furniture Company, 126
Baker, Newton D., 208
Baldwin, Roger, friendship with Ryan, 142–143, 153; quoted, 141
Barnes, Harry Elmer, 135
Beckman, Francis J. L., 258–259
Belloc, Hilaire, 88
Benedict XV, Pope, 103–104, 108
Bernardini, Filippo, 177, 205n.
birth control, Ryan on, 38, 148–150
"Bishops' Program for Social Reconstruction," 105–107, 155
Black, Hugo L., 244; and 30-hour bill, 212; appointed to Supreme Court, 233; honored, 275
Black, John D., 198–199
Boland, Francis J., 247
Bouquillon, Thomas, 25, 28, 31–32
Brandeis, Louis D., 81, 85–86; Ryan lauds, 240–241

Brown, Rome G., 68
Burke, John J., 108, 120

Callahan, Patrick H., 126, 146; in campaign of 1928, 181, 183, 186
Cannon, James E., Jr., 180, 183, 188–189
"Catechism of the Social Question, A," 121
Catholic Action. See N.C.W.C. Bulletin
Catholic Association for International Peace, 137–138
Catholic Charities Review, 95, 164, 200
Catholic Church and the Citizen, The, 179
Catholic Conference on Industrial Problems, 121, 164, 200, 209
Catholic Principles of Politics, 247–248
Catholic Review, Baltimore, 114; attacks Ryan, 228, 230–231; praises Ryan, 245
Catholic University of America, Ryan as student at, 27–36, 45–46; on faculty, 89–90; described, 93–94; academic freedom at, 159; tensions at, 201, 204–208, 245–246; gives degree to FDR, 213
Cathrein, Viktor, 24, 53, 66, 172
Central Conference of American Rabbis, 194, 197–198
Central Verein, German Roman Catholic, 62, 63, 156
Chambliss, A. W., 142
child labor, laws forbidding, 97–98, 126–127; amendment, 128–129, 154–159
Christian Century, 171–172, 183
Church and Labor, The, 95

288

Roosevelt, Franklin D., in campaign of 1928, 173; in campaign of 1932, 208–210; Ryan approves of, 217, 220; inauguration of, in 1937, 229–230; lauds Ryan, 245, 264
Rural Life Bureau (NCWC), 121
Ryan, Desmond, quoted, 240
Ryan, James H., 201, 205–207, 214–215, 261
Ryan, John A., boyhood of, 3, 6–10; at St. Thomas Seminary, 10–12; at St. Paul Seminary as student, 16–25, on faculty, 35–37; ordained, 25–26; at C.U. as student, 27–36, 45–46, on faculty, 89–91, 93–95, 116–118, 124, 204–208, 245–246; at Trinity College, 94–95; at NCSSS, 118, 246–247; at NCWC, 108–109, 120–122, 161, 249; becomes monsignor, 214–216; death of, 275–276
on birth control, 148–150; child labor laws, 97–98, 126–129; church and state, 118–120, 170–174, 247–248; in Mexico, 143–147; in Italy, 147–148; civil liberties, 113–115, 142–143, 236–237; compulsory arbitration, 34–35; depression of 1929, 190–199, 208–210; election of 1928, 170–185; election of 1932, 208–209; election of 1936, 225–229; election of 1940, 257–258; election of 1944, 274–275; immigration restriction, 96–97; industrial democracy, 125–126, 196, 198, 216–217, 220–221, 257, 263; interest, 50–51; Ireland, 122–123, 203–205; just price, 49; labor unions, 34, 234–235; liberalism, 150–152, 233–234, 265–269; living wage, 35, 37–44; minimum-wage laws, 80–86, 238–239; modernism, 70–72; monopoly, 49–50; New Deal, 212–214, 216–217, 218–222; peace movement, 103–104, 135–138, 159–160; Populism, 18–19; prohibition, 99, 165–170; public power, 134; railroad regulation, 50, 130–134; Scopes trial, 140–142; socialism, 86–89, 208; social reform by Catholics, 23–24, 52–57, 64–75; speculation, 35; stockwatering, 50; women's suffrage, 98–99; World War I, 101–104, and reconstruction, 103–106; World War II, 254–256, and reconstruction, 263–269, 272–274
writings of: A Living Wage, 37–44; Distributive Justice, 91–92, 252; The Church and Socialism, 95; The Church and Labor, 95; Social Reconstruction, 107; The State and the Church, 118–120, 170–171, 173–174, 177–178, revised as Catholic Principles of Politics, 247–248; Declining Liberty, 169; The Cath-

Ryan, John A. (cont.)
olic Church and the Citizen, 179; Questions of the Day, 202; Seven Troubled Years, 198n.; Social Doctrine in Action, 250–252; "A Programme of Social Reform by Legislation," 57–60; "Bishops' Program for Social Reconstruction," 105–110; "The Norm of Morality," 252
Ryan, Katherine (Sister Mary John), 76, 77–78, 108, 110, 123, 216; quoted, 125
Ryan, Lawrence F., 76, 77–78, 91, 124, 244, 250–251
Ryan, Maria Luby, 3–5, 76–77, 123–124, 191
Ryan, Mary Jane (Sister Constance), 76–77, 123, 216
Ryan, Maurice, 76, 212, 228, 244
Ryan, William, 2–6, 76–77, 123

St. Paul Seminary, 16–17; Ryan teaches at, 36–37
St. Thomas Seminary, 10–11
Salvemini, Gaetano, 266–267
Sarton, George, quoted, 228
Scanlan, Patrick F., 182, 231
Schumacher, Henry, 206–208
Scopes trial, 140–142
Sedgwick, Ellery, 133, 174, 185
Shahan, Thomas J., 28, 61–62, 94, 201; quoted, 196
Sheehy, Maurice S., 206, 214, 232, 244, 257–258
Shotwell, James T., 137
Siedenburg, Frederick, 62, 64
single tax, 22–23, 24–25, 61
Sister Mary John. See Ryan, Katherine
Slater, Thomas, 71–72
Smith, Alfred E., in 1928, 172–175, 179–185
Smith, E. Harold, 265, 271
Smith, T. V., 142
Social Action, Department of (NCWC), created, 108–109; Ryan at, 120–122, 137, 161, 200, 216, 258
Social Doctrine in Action, 250–252; quoted, 72, 75
social justice, 41n., 196. See individual reforms
Social Justice, 223, 259, 260–261
Social Reconstruction, 107
socialism, Ryan comments on, 22–23, 53, 208; reform differs from, 59–60; Ryan viewed as friendly to, 67–69; Ryan debates Hillquit on, 86–89
Spalding, John Lancaster, 14, 15–16
Spanish Civil War, 233–234

290

speculation, 34
Splaine, Michael J., 156–157
standard of living, 55–56; minimum, 80
State and the Church, The, 118–120, 124, 170–178; revised, 247–248
state-church relations, Ryan on, 118–120, 170–172, 174–182, 278; in Mexico, 143–147; in Italy, 147–148
stockwatering, 50
Stone, Harlan Fiske, 114
Stratmann, Franziskus, 137–138
Stritch, Samuel A., 199
Sutherland, George, 127

Tablet, Brooklyn, 254, 261
Taft, William Howard, 127
taxation, 61. *See* single tax
Testem benevolentiae, 29
Thomas, Norman, 144–146
Thompson, Carl D., 134
Times, New York, chides Ryan, 264
Tippy, Worth M., 136
Trinity College, 94–95, 117–118
Truman, Harry S., quoted, 277

underconsumption, theory of, 33–34, 193–194

Union Advocate, Minnesota, 47, 52, 78–79

Veblen, Thorstein, 55
Vermeesch, A., quoted, 69–70
Villard, Oswald Garrison, 144, 145–146
Volstead Act, 166–167, 187–189

Walsh, Frank P., 86–87, 89, 107, 228
Walsh, Thomas J., 128, 155
Ward, Wilfrid, quoted, 109
Webb, Sidney and Beatrice, 41
Weiss, A. M., 70
West, George P., 265
White, William Allen, 114, 180, 190, 256
White, William J., 65
Wilbur, Russell, quoted, 242
Willard, Daniel, 125–126
Willebrandt, Mabel Walker, 180–181
Wilson, Woodrow, 85, 96; and World War I, 100–104
Wisconsin, University of, 217
Witte, Edwin E., 217
women, legislation for, 58–59, 98–99; bishops support, 106
World Court, 224
World War I, 100–104; II, 254–256, 258–262